Sterling Price: Portrait of a Southerner

STERLING PRICE

Portrait of a Southerner

Robert E. Shalhope, *1941*

University of Missouri Press
Columbia, Missouri

Copyright © 1971 by
The Curators of the University of Missouri
University of Missouri Press, Columbia, Missouri 65201
Library of Congress Catalog Number 79–130670
Printed and bound in the United States of America
ISBN 0–8262–0103–2

For my mother and father

Acknowledgments

This book has greatly benefited from the assistance of others. Since the bulk of Sterling Price's personal papers was destroyed by fire in the 1880's, it was necessary to visit a great many manuscript repositories in order to gather the many scattered letters of Price and his contemporaries. I would like, therefore, to express my deep appreciation to the curators of the repositories listed in the Bibliography for making the search for materials an enjoyable one. A special note of thanks is due Ruth Rollins Westfall of Columbia, Missouri, for permission to see various letters in the Rollins Collection at the University of Missouri Library. Miss Hazel Price of Glasgow, Missouri, great-granddaughter of Price, gave generously of her time and knowledge of her great-grandfather and loaned me family photographs that would have been otherwise inaccessible. I would also like to thank the editors of the *Missouri Historical Society Bulletin* and *Civil War History* for permission to quote material that appeared in their journals.

While I assume sole responsibility for errors of fact and interpretation, I owe much to those who have advised and assisted me in the preparation of this study. I profited immensely from my association with Thomas C. Barrow and from the valuable suggestions of Noble E. Cunningham and Allan R. Millett, and my colleagues John S. Ezell and Arrell M. Gibson, who read the entire manuscript and offered useful advice. I owe a special debt of gratitude to Lewis E. Atherton who offered painstaking criticism of both style and content of the manuscript; more important and less evident is a debt to the man himself—a wise and dedicated teacher.

It is difficult to express adequately the debt owed to my family. My parents gave me constant aid and encouragement to study history and to pursue my own course; my wife Emma helped more than she can possibly know, and Adelaide's regular visits to my study proved to be cheering diversions when I needed them most.

R.E.S.
Norman, Oklahoma
November, 1970

Contents

List of Maps

Prologue

Pap Price Is Dead

The six black horses stamped nervously as they waited, harnessed to a gleaming black hearse. The clatter of their hoofs on the pavement shattered the strange hush that had fallen over the corner of Eighth and Washington streets in St. Louis. This silence was occasioned by the opening of the doors of the Methodist Episcopal Church and the slow descent of twelve pallbearers bearing a silver-trimmed mahogany casket toward the waiting hearse. A grieving woman and her family followed, descended the steps of the church, and stepped into a carriage drawn by a set of matched grays. In turn came hundreds of lean, hardened men who entered carriages and followed the hearse up Washington Street as it made its way to Bellefontaine Cemetery. The largest funeral procession in the city's history made its way through the streets of St. Louis.

After the coffin was lowered into the open grave and the minister had uttered last words over it, the attendants began to cover the grave. As the dirt echoed hollowly on the coffin, Sterling Price, whose public life had been filled with controversy and his private life with anxiety and tension, came to a final rest.

In many ways his life, both public and private, represented a series of paradoxes. Price had been born into an old republican environment and throughout his life observed the Jeffersonian world he so admired being dissolved by the economic opportunities of a burgeoning young nation. While attempting to guide his life by republican principles, he constantly faced anxiety, for he too was a part of the rootless, mobile society that was destroying the values of the Old Republic. Price was a capitalist who maintained anticapitalistic principles, thus suffering the anxieties involved in being both an entrepreneurial Democrat and a doctrinaire republican; he was also at once a democratic-nationalist and a slaveholder. This last tension, which wracked so many Southern republicans during the antebellum period, became even more disturbing to Price since he possessed a nearly insatiable desire for personal status. Born into a family on the fringe of gentility in Virginia, the social position he so desired and finally attained as a slaveholding Missouri tobacco planter faced constant threats from the nationalism to which he so ardently adhered.

Price became the storm center for controversies in both his public and military careers. His peculiar habit of keeping his own counsel, combined with his known ambition and vanity, caused his opponents continually to weave power plots about him. During the Civil War he engendered blind devotion and loyalty from the common soldiers, who affectionately nicknamed him "Old Pap," while he alienated nearly every member of the Confederate command system from President Jefferson Davis to commanders in the field.

Price's soldiers, and most Missourians, would not desert him either during or after the war. When he returned to St. Louis after the end of hostilities and an interlude in Mexico, his former soldiers joined other Missourians to purchase a home for him. The indomitable spirit that had carried him through life could not sustain his disease-wracked body, and he succumbed within a year after his return to the state. At the time of his death he was the most revered man in the state, and many battle-hardened veterans who had served with him through grueling campaigns wept when they learned that Pap Price was dead.

· 1 ·

A Southside Heritage

The years 1815 and 1816 were good ones for the tobacco planters of Virginia. Prices had risen beyond the highest expectations and crops were sold even before they had been prized. Pugh Williamson Price of Prince Edward County enjoyed unusually good fortune, thus enabling him to send his sons to school, provide well for his family, and buy an expensive new carriage. The last was particularly important to Price for he was an ambitious and acutely status-conscious individual. Now when he drove his family to his nephew Charles' fine plantation there would be no cause for embarrassment, as earlier had been occasioned by the old two-wheeled family carriage.

Had Price been introspective, he might well have paused to reflect upon his family's position in Virginia society. From his front porch he could glance down the sloping fields of tobacco to the Buffalo River, or perhaps wander over to the fine house in which he had been raised, now occupied by Charles. The Price family had done well in the five generations since their ancestors first landed at Jamestown. Price was not of the local oligarchy, but the family did epitomize the advance from immigrant, to yeoman, to gentleman freeholder that was taking place in Virginia.

II

Like countless other immigrants, John and Mary Price had been driven by individual impulses to leave their native Wales and risk their lives and fortunes in the New World. Stories of hardship, suffering, and death certainly must have filtered back to Wales, but the Prices were determined to go. The incomplete records of the period do not indicate whether their sons Matthewes and William accompanied them. There may have been some fear on their part for their children's safety. This apprehension was to prove well-founded, for within two years after landing at Jamestown tragedy did strike the couple, and Mary died in the great Indian massacre of 1622.

As immigrants were forced to do on a ruthless frontier, John could only start anew. By 1624 he had remarried and was farming a plot of 150 acres in Henrico County. Within a few years Matthewes joined John and Ann, the second wife, and took up a grant of 150 acres in the same county; by 1650 he had married and had a son whom he named after his father.[1]

The second John Price also remained in Henrico County. He was a hard-working, religious man of the yeoman class who would provide only simply for his children upon his death. John's will divided his household items among his four children with the youngest, Pew [Pugh], receiving a feather bed and bolster, one red yarn rug, a blanket, a large chest, one "great pot" with racks and hooks, two pewter dishes and two plates, one "short" musket, one large iron spit, one large brass kettle, a large dripping pan, one cow, one yearling, one couch, and one oval table.[2]

Pugh Price—ambitious, restless, avaricious, adventurous—embodied the qualities that were impelling Americans to conquer their nation's frontier. Although only twenty-one when his father died and still a resident of Henrico County, he evidently was considered a solid citizen, for a 1743 St. John's Parish vestry meeting gave him and two others responsibility for processioning, or walking the boundaries "all between Four Mile Creek, Bailey's Run, and White Oak Swamp."[3] Pugh, nonetheless, was not satisfied in Henrico, since this was a time when Virginians were moving south and west of the James River. In 1743, Pugh purchased 328 acres of land that had been formed nine years earlier out of Prince George County on the Buffalo River in Amelia County and still constituted a frontier area.[4]

Pugh continued to add to these holdings and moved there some time after 1743, a fact substantiated by a deed in 1750 that read Pugh Price "of Amelia County." This purchase of 200 acres on the Buffalo River included the "plantation with all houses, orchards, and gardens."[5] Pugh was beginning to build one of the finest plantations in that part of Amelia County, later to become Prince Edward County.

Meanwhile Pugh was entrenching himself with the local elite that had preceded him. The Morton family had arrived in the early 1730's and the Peyton Randolphs shortly thereafter. By 1760, both Pugh and his eldest son, Pugh, Jr., were listed as "gentlemen freeholders" in St. Patrick's Parish vestry book, indicating that Pugh had achieved status among the Mortons, Venables, Randolphs, and others of the local oligarchy.[6]

As was common in his day, Pugh sired a large family. His first wife gave birth to seven children and his second, Jerusha Penick, to nine.

1. Benjamin Luther Price, *John Price the Immigrant*, 7.
2. Will of John Price, Henrico County Records, Deeds and Wills, 1710–1714, 79–80.
3. St. John's Parish Vestry Book, 31.
4. Amelia County Deed Book #2, 24.
5. *Ibid.*, 552–53.
6. St. Patrick's Parish Vestry Book, *passim*.

They lived well, if not ostentatiously; the homes in the area reflected the newness of the country, being comfortable rather than pretentious, but none matching the grandeur of the tidewater plantation homes. While most lived in comfortable two-story frame dwellings, Pugh built a large three-story brick mansion, surrounded it with fine outbuildings, and framed his front walk with boxwoods. He was able to leave sizable estates to his children when he died; several sons received plantations of over 500 acres. None, however, came immediately into possession of the main plantation and none would ever be able to rival the original estate.[7]

III

Pugh Price died shortly before the birth of his last child, Pugh Williamson. According to Pugh's will, Pugh W., mentioned as the "child that my wife is now big with," was to remain on the plantation until the death of his mother or until he attained his majority when he would receive "one negro boy named Guy, one feather bed and furniture, and one young horse." When Jerusha died the remainder of the estate was to be divided among the family.[8] Pugh W., raised and schooled as befitted the child of one of the gentry, grew accustomed to that style of life. He lived on one of the finest plantations in the area and associated with the local elite. However, by the time he came of age, the home plantation had passed to the family of his brother Charles and the remainder of old Pugh's land had been divided. Pugh W. received a small plot of land on the Buffalo River and cash for the value of Guy.

His father had been impelled by the spirit of the age but Pugh W. was driven by an even stronger impulse for advancement. Born into established gentility, he was to feel the pangs of deprivation. Instead of being a recognized member of the local elite he became simply another freeholder, living on the fringe of gentility. Partially, rather than totally dispossessed, Pugh became determined to regain his social position. Behind his strained lunging at propriety and status lay not only the yearnings of the disinherited but also the pent-up ambitions of the gentleman *manqué*. Thus fired with a deep desire for gentility, Pugh W. became hypersensitive of his status.

Pugh was not yet twenty-one when he found himself on his own with his small tract of land. He soon married Elizabeth Williamson, a daughter of one of the oldest and most respected families in the county, and the couple settled down to tobacco farming and raising a family. Their first child, Edwin, born in 1795, was followed during the next ten years by two more children, Pamela Williamson and

7. Will of Pugh Price, Prince Edward County Will Book #1, 173–74.
8. *Ibid.*

Robert Pugh. Pugh, like many other ambitious young Virginians, faced the difficult task of advancing in society and enlarging his estate. His father and others of his time had been able to acquire large tracts of cheap land as a basis for their extensive plantations, but by 1800 this method of advancement was closed. Now one could add to his holdings only by shrewd, sometimes risky, and always expensive, purchases. In 1808, 60 acres near the courthouse cost Pugh "100 pounds lawful money."[9]

By the time of the birth of their third son, Sterling, in 1809, Pugh and Elizabeth were established in a comfortable two-story frame house overlooking the Buffalo River. Pugh continued to add small tracts to his holdings and to purchase slaves. In a county where nearly one-third of the families possessed no slaves and the vast majority of slaveholders owned only half a dozen, Pugh managed to acquire twelve. Still, Peyton Randolph owned more than seventy and the Venables more than forty.[10] Although Pugh defeated Peyton Randolph in an election for first sergeant during the War of 1812, when they both served in Captain Samuel Allen's company, the commanding officers were selected from the county elite, William Venable and Henry Watkins serving as lieutenants.[11] A gentleman freeholder like Pugh might be asked to sign important petitions or to grace local functions by his presence, but he could scarcely hope to compete with the oligarchy for membership on the county court.[12]

IV

Young Sterling would remember little of his father and elder brother Edwin going to war in 1812, for he was only three years old. His early childhood spanned the flush times following that conflict; he spent his time playing with his younger brother, John Randolph, and his sister Pamela, although being nine years his elder she probably had little time for him. If things became tedious around the house the children could fish in the river or play with their cousin Charles at the big house. Sterling enjoyed still more a ride to the courthouse with his father in their new carriage to see the hustle and activity in Farmville during the sale of tobacco. At such times the site swarmed with planters and their retainers, all eager to learn what price their leaf would bring. Occasionally Sterling accompanied his father on one of his frequent trips to the courthouse to sue for debts or to seek redress in a land dispute.

All too soon Sterling, like other youngsters, learned that there was

9. Prince Edward County Deed Book #14, 225.
10. Virginia Census, 1810.
11. Muster Rolls of the Virginia Militia in the War of 1812, 88.
12. For an excellent description of the oligarchic nature of Virginia society, see Charles Sydnor, *Gentlemen Freeholders*.

more to do than play; he must learn to help with the tobacco crop. At first his chore would only entail shooing a flock of turkeys through the fields so that the birds could pick the leaves clean of worms; but greater responsibility quickly followed, for every planter's son must learn the intricacies of growing a vexatious and difficult crop. Sterling was to be involved in raising tobacco for the major part of his life, and this early training was an indispensable part of his education.

Although the Prince Edward planters considered it important that their sons learn tobacco raising, they had no intention of slighting their formal education. The gentry considered formal schooling necessary for a gentleman. Old Pugh Price had been careful to stipulate in his will that his plantation was to support his wife and take care of the "schooling of [his] children."

There are no surviving records to indicate which of the several grammar schools in the area Sterling attended, but he undoubtedly attended one of them in order to pass the entrance examination to gain admittance to Hampden-Sidney College, located in the nearby village of the same name. Because of the proximity of that school he may have attended its grammar department. In order to qualify for entrance into the college division a prospective student had to undergo an examination given by the faculty covering "Caesar's Commentaries, six books; Narrationes Excerptai; Virgil, through the sixth book of the Aeneid, Mair's Introduction; Greek Testament, John, Acts, Romans, and Hebrews; and thirty-three Dialogues of Lucian; or their equivalent."[13] Such was the type of education that planters expected of their sons and Pugh W. Price was no exception, for both Edwin and Robert graduated from Hampden-Sidney.

The college itself reflected the atmosphere of Prince Edward County. While not nearly as grand as William and Mary and soon to be overshadowed by the state university at Charlottesville, Hampden-Sidney strove for both respectability and gentility. Pugh Price and many others continually affixed their signatures to petitions to the Virginia Assembly asking for money from the state library fund for the college. They invariably extolled the college's "superior" education and lamented the manner in which the state neglected it.[14]

When Sterling entered Hampden-Sidney in the fall of 1826 he could not have been unfamiliar with its surroundings. Even if he had not attended its grammar school, he had passed through the local community innumerable times and his father owned land adjoining it. The village itself consisted of two commodious taverns and a dozen

13. "Laws of Hampden-Sidney College," Prince Edward County, Virginia, 1800–1824.
14. Petitions dated December 15, 1825, December 30, 1829, December 20, 1830, Prince Edward County.

or so residences, all shaded by stately oaks and hickories. The college proper had originally been a three-story brick building of twelve rooms. In 1822 a new brick dining hall was added, and there were three other small wooden buildings and one house occupied by students. The library, a small, two-story brick building, housed 450 volumes. The faculty consisted of the president, Jonathan Cushing—who also taught chemistry and natural philosophy—tutors of mathematics, Latin and Greek, and one who was preceptor of the grammar school division.[15] Sterling paid forty dollars tuition and ten dollars room rent and servant's fee per session.[16]

Most of the students were housed in the "new college," the upper floors of the dining hall built in 1822. Sterling's room had only one window and a fireplace and was furnished simply with andirons, shovel and tongs, two pine tables, two pitchers, a wash bowl, two glasses, a looking glass, two chairs, three brooms, and other necessities.[17] New students were soon solicited by upper classmen "electioneering" for either the Philanthropic or the Union debating society.[18]

The first-year curriculum included recitations on three books of Xenophon, Sallust, English grammar and selected parts of rhetoric. The winter session added arithmetic and algebra. With a composition, perhaps on frugality or procrastination,[19] due every four weeks throughout the year, the course of study kept the students occupied. At the close of each session every scholar was required to take a public examination before the faculty.

The social atmosphere of the school, if it met in any manner the rules prescribed by the administration, would have been puritanical indeed. Since the school was Presbyterian endowed, its catalog reflected the sternness of that sect. All students were required to attend morning and evening prayers and to behave "with gravity and reverence during the whole service." All were to be present at public worship on Sundays and strict attendance both at church and in class was mandatory. Students were to be immediately expelled for such things as duelling, robbery, playing cards, dice, or gambling. Strict

15. "A Report of the Condition of Hampden-Sidney" (report submitted by William Morton in an undated petition to the Virginia Assembly), Legislative Petitions, Prince Edward County, 1800–1824, Archives Division, Virginia State Library.

16. *Ibid.*

17. Robert Hubard to his mother, November 6, 1827, Hubard Family Papers.

18. *Ibid.*

19. Edmund Hubard to Robert Hubard, October 10, 1824; a composition on "economy (frugality)" written by Edmund Hubard, dated February 8, 1825, Hubard Papers.

regulations prohibited drinking or indecent dress and there was to be no cooking of meals by the students.[20]

If the officers of the school attempted to enforce these rules to the letter they must have been a frustrated group, for the young men disliked such strict regulations. One scholarly student continually complained of the noise in the "college" and how he was constantly disturbed by his fellow students.[21] One group of pranksters drove a flock of turkeys into the dining hall and another carried off the 500-pound school bell. Even after President Cushing specifically warned the students that the rules prohibited having a "frolic," a group of them held a dinner, with "plenty of liquor," at one of the local taverns and invited a great number of their companions to attend; several reportedly staggered back to their rooms.[22] At another party a student became tipsy, started a fight with a pastor and several others, and "came off with terrible bruises."[23] The planters' sons were bound to have their "frolic" no matter what the rules. Sterling, as prone as his fellow students to disregard the strict regulations, found few of them restrictive, but he greatly disliked the enforced prayers and church attendance. His college experience may well have contributed to his lack of a religious commitment, or at least of regular church attendance, throughout his life.

The college records do not reveal Sterling's performance on his public examination at the end of the term. For some reason, perhaps failure of the examination or a shortage of money, he did not return for the 1827–1828 session, but instead attended Creed Taylor's law school at the latter's home, Nedham, in Cumberland County. Taylor, an intimate of John Randolph of Roanoke and a prominent figure in the Republican party of an earlier period, was a leading Virginia jurist and circuit judge at the time he founded his law school. The school itself was a unique institution since it placed a great deal of dependence upon moot courts, a novelty in that period. Aware of this uniqueness, Taylor sent his school journal to prominent lawyers for their opinions; all, including Thomas Jefferson, answered favorably.[24] Taylor divided his program into three courses involving rigorous training and reading. There is no record of a session of the school

20. "Laws of Hampden-Sidney," 10–11.

21. Robert Hubard to his mother, November 6, 1827; Edmund Hubard to Robert Hubard, October 10, 1824, Hubard Papers.

22. Robert Hubard to Edmund Hubard, March 1, 1828, Hubard Papers.

23. Robert Hubard to Louisiana Hubard, February 29, 1828, Hubard Papers.

24. Thomas Jefferson to Creed Taylor, March 27, 1823; numerous letters from other Virginia jurists throughout the collection, Creed Taylor Papers.

for 1828–1829 and Sterling evidently did not graduate or gain more than a minimal legal education. In 1828 he became an assistant to Branch J. Worsham, clerk of the Prince Edward county court.

V

The most lasting influence on Sterling's life came not from his formal education but from the environment of his youth. In an age when Jeffersonian society was being dissolved by the economic opportunities of a nation drawn to the main chance, the planters of Prince Edward turned to the principles of the Old Republic to anchor themselves. Sterling's formative years brought him into contact with such doctrinaire republicans as Creed Taylor, Branch Worsham, and John Randolph of Roanoke. His own father was also a stalwart old republican.

Of immediate interest to the planters of Prince Edward were internal improvements to make the marketing of their tobacco easier and more profitable, and they did not hesitate to turn to the state government for aid. Pugh signed several such petitions and even Sterling's mother, Elizabeth, signed one.[25] While they favored those projects, they distrusted a large state debt and considered it symptomatic of an oppressive government granting special privileges to the few at the expense of the many. In order to guard against this, they felt the need for constant vigilance against deviations from the state constitution. This need was exemplified in a petition to the Virginia Assembly strenuously objecting to a grant made to a company that had not subscribed two-thirds of the sum needed for its project by other means, as was required by the Virginia constitution.[26]

While Prince Edward planters were eager for improvements, they would approve only those that were deemed necessary and that adhered to rigid principles. John Randolph, their representative in Congress, expressed these views when he asked that body to "leave the profits of labor in the pockets of the people, to rid them of the private embarrassment under which they so extensively suffer," and continued by asking them to "apply every shilling of the revenue, not indispensable to the exigencies of the Government, to the faithful discharge of the public debt, before we engage in any new scheme of lavish expenditure."[27] To Randolph and the Prince Edward planters debt meant subordination of their interests—the transfer rather than the exchange of wealth. Once Randolph exclaimed: "Mr. Speaker, I have discovered the philosopher's stone. It is this, sir—Pay as you go!

25. Petition, December 2, 1812, Legislative Petitions, Prince Edward County.
26. Undated petition, Legislative Petitions, Prince Edward County, 1800–1824.
27. *Annals of Congress*, 18th Cong., 1st sess., Pt. 1:1310.

Pay as you go!"[28] This phrase was to motivate the Prince Edward planters and would be the touchstone of Sterling Price's political life.

Another watchword was that "change is not reform."[29] Southside planters felt that their agrarian, deferential society represented the ideal and they dreaded and mistrusted change. When faced with the movement in the 1820's for a constitutional convention, Prince Edward leaders sent petitions to the assembly vehemently protesting such a gathering. Pugh Price signed a petition stating that the memorialists were certain that the people of Virginia were "perfectly content with their ancient institutions, and most jealous and fearful of the spirit of innovation." In the same document they declared their "content with the good, the very good, which they now possess and enjoy; and can never consent to put it to any risk or jeopardies, in the vain hope of unattainable perfection."[30]

Prince Edward planters watched with anxiety and apprehension when the Virginia constitutional convention met in 1829, because another sensitive subject had arisen—slavery. This institution had been questioned on economic grounds in the early 1820's, but never had such a direct attack been made upon it. Randolph, reflecting the Southside's anxiety, voiced the compelling fear of his constituents: the fear of the Negro. Randolph wrote: "We must concern ourselves with what is, and slavery exists: We must preserve the right of the States, as guaranteed by the Constitution, or the negroes are at our throats. The question of slavery as it is called, is to us a question of life and death."[31] In counties such as Prince Edward, where over half of the population was Negro, whites displayed a morbid sensitivity toward any threat, real or implied, to the institution of slavery. Pugh and his son Sterling were deeply imbued with this same fear.

Randolph mirrored the desires and feelings in more than his positions on internal improvements and slavery; the planters of Prince Edward were in perfect accord with the Burkean philosophy of government and society exemplified by their congressman. From the time that Creed Taylor first urged him to run for Congress,[32] to his defeat by John Eppes in 1813, and through the 1820's, Randolph had the support of Prince Edward County. Randolph seemed the very embodiment of their political and social beliefs; he epitomized the strict construction, State rights ideals that seemed to be the only de-

28. Edmund Quincy, *Life of Josiah Quincy*, 343.
29. This phrase is the title to Chapter Seven in Russel Kirk, *Randolph of Roanoke*. My analysis of Randolph's ideology draws heavily on Kirk's work.
30. Petition, June 16, 1826, Legislative Petitions, Prince Edward County.
31. Quoted in Quincy, *Josiah Quincy*, 212–13.
32. John Randolph, Jr., to Creed Taylor, September 16, 1799, Creed Taylor Papers.

fense against the decay the planters felt around them. While it might seem strange to other Americans that a man as eccentric as Randolph could be elected to the Congress, Prince Edward planters admired his aristocratic ways and never wavered in their loyalty to the man. Pugh W. Price was as ardent a follower of Randolph as any and in 1827 served on a committee to organize a testimonial dinner for him. Branch Worsham epitomized the feelings of those present when he toasted: "The blessings of civil liberty; secured by the constitution as written, not as construed."[33]

As the Administration of John Quincy Adams drew to a close, the planters of Prince Edward were convinced that it embodied special privilege for the few and represented a serious threat to republican principles.[34] In their minds the restoration of lost principles and the regaining of lost status by Southern agrarians would require the election of Andrew Jackson in 1828. A freeholders meeting voted to approve the vigorous measures being taken in Virginia for the election of Jackson and requested that their representatives and senator attend a Jackson meeting to be held in Richmond.[35] When an anti-Jackson convention met in Richmond in June, no delegates attended from Prince Edward.[36] Young Sterling, as an assistant to Branch Worsham, who was on the corresponding committee for the Jackson campaign in Virginia, became caught up in the excitement for Jackson and the Democratic party.

VI

The Southside had fallen on hard times and looked to Jackson to remedy more than political wrongs. The excitement of the tobacco markets from September, 1815, to April, 1816, had been without parallel in the history of leaf tobacco. There had been an almost vertical rise in price from 1814 to 1816; the price per pound before the War of 1812 had been around four cents. In 1815, it soared to over twenty cents, with prime leaf bringing over twenty-five. Dealers drove around the countryside engaging unprized leaf for twelve to fifteen cents a pound; speculation was rampant.[37]

The boom was short-lived. By 1817 the bottom dropped out of the market and prices plummeted. Many shippers and merchants, having utilized the overexpanded credit facilities of the Bank of the United States and state banks, were destroyed in the contraction of credit. An observer noted: "Distress spread almost universally throughout Vir-

33. *Daily Richmond* (Va.) *Enquirer*, April 26, 1827.
34. This may be clearly seen in a series of toasts offered during an Independence Day celebration at Farmville, *ibid.*, July 17, 1827.
35. *Ibid.*, December 25, 1827.
36. *Ibid.*, January 22, 1828.
37. Joseph Clark Robert, *The Tobacco Kingdom*, 132–34.

ginia in 1818–1819, in consequence of the heavy reduction in price of tobacco. . . . Some of the first families were reduced to a state of extreme embarrassment and distress."[38] Although prices recovered slightly in 1820, by the end of that year they showed a tendency to decline—an ominous prophecy of a lean decade to come.

The decade of the 1820's was indeed a lean one, worsened considerably by a feeling of hopelessness that pervaded Southside Virginia. In 1828, the *Daily Richmond Enquirer* proclaimed the futility of denying that the section was far behind others and that "benumbing poverty" and "broken spirits" characterized the area.[39] The *American Farmer*, the most influential agricultural journal of the section, asked its readers, each in his own county, to recall the period twenty to thirty years previous and queried, "did it not then abound in well bred gentlemen farmers, living in good dwellings well supplied; their families genteely clad and well educated; their churches in good repair and well attended; the intercourse of neighboring families social and frequent, and their manners and amusements comparatively refined and elegant?" It then asked: "What is *now* the state of the country? Does anyone build substantial dwellings on a scale, and with conveniences for the genteel accommodation and hospitable entertainment of friends? . . . Have not truck patches with worm fences and cabbage and potatoes taken the place of all the old fruitful paled gardens . . .?" The editor continued: "Formerly there were very many farmers and planters in every county in the state, who could maintain their families in a style of at least comparative affluence, enjoying leisure for mental improvement, and a taste for social pleasure."[40] These were discouraging words for a status-conscious individual such as Pugh Price.

By 1826 many Southerners began to speculate on possible causes of such bad times. The editor of the *American Farmer* suggested that it may have resulted from the subdivision of estates, the existence of slavery, with "the more and more unprofitable results of that species of labor," and the desertion of the region by the "*elite*" for richer soils. A later editorial concluded that the whole character of the area was undergoing a complete transition and that Virginia must adapt her institutions as soon as possible. The change must be away "from large possessions, well disciplined and profitable slave labor, elegance of manners and luxury of living condition in which estates will be cut up." He prophesied that "Slavery will disappear . . . a condition in which *every mother's son*, as in the *country* of New England, must put his own hand to the axe and the plough—and every mother's daughter must give up her silks and her satins and betake herself to

38. *American Farmer*, 1 (1824–1825), 1.
39. *Daily Richmond Enquirer*, March 1, 1828.
40. *American Farmer*, 8:46 (January 26, 1827), 360.

the churn and the wheel. . . ."[41] The *Daily Richmond Enquirer* pointed
out that slavery was adversely affecting the agricultural conditions of
the section and further noted that this was the first time in twenty-
seven years that the paper had touched on the subject of slavery.[42]

To make matters worse, the West was becoming increasingly com-
petitive. In the eyes of the Virginia planters the most ominous development in the first three decades of the nineteenth century was the
opening of new tobacco districts in the western states; this threatened
to eventually eclipse the old areas.[43] Kentucky and Missouri tobacco
drove Virginia tobacco out of certain markets and competed successfully in others.[44]

While the idea that Virginia might become like "the *country* of
New England," causing each man to become a yeoman and to give
up elegant living, genteel pastimes, and, more importantly, slavery,
was repugnant to most Prince Edward planters, it was anathema to
Pugh Price. He had strived to regain the status of his father, only to
meet what he hoped were temporary frustrations. However, in the
1820's these began to assume permanency and even carried with them
a threat to the degree of status he had managed to gain. His hope of
achieving gentility was slipping away.

Through the late 1820's Pugh could only ponder his situation and,
with many others, remain anxiety-stricken. Perhaps, however, what
many Virginians considered the bane of their existence might in
reality prove to be the means by which Pugh could yet achieve the
position he so eagerly desired. If Missouri was the center of excellent
tobacco lands, with slavery firmly entrenched, why not move there?
Surely a man of some means and background could quickly become
prominent in such an environment.

Thus, by late 1830, Pugh had decided to move his family to Missouri; he settled his affairs in Virginia and prepared for the long and
arduous journey. John and Sterling accompanied their parents, the
other children having families of their own, and Elizabeth rode an
ox-drawn wagon containing the household goods and farm imple-
ments. The men rode horseback, while the slaves drove the livestock.

VII

When he left Virginia Sterling had few material possessions: he
was still a member of his father's house. Though he lacked worldly
goods, he carried with him something of far greater importance in
shaping his future—a Southside heritage. He had lived among what
he perceived to be the aristocracy and the gentility of the South and

41. *Ibid.*, 8:46 (February 9, 1827), 375.
42. *Daily Richmond Enquirer*, January 27, 1828, January 11, 1832.
43. Robert, *Tobacco Kingdom*, 142.
44. *Ibid.*, 150.

his father's insatiable desire for status had been instilled into his character; he also brought with him a doctrinaire attachment to old republican principles. These two elements, hunger for status and an attachment to republican principles, were to become the guiding forces in Price's life. When he became caught up in an environment of restless mobility and strident opportunism, he turned to the verities of the Old Republic. However, these two inherently contradictory influences on his character were to create an ambivalence in his personality that could be resolved only after much anxiety and soul-searching.

· 2 ·

Young Leader in Chariton

An overland trip from Virginia to Missouri in 1830, while less dangerous than formerly, still remained strenuous. Hundreds of immigrant wagons might lessen the boredom of the long journey, but they created rutted gullies in the roads during dry weather and quagmires when it rained. Occasionally wagons would fall in together and form companies to ease the inconveniences of travel.

When the Prices reached St. Louis they undoubtedly were impressed with the activity and size of the city, which by 1830 had become a bustling commercial entrepot for the growing hinterland of the Missouri and Mississippi rivers. The city and the state, on the verge of a tremendous period of population growth, would more than double in the next decade.

An urban environment held no attraction for the Southern agrarians, and the Prices remained in the city only long enough to purchase needed supplies for their journey on to Fayette in Howard County. Taking the old Boonslick Trace out of the city, they passed through St. Charles and continued on through the tier of counties north of the Missouri River to Fulton in Callaway County; from Fulton the road led to Fayette.

Upon reaching Fayette the Virginians found only a tiny farm village. The town, laid out just eight years previously, still bore vestiges of its frontier past. Crude log cabins dotted the hamlet, although they were being replaced by neat frame dwellings. Nearly a dozen homes and another dozen or so stores and mechanics' shops surrounded the public square and the new brick courthouse.

Pugh decided to settle only temporarily in Fayette, in order to make a careful selection of land. Having every intention of re-creating as closely as possible his old Virginia life, Price desired fine soil for raising tobacco. Since most of the best land in the Fayette area was already taken, Pugh began to search in Chariton County to the west. There he found broad undulating prairies watered by several small rivers. Within several months Pugh purchased nearly 700 acres in Chariton County and began making preparations to move his family there.[1]

1. Chariton County (Mo.) Deed Book C, 352, 404; Land Journal of James Keyte, Keyte Papers.

In the summer of 1831 the Price family crossed the Grand River at old Chariton and proceeded north over several miles of bottom land. The last dozen miles of their journey, through rich timber land, gradually rose to where the newly founded town of Keytesville nestled among the trees. The earliest village in the county was old Chariton but, by 1831 when the Prices crossed the river, the hamlet, due to constant flooding and a sickly environment, had declined to a single tavern. Earlier in that same year James Keyte, a Methodist minister and farmer, constructed a log cabin on the Mussel Fork of the Chariton River several miles above where it flowed into the Missouri; in addition, he erected a small business house and began to lay out the town of Keytesville. Pugh had selected his land on an expansive prairie several miles south of the budding village. The locality was just beginning to fill up since its settlement, like much of the county, had been retarded by speculative purchases through military bounty land warrants, and those desirous of settling there had found it difficult to get in touch with the absentee owners.

Once established in Chariton County, Pugh quickly began to add to his holdings. Since his land in Virginia had been valuable, money from its sale enabled him to purchase a large acreage. Within a year Pugh owned 4,886 acres valued at nearly $3,000, and ranked seventh in the county in total land valuation.[2]

During this same time the county itself began to show signs of prosperity. The land, well timbered and watered, was excellent for raising corn, wheat, and other crops, but tobacco, its future cash crop, was just beginning to boost the area's economy. Keytesville also began to evidence growth: Isaac Redding built a double log house hotel in 1831 that in turn seems to have encouraged Keyte to erect a mill; within a few months a blacksmith, a doctor, a lawyer, and several businessmen appeared and the village began to prosper.

Both Pugh and John recognized the potential value of town lots and began to purchase such property in Keytesville. In September, 1831, John married Patience Owen, whom he had met while the family was living in Fayette. Soon he built a large two-story frame building in Keytesville and opened it as a hotel. Sterling remained on the farm to supervise the raising of tobacco, wheat, and corn, although he, too, was aware of the possibilities of commercial property.

II

When Sterling arrived in Keytesville he was a handsome young man of twenty-two, over six feet tall with an easy, genteel, yet prepossessing manner about him. Although not a fluent or overpowering speaker, his striking presence commanded respect when he expressed

2. Chariton County Tax List, 1833. There were 162 landholders in the county.

himself. In this new and roughhewn country a man with Price's background and education was certain to prosper if he had the ability and ambition, and Price lacked neither. Within two years after his arrival he moved easily among the county's leading men, and was elected to command the county militia unit.

Sterling, anxious to achieve status comparable to the Virginia gentry from which he had been excluded, found a favorable environment in the Boonslick area of Missouri—a region populated almost exclusively by Virginians who shared much the same aspirations as Price.[3] There was a conscious effort by these people to re-create the gentry society of Virginia. New arrivals were struck by the richness of the land and the affluent lifestyle emerging in the area. One recent Virginia immigrant, expecting to find nothing but "a parcel of ruffians," wrote to those he had left behind that he had seen "more wealth and splendor in one neighborhood [Boonslick area] here than ever I saw in Virginia."[4]

Sterling, anxious to take advantage of his position in this newly developing society, quickly began to search for business opportunities. He spent a good deal of time at Huntsville in neighboring Randolph County, where he discussed a partnership with Walter Chiles, a local merchant. However, it was more than potential business connections that drew the young man to Huntsville. While there he was most often seen at the gay "fandangoes" given by Walter Head, a judge on the Randolph county court and recent immigrant from Orange County, Virginia. Head made every effort to emulate the gentry of his native state; his gatherings would sometimes last for several days and his guests, when not dancing the quadrille, could partake of nuts, cakes, plums, ice creams, candies, and other delicacies that abounded.

While Sterling enjoyed mixing in such company, described by another status-conscious young Virginian as "decidedly the most genteel" he had ever enjoyed,[5] he was much more interested in Martha, the younger of the judge's two attractive daughters. Martha returned his affections and the young couple was married in the judge's home on May 14, 1833. Following the marriage celebration they returned to Keytesville and settled on the Price family farm.

Shortly after his marriage Price formed a partnership with Chiles to engage in general merchandising at Keytesville. Sterling's brother John had sold him his hotel and moved back to Fayette. Sterling shipped most of the furnishings from the hotel to his brother and con-

---

3. The Boonslick area is that region where the counties of Chariton, Saline, Howard, and Cooper converge.

4. Ethelbert W. Lewis to William W. Lewis, January 20, 1837, Lewis letters, printed in *Kansas City Star*, January 21, 1937.

5. *Ibid.*

verted the building into a general store. For the next several years Price and Chiles prospered along with the village. Within five years after its founding, the town contained four general stores, three taverns, and a number of mechanics' shops. In 1832 Keyte's donation of fifty acres of land to the county won the county seat for Keytesville and resulted in the building of a fine two-story brick courthouse.

Not satisfied with his landholdings and partnership, Sterling began to buy land at what was becoming known as Keytesville Landing. The landing came into existence shortly after Keytesville was founded to aid transportation over the considerable distance between the town and the river. Goods imported by the merchants were unloaded from riverboats at the landing and transported by wagon the six miles to the village. Realizing the potential of the area, Price bought property both at the landing and on the rich prairie to the south. The location soon became a bustling riverboat landing and continued to prosper long after Brunswick, another town founded by Keyte on the Missouri River, overshadowed Keytesville.

Price quickly achieved an important position in the community, typical of most successful merchants, and served a variety of community functions.[6] In doing this he emulated the firm of Morton and Venable in his old home in Prince Edward County. These two men had been the richest planters and also the most respected and wealthiest merchants in the county. While having no intention of remaining a storekeeper all his life, Price well knew the value of establishing himself as a merchant in order to provide a stable base for later specialization. Merchandising could provide operative capital to invest in other enterprises. His militia position brought him into contact with the people of the county, thus aiding him in another pursuit which could bring status and success—politics. Within several years after establishing himself in business, Price began to mix in local Democratic politics.

III

In the late fall of 1834 Chariton County voters elected Price their representative at the Democratic state convention to be held in Jefferson City in January, 1835. Thus began a political career that would span two and one-half decades. Like other Missouri Democrats, Price soon became enmeshed in the struggle to forge a unified, cohesive party.

After the presidential election of 1824 an increasing number of Missourians became followers of Andrew Jackson. To them Jackson represented an old Roman republican struggling against a privileged

6. For an excellent description of the merchant and his role in the community, see Lewis Atherton, *The Pioneer Merchant in Mid-America*, 7–30.

elite. The "corrupt bargain" charge helped crystallize feelings of uncertainty, which permeated the rapidly growing state, against Adams.
Thus, by 1828, Jackson was able to carry the state with over 70 per
cent of the vote, and a definite Jacksonian movement had emerged
in Missouri. To say that a Jacksonian "party" existed would, however,
be false. The state had been carried by an amorphous assemblage of
groups, with neither coherent organization nor guiding principles, but
all claiming loyalty to Jackson. The fact that nearly every politician
professed to be a "Jacksonian," while paying only lip service to the
Old Hero, greatly complicated the political situation.

This lack of cohesion allowed the "Opposition"—those who would
form the Whig party in Missouri in 1840—to play one Jacksonian off
against another in order to elect the one most amenable to their interests. Indeed, Opposition men often ran for office claiming to be
Jacksonians,[7] and leading Democratic politicians warned that the
party must unify in order to flush out these "counterfeit Jacksonians."[8]
Congressional and state elections only resulted in further Democratic
disillusionment. It seemed as if one man's announcement of his intention to run for office only led to another's, and so forth until a
vicious circle was formed that played into the hands of the Opposition.

Missouri Democrats looked to the nominating convention in 1835
to bring unity to the party. Many politicians looked to "Boonslick" to
accomplish this.[9] The influential Boonslick leaders, the "Boonslick
Democracy," had purged their faction of "counterfeit Jacksonians"
and were intent upon unifying the party. The leading members of
this faction, composed of the most influential planters and merchants
in the Boonslick region, included Dr. John Lowry, Thomas Reynolds,
Claiborne F. Jackson, Joshua Redman, and Owen Rawlins of Howard
County; Dr. George Penn, Meredith M. Marmaduke, and Dr. John
Sappington of Saline County; and William B. Napton of Cooper
County. Price had already had social and commercial contact with
several of these men, who represented that to which he aspired, and
Lowry had urged him to become a delegate to the convention.

IV

When Price arrived in Jefferson City in January, 1835, he found
the delegates excited with the prospect of unifying the party and
establishing a strong slate.[10] He began to mix with the Boonslick

7. The tactics of the "Opposition" during this period are ably discussed
in John Volmer Mering, *The Whig Party in Missouri*, 28–40.
8. John Miller to Daniel Dunklin, September 16, 1832, March 8, 1832,
Dunklin Collection.
9. Lewis Linn to Daniel Dunklin, September 13, 1831, Dunklin
Collection.
10. Account of the nominating convention taken from the Jefferson
City (Mo.) *Jeffersonian Republican*, January 17, 1835.

leaders who were working behind the scenes and would prove to be the dominant force in the convention. Lowry, unofficial leader of the Boonslick group, was unanimously named presiding officer. Price then moved that a committee be appointed to prepare an address to the people of the state, and Lowry, already acquainted with Price's political beliefs, appointed Price, Redman, and Penn to the committee.

The Boonslick politicians, certain that the party could be unified solely on principles, convinced the delegates that party stability could be attained only by concentrating on issues. Prospective candidates, both state and national, consequently had to answer certain questions to the satisfaction of the convention. The delegates quickly agreed that each candidate must express his views on the recharter of the National Bank, the power of the federal government to create a protective tariff, paper currency, corporations, and "Clay's Land Bill"; a suitable candidate would have to oppose all of these. The assemblage then nominated Martin Van Buren for President, Thomas Hart Benton for vice president, Lilburn Boggs for governor, Franklin Cannon for lieutenant governor, and George Strother and Albert Harrison for Congress.

After the nominations the convention passed a series of resolutions, the most important of which stated that no person could be considered friendly to the Democracy if he put himself forward as a candidate in opposition to the choice of the convention. The remaining resolutions praised Jackson and railed against a national bank.

The address to the people of the state avoided concrete issues in favor of abstract principles.[11] Price, Penn, and the others who drafted the address felt it necessary that the party's general views on government be placed before the people. The resulting statement stressed the sovereignty of the people and urged that Missourians, in order to protect themselves from the "encroaching aristocracy," give up their individual preferences for the common good. The United States Bank and the bank party were said to represent the greatest threat to democratic principles.

The address reflected the basic thinking of most Missouri Democrats. Just as Price felt pleasantly at ease among Missouri planters and their society, he also found the state political environment compatible. Missouri Democrats pledged themselves to the principles of Jefferson. Indeed, in order to gain acceptance by the Democracy, a candidate had first to establish himself as a Jeffersonian. One citizen, in announcing his candidacy for Congress, explicitly stated that he "was born and raised in Virginia, a true Jeffersonian Republican, and in my youth, had those republican principles so deeply impressed upon my mind, that I have not yet forgotten them. . . ."[12] Another

11. *Ibid.*, January 24, 1835.
12. *Ibid.*, June 11, 1831.

potential candidate wrote that "on the subject of my political creed, I profess to be a Republican of the Jeffersonian school."[13]

Missouri Democrats viewed politics in much the same way as their fathers had before them: a struggle between democracy and aristocracy, between Federalists and Republicans. In a column entitled "The Aristocracy Moving," Napton, editor of the *Boon's Lick Democrat*, attacked those men who wanted a branch of the Pennsylvania Bank in St. Louis.[14] Lowry struck the same chord in his impassioned public letters. To him the *ne plus ultra* of disciples of the Jeffersonian school was the sovereignty of the people, while the other party adhered to a "coerced construction of the U. S. constitution." He railed against Clay, Calhoun, Webster, and others whom he felt professed "monarchical principles" for "hurling their poisonous darts at every prominent man in the U. States of the Jeffersonian school of politics, (in common parlance Jackson men)."[15]

Although Price felt comfortable in this political milieu, there were disturbing tendencies among many Missouri politicians. Just as some men professed to be Jacksonians while adhering to anti-Jackson principles, others covered their actions with the cloak of Jeffersonianism. Price, through his growing intimacy with the Boonslick faction, found himself aligned with a group that could effectively combat this unsettling condition. He discovered that he had a great deal in common with these men; they were Southerners, slaveholders, and merchants, but what provided the strongest bond of union was their adherence to a common political ideology: They were doctrinaire old republicans.

This group of individuals from the central part of the state would unify the Democracy; they would become the most powerful faction in the Democratic party and impose their principles upon it.[16] Drawn

13. *Ibid.*, June 18, 1831.

14. Fayette (Mo.) *Boon's Lick Democrat*, August 23, 1836.

15. John Lowry to Abiel Leonard, printed in the *Jeffersonian Republican*, August 26, 1834.

16. When dealing with Missouri politics in this period historians have been misled by the imposing figure of Thomas Hart Benton. The standard interpretation maintains that Benton completely dominated the Missouri Democracy from 1820 to 1850. This belief becomes a controlling factor in Richard McCormick's analysis of Missouri in his provocative *The Second American Party System: Party Formation in the Jacksonian Era*. After noting that secondary sources relating to Missouri politics "are less than adequate" (page 372), McCormick states with certitude that "beyond all conventional influences, Missouri bore the imprint of the personality of Thomas Hart Benton, who dominated political affairs in the state to a degree that has rarely been equalled" (page 304). Later he refers to Missouri as the "political fief" of Senator Benton (page 325).

Thus, even one of the finest recent works on Jacksonian politics succumbs to the legend of the "power" of Benton and provides an excellent

together by their republican principles, the Boonslick politicians were determined to rule the party by these same principles. The relative ease with which the Boonslick group gained control of the 1835 nominating convention, and subsequently the entire state party, is most easily explained by noting the striking similarities between the social and political milieu in Missouri in the 1830's and that of Virginia. Both were gentry-controlled.[17]

Since early settlement in Missouri followed the Missouri River, the river counties comprised the oldest, most populous, and most powerful political area in the state. Almost the entire population of these counties came from the upper South, and most Missouri Democrats brought with them both an ingrained republicanism and an acceptance of political leadership by the social elite. The Boonslick politicians, being the leading planters and merchants in their respective counties, were thus able to exert great social, economic, and political influence.[18] The convention system that arose in Missouri, combined with the general ticket system of nomination and election, was made to order for their oligarchic style of politics. They remained masters of the convention technique for several decades.

V

When the convention adjourned, Price returned to Keytesville to attend to his mercantile business. Soon thereafter Pugh Price divided

---

example of inferring the particular from the general. A cursory glance at Missouri politics shows the Democratic party completely dominating state affairs and Benton representing the state in the United States Senate for thirty years. This view has led historians who study Benton almost exclusively from a national point of view to conclude that he must therefore have dominated the Democratic party of Missouri. A closer examination, however, reveals that the "Boonslick Democracy" played the key role in the formation of the Democratic party in Missouri and controlled party politics within the state. Benton aligned himself with them, and each traded off of the influence of the other. For a detailed analysis of this relationship, see Robert E. Shalhope, "Thomas Hart Benton and Missouri State Politics: A Re-examination," *Missouri Historical Society Bulletin,* 25:3(April, 1969), 171–91. For an analysis of McCormick's entire thesis as it relates to Missouri, see Robert E. Shalhope, "Jacksonian Politics in Missouri: A Comment on the McCormick Thesis," *Civil War History,* 15:3 (September, 1969), 210–25.

17. For an excellent discussion of Virginia life, see Charles Sydnor's *Gentlemen Freeholders* and *The Development of Southern Sectionalism.* For a provocative discussion of the workings of "democracy" in the South, see Stanley Elkins and Eric McKitrick, "A Meaning for Turner's Frontier: The Southwest Frontier and New England," *Political Science Quarterly,* 69:4 (December, 1954), 565–85.

18. A classic picture of the manner in which the Southern social elite "managed" the yeoman may be seen in W. J. Cash, *The Mind of the South,* 41.

his land between John and Sterling, with Sterling receiving most of the land and gaining possession of the home farm because of his interest in tobacco farming. With his earlier purchases, Sterling now became the eighth-ranking landholder in the county, with over 3,000 acres.[19]

All aspects of his life seemed to prosper during the year 1835. In April the political connections made at the convention paid off handsomely and he was appointed Keytesville's first postmaster. The post office was located in Price's store, and helped in attracting customers for his merchandise. On June 10 Martha gave birth to the Prices' first child, a son whom they named Edwin for Sterling's eldest brother.

By August, Sterling decided to continue his career in politics and canvassed the county for election to the Ninth General Assembly. His positions as postmaster, merchant, militia colonel, and leading landholder gave him standing with the voters. Price had risen quickly to a place of prominence in Chariton County and his easy manner, taken by some as vanity, won admiration throughout the area; he easily gained election.

Once again Price set out for Jefferson City. On his way he stopped in Fayette to confer with Lowry and other Boonslick leaders. Since the Boonslick faction had gained control of the 1835 nominating convention, its slate of candidates had been unopposed for the first time by other Democrats. At last some degree of unity was being brought to the party, and the Boonslick group intended to tighten its control in the coming assembly.

Price accompanied Joshua Redman and Owen Rawlins, Howard County's representative and senator respectively, to Jefferson City. On their way they may well have discussed the pressing political issues of the day. They faced the problem of a growing clamor for a constitutional convention to reapportion the state legislature. The Opposition wished to call a convention because each time the legislature created a new county the Democrats gained a seat in the House, and the Opposition lost one.[20] The issues of a state bank and paper currency, having agitated the state for the last four years, were still uppermost in their minds.

After the adjournment of the Eighth General Assembly in 1834, the bank issue remained intense due to the failure of the legislature to write a bank bill. Business in St. Louis had grown to such a degree

19. Chariton County Tax List, 1837.
20. The Missouri State Constitution limited the total number of members in the House of Representatives to 100 and stipulated that each county must have at least one representative. Thus, whenever a new county was created, an old county—usually dominated by the Whigs— lost a representative.

that hard money policies were inadequate, and its Chamber of Commerce petitioned Congress to establish another national bank. Illinois banking institutions were asked to open offices in St. Louis and Illinois bank notes were welcomed. By 1836 Illinois notes became so numerous that they nearly displaced specie circulation and caused much concern to hard money advocates. It became evident to all observers that the failure of the Eighth General Assembly to pass a banking law had only served to intensify the demand from the business community. It also became apparent that many St. Louis Democrats, becoming known as "business Democrats," were extremely unhappy with the hard money attitude of state leaders and intended to press for a change. Lilburn Boggs, the Democratic gubernatorial candidate in 1836, recognized the problem and stated it precisely: "Missouri is the only state without a bank, so we are at the mercy of the money of other states. We get all the evils of a state bank and none of the benefits."[21] This was a telling point. Price and other republicans were suspicious of banks but felt it better to have a republican institution, where currency issue could be controlled, than to suffer from the depreciated currency of other states. By the time of the Ninth General Assembly, there had been a great deal of soul-searching by many Democrats.

As the legislators began congregating, it became apparent that the chartering of a state bank would be the overriding issue of the session. Boggs, having been elected governor, stressed the bank issue in an address to the combined session of the assembly following its convening on November 21, 1836. He had campaigned in favor of a bank and now stated that the incorporation of such an institution was of the utmost importance. Voicing the conclusion of a great many Missouri Democrats, the Governor stated that although "moneyed monopolies may justly be regarded as anti-republican in their spirit and tendency, it may yet be reasonably doubted whether they are not so interwoven with the business and interests of the people, as to render their immediate abandonment productive of great inconvenience."[22]

Soon afterwards the House organized and appointed committees. The Speaker appointed Price to the Committee on Ways and Means and the Committee on Enrolled Bills on the Part of the House. In order to facilitate action on the bank question the Speaker named a select committee on banking but, unfortunately, it seemed impossible for this committee to come to any agreement; there were daily calls for a report but without results. Finally, on December 7, Price introduced a successful resolution calling for the bank bill to be made

21. St. Louis *Missouri Argus*, May 20, 1836.
22. *Journal of the Missouri House of Representatives*, 9th Assembly, 1st sess., 1837, 31.

the standing order of the day after previous business was completed.[23] On January 7, 1837, the committee reported that it could reach no agreement and asked to be relieved. This being done, the matter was placed in the hands of another select committee of five members.

By that time it was becoming evident that the House was divided into three loose coalitions on the issue, although the nature of the assemblage caused these groupings to be vague and transitory. One, for abstract reasons, opposed any bank; the second, led by the Boonslick politicians, favored a republican-type institution with its accompanying strict legislative controls over the management and note issue of the bank; the third group, composed mainly of Opposition members, opposed the creation of a state bank, feeling that such an action would preclude the establishment of a new national bank.

The bank struggle afforded Price the opportunity to become acquainted with the style of politics that would characterize the state for over a decade. The legislature, a reflection of state society, was roughhewn, young, and aggressive. The House met in a crowded room lined with rows of tables and crowded with men talking, laughing, writing, drinking, or congregating in groups in deep conversation. At times the assemblage would become so boisterous that the uninitiated mistook it for a "grog shop."[24] A then-recent Virginia immigrant, attempting to describe the "Physmagog" of the House, felt that one must "picture every kind of mortal from the serene old statesman to the most rough-hewn backwoodsman; with now and then a pert little dandy; . . . ." While laughing at the speech of many of the members, comparing it to that of a common schoolboy, he was impressed with a number of "very smart or rather talented men."[25]

It was within this environment, while seemingly chaotic, that the Boonslick politicians prospered. They gathered support for their position by circulating from group to group or cornering a representative at his table. Price proved uncommonly adept at this style of politics, since his impressive physical appearance and prepossessing manner made him especially suited to this milieu. Soon the Boonslick politicians had gathered enough support to pass their bank bill.

During the third week in January, 1837, a bill entitled an "Act to Charter the State Bank of Missouri" easily passed in the Senate and House, with all but two members of the Opposition voting against it.[26] In the meantime, the House passed a bill excluding all banking agencies from other states, and the Senate concurred. Those favoring

23. *Ibid.*, 250.
24. Ethelbert W. Lewis to William W. Lewis, January 20, 1837, Lewis Letters.
25. *Ibid.*
26. *House Journal*, 9th Assembly, 1st sess., 315.

a republican-style bank thus gained their desire, while at the same time eliminating the hated foreign bank notes from the state.

Compared to similar banks of the day the State Bank of Missouri was a conservative institution.[27] This republican-style bank could issue no paper money in denominations of less than ten dollars; if the bank refused to redeem its notes in specie its charter became null and void. The governor and the General Assembly, through the powers of electing the bank's officers, requiring statements, and appointing investigating committees, were given control of its general policies. Most important to Price and his political intimates was the fact that the bank's very existence required that it must not suspend specie payments.

The passage of the bank bill somewhat mollified the business Democrats and revealed the growing power of the Boonslick faction over the party. They not only had gained the bank they desired but they also controlled the elections of its officers. Indeed, they gained complete control of the branch bank in Fayette, their political capital in Howard County. John Lowry became the branch bank's president and several other Boonslick politicians were elected to its board of directors.[28]

Although the bank bill overshadowed all others in the Ninth General Assembly, several others enacted were pleasing to Price's group. These included an act making it a crime, punishable in extreme cases by death, to foment rebellion among the state's slave population.[29] While the majority of Missourians did not own slaves, Price and the Boonslick group were especially sensitive regarding the institution. Price, realizing the opportunity existed in Missouri for him to attain the status of an aristocrat, knew he must protect slavery, without which there could be no Southern aristocracy. Price, quicker to oppose any jeopardization of slave property than others who were not as status conscious as he, amended a resolution regarding slaves executed by the state to require the government to reimburse their owners.

Issues dealing with internal improvements were also in evidence, although not to the extent they would be later. Like his father, Price was not inherently opposed to internal improvements at public expense, but his republican background taught him to be suspect of them. As evidence of this, he offered an amendment that read "if practicable at a reasonable expense" to a bill providing for a railroad.[30] This presaged the view he would take throughout his public career.

27. John R. Cable, *The Bank of the State of Missouri.*
28. *House Journal*, 9th Assembly, 1st sess., 432–39.
29. *Ibid.*, 228.
30. *Ibid.*, 261.

The Ninth General Assembly adjourned on February 6, 1837, with the Democracy secure. The Boonslick faction had brought unity to the party, and its business and agrarian branches were in accord. Price could feel satisfied with his part in this; while playing no large role in the legislative arena, he had become an intimate of members of the Boonslick group who were assuming the leadership of the party. Price returned to Keytesville after the legislative session.

VI

Tremendous growth had taken place in Missouri during the seven years that Price had been a resident and much of society seemed to be in flux. In the decade of the thirties Missouri more than doubled in population, with Chariton County and Keytesville nearly tripling. The slave population greatly expanded and many new businesses sprang up. Price himself prospered with the times, but he could not escape the uneasiness pervading the nation. This was a time of laissez-faire individualism, with disturbing questions arising from this environment: What was to prevent this seemingly boundless liberty and individualism from completely destroying the values and landmarks provided by the founding fathers? In this mobile and rootless society how was the individual to retain a feeling of continuity with the past? In fact, how could he be certain that there was anything in society that would ensure a fundamental unity and a common loyalty among the people?

While the majority of Americans prided themselves on their material progress, they also yearned for the reassurance and security that could be found in the unity afforded by a cause transcending individual self-interest. A perceptive scholar noted that with "only a loose, and often ephemeral attachment to places and institutions, many Americans felt a compelling need to articulate their loyalties, to prove their faith, and to demonstrate their allegiance to certain ideals and institutions. By so doing they acquired a sense of self-identity and personal direction in an otherwise rootless and shifting environment."[31] For Price, insecure and status-conscious, this need took on a special urgency. He constantly faced tension between his desire to follow the main chance and the republican ideals that contradicted his entrepreneurial wishes.

An opportunity arose in northwestern Missouri that afforded Price and others an opportunity to prove their attachment to American ideals by defending them against what they perceived to be sub-

31. David B. Davis, "Some Themes of Counter-Subversion: An Analysis of Anti-Masonic, Anti-Catholic, and Anti-Mormon Literature," *Mississippi Valley Historical Review*, 47 (September, 1960), 205–24. My analysis of individual and group motivation in the anti-Mormon disturbances in Missouri draws heavily on Davis' keen perception.

versive elements. In 1831 Mormons began to arrive in Jackson County and within two years became involved in friction with their neighbors. The editorial policy of a local Mormon newspaper, *The Evening and Morning Star*, touched off a crisis that resulted in the expulsion of the Mormons from the county. This paper's editorials, bolstered by rumors circulating around the county, convinced many Missourians that the Mormons planned to lead an uprising of the Indians to wipe out the gentile population. In July, 1831, a mob attacked the Mormons and threw the newspaper press into the Missouri River. The Missourians then destroyed neighboring Mormon shops and several houses. Later the people of Jackson County held a meeting and passed several resolutions dealing with the "menace." Those in attendance declared that they felt "called on by every consideration of self-preservation, good society, public morals, and the fair prospects that, if not blasted in the germ, await this young and beautiful country . . ." to defend their attitude toward the Mormon "threat."[32]

The Mormons eventually left Jackson County and settled in newly-organized Caldwell County. By 1836 matters seemingly had quieted down, but within two years the Mormons gained domination of Caldwell County and began to spill over into surrounding counties. Northwest Missouri became alarmed and sporadic incidents erupted; Chariton County did not escape the ferment. Daniel Ashby, James Keyte, and Price, reflecting the local alarm, requested the governor to call out the militia. The three men declared that they were "strongly of the opinion that there is a deeply laid scheme existing among these fanatics, that will be highly destructive of character and at once subversive of the rights and liberties of the people."[33]

Governor Boggs did not attempt to quiet the agitation, instead he ordered the militia to punish the Mormons.[34] The first brigade of the Missouri militia, consisting of men from Howard County, rendezvoused in Fayette and rode for Chariton County. In the meantime, Price, commanding the Chariton militia, helped General Robert Wilson gather the second brigade. The entire division then met at Keytesville on October 30 and marched for Far West, arriving there five days later. On the night of their arrival the division commander, General John B. Clark, took his field officers and a few men into the Mormon village to ferret out the guilty Mormons. For several days Clark held what amounted to an inquisition; all the Mormons were paraded before him and he had certain ones he deemed guilty

32. *Jeffersonian Republican*, August 17, 1833.
33. Ashley, Keyte, and Price to Governor Lilburn Boggs, September 1, 1838, printed in *Document Containing Correspondence, Orders, etc. in relation to the disturbance with the Mormons. . . .*
34. My analysis of the action against the Mormons is drawn from the letters and orders *ibid.*

pulled out to be tried. While this went on the militiamen ransacked the town.

Price accompanied General Clark and the division to Far West. There Clark ordered him to take two companies to Richmond to receive arms and prisoners taken by General Samuel B. Lucas in action to the West. When Price reached Richmond he discovered that Lucas had not arrived, so he led his mounted men to Independence where they found Lucas and his captives. Price's companies escorted the prisoners back to Keytesville and Price remained in charge of the guard while the Mormons awaited trial. This action took place in bitterly cold weather accompanied by heavy snow, with the Mormons incarcerated in empty warehouses with no heat and few comforts. The Missourians treated them roughly and Price took no steps to intervene.[35]

General Clark, in a letter to the Governor, reflected the attitude Missourians held toward the Mormons. The General described "societies formed under the most binding covenants in form, and the most horrid oaths to circumvent the laws, and put them at defiance, and to plunder and burn and murder, and divide the spoils for the use of the church."[36] The Missourians were certain, if deluded, that they were protecting revered institutions against fanatical subversives and in combating such a dreaded menace they felt no regret in using the same methods attributed to their enemy.

In January, 1839, Keytesville citizens held a mass meeting and felt compelled to express their feelings toward the Mormons. Price and three others drafted the resolutions. Their report denied that the county had been unnecessarily harsh in putting down the Mormons, stating that it had been lawfully proven that the Mormons were "a set of lawless fanatics who had everything other than religious purposes in view." They highly approved of Governor Boggs' harsh measures and went on to say that they felt those who sided with the Mormons had "some hidden purposes, other than friendship to law and justice."[37] Reflecting the tensions of the period, Price and the others were convinced that their behavior reflected courage and honor.

VII

Price's militia activities precluded his serving a second term in the legislature, but his role in dealing with the Mormons elevated his

35. *Autobiography of Parley Parker Pratt*, Parley P. Pratt, ed., 210; B. H. Roberts, *History of the Church of Jesus Christ of the Latter Day Saints*, III, 205–6.
36. Major General John B. Clark to Governor Lilburn Boggs, November 10, 1838, in *Document regarding Mormons*.
37. *Jeffersonian Republican*, January 19, 1839.

standing in the county more than if he had served in the assembly, and his political friends attended to his interests. During the Tenth General Assembly the Boonslick politicians secured his election to a directorship of the branch bank at Fayette.

After the Mormon difficulties, Price took steps to improve his own financial position. His mercantile partner Chiles had contracted huge debts for which the partnership was held liable.[38] Displeased with the arrangement, but nonetheless liable, Price met his financial obligations, then dissolved the partnership and formed another with Lisbon Applegate, a prosperous merchant and leading figure in Keytesville. This proved much more satisfactory and the new firm prospered.[39]

As the first decade of Price's life in Missouri drew to a close his position in society seemed secure. He had achieved a status he could never have attained in Prince Edward and he appeared to be on the verge of even greater achievements. Only a personal tragedy dulled Price's happiness: Little Amanda, Sterling and Martha's daughter born in August, 1837, died a little more than a year later.

38. Records of debts totaling over $3,000 may be found throughout the Abiel Leonard Papers; Leonard was engaged by eastern firms to prosecute their debts. Leonard Papers.

39. Accounts of this partnership may be found in the Lisbon Applegate Collection.

· 3 ·

Speaker for the Boonslick Democracy

During the months after the cessation of fighting with the Mormons, Price often visited Fayette and became intimate with John Lowry, who encouraged him to remain in politics. Consequently he decided to run for the Eleventh General Assembly and began his canvass in the summer of 1840. He won easily in the August elections, as did the Democratic state ticket.

After their successes in the August elections the Democrats called a young men's convention to meet in October in Jefferson City. Price accompanied Lowry to the capital. En route they may have discussed Price's role in the coming assembly; many people felt he should be Speaker, even though he had served only one term and was only thirty years of age.[1] His activities during the Ninth General Assembly and his role in the Mormon difficulties had worked greatly to his advantage.

Even before the meeting convened the Boonslick politicians began circulating among the delegates, making their presence felt by joking and talking with all in attendance. Lowry, Price, and D. R. Scott soon found themselves on a committee to invite members of the congressional delegation to address the gathering; Price was appointed to chair the committee to draw up resolutions expressing the sense of the meeting.[2] Thomas Harvey, an associate of the Boonslick group from Saline County, introduced a series of resolutions to provide for a more thorough party organization, thereby hoping to obviate future party schisms. These resolutions, prompted by the Boonslick leaders,[3] reflected the oligarchic nature of the party and the growing power of the Boonslick faction within the organization. Harvey's resolutions, which passed easily, created a state central committee with power over similar county and township organizations. All nine men making up the state committee were to be residents of Howard County empowered to fill any vacancies that might occur within their committee. Lowry became chairman of the state

1. St. Louis *Missouri Argus*, September 14, 1840.
2. Account of convention, resolutions, and address to the people in the Jefferson City (Mo.) *Jefferson Enquirer*, October 15, 1840.
3. C. F. Jackson to M. M. Marmaduke, August 7, 1840, Sappington Papers.

committee, which also included C. F. Jackson and D. R. Scott. With these matters concluded the assemblage marched to the Capitol and Lowry introduced Senator Thomas Hart Benton, who delivered one of his most powerful speeches on the currency question. In soaring phrases Benton called for every state to suppress the circulation of paper money in denominations of less than twenty dollars. "Old Bullion" labeled the currency problem the "great question of the age" and called for the Democratic party to "purify and protect" hard money in order to save labor, industry, and commerce "from the depredations of depreciated paper."[4] Price, asked by his committee to obtain Benton's permission to print his speech, met with the Senator following his oration. The two men, so close in their political principles and so alike in their personalities, were soon engaged in friendly conversation. This initiated what was to be a stormy relationship.

As chairman of the committee to present the sense of the meeting, Price introduced the committee resolutions and these were adopted by the delegates. Thus the convention resolved to support Martin Van Buren for the Presidency, expressed its approval of his ten-hour work day for federal employees, and called for paper money of less than twenty dollars to be replaced by gold and silver. The group also warned St. Louis corporations that had assumed banking functions in violation of their charters that their charters might be revoked.

Chairman Price was largely responsible for a resolution linking the Whig presidential candidate, William Henry Harrison, with abolitionism. This resolution railed against the juncture of "federalists and abolitionists" and their union with English abolitionists. Price, exhibiting the stance he would assume throughout his life on this question, declared that this was just cause for alarm "not only to all the slaveholding States, but to all the friends of our constitution, and all who desire the duration and perpetuity of our union." Price may also have been instrumental in drafting the "Address to the People of the State of Missouri," for it reiterated the resolutions in Jeffersonian rhetoric. The address warned Missourians that paper currency and illegal corporations were the instruments of the "aristocracy" and pictured Harrison as tainted with Federalism and a threat to slavery.

II

Representatives and senators of the Eleventh General Assembly began to gather in Jefferson City the second week in November and the subtle persuasion of the Boonslick politicians became apparent

4. Benton's currency speech printed in the *Jefferson Enquirer*, August 31, 1843.

when the session commenced and the houses organized. The Senate elected Owen Rawlins as president pro tem and the House unanimously selected Price its speaker. With Thomas Reynolds, elected in August, in the Governor's Mansion and Meredith M. Marmaduke his lieutenant governor, the Boonslick group also controlled the executive branch. John C. Edwards and John Miller, Missouri's representatives in Congress, both resided in the central part of the state and were close associates of the Boonslick group. With Lewis Linn and Benton, both ideological allies of the Boonslick faction, in the United States Senate, republican control of the Missouri Democracy was secure.

Reynolds' inaugural address enunciated his faction's political ideology;[5] reminiscent of the thought of John Taylor of Caroline, it warned against the central government's encroachment, "by almost imperceptible degrees, upon the reserved rights of the states. . . ." Reynolds called for strict vigilance by the people and, further, for them to demand strict economy in public spending. Extravagance could only create a public debt that would lead to the loss of "that high-toned spirit of independence which a republican government, of all others, should take a pride in maintaining." This debt would also create burdens on the people, "particularly upon the cultivators of the soil." His view of public spending was no less applicable for state government. Thus he refused to spend money for unnecessary internal improvements and called for hard money and the suppression of what he considered to be fraudulent corporations.

Reynolds' closing sentences illustrated the Southerner's proclivity to interrelate the issues of slavery and State rights. They also revealed the Boonslick group's passionate adherence to the South's peculiar institution. The Governor lashed out at the abolitionists' "head long fury," fearing that they would "trample upon the rights of the slave-holding states and expose us to all the horrors of a servile war." Reynolds considered the institution of slavery the sole prerogative of the states in which it existed and declared that Missourians would "be wanting in self-respect, and regardless of our undoubted rights, were we to suffer the least interference with this delicate question, from any quarter."

After Reynolds' speech the General Assembly organized itself into committees to carry out the Governor's suggestions. Price was fair in his committee choices, but took care to appoint Joshua Redman to chair a special committee appointed to handle questions regarding the state bank and currency issues.[6]

Shortly after the legislative session began Redman introduced a

5. *Journal of the Missouri House of Representatives,* 11th Assembly, 1st sess., 1841, 28–33.
6. *Ibid.,* 27.

resolution to tighten restrictions on the state bank.[7] On December 4, 1840, he introduced another bill to prevent the circulation of small bank notes and depreciated currency and to compel corporations to obey their charters. W. B. Napton, Missouri supreme court judge and prominent member of the Boonslick group, felt it should be defeated because of the ease with which lawyers would be able to pick it to pieces.[8] Evidently many others shared Napton's opinion, for the bill failed to pass.

On the same day that Redman introduced his currency bill Governor Reynolds sent a letter to the House regarding the refusal of Governor William H. Seward of New York State to surrender fugitive slaves that had escaped from the South. Responding to a letter from the governor of Virginia that requested the slave states to cooperate in measures that Virginia might adopt, Reynolds asked that the House consider Missouri's response. Seward's position—that slaves were not property and therefore not subjects of larceny—greatly distressed Reynolds and he feared that, unless Missouri responded strongly, her non-slaveholding neighbors might adopt this same dangerous doctrine.[9] The House left the matter in the hands of its Speaker.

On December 8 the combined assembly met to elect officers for the state bank and its branches. For the first time there were regular slates of candidates in opposition to those named by the Democratic majority. The Democratic candidates, named by the Boonslick group, won handily,[10] but the opposition, led by prominent members of the newly-formed Whig party, reflected the growing divergence between the business interests of St. Louis and the agrarian outstate region.

On January 17, 1841, Wade Jackson, Claiborne's brother, reflecting the essentially anti-capitalistic bias of the Boonslick faction, amended a bill incorporating an insurance company to include unlimited liability for that company's officers, directors, and stockholders. A bill calling for limited partnerships appeared at about the same time and brought the ambivalence of Price and others to a crisis; Price was not the only man who had suffered as a result of the unlimited liability of partnerships and was certainly not the only Democratic leader involved in commercial ventures. Price's entrepreneurial impulses now confronted his doctrinaire republican political principles. His republican principles prevailed as he voted with the Democratic majority to defeat the bill.[11]

7. *Ibid.*, 52.
8. Napton to M. M. Marmaduke, December 30, 1840, Sappington Papers.
9. *House Journal*, 11th Assembly, 1st sess., 113–14.
10. *Ibid.*, 115–39.
11. *Ibid.*, 431.

This session saw issues come to the fore that greatly troubled Price. While the business liability bills caused him some agitation, it was Seward's action and Reynolds' letter that most deeply disturbed him. Having assumed personal responsibility for directing the House's action on this matter, Price introduced a series of resolutions constituting the General Assembly's response to the Virginia governor's request. These accused Seward of demonstrating an utter disregard for the Constitution and the rights of the slaveholding states, thereby endangering the harmony of the Union. In Price's opinion any state that required a master to establish a claim before a jury, "who might and frequently would be Abolitionists, and who are known wholly to disregard the rights of a master," was a mockery of the rights of all slave states, as was the contention that slaves were not property. The resolutions further stated that Missourians, greatly upset by the New York governor's conduct and by his "dangerous and alarming doctrines and principles," would make "common cause with the said slaveholding States until redress is afforded." Price's final resolution called for a boycott of New York goods by Missourians. After striking this last measure the House passed the resolutions by a vote of 90–3.[12]

Meanwhile the struggles within the legislature over currency, banking, and corporations began to assume the definite shape of St. Louis against the agrarian outstate area. The agrarian majority greatly aggravated this conflict by passing an incorporation amendment affecting the ward bounds and the suffrage qualifications within the city.[13] Feelings now began to run high outside the assembly and Abel R. Corbin, powerful Democratic editor of the *Missouri Argus*, began to align his newspaper with the city against the center of the state.

The state bank president, John Smith, elected by the agrarian majority, recognized the antagonism toward the outstate area that existed in the city and was apprehensive lest his directors turn against him.[14] This fear proved well-founded: On January 10, 1840, Smith's directors overruled him and the bank began to receive depreciated currency. This decision reflected the growing consensus among St. Louisans that the politicians of the center were antagonistic to their best interests.

When the directors decided to accept paper money the *Argus* came out in their favor. To make matters worse, Corbin widened the breach between the city and the agrarians by attacking Lowry, the *Jefferson*

12. *Ibid.*, 357–58.
13. *Laws of Missouri, 1840–1841*, 129–41.
14. John Smith to M. M. Marmaduke, January 10, 1840, Sappington Papers.

Enquirer, Reynolds, and the *Boon's Lick Democrat* as constituting a "Central Clique."[15]

Corbin's actions prompted the *Enquirer,* the leading organ of the central group, to make a series of attacks on Corbin for "squinting" toward "bank aristocracy."[16] Governor Reynolds, also agitated, feared that Corbin had "sold himself to the Federalists" and wanted to unite the various sections of the state against the center to break down the "Democracy of Boonslick."[17]

As late as August, 1840, George Penn, a Boonslick stalwart, had attempted to persuade Corbin to change his policy, but the editor remained adamant. By October Corbin had sold the *Argus* to Shadrach Penn, a Kentucky editor recently arrived in St. Louis. George Penn, no relation to the new editor, was so flushed by this good news that he solicited Marmaduke, Sappington, and Thomas Harvey for $3,000 to aid Shadrach Penn in getting established.[18] Little did the Boonslick men suspect that they were pressing a viper to their bosom.

III

By the winter of 1841–1842 it appeared as if an open rupture in the Democratic party was imminent. The St. Louis city elections in 1840 had seen a noticeable disaffection among bank Democrats, whose actions aided in a Whig victory. The Whigs were hoping for a return to the halcyon days of the early 1830's when a coalition of bank Democrats and Whigs had gained numerous victories. Adding to the currency dispute was the growing discontent that arose in St. Louis and other regions against the central part of the state. This stemmed from the fact that Missouri still elected her representatives to Congress by the general ticket system. The Boonslick group's control of the party machinery and the nominating conventions was greatly augmented by the general ticket system of nominating and electing congressmen. The *Ozark Eagle,* a Democratic paper published in Springfield, reflected this unrest by grumbling about "centralism" and aiming denunciations at the "Central Clique."[19] This area favored hard money but endorsed the creation of congressional districts, thereby providing a lever to be used against the Boonslick group by the revolting business Democrats.

The position of the business Democrats was greatly enhanced by a split in the Whig party caused by nativism, thus allowing the Demo-

15. St. Louis *Daily Missouri Republican,* April 21, 1841.
16. *Jefferson Enquirer,* March 25, 1841.
17. Reynolds to M. M. Marmaduke, April 12, 1841, Sappington Papers.
18. Penn to M. M. Marmaduke, August 23, 1841, October 8, 1841, Sappington Papers.
19. *Eagle* articles reprinted in Columbia (Mo.) *Patriot,* June 17, 1842.

crats to carry the St. Louis legislative elections. For the first time the entire St. Louis delegation to the state assembly consisted of Democrats. It was not long before the agrarian Democrats had cause to wish that the Whigs had been victorious, since the St. Louis Democrats, soon to be known as "soft" Democrats, assumed the leadership of the opposition to the hard-money agrarians. A year after the election David Rice Atchison lamented the fact that whenever St. Louis elected Democrats to the legislature "confusion always follows."[20]

While the Boonslick group was able to still the discord for the time being by making shrewd use of an increase in representative positions after the 1840 census, the faction received a setback from Congress when that body passed a law requiring state legislatures to create single-member congressional districts. This was anathema to the Boonslick group and provided ammunition to the rebellious softs. The issue was drawn, and it would take a great deal of political finesse for the Boonslick politicians to control it.

IV

In 1842 Price was prospering. He received good profits from his partnership with Applegate and his tobacco production had expanded. As one of Chariton's first citizens he easily gained re-election to the Eleventh General Assembly and was rising rapidly in the state Democracy. His family life was also much happier—Martha had given birth to a second son in March, 1841, whom they named Celsus. Price, nonetheless, was still affected by the loss of his daughter Amanda and formed a fond affection for his niece Elizabeth, daughter of Patience and John. In 1840 Sterling's brothers Edwin and Robert Pugh moved their families to Missouri; Edwin settled in Brunswick and Robert started a meat-packing business in Glasgow; and Pamela and her husband John B. Royall settled in Columbia in Boone County.

Though 1842 was a good year for Price, it was not for the region as a whole. Hard times had reached the state, accompanied by a currency shortage, falling prices and wages, and sheriff's sales. Robert's business in Glasgow failed. Missourians began to ask for relief, and to many this meant easy money. The conflict between "hards" and "softs" sharpened into more than an antagonism between St. Louis and the outstate region, thus causing the Boonslick group serious anxieties.

Governor Reynolds, concerned with the coming assembly and desiring Price to remain its leader, wondered if he would serve again as Speaker. Price assured Benjamin Stringfellow, the Governor's correspondent, that he would be pleased to know his friends were satisfied with the way he had handled the office. For Price, the speak-

20. Atchison to Thomas Reynolds, April 6, 1843, Reynolds Papers.

ership no longer represented simply a desire for office; he would view a defeat as an implied censure. His growing vanity caused him to become more and more sensitive regarding his public image.[21]

The Boonslick faction was well aware that the bank issue would again be explosive. Its consensus was that George Penn should be elected president of the state bank, since he would administer it in a conservative manner. William Napton concluded that: "We must either have a bank of our own or exclude all Bank paper from the State and rely on hard money soley [*sic*]—or a Bank of the U. S. must come." Reflecting the views of his faction, he definitely felt that the first was the more practical choice.[22]

In August, 1842, Benton increased the faction's problems by returning to the state to agitate for currency reform. In a public statement he proclaimed that "a base currency afflicts the state," and that those who favored easy money represented a "Federalist" plot to force the people to call for a new national bank. The Senator then exclaimed: "I began the war against this Bank almost '*solitary and alone*' twelve years ago (for I had but few backers, but among them Jackson and Van Buren) and have lived to see the institution in dust and infamy. . . ."[23]

Benton's statement prompted A. B. Chambers, editor of the *Daily Missouri Republican,* the most powerful Whig paper in the state, to call it "a specimen of bombast and egotism which could hardly be excelled . . . the pronouns *I* and *me* are the most conspicuous words in the letter, and it is evident the writer thinks himself the Hercules of the day."[24] Unfortunately, not only Whigs took offense at Benton's statements. Shadrach Penn and his *Missouri Reporter,* several months after taking over from Corbin, energetically took up where the latter left off. On November 1, the *Reporter,* now the most prominent soft Democratic paper in the state, carried an angry editorial. No man, it declared, should be allowed "to dictate to a party . . . men of the same party often differ," and no one should be permitted to act as "an arrogant and arbitrary dictator."[25] This would not be the last time Benton's tirades would interfere with the Boonslick faction's efforts to conciliate the state in order to preserve its hard-money policies.

V

When the Twelfth General Assembly convened, Thomas English nominated Price for Speaker. Thomas Wash, a St. Louis soft, nomi-

21. Stringfellow to Reynolds, September 20, 1842, Reynolds Papers.
22. Napton to Thomas Reynolds, October 6, 1842, Reynolds Papers.
23. *Daily Missouri Republican,* November 1, 1842.
24. *Ibid.*
25. St. Louis *Missouri Reporter,* November 1, 1842.

nated Jesse B. Thompson, but Price gained election 72–11.[26] This seemingly easy victory for the Boonslick faction proved deceptive since no divisive issue had been involved and Price had proven to be a popular Speaker. The next day Governor Reynolds presented his message to the combined assembly; he warned against circulation of paper money, against corporations assuming banking functions, and pointed out that the state bank was circulating and accepting currency from non-specie-paying banks. He believed the federal law to district the state was unconstitutional and suggested that the state decide the issue for itself.[27]

The day after the Governor's message the combined assembly met and elected Lewis Linn to the Senate with only a scattering of opposition. The House was equally harmonious in opposing the congressional call for districting. Joseph Wells of Warren County offered a preamble and joint resolutions that later made up the bulk of the report of a committee chaired by Thomas Hudson. In essence the House voted that submission by the state would be a surrender of sacred principles and that Missouri would not submit; instead, the legislators would regulate themselves by "correct principles," in utter disregard of the provisions of the federal redistricting act.[28]

The divisive issue of the meeting was to be the state bank and its policies as determined by its officers. The hards were determined to elect George Penn and the St. Louis Democrats objected strenuously to a hard from the outstate area becoming president. Thomas Hudson, a prominent St. Louis soft, led an opposition that wanted to elect Ferdinand Kennett, a director who had voted to accept depreciated paper currency. Since both groups were still conciliatory, and neither wished to disrupt party unity, hard and soft leaders agreed to submit the issue to a party caucus. Before it could meet, however, a series of disruptive incidents occurred.

Prior to the assembly meeting Governor Reynolds had appointed a special committee to investigate the bank's decision to accept depreciated currency. S. H. Whipple, a hard, called for the committee's report prior to the day scheduled for the caucus, and Hudson and the softs, to avoid incrimination, voted in favor of Whipple's resolution.[29] Claiborne Jackson hoped to expose loose business practices in the main bank in St. Louis and called for a detailed report from the cashier; Hudson countered by amending Jackson's motion to include the Fayette branch.[30] The investigating committee's report criticized the management of the bank and, by inference, Kennett.

26. *House Journal*, 12th Assembly, 1st sess., 1844, 5.
27. *Ibid.*, 19–36.
28. *Ibid.*, 56.
29. *Ibid.*, 92–94.
30. *Ibid.*

Hudson, probably suspicious of the Boonslick faction's power in caucus, led a soft refusal to go into caucus. Evidently the softs felt that Kennett would have a much better chance on the open floor where he would have the support of the Whigs.

On December 5, the day set for the election of bank officers, both houses convened in a combined meeting. Shortly after Hudson placed Kennett's name in nomination, Carty Wells, a Lincoln County hard, offered a resolution to postpone the election until the second Monday of January in order to give the assembly time to receive the report of the cashier.[31] Price and the hards favored this, but it failed. After this setback the hards feared a defeat of Penn and instead supported Robert Campbell of St. Louis, who lost 91–38.[32] The remaining elections went much better for the hards, who gained many of the directorships and easily re-elected Lowry president of the Fayette branch.[33]

The bank elections of 1842 illuminated the obstacles the Boonslick faction faced in the assembly. Party organization in Missouri never attained a point where continued regularity of voting was assured. Democrats in the assembly, with the exception of several cohesive factions, constituted a formless collection of unaligned individuals. Issues of orthodox Democracy such as opposition to a national bank, a protective tariff, internal improvements at federal expense, soft currency, and corporations formed broad outer limits within which there existed innumerable individual preferences. Only when an issue clearly involved questions of orthodox Democracy could a vote be expected to adhere to party lines. When this was not the case individual legislators continued to vote on the merits of each question as they saw them, rather than in consideration of a larger interest.

In the eleventh and twelfth assemblies, Price represented the closest thing to a party manager that existed. While C. F. Jackson served as floor leader and parliamentarian for the hards when the House was actually in session, it was Price who rounded up support for hard measures and brought recalcitrant legislators into line. Although only an adequate parliamentarian and a poor orator, Price displayed a special adroitness for party management. Shunning oratorical persuasion he moved among legislators during House recesses and after-hours, exerting an unobtrusive but relentless pressure. His commanding presence and aura of leadership made him singularly suited for this task.

Throughout his public and military career Price possessed a unique facility for eliciting almost blind loyalty among many Missourians. Even though his opponents viewed him as vain and pompous, he was already beginning to evince a growing charisma that would prompt

31. *Ibid.*, 100–101.
32. *Ibid.*, 101–2.
33. *Ibid.*, 101–28.

many Missourians to turn to him in times of crisis. Price's persuasive skills and powerful presence were perfectly suited to the legislative milieu existing in Missouri in the 1840's. With the bulk of Democratic legislators drawn from the upper South and thus already amenable to his principles, his task was made much easier. Many Missourians, however, especially those from the newly-created counties, occasionally displayed a stubborn individualism and could not be swayed even by so persuasive and prepossessing an individual as Price.

Such was the case in the election of president of the Bank of Missouri in 1842. Price and the other hards realized they had not gained sufficient support for Penn because the legislators did not feel any clear principles were at stake. Rather than risk the defeat of a Boonslick friend, Penn was not nominated.

While the hards were not successful in electing Penn they did gain a bill regulating currency. Claiborne Jackson reported it out of the special committee on currency and banking after similar measures by Redman and G. W. Huston had failed. Jackson's bill, although a revision of previous ones, differed from the others in that it did not illegalize the passing of depreciated currency of less denomination than ten dollars by private citizens; instead, this measure assessed heavy penalties on corporations for so doing. The bill would be as effective as the others but eliminate the odious elements of previous ones that had inflicted heavy penalties on individuals as well as corporations. Jackson's bill passed the House 53–40, and the Senate by an unrecorded vote.[34] At last the hards had accomplished the regulation of currency and the suppression of illegal banking by corporations.

If the hards gained success on the currency dispute, their cardinal desire, they suffered a setback in their opposition to the calling of a constitutional convention; a bill for that purpose passed 57–23.[35] On February 22, 1843, a bill to create congressional districts arrived from the Senate. Price ruled it out of order on grounds that the House had indefinitely postponed one containing the same provisions during the session and therefore could not consider the measure. Hudson appealed the decision but the House sustained its Speaker 54–39.[36]

If the divisions within the assembly were shifting and somewhat conciliatory, those outside were not. The bank issue touched off a vitriolic newspaper war that resulted in hard and soft alignments throughout the state. With Benton up for re-election in the next assembly, the softs had a convenient target upon which to focus their discontent, although they vented equal spleen upon the Boonslick group. "Centralism" became the rallying cry of the softs as they dili-

34. *Ibid.*, 533.
35. *Ibid.*, 334.
36. *Ibid.*, 509–10.

gently attempted to win over hard areas that favored districting or a convention. Shadrach Penn bitterly denounced the sins of the "Central Clique," thus assuming the leadership of the soft forces.

VI

After the legislature adjourned, Price returned to Keytesville and his business affairs. He began to put his land at Keytesville Landing to profitable use by constructing a tobacco warehouse to facilitate storing and shipping tobacco for himself and others. He also began to develop what was to become one of the finest tobacco plantations in the region. Earlier in the year Martha had borne him a third son, whom they named Heber.

Price had become a leading figure in the state Democratic party, but his own ambition impelled him to strive for a larger and more profitable role. He talked with Claiborne Jackson regarding an appointment as land commissioner. When Jackson informed him that this office required a practical knowledge of surveying Price asked him about an appointment as tobacco inspector and superintendent of tobacco warehouse construction, remarking that "he must have something out of the general distribution of favors." Jackson jokingly asked him if he would settle for a pan of old brushes, to which Price, responding in the same vein, replied that he would be grateful for any favors.[37]

Price, identifying his own political future with Benton's, canvassed Chariton County for the Senator. Nearly every county in the state held meetings during the early months of 1844 and declared their feelings in resolutions printed and circulated in local newspapers. In several counties feelings ran so high that separate meetings convened and two sets of delegates were appointed to the approaching state Democratic nominating convention. Three names circulated as possible choices for governor: Meredith M. Marmaduke, an out-and-out hard and an uncompromising opponent of districting and a constitutional convention; John C. Edwards, a hard, who held no particular views on the convention issue and favored nomination by district and election by the general ticket; and Austin A. King, a moderate on the currency issue, who favored districting and a constitutional convention.

When the Democratic nominating convention met in Jefferson City on April 1, 1844, an air of tension pervaded the hall.[38] The first and most important action was the election of a presiding officer, for his selection would indicate the direction the convention would take. The Boonslick faction's strenuous behind-the-scenes work among the

37. Jackson to Reynolds, March 12, 1843, Reynolds Papers.
38. Account of the convention taken from the Boonville *Missouri Register*, April 16, 1844.

delegates paid off handsomely and the convention elected Price its presiding officer. The Boonslick group, recognizing the tremendous appeal Price seemed to have for most of the delegates and hoping to capitalize on his vote-getting ability, had pressed his election. The post would enable him to name the important committees, including those on credentials and resolutions, and his biased use of the gavel could help silence the softs.

Immediately after his election Price and his faction began to exert their control. They gained passage of a resolution stating that all persons must submit their right to a seat in the convention to the credentials committee and must abide by its decision. With the passage of this resolution the Benton County soft delegation realized the futility of hoping for a Price-appointed committee to rule in its favor and walked out. Not long after this the credentials committee approved the hard delegation from St. Louis and refused to seat the soft delegation led by Thomas Hudson. Price's appointees did not disappoint him.

The third day of the convention brought the nomination of candidates for Congress and saw the Boonslick politicians, after running roughshod over the softs, proceed with great tact. The convention nominated by districts to allay the fears of some, although the election would be according to the general system. Price received the first nomination; he apparently was to have much more than the speakership of the state assembly, a tobacco inspectorship, or a pan of old brushes. Finishing the congressional nominations, the convention moved to the state offices. The Boonslick group then made a tactical move and threw its support to John Edwards, who received the nomination for governor, rather than nominate Marmaduke. By doing this the Boonslick politicians cemented relations with those hard areas that favored districting and a convention. With their influence they may well have been able to nominate Marmaduke, but this would have been at the risk of creating disunity among the hards. The Boonslick men were willing to compromise on districting and a convention in order to protect their hard-money principles.

When resolutions were in order to express the sense of the convention a fight developed on the floor. A delegate from Cooper County called for a resolution against the bills regulating currency and asked that no Democratic editor be proscribed for coming out against the general ticket system of electing congressmen or being in favor of a constitutional convention. At this point Price recognized a call from the Howard County delegation for the previous question, thus preventing the Cooper resolutions from coming to a vote. The resolutions that did pass were typical of past Democratic proposals. They endorsed strict construction of the Constitution and the subtreasury system, opposed protective tariffs and a national bank, and favored graduation of land prices and pre-emption. One resolution that caused no comment at the time but would create a furor later called for prompt occupation of Oregon and annexation of Texas. Price, having previously laid the groundwork among the delegates, pushed through a final resolution stating that no man should be considered for nomination to the Missouri assembly who, if elected, would not vote for Benton and David R. Atchison for the Senate. To preserve at least the outward appearance of unity the convention voted to keep its proceedings out of the press and to allow only unanimously passed resolutions to be printed.

Not long after the convention closed, independent candidates began to enter the various races. By late April soft Democratic newspapers were publishing an entire slate of independent Democrats for the state offices. These candidates ran on slates against the bills of "pains and penalties" [hard currency bills passed in the assembly] and in favor of districting the state and calling a constitutional convention.[39] By May it became obvious that the state elections in August would involve a test of Benton and anti-Benton strength. The Boonslick faction faced its greatest test, since control of the legislature with its accompanying election of Benton was entirely in their hands.

VII

The Boonslick faction weathered the storm well for a period of time. With prosperity returning to the state the currency issue began to fade and the Boonslick politicians proved adept at conciliating the other issues. Late in June, however, a thunderbolt struck the Missouri Democracy and once again the central group faced a crisis brought on by Benton.

In an answer to a letter from the Texas Congress, Benton had set out his position on the Texas issue. In a blunt and egotistical manifesto Benton came out against immediate annexation for fear of war with Mexico. He followed this with a three-day harangue in the Senate in which he attacked the Tyler-Calhoun treaty for annexing Texas. Debates in Congress muddled on into June and finally, on June 8, the Senate, along with Benton, voted down the treaty. Two days later Benton presented his own plan and a violent attack on John C. Calhoun and President John Tyler.[40]

Benton's opposition to the immediate annexation of Texas provided the Whigs and the revolting softs with an added issue, since Missourians greatly favored immediate annexation. Thus, while assuming an honorable stand, Benton placed the Boonslick group in a

39. *Ibid.*, May 7, 1844.
40. William N. Chambers, *Old Bullion Benton: Senator from the New West*, 271–79.

difficult position. Claiborne Fox Jackson's actions while running for the Missouri legislature in Howard County were indicative of just how difficult the Boonslick group's dilemma really was. Howard County, one of the few truly two-party counties in the state, greatly favored immediate annexation. Jackson was therefore forced to campaign for immediate annexation, thereby appearing to lead an insurgency against Benton.[41] There was to be a direct confrontation between Benton and Jackson, for both meant to attend a mass rally at Boonville.

The rally met at the courthouse on July 17.[42] At noon the participants formed a procession and marched to a hill west of town to hear addresses by their leading speakers. Benton led off, followed by the congressional candidates and Jackson. In a three-hour speech Benton declared himself passive as to his own election and lauded James K. Polk's declaration to run for only one presidential term. He recommended a northern Democrat for the presidential nomination in 1848—possibly Silas Wright. Continuing, he damned Tyler's treaty as designed to present the acquisition of Texas as "wholly directed to the extension, perpetuation, and predominance of slavery" and attacked this as endangering the Union. The others, including Price, avoided this issue by castigating the softs.

Jackson, denying that he had ever pledged himself to vote against Benton, came out strongly for him, but he hinted that Benton would vote for immediate annexation if the Missouri General Assembly so instructed him. All felt certain that Benton sincerely wanted the annexation of Texas and they were willing to wait for the legislature to meet.[43] The Boonslick leaders had been certain for some time that Benton favored annexation, although wishing it done according to certain principles and most considered Jackson's inordinate ambition the cause for his previous dilemma.[44] Benton was content to leave his election to the Boonslick group, confident that any instruction emanating from the assembly would, as usual, be more to his liking than not.

41. Jackson's actions have been greatly exaggerated by C. H. McClure, *Opposition in Missouri to Thomas Hart Benton*. Though little known, this book takes Benton at his word on all issues and has exerted significant influence on writers who have dealt with Missouri politics. McClure sees Jackson as leading an insurgency against Benton that eventually culminated in the Senator's overthrow in 1851.

42. Account of this rally in *Jefferson Enquirer*, August 1, 1844.

43. While there is no record of such a meeting, it seems likely that Lowry, Price, and others in the faction met and arranged with Benton and Jackson that there would be instructions from the next Missouri Assembly on the Texas issue. The faction probably assured Benton that the instructions would not offend him.

44. John Lowry to M. M. Marmaduke, June 12, 1844, June 29, 1844, Sappington Papers.

VIII

When the Thirteenth General Assembly opened, the Boonslick faction again demonstrated its mastery of the situation. Jackson received the speakership and thus assured the support of those Democrats who had some doubts about Benton and Texas. In return for votes for Benton the Boonslick men agreed to vote for districting the state and claimed that their opposition had been to federal intervention; this allowed them to give in to pressure from within the state. To further ensure Benton's election, the central group also agreed to support resolutions instructing Missouri's congressional delegation to vote for Texas annexation. Then, after securing Benton's re-election, the central group still insisted the instructions read "at the earliest practicable moment" rather than "immediate annexation." In this they were successful.[45]

Thus the Boonslick faction survived and remained firmly in control of the state party. They had proven themselves flexible enough on the difficult problems of a constitutional convention, the general ticket system, and Benton's stand on Texas to conciliate the party without sacrificing their hard-money principles—their dominating concern. The events of 1844 would prove to be a portent. As long as the Boonslick politicians remained convinced of Benton's principles, regardless of his actions, they would give him their support. However, far from being the slavish followers of Benton as pictured by contemporaries and later historians, it was the Boonslick politicians who held the balance of power in the state and could break a man as prestigious as Benton if he opposed their interests.

With Benton safely re-elected and the state once again prosperous, Price returned to Chariton to await his trip to Washington. While the party was once again harmonious, the soft revolt having disintegrated, there were imperceptible changes taking place—changes that would demand new approaches from Price and his cohorts; with the currency issue dead, it would no longer be a question of hards against softs. Challenges seen in the Texas controversy that would rend the Missouri Democracy as none other had and would cause Price and other Missourians the deepest soul-searching were still to appear.

45. William Monroe to M. M. Marmaduke, January 24, 1845, Meredith M. Marmaduke Collection.

· 4 ·

Congressman and Colonel

In the year between his election to Congress and his departure for Washington Price remained comparatively inactive while enjoying the first lull in his political career in nearly a decade and spending considerable time caring for his business enterprises. His mercantile partnership with Lisbon Applegate remained prosperous and his tobacco interests, both the warehousing venture and his own farm, brought in even greater profits as tobacco prices soared in Missouri.[1] During the decade of the 1840's Missouri tobacco production increased more rapidly than in any other state. While production in Virginia, Maryland, and Tennessee decreased in volume, Missouri's increased by over eight million pounds and it became the fifth leading tobacco-producing state in the Union.[2]

Tobacco production and marketing had made great advances since Price first came to Missouri. When Missourians first began growing tobacco they shipped it on consignment to New Orleans and had a lengthy wait for payment. Soon, however, the Missouri planters, impatient at this delay, began to sell to local manufacturers and middlemen. This change in trade patterns brought Price and many others into the warehouse business, and warehouses appeared all over central Missouri. As tobacco manufacturing grew, Fayette and St. Louis became the state's major trade centers.[3]

Although Price devoted much time to supervising his businesses, he also enjoyed the opportunity to be with his family. His sister-in-law Patience died in April, 1845, bringing Sterling's niece Elizabeth even closer to her uncle; she visited Keytesville often. While the elder Price remained around the farm, Elizabeth conducted a school that

1. Feazel and Lewis Journal, 1843–1847 (microfilm); ledger and contracts for purchases of tobacco, 1841–1842, Applegate Collection. During the three decades prior to the outbreak of the Civil War, the number of slaves owned by Price fluctuated betwen twelve and twenty. Throughout these years he employed between one-fourth and one-third of his slaves in commercial practices. This would indicate that he gained a good portion of his income from his warehouse ventures and did not depend entirely upon his own tobacco farm. Manuscript Census, Missouri, 1840, 1850, 1860.

2. Joseph C. Robert, *The Tobacco Kingdom*, 147, 152.

3. Joseph C. Robert, *The Story of Tobacco in America*, 68, 79–80.

young Elizabeth could attend when in Chariton. Price also had time to visit with John Lowry in Fayette and to go to Jefferson City to confer with legislators after the session opened. While on these trips he would also settle business affairs for various of the Boonslick group.[4]

The leading political issue in the state in late 1845 was the constitutional convention scheduled for November of that year. The Boonslick faction was vitally interested in the outcome. Price's coming trip to Washington to attend Congress precluded his being a delegate to the convention, but Chariton and Howard counties were well represented by Claiborne F. Jackson and Price's business partner Lisbon Applegate.[5]

With the year 1845 drawing to a close Price made ready for his trip to Washington. As he packed and left his family for the capital, he had no way of knowing that it was to be more than three years before he could return to Chariton permanently, and that he would then return as a military hero—not a congressman.

II

When Price, the agrarian, arrived in Washington in late November, 1845, he was probably little impressed with the capital and certainly not awed by an urban environment.[6] Washington still resembled more a sprawling town than a city or a nation's capital. Price was also much at home in the social aspects of the capital, which greatly resembled a southern city. Slave pens and auction blocks were prominent on public thoroughfares and many families owned slaves they used as domestics or hired out.

Washington was at an unattractive stage in between losing its rural simplicity and not yet attaining the tasteful elegance of maturity. Pennsylvania Avenue was the only paved and lighted street in the city, and even it became a straggling mudhole in rainy weather or a source of billowing clouds of dust when the sun shone. Cattle pastured in the streets and bullfrogs croaked in the side lanes. Pretentious mansions stood next to crude cabins, their back yards crowded with cowsheds, pigsties, chicken runs, and privies, reflecting the helter-skelter spacing of the city. The maze of unpaved streets, with their scattering of detached houses, was made even more difficult for

4. Sterling Price to ——, February 21, 1844, Sappington Papers.
5. Missouri remained under its old constitution when the new one, written in 1845, was voted down by the people.
6. My description of Washington is drawn from sketches in Wilhemus Bogart Bryan, "Washington on the Eve of the Civil War," in *Washington During War Time*, Marcus Benjamin, ed., 3–12; Frederick Seward, *Seward at Washington*. An excellent feeling for the life and tempo of the city may be gained from Constance McLaughlin Green, *Washington: Village and Capital*, 1800–1878, 152–77.

the uninitiated by the lack of numbering; directions had to be obtained from a hack driver or a resident.

The Capitol building itself, just as unpretentious, lacked the great marble wings that would later house the Senate and the House, and the projected colonnaded dome had not yet replaced a much less imposing affair of brick and iron. While the white fronts of the Capitol and Executive Mansion gleamed through the foliage at each end of Pennsylvania Avenue, and the substantial Post-Office Building and the long colonnade of the Treasury were finished and imposing, the old brick edifices for the State, War, and Navy departments were still standing.

Most of the legislators quartered in "messes" on Capitol Hill or near the eastern end of Pennsylvania Avenue just under the Hill. These quarters, in converted private homes, suffered from the same conditions as did most of the other private dwellings. The intense heat of the summer season caused homes to be built with high ceilings, and the rooms were usually long, narrow, and badly proportioned. Each congressman generally had a sitting room, bedroom, and drawing room on an upper floor. The men took their meals at a common dining room where spirited conversations were commonplace.

None of the Missouri congressional delegation stayed together. Price chose to live at Mrs. Owner's on Capitol Hill, where Lewis Linn and Albert Harrison, the latter a Missouri representative, had lived when they were in Washington. This may have affected Price's choice, but the composition of the mess probably played a more important part in his decision. Mrs. Owner's had generally been inhabited by Southerners and 1845 was no exception. The bulk of the mess were from North Carolina and shared Price's republicanism; they were James McKay, James C. Dobbin, Asa Biggs, and David S. Reid. Joining the Carolinians were Archibald Yell of Arkansas, Robert Smith from Illinois, Howell Cobb of Georgia, and two Northerners, Mace Moulton and Benning W. Jenness from New Hampshire.[7]

III

When the Twenty-ninth Congress convened at noon on December 1, 1845, the first order of business was to elect a Speaker. The House did this immediately with John Davis, an Indiana Democrat, winning over Samuel Vinton, a Whig from Ohio. Price voted with the Democratic majority.[8] Howell Cobb offered a successful resolution to permit members to choose their own seats in the order in which their names were drawn out of a hat.[9] Price chose a seat in the third row

7. *Congressional Directory*, 29th Cong., 1st sess., 1846.
8. *Congressional Globe*, 29th Cong., 1st sess., 1846, 2.
9. *Ibid.*, 4, 22–23.

on the left aisle, directly across from his messmate Howell Cobb, next
to Seaborn Jones of Georgia, and directly behind Archibald Yell.
Others of the mess were in the immediate area.[10]

Within a week, when the Speaker announced the committee appointments, Price came into close association with a man who was to
exert a strong influence on him: Stephen A. Douglas, the Illinois representative chairing the Committee on the Territories to which the
Speaker named Price. Price also became a member of the Committee
on Expenditures in the War Department, chaired by Owen Leib, a
Democrat from Pennsylvania.

The Twenty-ninth Congress contained a great many men who
would become prominent in the secession crisis and the formation of
the Confederacy in another decade and a half. William Lowndes
Yancey and Robert Rhett, Southern nationalists, represented Alabama and South Carolina respectively. John Bell, a moderate Whig
who would run for the Presidency in 1860 on the Constitutional Union
ticket, came to the session from Tennessee. Price had no way of
knowing it, but many individuals who would be his superiors in the
Confederate government were also in the House. Some—Jefferson
Davis, Alexander Stephens, Robert Toombs, Robert M. T. Hunter,
James Seddon, and Howell Cobb—would attain high positions in that
government.

It was, nonetheless, the Carolina republicans and certain western
figures who attracted Price, rather than the firebrands Yancey or
Rhett or the followers of John C. Calhoun. Price became close friends
with Archibald Yell and felt a great respect for Douglas. Another
messmate, Howell Cobb, represented all to which Price aspired; an
urbane and polished lawyer, he was the scion of one of Georgia's
first families. Price may also have come into contact with the future
vice president of the Confederacy, Alexander Stephens, through
Cobb, who spent many hours lounging with Stephens in the latter's
sitting room.[11] Of all the men he associated with, Price may well have
felt the most respect and admiration for "General" John McKay, the
powerful chairman of the Ways and Means Committee and a republican of the Silas Wright-Martin Van Buren mold. McKay dominated
the mess and probably exerted the greatest influence on the freshman
congressman from Missouri.

IV

Price felt a keen interest in several of the first votes he cast. The
notorious "gag" resolution had been repealed by the previous Con-

10. *Congressional Directory*, 29th Cong., 1st sess.
11. Rudolf Von Abele, *Alexander H. Stephens*, 94.

gress, but Reuben Chapman, an Alabama representative, offered an amendment to a resolution on House rules that would have reinstituted the gag. Price, ever sensitive toward abolitionism, voted for Chapman's proposal, but the measure failed by a sectional vote of 84–121.[12] Several days later Price voted with the majority to table a resolution calling for an investigation of the credentials of all representatives who were elected by the general ticket system.[13]

A report from the Committee on the Territories calling for consideration of the admission of Texas brought about the first major legislation of the session. The last session of the Twenty-eighth Congress had passed a joint resolution consenting to the creation of a new state in Texas upon the organization of a republican form of government. This resolution was still pending and formed the basis of the committee's report in the Twenty-ninth Congress.

The interval between sessions had provided sufficient time for various Northern opposition groups to organize around the slavery issue. Their position was evident in the Twenty-ninth Congress in the debate on the resolution for the admission of Texas when John Quincy Adams presented memorials from various northern states against the proposal. Price, exhibiting his Southern slaveholding bias, voted with the majority to defeat the memorials.[14] The day after Adams' presentations Erastus Culver, a New York representative, presented memorials calling for the abolition of slavery and the slave trade in the District of Columbia. The House immediately tabled these 107–59 with Price again voting with the majority.[15] On December 5, Adams presented another memorial protesting the admission of Texas as a slave state; Price again voted to table the measure in an 83–67 vote.[16] Adams then presented a resolution asking for federal intervention in South Carolina and Louisiana, where he felt the liberties and rights of Massachusetts citizens had been violated.

---

12. *Congressional Globe*, 29th Cong., 1st sess., 4. Price's voting record becomes more meaningful when considered in the larger context of party voting in this period. Thomas B. Alexander's *Sectional Stress and Party Strength: A Study of the Roll-Call Voting Patterns in the United States House of Representatives, 1836–1860*, and Joel H. Silbey's *The Shrine of Party: Congressional Voting Behavior, 1841–1852*, are essential for understanding the voting behavior of both parties during the 1840's. Both authors, through sophisticated use of computers, maintain that party voting was able to withstand the stress of sectional issues throughout the 1840's. Price's voting behavior bears out their analyses, but does present an added dimension. His republicanism and that of others provides a provocative variant that could not be dealt with through computers.

13. *Congressional Globe*, 29th Cong., 1st sess., 4.

14. *Ibid.*, 41.

15. *Ibid.*, 43.

16. *Ibid.*, 53.

Price voted with the majority to table this proposal, 90–68.[17] Finally, on December 19, action on the joint resolution to admit Texas carried 141–56 with Price joining the majority in passing the measure.[18]

On proposals dealing with internal improvements Price voted in keeping with his republican background. Here the main piece of legislation was the Rivers and Harbors Bill. On the third day of the session John W. Tibbatts of the commerce committee gave notice of his intention to introduce a bill "making appropriations for the improvement of certain rivers and harbors," and two or three related measures.[19] The bill was actually reported on December 31 and finally taken up as the special order of business to be followed until disposed of on February 24, 1846. By March 18, the bill was ready for amendments, which came in great abundance, and the ensuing discussion reflected the struggle for and against a mixture of special projects. On March 18, debate ended and the bill came to a first vote. With its sundry amendments, the measure contained a motley collection of a few worthy and many unworthy projects.

During the amending process members had sought to obtain appropriations that would benefit their home districts, and the final bill contained provisions for the improvement of "Little Sodus Bay," "Oak Orchard Harbor," and many other local projects.[20] Like many other congressmen, Price had to evaluate the proposed amendments, and in doing so he voted for those that concurred with his principles;[21] he favored those he felt would benefit the nation at large and thus would justify financial support by the federal government. While voting for amendments to improve the major waterways, such as the Ohio, Mississippi, and Missouri rivers, when the time came to vote on the entire measure Price cast a negative vote. He could only view the bill in its entirety as a collection of measures to aid special interests and it was thus offensive to his principles. This vote reflected his Southern republican rather than Western identification.

The vote on this and other bills showed the ideological affinity of the members of the mess. On the Rivers and Harbors Bill only Yell and Smith, both westerners, voted for the measure. Even two men not voting in consonance with the rest of the mess was unusual, for the individual members voted together over 95 per cent of the time.[22] Price's affiliation with his mess served to solidify an already firmly held political faith.

17. *Ibid.*
18. *Ibid.*, 65.
19. *Ibid.*, 23.
20. Amendments to the measure may be found *ibid.*, 524–31.
21. *Ibid.*
22. These conclusions result from an analysis of the votes on nineteen major pieces of legislation.

V

In the Twenty-ninth Congress, as in the nation at large, the Oregon conflict raged anew. In his message to Congress President James K. Polk urged an end to the British-American joint occupation, and asserted claims to the whole region, presumably to 54°40'.[23] Congressional "ultras" led by Lewis Cass and Edward Hannegan in the Senate and Stephen A. Douglas in the House renewed their demands for the whole of Oregon to be annexed. New talk of war rumbled like ominous thunder and Polk worried over reports that Britain was already engaged in warlike preparations. In this tense atmosphere, and especially in Missouri, a dramatic slogan swept the land: "Fifty-four Forty or Fight!" In the Twenty-ninth Congress, five separate measures relating to the Oregon issue were under consideration more or less concurrently. However, the primary point of dispute was whether the United States should press for the whole of the region or only for the forty-ninth parallel.

This last question aroused divided personal loyalties in Price and placed him in an anxious situation. When he had arrived in Congress, he believed that the United States should make good its claim to the whole region, and he received valuable support from Douglas. Another man whom Price also respected, Thomas Hart Benton, remained adamant against the "54–40" position, and in his indomitable manner attacked both it and its individual supporters. Benton must have attempted to persuade Price to change his stand and eventually the younger man did come to feel that Benton was "unquestionably right."[24] Price finally reached the conclusion that the best interests of the country would be served by adopting the forty-ninth parallel, even though this position was extremely unpopular in Missouri.

VI

The finale to the Texas annexation question resulted in a crisis between the United States and Mexico; all through the spring of 1846 American relations with Mexico worsened. On January 13, American troops received orders to move to the Rio Grande. This necessitated marching through territory claimed by Mexico, which they did and arrived in late March. Mexico protested, but the troops under Zachary Taylor remained. In March, 1845, Mexico broke off diplomatic relations, with long-standing unsettled claims by Americans against Mexico further complicating the matter. In addition, the Mexican administration insisted that the proper border of Texas

23. *Congressional Globe*, 29th Cong., 1st sess., 2–11.
24. Sterling Price to the Editor of *The* Brunswick (Mo.) *Weekly Brunswicker*, July 22, 1849, printed in the Jefferson City (Mo.) *Jefferson Enquirer*, August 4, 1849.

was the Nueces River, north of where the American troops were camped.

Trouble arrived through a fateful series of events occurring after the troops arrived on the Rio Grande. In April an American scouting party was ambushed just north of the Rio Grande. When news of this encounter reached Washington, Polk sent his war message to Congress on May 11, 1846. Within a few hours the House responded with a bill that echoed the President's declaration of the pre-existence of war and its origin, and provided troops and money. Price and the other members of his mess, with the exception of Cobb, had long been excited over the prospects of strong measures being taken against Mexico.[25]

Although he was unaware of it, the same day that Price voted for Polk's war measure the Third Congressional District of Missouri held its nominating convention in Huntsville with John Lowry presiding over the three-day meeting. Delegates from the various counties came to Huntsville with instructions to vote for certain candidates and Price, the choice of Chariton and Randolph counties, was one among several men nominated.[26]

Even prior to the meeting Price did not lack enthusiastic supporters. "A Democrat," writing several months before the convention, declared that Price had "given evidence, on several occasions, of the same devotion to the republican cause which has marked his whole life."[27] "Mentor," writing from Washington in early May, considered "Colonel" Price a conscientious representative and felt that Missourians could not place their confidence in a more faithful servant: "His conciliatory principles, urbanity of manners, and gentlemanly address, have won for him the full confidence of every Missourian, both in and out of Congress here."[28]

Price left his nomination to his Boonslick cohorts, although those favoring his re-nomination faced a difficult struggle, since the Third District included eighteen counties constituting an irregular slab running north and south through the center of the state. Most of these counties had never been given a real voice in the choice of candidates and were amenable to the old cries of "centralism."

Price's congressional career did nothing to aid his candidacy. While freshmen congressmen rarely assumed dynamic roles, Price played only a minimal role in the House. His floor appearances were limited

25. Howell Cobb to his wife, May 10, 1846, in *The Correspondence of Robert Toombs, Alexander H. Stephens, and Howell Cobb*, II, U. B. Phillips, ed., Annual Report of the American Historical Association for the Year 1912.
26. *Jefferson Enquirer*, March 25, 1846.
27. *Ibid.*, March 11, 1846.
28. *Ibid.*, May 27, 1846.

to raising points of order, calling for the previous question to speed the legislative process, and the introduction of memorials from Missouri citizens. He introduced only two bills. The first called for the Committee on the Post and Post Roads to be instructed to inquire into the expediency of establishing a mail route from Quincy, Illinois, to St. Joseph, Missouri.[29] The second requested that Missouri volunteers who had served in Florida during the Seminole campaigns be paid for the horses they had lost.[30]

While in Congress he had been a diligent worker, faithfully answering roll calls and tending to his committee assignments; he had also, as "Democrat" mentioned, adhered to his republican principles. However, this appealed to few other than the Boonslick faction. Indeed, his vote on the Rivers and Harbors Bill was detrimental to his cause,[31] as was his vote to accept the forty-ninth parallel. Regardless of these handicaps, Price remained in close contention for three days and through fifty-nine ballots. On the final ballot James S. Green received the nomination.[32]

Upon learning of this result Price addressed a letter to the voters of his district. In his best form he declared that he "rejoiced" at the harmony and unanimity of the Huntsville convention, and continued: "The consistent advocate for union and harmony in the Democratic ranks at all times, I cordially acquiesce in the decision of the convention, and shall give to its nominee, a support commensurate with my ability to advance the cause in his person, as our chosen standard bearer."[33] His words concealed his true feelings. A sensitive and ambitious man, Price was both hurt and disgusted by the convention's action. This was a setback to him and he viewed the action of the convention as a personal censure, so much so that he decided to resign his seat before the end of his term.[34]

VII

While Price brooded over his failure to be renominated, Benton worked for his cause in another way. The same day that Price wrote his letter to the voters of Missouri, Benton conferred with President Polk. Earlier, the President and his cabinet had planned a three-pronged attack against Santa Fe, Chihuahua, and the lower Rio Grande. Stephen W. Kearny and his First Dragoons, stationed at Fort Leavenworth, were to capture New Mexico with the aid of

29. *Congressional Globe*, 29th Cong., 1st sess., 195.
30. *Ibid.*, 196, 221.
31. St. Louis *Daily Missouri Republican*, September 17, 1846.
32. *Jefferson Enquirer*, June 17, 1846.
33. *Ibid.*
34. Thomas C. Reynolds, "General Sterling Price and the Confederacy," 1.

several regiments of mounted Missouri volunteers. Benton, spying a chance to aid his young protégé, suggested to Polk that Price would be a fine choice to lead one of the Missouri regiments.[35] The next day Price met with Polk and Secretary of War William Marcy to arrange for him to raise a regiment if it could be done without delay.[36] Once it was agreed that Price would lead a regiment, Marcy immediately informed Governor John C. Edwards that Price had been "highly recommended to the President, as in every respect qualified to be placed at the head of a regiment."[37] Shortly thereafter Price left Washington with Archibald Yell, who was also to lead a regiment from his state.

Although Price had not advanced his career in Congress, he received an opportunity to do so through military achievement. In an age when military glory meant almost certain political and personal advancement, Benton had saved Price from possible oblivion.

35. *Diary of James K. Polk*, I, Milo Quaife, ed., 440.
36. *Ibid.*, 440–41.
37. *Daily Missouri Republican*, July 27, 1846.

· 5 ·

Hero by Design

When Price arrived in Missouri in the second week of June, 1846, he discovered tremendous enthusiasm for the war and great indignation, especially among Whig editors, regarding his appointment to command a regiment. The *Daily Missouri Republican*, an old enemy, set the tone for the opposition. Its editor commented that Price had not resigned his seat in Congress and that he very likely would not unless he was successful in obtaining the command of a regiment, "the game of which he is now in pursuit."[1] While the Whig press in Missouri supported the war, Whig editors repeatedly castigated the "high-handed course of Mr. Polk" in his appointment of Price and continued to attack the President for attempting to turn the war into a political affair to enhance Democrats.[2] The editor of *The Weekly Tribune* asked: When "has the *necessity* of an invading, or defensive force, been suspended upon the acceptance, by such force (of *volunteers* mark you) of this, or that man, for command?"[3]

In spite of this indignation at what they believed to be an evasion of their militia rights, Missourians remained enthusiastic about the war and rushed to enlist. Responding to the call for troops with tremendous enthusiasm, zealous volunteers quickly filled the quotas of those engaged in raising companies. The *Republican* commented that the only problem was that the number of men requested bore no proportion to the number who wanted to go: "Several thousand can be readily raised,—indeed, there will be difficulty in restraining them, rather than to fill up the ranks."[4]

This enthusiasm was bipartisan. While the Whig press took occasional swipes at Democratic leaders, its general attitude was that the "enemy is upon our soil," and that the war should be fought to a speedy termination.[5] Alexander Doniphan, who led the first regiment of Missouri volunteers, was a Whig leader in the state and, much to Price's later discomfort, many of the second regiment's company commanders and men were also Whigs.

1. St. Louis *Daily Missouri Republican*, June 13, 1846.
2. *The* Liberty (Mo.) *Weekly Tribune*, July 11, 1846.
3. *Ibid.*
4. *Daily Missouri Republican*, August 13, 1846.
5. Fayette (Mo.) *Boon's Lick Times*, May 16, 1846.

In their eagerness, Missourians responded to a variety of impulses. The most prevalent attitude, reflected in newspapers, journals, and letters of volunteers, was that of self-righteous indignation. Most Missourians felt that Mexican insults had been borne by the United States quite long enough and that it was time to strike back. John Hughes, a volunteer, reflected this attitude when he commented on the "repeated insults offered our national flag." Hughes disliked Mexico's "supercilious and menacing air uniformly manifest towards this government, which, with characteristic forbearance and courtesy, has endeavored to maintain a friendly understanding."[6]

James Lusk, editor of the *Jefferson Enquirer*, fumed that immediately upon the annexation of Texas Mexico began depredations and insults "assuming the position that two free and independent republics had no right to form a union, and proclaimed her honor insulted." Incensed by this, Lusk wrote: "Where it becomes the *duty* of a free republican people to consult the caprice of a priest-ridden and deluded nation before transacting any affairs, we may bid farewell to freedom and national honor."[7]

These "insults" appeared even more unbearable to Missourians because they considered Mexicans an inferior race. The neighboring *Illinois State Register* expressed Missourians' views when it referred to Mexicans as "but little removed above the negro."[8] The *Missouri Reporter* thought that Mexico would eventually be "absorbed by the Anglo-Saxons, now overspreading the continent."[9] Richard Elliott, a St. Louis Whig and first lieutenant in the Laclede Rangers, graphically summed up these feelings when he commented that "the general sentiment was, that the Mexicans were a half-barbarous set anyway, and had no business to send their greasy and ragged soldiers over the Rio Grande, in a territory, already owned by them, but constructively conquered by the Texans who were the advanced guard of our superior civilization."[10] The Mexican dispute took on a greater meaning to Missouri than to many other states because of her connections with the Santa Fe trade. Many Missourians had relatives or friends who were detained in Mexico or whose goods had been confiscated.

Upon his return to the state Price had very little time to spend in Keytesville to enjoy his new baby girl, Martha Sterling, who had been born in April, and by early June he became involved in a new political controversy. Stephen W. Kearny and the First Missouri Volunteers had just gotton underway from Fort Leavenworth. A

6. John Hughes, *Doniphan's Expedition*, 23–24.
7. Jefferson City (Mo.) *Jefferson Enquirer*, September 15, 1846.
8. Springfield (Ill.) *Illinois State Register*, December 27, 1844.
9. St. Louis *Missouri Reporter*, reprinted *ibid.*, August 1, 1845.
10. Richard Smith Elliott, *Notes Taken in Sixty Years*, 218.

shortage of forage had caused Kearny to request that the second regiment consist of at least four-fifths infantry.[11] An additional letter made his wishes still more definite,[12] and he evidently assumed that infantry would be raised since he requisitioned the St. Louis arsenal for 800 muskets and only 300 cavalry carbines.[13] Having commanded cavalry against the Mormons and being repulsed by the idea of leading foot soldiers, Price proceeded to raise mounted troops. Once again the Whig press castigated him. Price was in a position in which he should have deferred to his superior's request, but he was still able to exercise his own judgment. He was already evincing a certain vanity regarding his own judgment that would cause him problems throughout his military career.

II

The companies from the various counties arrived at Fort Leavenworth at different dates, but all had rendezvoused by August 5 when Price arrived. On that date, following custom, the men elected him colonel. Some of the troops felt he would not have been elected if the men had not feared dissolution of the regiment as a consequence.[14] After choosing the remaining officers, the regiment formed; the force consisted of one regiment and an extra battalion of calvary numbering around 1,200 men with a considerable amount of artillery and a great number of provision and baggage wagons.[15]

To facilitate the march across the prairie, Price followed Kearny's example and split his force into sections, which left the fort at intervals between August 10 and 23. Price and his staff departed with the last companies. All except two companies took the Cimarron route; the other two went by way of Bent's Fort to escort supplies from that point. Francis Parkman met these companies at Bent's Fort and described them as a "set of undisciplined ragamuffins."[16] Farther along the trail Parkman met another of Price's companies "straggling along in their usual manner."[17]

The various detachments had their peculiar adventures, but all traveled under common conditions. Initially the men were thrilled at the sight of the Great Plains, but soon grew tired of the monotony

11. Stephen W. Kearny to Governor John C. Edwards, June 16, 1846, Kearny Letter Book, Kearny Papers, 25–26.
12. Kearny to Edwards, July 2, 1846, *ibid.*, 43.
13. H. S. Turner to Captain W. H. Bell, June 26, 1846, *ibid.*, 38–39.
14. *The Weekly Tribune*, August 22, 1846; Columbia *Missouri Statesman*, August 21, 1846. It is very likely these were Whigs.
15. Louise Barry, "Kansas Before 1854: A Revised Annals," *Kansas Historical Quarterly*, 30 (Autumn, 1964), 382.
16. *Journals of Francis Parkman*, I, Mason Wade, ed., 478.
17. *Ibid.*, 479.

of the landscape. They were constantly bothered by swarms of gnats, flies, and mosquitoes. Rattlesnakes swarmed over the prairies and it was not uncommon for a man to wake up and discover a rattler coiled in his blankets. Many of the men were not equipped to deal with the heavy rains and often had to sleep in wet clothes without eating because the green cottonwood used for fuel failed to ignite in the rain. One volunteer recalled after a long march in the rain that his feet were so swollen he had to cut his boots off.[18]

During the greater portion of the march the men were not bothered by too much water, but by the lack of it. Lieutenant Colonel David Willock, commander of the extra battalion, reported that he rarely saw timber after crossing the Arkansas River and that the troops went for seven days "during which I never saw a shrub."[19] Horses failed for want of grass and many times the men were short of rations and water. Some had to drink water found in wagon ruts.[20] Sandstorms buffeted the troops and they suffered with dysentery, measles, and other diseases. The troops, for the most part young and vigorous, overcame the hardships of the trail and found time for such diversions as card playing, fishing, hunting, or occasionally chasing a buffalo.

Price did not endure the trip as well as most. Several days before he reached Santa Fe, he fell seriously ill; reports circulated that he was near death.[21] When he arrived in Santa Fe on September 28 he was in a very feeble condition. He had contracted cholera and was to suffer severe intestinal disorders for the remainder of his life.

By October 12 all the troops were in Santa Fe. Their arrival intensified an existing bad situation in a city already overcrowded with volunteers, with a great deal of time on their hands. One volunteer noted that: "Want of employment engenders idleness amongst the men and it is followed by want of discipline, insubordination, drunkenness, and crime . . . . Not a day passes but what some outrage, some crime is committed by the American soldiers, whose victims usually are Mexicans."[22] If a Mexican attempted to gain redress from the American officers, he received none. It was not long before American soldiers were being found beaten to death by unknown assailants.[23]

With Kearny's departure for California, Colonel Alexander Doniphan held the post of commander when Price arrived. Prior to his

18. George R. Gibson, "Journal of a Soldier under Kearny and Doniphan," in *Southwest Historical Series*, III, Ralph Bieber, ed., 140.
19. David Willock to his wife, September 25, 1846, Mexican War Letters.
20. Marcellus Ball Edwards, "Journal of Marcellus Ball Edwards," in *Southwest Historical Series*, IV, Bieber, ed., 144.
21. Palmyra *Missouri Courier*, October 15, 1846.
22. Christian Cribben to ———, October 20, 1846, Mexican War Letters.
23. *Ibid.*

departure Kearny reconnoitered as far south as Tomé to ascertain
the military situation in the territory. He found no evidence of any
organized resistance and reported that the American commander
would have nothing to do except defend against an occasional Indian
raid.[24] Events were to prove him a poor prophet.

III

Soon after Kearny's departure conditions indicated that he had
been overly optimistic. Early in October an American teamster discovered a group of Mexicans drilling in the mountains;[25] later in
the month a Missourian found the body of an American teamster
who had been robbed and beaten to death.[26] By this time there was
"no good feeling for the native population"[27]—a sentiment the populace returned with equal fervor. George Ruxton, an English lieutenant on leave, commented that throughout the territory there existed
the most bitter feeling and determined hostility toward the Americans. When Ruxton asked a Mexican woman for lodging, she hesitated until she discovered that he was not an American. Then she
exclaimed: "Gracias a Dios! a Christian will sleep with us tonight and
not an American." Ruxton felt that the Missourians' bullying and overbearing attitude contributed greatly to this hostility.[28] Rumors of a
native revolt aggravated the already tense situation and by late
October so many rumors were afloat that many Missourians slept
with loaded guns.

At the height of his excitement Doniphan received orders from
Kearny to proceed against the Navajos, and on October 26 he led the
First Missouri out of Santa Fe. Price, reasonably well recuperated,
assumed command of the territory and immediately took steps to
end the friction between the volunteers and the natives. Hoping to
prevent an uprising, he instituted martial law and paraded the troops
twice a day, with extra drill for officers, to maintain discipline. Price
doubled the guards, stationed outposts on all roads leading into the
city, forbade the soldiers to drink, enforced a 10:00 P.M. curfew on
natives and volunteers, and placed artillery in strategic and conspicuous spots around the city. The Missourians maintained strict vigilance day and night for several weeks and by the middle of November
the danger of revolt had subsided and the soldiers relaxed their guard.

24. Kearny to Adjutant General Roger Jones, September 16, 1846, 29th
Cong., 2d sess., 1846–1847, House Exec. Doc. No. 19, 24–25.
25. St. Louis *Weekly Reveille*, December 21, 1846.
26. *The Weekly Tribune*, November 14, 1846.
27. Gibson, "Journal," 256–57.
28. George Ruxton, *Adventures in Mexico and the Rocky Mountains*,
197.

Conditions now enabled Price to send out grazing detachments and to reinforce outposts in Indian country. The remaining troops stayed in Santa Fe on garrison duty, their main activity being the construction of Fort Marcy, but the Missourians much preferred Señora Barcelo's gambling house to pick-and-shovel work around the fort.[29] They adhered to strict discipline at times of apparent necessity, but after the crisis passed they saw no need to conform. The troops quickly became bored, restive, and irritated by discipline. Some started a theatrical project, others a minstrel group, but most turned to drinking and gambling to pass the time.[30] Ruxton described crowds of drunken, brawling, volunteers as "the dirtiest, rowdiest, crew I have ever seen collected together . . . every other house was a bar disgorging reeling, drunken men."[31] An epidemic of measles broke out and for a short time the garrison buried a man a day. Continual Indian raids and short supplies worsened morale considerably, as did the crowded, uncomfortable, quarters where the volunteers lived.

Price faced a difficult situation, for he and his officers had very little military experience. Indeed, a member of the First Missouri wrote that many of Price's officers came to the noncommissioned officers of the First Missouri for advice;[32] he also commented that Price himself at this early stage of his career "knew very little about soldiering."[33] Price was handicapped because many of his officers and men harbored ill feelings regarding his appointment and did nothing to help; indeed, many went out of their way to thwart him. Price was, after all, in command of volunteer troops. These men had eagerly enlisted to fight, but grew restive under the inactivity of garrison duty. The volunteers shirked work on the fort and scorned regulations when the urge struck them. This independent spirit even carried over to the officers. To be liked, an officer had to be lax; to be unpopular meant a pistol or a saber in the face and a petition for his removal. Lewis Garrard, author of "Wah-To-Yah and the Taos Trail," could not resist commenting that Americans "were never intended to fight under strict discipline of the regular service. Deference and subordination they learn neither as children nor as men—and an army of invasion is a poor school to remedy the defect of education."[34]

Many officers resented Price's influence in Washington and the

29. William C. Kennerly, "Recollections of Our War with Mexico," Mexican War Letters.
30. *Ibid.*, 10.
31. Ruxton, *Adventures*, 190.
32. Kennerly, "Recollections," 6.
33. *Ibid.*, 7.
34. Lewis Garrard, "Wah-To-Yah and the Taos Trail," in *Southwest Historical Series*, VI, Bieber, ed., 321, 322.

"trickery" involved in his appointment. One Missourian hoped affairs would blow "sky high" and intimated that other officers generally held this same view. As a result constant friction existed between the officers who favored Price and those who did not. Those opposing him spent most of their time in saloons or openly flaunting mistresses.[35] Price's inexperience handicapped him, and the political pettiness of his command greatly aggravated the natural individualism of the men. To make matters worse, Price suffered a relapse and remained seriously ill throughout November and December. Nevertheless, he was still castigated by the Whig press in Missouri, which published damning letters from those opposed to Price.[36]

By late November New Mexico seethed with frustration and hatred. Although no gross outrages occurred, the Missourians were contemptuous of the Mexicans and made no attempt to hide it. Many displaced Mexican officials hated the territorial officers and numerous disbanded Mexican militiamen lingered in the area waiting for a chance to strike. Rumors of revolt again began to circulate, but volunteers felt such contempt for the populace that they did not take the warnings seriously.[37] Many American residents in the territory feared for their lives.[38]

These people had good reason to be apprehensive since latent hostilities were rapidly coming to the surface. Early in December a cabal of native leaders began to plot to overthrow the Americans. On December 15 a prostitute betrayed these men to Donaciano Vigil, secretary of the territory, who in turn informed Price.[39] Earlier, Captain Edwin Burgwin and his dragoons had captured Ambrosiso Armijo and several other Mexicans with a letter to Manuel Armijo, the former governor of the territory, which said that the American troops were scattered and the people, ready to revolt, just needed a military demonstration or assistance from the south to spark an uprising. The captured men also carried a list of all the disbanded Mexican soldiers in Santa Fe. Charles Bent, recently appointed territorial governor, felt that the revolt was confined to the four northern counties and did not include any important men,[40] but when the plot

35. Baltimore (Md.) *Niles Weekly Register*, March 6, 1847; Philip Gooch Ferguson, "Diary of Philip Gooch Ferguson," in *Southwest Historical Series*, IV, Bieber, ed., 348–49.

36. A sample of these letters may be seen in *Niles Weekly Register*, March 6, 1847.

37. *Missouri Statesman*, February 26, 1847.

38. Lieutenant J. W. Abert, "Examination of New Mexico," 30th Cong., 1st sess., 1847–1848, House Exec. Doc. No. 41, 451.

39. Ralph Emerson Twitchell, *Leading Facts of New Mexican History*, II, 232–33.

40. Charles Bent to James Buchanan, December 26, 1846, 30th Cong., 1st sess., House Exec. Doc. No. 70, 17–18.

was exposed Bent discovered that many of the most prominent men in the territory were implicated. Price moved quickly to arrest the key figures involved and thus, much to the regret of many of the volunteers who were spoiling for a fight, extinguished the spirit of revolt for a time.[41]

IV

The calm that settled over the territory was deceptive, for many restless and dissatisfied spirits remained yet to express themselves. Governor Bent, aware of the prevailing discontent, felt his long residence among the people would enable him to prevent any outbreak,[42] but he greatly misjudged the temper of the people—a mistake that cost him his life.

On January 14, 1847, several American officials traveled to Bent's home in Taos. Mexican leaders in the north had been stirring up the Indians at Pueblo de Taos and by January 18 Taos was in an uproar. Nearly all the Indians from the pueblo were in town, the saloons were crowded, and demagogues harangued the people. During the night of January 18 a friend warned Bent and the others that their lives were in danger, but they were still confident that they could calm the people.

Early the next morning a mob approached Bent's home and the Governor stepped out to speak with them. Shots rang out and Bent staggered back into the house; his assailants entered the house and scalped him alive. Bent's wife and Mrs. Kit Carson, Bent's sister, crawled through a hole into an adjoining house. Holding his hands to his bleeding head, Bent followed them. The mob broke into the house and fired repeatedly at Bent, but left the women and children unharmed. After slaying Bent, the mob tortured and killed five other officials. James Liel, prosecuting attorney for the northern district, was stripped naked and forced to walk through the streets while Indians shot arrows into his flesh. They scalped him alive, left him for a time, and then returned and killed him.[43]

The people in the Taos Valley and the small towns in the vicinity rose en masse to join the Pueblos. The same day as the massacre at Taos a mob attacked Turley's Mill at Arroyo Hondo and after a pitched battle killed seven Americans; at Rio Colorado a group killed and mutilated two American mountainmen. Gradually the insurgents formed into an *ad hoc* revolutionary army and sent circulars to various parts of the country to incite the people to rebel. All the towns in the northern part of the territory declared in favor

41. William Vaughn to his sister, January 7, 1847, Mexican War Letters.
42. Twitchell, *Leading Facts*, II, 233.
43. *Ibid.*, 234–35.

except Tecolote and Las Vegas, where American grazing detachments were stationed.

Price learned of the massacre on January 20.[44] That same day he intercepted a circular indicating that Santa Fe was to be attacked as soon as the revolutionaries could concentrate their rapidly growing forces. Since sickness and the departure of grazing parties had greatly reduced the garrison in Santa Fe, Price issued orders to Major Benjamin Edmonson and Captain Burgwin to come up from Albuquerque. Burgwin was to leave one company of dragoons in Santa Fe and Edmonson was to remain in Santa Fe under the command of Lieutenant Colonel Willock and his five companies of the Second Missouri.

On January 23 Price left Santa Fe with 350 men and four mountain howitzers. All the men were dismounted except a company of Santa Fe volunteers commanded by Ceran St. Vrain, the late Governor Bent's business partner. The next day St. Vrain's company, riding in advance, discovered enemy forces in the town of Cañada. Price rushed the remainder of his troops to the village, leaving his provision and ammunition wagons behind. When Price arrived he found the Mexicans fortified in three houses at the base of a hill beyond a creek in the village. The remaining Mexicans had taken positions on the heights immediately beyond and above the village. While his force advanced Price placed the artillery on his left flank to enable it to open on the houses in the village and the heights above. He positioned his infantry under a high bluff bank of the stream. The artillery opened fire on the houses at nearly the same time that a force of Mexicans advanced on Price's trailing supply wagons. Price sent St. Vrain and his men back and they brought up the wagons safely. With his supplies now secure, Price ordered his infantry on a successful charge to capture the houses. After this a general charge carried the other points. The Missourians killed thirty-six Mexicans while losing only two men.

The next day Price moved his force up the Rio del Norte as far as Luceros. On the twenty-eighth Captain Burgwin arrived with a company of dismounted dragoons, while another company of dismounted volunteers also reached Luceros. On January 29, Price learned that there was a small enemy force in the pass that led to the village of El Embudo. Since the gorge was impassable for wagons and artillery, he dispatched a force under Captain Burgwin and led the main force farther south to find a route through the mountains. Burgwin's men scattered the Mexicans and marched into El Embudo.

44. The account of the Taos campaign is drawn from Price's official report, 30th Cong., 1st sess., 1847–1848, House Exec. Doc. No. 1, 520–26.

On January 31, the American force rendezvoused at Las Trampas and pushed on toward Taos. For the next three days the troops marched through snow two feet deep, the men breaking a path in front of the wagons and artillery. By February 3 Price's men, many suffering from frostbite and fatigue, reached Taos, where they learned of a large enemy force at the pueblo outside the town.

Pueblo de Taos constituted an extremely formidable position. The entire complex was surrounded by thick adobe walls pierced for rifles. Within the walls there was a large church in the northwest angle, and near the north and south walls were large seven-story buildings capable of holding many defenders. Immediately upon his arrival Price ordered an artillery barrage on the church where the enemy was concentrated. Since the supply wagons had not arrived, the artillery soon ran out of ammunition. Moreover, the men were extremely fatigued, so Price ordered his force back to the village.

Early the next day Price returned with his troops. Reconnoitering on the previous day convinced him that the church was the key to the whole area; if it could be taken, the entire village would be helpless. Price placed Burgwin and his dragoons on the western flank of the church with two howitzers and the remainder of his troops opposite the northern wall, with the exception of St. Vrain and his mounted men whom he ordered to the opposite side of town to cut off any fugitives.

Shortly before 9:00 A.M. Price ordered his artillery to open fire. After two hours it became apparent that the light artillery pieces were having no effect on the adobe walls. On the previous day Price had noticed a space between the walls of the church and the outer walls that surrounded the village. If his men could get to the outer wall they would be hidden from the enemy fire. Taking advantage of this, Price ordered part of his forces opposite both the north and west walls to charge the outer walls. They did so and upon gaining the protection of the outer wall began to chop holes through the adobe with axes. Burgwin led a reckless group inside and tried to force the door of the church. Several men were wounded, including Burgwin who later died, and the group withdrew. In the meantime, small holes had been made in the west wall and the men threw in shells by hand. Price ordered an artillery piece brought around and it began to pour in charges of grape shot. By 3:00 P.M. the men had pushed this artillery piece to within sixty yards of the church and it soon managed to open a gaping hole in the wall. The Missourians then pushed the gun to within ten yards of the hole and fired in several rounds of grape. Storming parties, shielded by the clouds of smoke from the gun, charged through the hole and swarmed into the church. Once these troops were inside the church the remaining

Missourians charged into the village and the Mexicans began to flee. St. Vrain and his men, who had been close friends of the Americans massacred at Taos, brutally cut down any who attempted to escape. Soon night came and the Missourians bivouacked in the abandoned houses of the village.

The following morning the Mexicans sued for peace, which was granted on the condition that Tomasito, the man most responsible for stirring up the Indians at Taos, be delivered up. This was done and the revolt came to an end. Price estimated that the Mexicans had close to 650 men in the pueblo, of whom 150 were killed. The Americans counted seven killed and forty-five wounded, many of whom later died.

V

Price displayed considerable skill in directing the campaign and the Missourians, in the excitement of the fighting, forgot their grievances. The revolt had been efficiently, although in some instances brutally, put down. With the exception of scattered Indian raids east of the mountains, New Mexico remained calm for the duration of the war.

The swift, sure, crushing of the revolt produced a subdued populace that remained so because of the vigorous prosecutions by the court that convened at Taos to try those responsible for the revolt. This was a mountainman's court with a frontiersman's sense of justice.[45] Don Carlos Beaubien, whose son had been murdered at Taos, presided over the court, and George Bent, brother of the slain governor, served as foreman of the jury—itself composed of many relatives and friends of the dead Americans. Frank P. Blair, attorney general for the territory, drew up the prosecutions and handled them in the courtroom. The court was in session for fifteen working days and hanged a man for each day of the session. Most appeals received short shrift, since the sheriff hanged all those convicted of homicide before a transcript could have been written.[46]

One of the appeals caused bad feelings between Blair and Price, led to Blair's arrest, and became the genesis of a long-running feud between the two men. Blair based his prosecutions on the fact that Kearny had declared New Mexico to be part of the United States and its populace to be United States citizens,[47] thus enabling him to try

45. Francis Cheetham, "The First Term of the American Court in Taos, New Mexico," *New Mexico Historical Review*, 1 (January, 1926), 23–41.
46. Garrard, "Wah-To-Yah," 239–40, 248–50; William B. Drescher, "Mexican War Recollections," Mexican War Letters.
47. Frank Blair to John Y. Mason, April 1, 1847, 30th Cong., 1st sess., House Exec. Doc. No. 70, 19–20.

the prisoners for treason. When Donaciano Vigil petitioned Secretary of State James Buchanan for a pardon for Antonio Trujillo, Buchanan left the matter up to Price, who pardoned the man.[48] Blair objected so strongly that Price placed him under arrest; this led to Blair's resignation and a smoldering hatred of Price.

After the excitement of the revolt subsided the troops settled down to garrison duty and once again slipped into their old habits. The volunteers, aroused by what they perceived to be the treachery of the revolt, showed even less respect for persons and property. Sickness, short supplies, and Indian harassment lowered morale once again. Many of Price's company commanders still nursed resentment toward him and one volunteer wrote that half of them did not know where their men were or even how many they had. Lewis Garrard met part of Price's command and his comments clearly illustrated this laxness of discipline: "Volunteer-like they were in the rear, at the side, and in advance of their commander; they disregarding military deference, he military control." As Garrard passed the baggage wagons, a first lieutenant who had assisted the sheriff at the Taos executions poked his head out of one of the wagons and shouted to Garrard: "How are ye—would ye like to hang any more Mexicans? Now wasn't that a tall time down to Touse [*sic*]!" Garrard, already repulsed by the Taos trials, could only observe that "altogether he was a rare specimen of that peculiar genus known as a Missouri volunteer officer."[49]

Donaciano Vigil, who became acting governor upon Bent's death, recognized the shortcomings of volunteers for garrison duty and requested that regular troops be sent to hold New Mexico.[50] Price would have had a difficult time if his officers had been loyal, but with many deliberately thwarting him he was in a serious predicament. Once again the Whig press in Missouri began to damn him.

VI

Price's difficulties lessened during August and September, since the terms of enlistment for the Second Missouri expired during these months. Price discharged the companies as soon as their term of service drew to a close, for the men, having "seen the elephant," were anxious to return to their homes. Evidently a good number of the volunteers did appreciate Price's services as several days before his own departure many Missourians held a mass meeting in his honor. At their last fandango the troops adopted a resolution expressing

48. Donaciano Vigil to James Buchanan, March 23, 1847, *ibid.*, 24–25; William L. Marcy to Sterling Price, June 11, 1847, *ibid.*, 31–32.
49. Garrard, "Wah-To-Yah," 321.
50. Vigil to James Buchanan, February 16, 1847, 30th Cong., 1st sess., House Exec. Doc. No. 70, 19–20.

their fond feelings for him and thanking him for "the fatherly protection" he had extended to the regiment under his command. The
troops felt further compelled to commend him for his coolness and
courage while under fire.[51] Three days later Price accompanied the
last departing companies, leaving three companies of dragoons and
a company of re-enlisted volunteers to garrison Santa Fe.

On the trail home the Second Missouri met elements of the Third
Missouri and the First Illinois infantry regiment commanded by Colonel John Ralls and Lieutenant Colonel Alton Easton. To alleviate
the crowded conditions in Santa Fe most of these troops proceeded
to El Paso. The crushing of the revolt had left the territory quiet,
but relations with the natives were still far short of cordial.[52]

VII

While on the march homeward Price received his commission as
a brigadier general—a promotion that touched off another storm of
protest from the Whig press in Missouri. These editors were beside
themselves with rage that, after the reports they had printed concerning Price and his command in New Mexico, he should even be
considered for such a promotion. In their minds the soundest explanation was that Price was a "devotee at the shrine of Benton."[53]
In all their wild fury the Whigs came close to hitting the mark. Benton and Price had kept up a steady correspondence during the war,
and Benton looked upon Price as his special favorite and protégé.[54] In
this case there could be little doubt that Benton was instrumental
in gaining Price's promotion.

Price had little taste for political battles when he arrived home,
and was anxious to be with Martha and his family in Chariton. He
reached his farm in the second week of September and rested for a
short time, but planned to return to Santa Fe as soon as he could
make arrangements and tend to some business affairs.

In the first week of October, Sterling and Martha left for a trip to
Jefferson City and St. Louis. In the capital Price visited with the
Governor, various legislators, and his old political intimate, now
Attorney General, Benjamin Stringfellow.[55] He received enthusiastic
welcomes from various groups and the public at large in the city.
From Jefferson City Sterling and Martha went on to St. Louis where
they took rooms at the Planter's House. The St. Louis newspapers
announced his arrival and, depending upon their political leanings,

---

51. *Jefferson Enquirer*, October 9, 1847.
52. John V. Masten to his father, December 17, 1847, Mexican War
Letters.
53. *Missouri Statesman*, August 13, 1847.
54. Thomas C. Reynolds, "Sterling Price and the Confederacy," 5.
55. *Jefferson Enquirer*, October 9, 1847.

lauded him or merely noted his presence.[56] The day after Price's arrival a group of prominent St. Louis Democrats sent him a highly approbative invitation to a testimonial dinner in his honor.[57] Although not averse to receiving such an honor, Price had to refuse the invitation in favor of handling his business affairs and spending more time with his family on the farm. However, this offer and the wild receptions given his troops were not lost on him; neither was the status of the First Missouri's men overlooked. Many were being pressed for high political office on the strength of their military service alone.

VIII

On November 10 General Price left Fort Leavenworth with a small escort of dragoons. After a long but uneventful journey Price arrived in Santa Fe two months later. According to the *Santa Fe Republican* that city had never been more orderly than while commanded by Colonel Edward Newby and Lieutenant Colonel Easton;[58] with his new commission and command Price meant to keep it that way. Six days after his return he issued Order Number Eight calling for drill, strict discipline, and court-martial punishment of offenders.[59] From this point on the local press commended Price for a well-run department. The political pettiness of the Second Missouri was in the past and Price had to contend only with the usual difficulties of commanding volunteers.

Although the troops now commanded by Price may not have harbored ill feelings toward him, they did behave in much the same manner as his previous command. The officers sported mistresses, the troops gambled, drank, and resisted attempts at discipline by their superiors. On one occasion a lieutenant ordered several of his men tied up in the guardhouse. When a crowd of soldiers gathered the officer picked up his musket and threatened to fire into the group, thus prompting the men to gather up their own arms. A bloody fight was barely averted.[60]

The Missourians continued to treat the natives with disdain. Responding to a slight altercation with some Mexicans, a group of Missourians rode into a native village, shot several of the inhabitants, stole chickens, blankets, and trinkets, and one even removed an image of a saint from a church.[61] Price was not blamed for these activities as he had been for those of the Second Missouri because these troops were not angered by his commission.

56. Compare the *Saint Louis Daily Union* and the *Daily Missouri Republican* for the dates October 12–16, 1847.
57. *Saint Louis Daily Union*, October 16, 1847.
58. *Santa Fe Republican*, September 17, 1847; December 4, 1847.
59. *Ibid.*, December 18, 1847.
60. Philip Gooch Ferguson, "Diary," 348–49.
61. *Ibid.*, 333.

IX

During his stay in Missouri Price had corresponded with Adjutant General Roger Jones, asking for permission to lead an expedition to Chihuahua.[62] Jones replied that Secretary of War Marcy favored the proposal but, before giving instructions on the subject, wanted Price's views in more detail.[63] To this Price answered that he intended to occupy Chihuahua, Durango, and provinces farther south.[64] In November Jones responded that the expedition to Chihuahua and Durango could be handled better and more economically from Monterey or Saltillo and ordered Price not to march south. However, Jones did indicate that should Price learn of an enemy force at Chihuahua, organized "with the design of marching on New Mexico, although it is not advisable that you should proceed there for the purpose of attacking it, you should make reasonable demonstrations and use your own discretion as to when it should be encountered."[65]

Price returned to Santa Fe prior to receiving Jones' last letter. Rumors were in the air that Mexican troops were making threatening movements to the south, and American residents in Santa Fe urged Price to lead an expedition to Chihuahua. In early October, 1847, the *Santa Fe Republican* noted that no "active measures" had been taken to control Chihuahua after Doniphan's departure and that since that time American citizens in Chihuahua had been badly treated and their goods confiscated. Reflecting the desire of American inhabitants in New Mexico, the *Republican* called for action to rectify this situation.[66] Merchants in Santa Fe also exerted great pressure on Price for an expedition to Chihuahua.

Price felt he could satisfy these people since, on the basis of Jones' last letter, he was confident that he would receive permission to move south. His inclination to lead an expedition south was greatly strengthened when rumors reached Santa Fe that General Urrea was advancing on El Paso with nearly 8,000 men.[67] A later rumor indicated that Colonel Ralls had been defeated by Urrea at El Paso.[68] The *Republican* claimed that these reports, coming from "highly respected

62. Price to Jones, August 14, 1847; September 18, 1847, Letters Received, The Adjutant General's Office.
63. Jones to Price, October 4, 1847, Letters Sent, The Adjutant General's Office.
64. Price to Jones, October 31, 1847, Letters Received, The Adjutant General's Office.
65. Jones to Price, January 21, 1848, Letters Sent, The Adjutant General's Office.
66. *Santa Fe Republican*, October 9, 1847.
67. John V. Masten to his father, February 7, 1847, Mexican War Letters.
68. *Missouri Statesman*, April 7, 1847.

sources" and being "based on very plausible ground," called for action.[69]

Price informed Jones that the enemy was making threatening moves and that he was going to take possession of Chihuahua if the express from Jones, which he expected daily, did not contain instructions to the contrary. He justified his action on the grounds that he could secure uninterrupted communications with General Taylor, bring tranquility to New Mexico, and afford protection to the many American citizens in Chihuahua.[70]

During a ball the night of February 4 a messenger rushed in and handed Price a dispatch from Lieutenant Colonel Lane, commander of the American troops at El Paso. Lane reported that he had seized documents from captured Mexican troops revealing that General Urrea was marching toward El Paso with 3,000 men and that reinforcements from the city of Chihuahua would join him.[71] Price decided to act immediately. He wrote Jones that he had waited for the latter's dispatch but now "Chihuahua taken and held is regarded by the American citizens here, of the utmost importance and a measure effecting their interests to a great extent."[72] Four days after receiving Lane's message Price left Santa Fe with his staff; a letter from Jones arrived at Santa Fe a few days later.

On February 23 Price entered El Paso, only to learn that Urrea's reported advance was just rumor. He also received Jones' November dispatch forbidding him to proceed south. Deliberately, but silently, he decided to disobey it. With no Mexican forces threatening Santa Fe, Jones' orders instructed Price to remain in El Paso, but he was determined to lead an expedition to Chihuahua and prepared his forces for the march. At the first opportunity he wrote to Benton, who approved of his course and promised to attempt to shield him from censure should he fail.[73]

X

Price decided to advance on Chihuahua before the Mexicans could become aware of his presence[74] and make forced marches with his best mounted troops in order to strike a blow before the Mexicans

69. *Santa Fe Republican*, February 12, 1848.
70. Price to Jones, January 21, 1848, Letters Received, The Adjutant General's Office.
71. Lane to Price, January 30, 1848, Letters Received, The Adjutant General's Office.
72. Price to Jones, February 6, 1848, Letters Received, The Adjutant General's Office.
73. Reynolds, "Price and the Confederacy," 3–4.
74. The following account of the Chihuahua campaign is drawn from the reports of Price and his company commanders, 30th Cong., 2d sess., House Exec. Doc. No. 1, 113–36.

learned of his intentions. The day after his arrival in El Paso he dispatched Major Walker with three companies of volunteers to occupy Carrizal, ninety miles to the south, in order to command all the passes leading to Chihuahua and thus cut off enemy communications with that city.

Price remained in El Paso for four days waiting for supply trains to arrive. Finally exasperated by this delay he decided to proceed and ordered the provision wagons and additional troops to catch up when they could. Price, more the romantic than the practical military leader, left with four companies of volunteers, two companies of dragoons under Major Benjamin Beall, and one company of volunteer light artillery. Traveling light, with only eight days' rations and no tents, the force entered Carrizal and joined Walker's force three days later.

The troops left at sunrise the next day and rode forty miles through a cold rain. The following morning they left at daybreak again and rode until 10:00 that night, covering fifty miles. At times they passed over high hills of pure sand where their horses sank to their fetlocks. On March 6 the troops ran into enemy pickets who managed to escape, thus causing Price to push his force on to Laguna, six miles north of Sacramento, where a Mexican delegation from Governor Trias met Price under a flag of truce. The Governor protested against the advance of American troops and asserted that he had received instructions from the Mexican government to suspend hostilities because of the signing of a peace treaty between the two nations. Price did not believe the messenger and, growing tired of the conference, sent several officers ahead into Chihuahua to arrange for the preliminaries of capitulation. Price, "fearful that dissimulation was the object of the interview," determined to move his command into Chihuahua that night. The men rode on rapidly and within an hour met a group of Americans from Chihuahua who informed Price that the Mexican army had retreated from the city the previous morning. Price urged his men on and the Missourians entered the city during the night.

Having anticipated the Mexican withdrawal, Price had dispatched Beall and his dragoons the previous day on a forced march through the mountains to reach the Durango road and cut off Trias. Early the next morning Price, after pressing some mules and horses into service to replace those spent from the hard rides, left in pursuit of Trias. He was able to take only 250 men with him because of the shortage of remounts, the remaining troops to follow when their horses were rested. By sunrise the next day Price and his men had ridden the sixty miles to Santa Cruz de Rosales, where they discovered the Mexican army entrenched in a fortified town.

Price made a reconnaissance of the town and decided to storm it. While he readied his troops for the attack he sent an officer under flag of truce to demand the surrender of the town. Governor Trias requested an interview and once again informed Price that he had learned in "an official manner" of the conclusion of a treaty of peace and that under the circumstances he could only act on the defensive.[75] Price, because of the arrival of more of his troops and supplies each day, was in an excellent position to wait confirmation of the treaty. He decided to besiege the town.

From March 9 to March 16 nothing happened. Small detachments of troops, after incredible marches, joined Price's force. Provision wagons began to arrive and with them more artillery. By the sixteenth Price decided to attack; he had received no word to confirm Trias' statements and his troops, with no shelter, were becoming restless under their constant vigil. On the morning of the sixteenth Price ordered his artillery to open on the town. The Mexican batteries returned the fire and a brisk artillery duel ensued. Price received word that a large Mexican force was approaching his rear and pulled his artillery back to meet this threat. The Mexicans, upon observing this, felt they were victorious and broke into furious cheers, but when Price discovered that no force was threatening him, he decided to take the town by storm.

The American encampment during the siege was on the east side of the town, where much of the Mexican fortifications were located. Price therefore decided to send his men in from the northern, southern, and southwestern approaches to the village. The reopening of American artillery fire was to signal the attack. In the late afternoon the American guns opened on the Mexican positions and kept up a constant shelling. At the sound of the guns the dismounted Missourians rushed the town amid loud shrieks and cheers. Lieutenant Colonel Lane and his men entered the town from the northern approach and ran into the heaviest resistance. Colonel Ralls and Major Walker entered from the southwest and the south, and in fierce house-to-house fighting made their way toward the plaza, where the main Mexican resistance was concentrated in a large church.

Every house was filled with Mexicans and they had also posted sharpshooters on the roofs behind barricades and parapets. The Missourians, advancing on the rooftops and through the streets, broke into houses with axes and crowbars and drove the enemy out, at the same time protecting themselves from Mexican fire by taking cover in the captured homes. The Mexicans threw long-fused grenades at the Missourians who had time to kick them into the houses filled with enemy soldiers. Walker had brought along a small mountain howitzer and handed out shells to his men to light and use as hand grenades. During the fighting the artillery duel continued, and each time the

75. Trias to Price, March 10, 1848; March 12, 1848, Letters Received, The Adjutant General's Office.

Missourians passed by a house or over a parapet they gave a loud cheer to let the American gunners know where they were.

Most of the troops made their way directly toward the plaza. Only Lane and his men, running into a fierce Mexican crossfire from their main batteries and those placed at right angles with the main street, were forced to fall back. They retreated to the outskirts of the village and then circled around to follow Ralls' men into the village.

Near sunset the Americans reached the edge of the plaza and prepared to storm the church. Walker's howitzer opened fire on the church, but at this point the Mexicans raised flags of surrender. The American officers had a difficult time restraining their men, who in the fierce fighting had become intent upon taking the church, and many Mexicans were brutally killed while attempting to surrender. Finally, the Missourians accepted the enemy surrender and secured the town.

The next morning the Americans surveyed their work. Piles of horribly mangled Mexican bodies lay throughout the village. Over 200 Mexicans had lost their lives while the Americans suffered only four dead and nineteen wounded. Governor Trias and many other principal officers surrendered and the Americans captured twenty pieces of artillery and over 500 small arms. Price had registered a stunning victory.

XI

With Price serving as the provincial military governor, the Missourians remained in Chihuahua until July, 1848, when they began their journey back to Missouri. Major Beall assumed command of the Ninth Military District, which remained under regular troops thereafter.

The Chihuahua campaign had been an incredible one. Price displayed great courage in his pursuit and defeat of Trias. He had made good use of his mounted troops, established a rapport with his volunteers, made judicious use of his regulars, and in general drew maximum co-operation from his men. Although his motives for the campaign were certainly questionable, no one brought this up in the fanfare that followed. For all practical purposes the war was over when Price started the campaign. Mexico City had fallen six months earlier and the Treaty of Guadelupe Hidalgo had been signed on February 2 and ratified by the United States Senate on March 10. Santa Fe was certainly in no danger and, if it had been, the occupation of El Paso would have been sufficient to prevent its capture without staging an extended and dangerous campaign. A defeat of Price might have provided the needed stimulus for Mexico to continue the struggle, or possibly complicated ratification of the peace treaty. On the other hand, Price's rapid march and complete triumph gave practical control of Chihuahua to the Americans and may have hurried Mexican ratification of the treaty.[76]

During his stay in Santa Fe Price had been under pressure from the inhabitants to lead an expedition to Chihuahua.[77] As early as August he had asked permission of The Adjutant General to lead such a force, ostensibly to protect the interests of American residents. Later, when rumors were circulating that a Mexican force was moving toward New Mexico, it seemed a matter of military necessity to move to meet them. When Price learned that there was no Mexican threat and received definite orders not to advance, something more than commercial pressure must have caused him to deliberately disregard orders from his superiors.

The answer lay with Price himself. He had been bitterly criticized in the press from the moment he accepted Polk's appointment; his promotion to brigadier general made short life of the respite gained after the Taos campaign. Moreover, while in Missouri in 1847 Price became aware of the tremendous possibilities that existed for a military hero to further his own position. His future could benefit enormously from a successful campaign such as Doniphan's. Thus, trusting his own military judgment rather than that of his superiors, Price set out on a wild campaign to risk everything on one daring venture.

XII

By October Price was back with Martha and his family, basking in the glory of his military success. President Polk considered the campaign one of the notable successes of the war[78] and Missouri newspapers were filled with acclaim for Price. The *Enquirer* printed a letter complimenting Price as a "bold, daring, and energetic officer" and predicting that he would retire from service "with a *higher military* fame and with *laurels more imperishable* than any other officer who *has been* or *is now* connected with the army of the west."[79] At celebrations given the returning volunteers Price was acclaimed as "the soldier, the patriot, and the friend of the volunteer . . ."[80] and the Missouri Assembly passed resolutions of thanks to Price and Don-

76. Frederick Merk notes that President Polk wanted to prod the Mexicans into ratifying the treaty and did this by sending reinforcements to Winfield Scott and pressing a large war loan through Congress. Price's expedition was consequently a windfall for Polk. Merk, *Manifest Destiny and Mission in American History: A Reinterpretation*, 188.

77. Justin Smith comes to the conclusion that commercial pressure was the sole reason for the campaign in *The War With Mexico*, II, 419.

78. *The Diary of James K. Polk*, II, Milo Quaife, ed., 481–82.

79. *Jefferson Enquirer*, May 27, 1848.

80. *Ibid.*, September 4, 1848.

iphan.[81] A comment in *The Weekly Tribune*, a Whig paper, must have been even more pleasing to Price. The editor, hearing that Price intended to oppose David R. Atchison for the Senate, concluded that if this were true "The hero of New Mexico will walk over the course."[82] Price had accomplished what he had set out to do. He had become a hero to Missourians and his personal future seemed secure.

While fully realizing the effect of his Mexican War experience upon his political career, Price could have no way to know that this experience would also have a profound effect upon his military behavior during the Civil War. Price's strengths and weaknesses as a Confederate general would strongly reflect his Mexican War background, which gave him valuable military experience and training. He had only minimal military knowledge prior to the war, yet by the time of the Chihuahua campaign he displayed remarkable resourcefulness and skill. The success of his rapid movements and his use of cavalry foreshadowed his raids into Missouri during the later conflict. Beall's dragoons were the precursors of Jo Shelby's gray-coated Iron Brigade. By far the most valuable lesson learned in the Mexican War, although certainly the most trying one, was Price's experience in handling volunteer troops. The majority of Confederate field commanders who served in the Mexican War led regular troops;[83] as a result they tended to expect too much from volunteer troops during the Civil War. Intricate battle plans proved far too complex to be executed by volunteers. Price knew only too well the strengths and weaknesses of these independent troops and the special handling they required.[84] He knew how to gain their confidence and their loyalty, as he gained experience in handling large groups of men, and his troops during the Civil War would idolize him.[85] Few of the Union and Confederate leaders who served in the Mexican War had led troops of company strength, while Price had commanded a regiment.

Price's success during the Mexican War in disobeying orders from superiors strengthened his opinion of his own abilities and prompted

81. Printed in the *The Weekly Tribune*, January 26, 1849.

82. *Ibid.*, November 10, 1848.

83. An analysis of biographical sketches of all Confederate generals reveals that of the 425 Confederate generals, 138 served in the Mexican War in some capacity while 184 of the 538 Union generals saw service in that war. Ezra Warner, *Generals in Gray*.

84. There is a striking similarity between the behavior of the Confederate soldier presented by David Donald and that of the Missouri volunteers in the Mexican War. Donald, "The Confederate as a Fighting Man," *Journal of Southern History*, 25 (May, 1959), 178–93.

85. Not all officers who later served in the Civil War learned this lesson. For quite a different experience, see Grady McWhiney, *Braxton Bragg and Confederate Defeat*, I.

his headstrong actions, bordering upon insubordination during the Civil War. During the latter conflict he had difficulty co-operating with his fellow officers and in obeying orders from his superiors. Kearny never brought Price to task for raising cavalry, and Polk and Marcy expressed their highest admiration for the Chihuahua campaign, which had resulted from direct disobedience on Price's part. Further, Price in his romantic dash after Trias had been successful while paying no heed to the more practical problems of warfare. He would never understand the need for proper logistical support of troops in the field. These successes that served to strengthen Price's confidence in his own judgment and skill would lead to problems during the Civil War.

· 6 ·

Return to a Political Maelstrom

Within a week after his return Price, who could not keep away
from the political scene, attended a rally in Fayette where David R.
Atchison, in a two-hour address, castigated Martin Van Buren as the
"arch traitor and apostate of democracy" for his acceptance of the
Free Soil party's nomination for the Presidency. He further denied
that Lewis Cass, the regular Democratic presidential nominee, had
ever favored the Wilmot Proviso forbidding slavery's expansion into
the territories gained from Mexico. Soon after the Senator concluded
his harangue a general call arose from the crowd for Price to speak.
Price mounted the speaker's platform to the accompaniment of thun-
derous applause. Always careful in his political expressions, he remarked that due to his lengthy absence from the state he could not be
expected to shed any additional light on the subject under discussion
and therefore he dealt with his Mexican War experience. Always a
party man, he did endorse Cass for the Presidency.[1]

Price avoided a political stand at Fayette, but it would not be long
before he would be forced to speak out. While he fought in Mexico
dangerous national issues had arisen that would soon engulf him. The
Mexican War revived the issue of slavery and its status in the territories. This issue, so full of portent, forced Price and his associates
to conceptualize their views on long dormant issues.

II

During Price's absence, party relations in Missouri had undergone
subtle and gradual changes. Shadrach Penn kept the old factional
struggle alive for a time, but with his death in 1846 the bitterness of
the hard-soft quarrels died away. A united Democracy, with the
Boonslick group firmly in control, emerged once again, but a new
and more divisive issue, which would rend both Missouri and the
nation, arose during the closing days of the first session of the Twenty-
ninth Congress.

When President James K. Polk sent a message to Congress requesting two million dollars to prosecute the war against Mexico a young
Pennsylvania congressman offered a proposal that precipitated a na-

1. Jefferson City (Mo.) *Jefferson Enquirer*, October 21, 1848.

tionwide controversy. David Wilmot's "proviso" called for the prohibition of slavery in all territory gained by the war. The proviso, which arose again in the second session of Congress, prompted a violent discussion between John C. Calhoun and Thomas H. Benton. Calhoun introduced a series of resolutions declaring that Congress had no right to legislate for the territories and insisted instead upon the positive protection of slavery. These resolutions elicited a disdainful response from Benton, who referred to them as "abstractions" obstructing more important work. Benton's retort led to an angry exchange between the two senators, ending with Benton stating that, rather than support such "firebrands," he would be found "on the side of my country and the Union."[2] When a vote finally came on the Wilmot Proviso, Benton cast his vote against it, considering it the twin evil to Calhoun's resolutions.[3]

During this period party relations remained harmonious in Missouri. At a rally in Fayette early in 1847 the Boonslick group nominated Benton for the Presidency in 1848. Immediately upon his return to Missouri in early May, 1847, Benton informed the Howard County Democrats that he desired a Northern man for the Democratic nomination. The Senator expressed a fear that the South was putting the North to a test over slavery in the territories and that if this test was adopted by the slave states it would end all Northern support for the Democracy and create sectional parties.[4] Benton followed this letter with a speech in St. Louis in which he outlined his position for the 1840's. He reviewed his course on Texas and Oregon and blasted Calhoun and his resolutions, calling them "a subversion of the Union" that would obviate all compromise on the slavery question. Stating that he had "sounded the alarm," he called for the people to do the rest.[5] Near the end of May Benton followed this bold position with an address at Jefferson City. There again he warned that the slavery issue would break up the parties and bring about the destruction of the Union, but he did express the conviction that Missouri, "for one slaveholding State, will not follow the lead of the slavery propagandist resolutions."[6]

While Benton remained in Missouri, Democratic newspapers offered no adverse comment on his stand on slavery as might have been expected; indeed, they maintained a strange silence on the entire issue. A Whig editor, evidently hoping to create dissension in Dem-

---

2. *Congressional Globe*, 29th Cong., 2d sess., 453–55.
3. William N. Chambers, *Old Bullion Benton: Senator from the New West*, 314–15.
4. Benton to Wade Jackson, May 7, 1847, printed in Fayette (Mo.) *Boon's Lick Times*, May 29, 1847.
5. *Saint Louis Daily Union*, May 11, 1847.
6. *Jefferson Enquirer*, May 29, 1847.

ocratic ranks, warned that Benton's declaration could not be "palatable" to the Democracy, but "palatable" it appeared to be.[7] John Lowry, writing after Silas Wright's death, referred to the New Yorker as "one of the greatest statesmen of the day" and felt that Benton should now be pushed for the Presidency.[8]

By December, 1847, it became apparent that not all Democrats shared Lowry's feelings toward Benton. Indeed, evidence that divisions existed even within the Boonslick group appeared—tension created by the ambitions of C. F. Jackson. At a meeting of Howard County Democrats held on December 6, Lowry's call for a resolution complimentary to Benton set off a heated debate. D. R. Scott, Jackson, and others opposed Lowry's resolution and voted it down. They were uneasy regarding Benton's position on slavery in the territories.[9] A Whig editor leaped at the chance to publicize this "repudiation" of Benton and speculated that Benton's popularity was "on the wane and that the ice is now being broken against him."[10] Doubtless, in his eagerness to foment discord in Democratic ranks, the editor exaggerated his account of the discussion, but nevertheless the fact that tension did exist within the Boonslick group could not long remain obscured.

Jackson, courting all Democratic elements in a drive for the gubernatorial nomination, soon had second thoughts about his action at the Howard County meeting and went to St. Louis to assure Democrats there that he did not oppose Benton.[11] However, since M. M. Marmaduke still continued to be the St. Louis group's choice for governor, Jackson felt compelled to take further actions to ensure his own nomination. Three weeks prior to the state nominating convention Jackson arranged another Howard County meeting that endorsed Benton. Regardless of Jackson's exertions, the gubernatorial nomination ultimately went to Austin A. King. It soon became apparent that Jackson was bitter over his defeat and that he held Benton supporters responsible. His alienation, which grew with the passage of time, would divide the Boonslick faction.

By August, 1848, the Missouri Democracy was filled with unrest. A Howard County convention nominated C. F. Jackson for the state

7. *St. Louis New Era* reprinted in *Boon's Lick Times,* September 11, 1847.
8. Lowry to M. M. Marmaduke, September 17, 1847, Sappington Papers.
9. *Boon's Lick Times,* December 11, 1847; John J. Lowry to M. M. Marmaduke, December 25, 1847, Meredith M. Marmaduke Collection.
10. *Boon's Lick Times,* December 11, 1847.
11. George Penn to M. M. Marmaduke, January 11, 1848; Thomas Gray to M. M. Marmaduke, January 9, 1848; John Krum to M. M. Marmaduke, January 10, 1848, Sappington Papers.

Senate. Lowry, certain that Jackson's friends looked upon this position seat as a stepping stone to the United States Senate, felt that Jackson, certain to "injure himself by his unbounded ambition," should not run. In Lowry's mind, he could only disrupt the unity of the state party.[12]

It was not only state affairs that were upsetting Missouri Democrats. Benton, desperately trying to obtain the organization of a government for Oregon, voted for one that included a version of the Wilmot Proviso. To compound this, Martin Van Buren accepted the nomination of the Free-Soil party. Benton's known attachment to the New Yorker caused many anxious days. The immediate reaction was to defend Benton from charges of free soilism.[13] But as time passed with no word from Benton, Missourians began to worry. The *Daily Missouri Republican* declared that Benton would withdraw his support from Cass and give it to Van Buren.[14] Samuel Treat, editor of the *Saint Louis Daily Union* and a member of the newly-formed Democratic National Committee, publicly declared that Benton would take "bold ground" against Van Buren's defection.[15] Privately, however, Treat maintained doubts that must have been shared by many others. Treat felt that Benton could have prevented Van Buren's defection by visiting him at Kinderhook while the Senator was in New York. Benton had refused to do this. Before long Treat became convinced that Benton's participation in the canvass for Cass was "half-hearted."[16]

Frank Blair, one of Benton's closest intimates in Missouri, greatly heightened the state Democracy's anxieties by establishing a free-soil campaign paper, the *Barnburner*, in St. Louis and invoking Benton's name in support of his cause. While Benton lent no aid to Blair's efforts, the questions of where Benton stood remained to plague Missourians.

From July through October Treat's *Union* ran reassuring articles that Benton would not support Van Buren, but was unable to produce any direct affirmation from the Senator. Everyone waited for Benton to come to Missouri to define his position as he had always done in the past. George Penn, assuming that Benton would turn against Van Buren, could not forget the Senator's affection for the

12. Lowry to M. M. Marmaduke, June 29, 1848, Sappington Papers.
13. This may be seen in the editorial policy of *The* Jefferson City (Mo.) *Metropolitan*, a paper that would become the most violently anti-Benton organ in 1850. See *The Metropolitan*, August 29, 1848.
14. St. Louis *Daily Missouri Republican*, June 5, 6, 1848.
15. *Saint Louis Daily Union*, June 30, 1848.
16. Notes made by Treat on July 3, 1848, and "n.d." on letter from Lewis Cass, Samuel Treat Papers.

New Yorker and his faction.[17] William Napton suspected Benton of free-soil tendencies[18] and when Treat announced that "business" would "detain" Benton and prevent his coming to Missouri that fall there were anxious times indeed.[19]

It was during these tense moments of watchful waiting that Price returned to Missouri. Since he could not escape the maelstrom, it would be necessary for him to clarify his own thinking on the points at issue.

III

Price, intent upon his plantation and businesses, remained close to Keytesville for several months after his return from Mexico. By this time Val Verde, as he named his plantation, was one of the finest in the region. Often guests would come up the Missouri River by steamboat from St. Louis and disembark at Price's wharf to spend several days with the Price family. Sterling enjoyed entertaining on a lavish scale. He was also greatly drawn to raising thoroughbred horses, and his guests could enjoy races among Price's stock on the Val Verde track. Regardless of how Price might enjoy the social life of his plantation, he would not long be able to delight in his leisure because of the political developments in the state and the nation.

The slavery issue began to agitate the state. Upon the convening of the Missouri legislature in December, 1848, David R. Atchison, an ardent proslavery advocate, received the Democratic caucus nomination for the United States Senate seat of the deceased Lewis Linn. He received the support of C. F. Jackson, who had stumped the state with him during the previous summer. Jackson's support came as no surprise, because the affinity of thought between the two men on the slavery question was well-known. On January 8, 1849, a Jackson Day celebration witnessed speeches reflecting the same tone as those of Calhoun in the Senate. The Missouri legislature was greatly distressed by the territorial problem and these expressions delineated its feelings.

The Boonslick leadership in Jefferson City had become quite concerned about Benton's silence regarding slavery in the territories. A group of them, including Carty Wells, William Napton, Benjamin Stringfellow, and C. F. Jackson came to the conclusion that, rather than waiting for Benton to announce his position, he should be compelled to stand with them. Shortly after the legislature convened these men gathered in Napton's office in the Capitol and pooled their thoughts on the slavery issue. After a lengthy discussion the group

17. Penn to M. M. Marmaduke, November 14, 1848, Sappington Papers.
18. William B. Napton Diary, Missouri Historical Society, 86.
19. *Saint Louis Daily Union*, October 25, 26, 1848.

decided that Napton should take all their suggestions and draft a set of resolutions to be passed in the legislature.[20]

It was at this time that Price, never able to resist the political arena, visited Jefferson City. Napton invited him into his office and showed Price the finished resolutions to elicit the latter's opinion. Price, never suspecting the consequences of the concluding resolution instructing Missouri's congressional delegation to vote in accordance with the proslavery resolution, offered no criticism. Indeed, the resolutions were quite similar in spirit to his own offered in 1841 in response to William Seward's actions regarding fugitive slaves and reflected his views on the territorial issue.[21]

On January 15, 1849, C. F. Jackson introduced the resolutions that thereafter bore his name. These measures, breathing the proslavery spirit of the legislature, stated that the territories were the common property of all the states and that it would be "inconsistent with the spirit of the federal compact as well as insulting to the sovereignty and dignity of the states thus affected, calculated to alienate one portion of the union from another, and tending ultimately to disunion" to prevent slaveholders from taking their property into the territories. For the sake of harmony Missourians would adhere to the Missouri Compromise. The resolutions then expressed the opinion that the right to prohibit slavery in the territories belonged only to the people of a territory and only upon forming a constitution prior to statehood. They further stated that if Congress passed any act conflicting with the principles of these resolutions Missouri would act in co-operation with the other slave states in any measures deemed necessary "for our mutual protection against the encroachments of northern fanaticism." The final resolution instructed Missouri's congressional delegation to act in conformity with the measures. When voted upon, the resolutions passed on party lines.[22] The Boonslick group could now only hope that Benton would recognize their feelings and stand with them as he had in the past.

Following the adjournment of the assembly Missourians held county meetings throughout the state to express their views on the Jackson Resolutions and the Wilmot Proviso. All castigated the proviso and some criticized Benton for his reactions to it. Late in March, 1848, Chariton County citizens held a meeting to discuss the disturb-

20. Account of this meeting given to Edward Bates by Carty Wells. Diary of Edward Bates, 1848–1852, October 25, 1849.
21. Price to Thomas H. Benton, August 8, 1849, printed in *Jefferson Enquirer*, September 8, 1849.
22. "Jackson Resolutions" in *Laws of the State of Missouri*, 15th Assembly, 1848–1849, 667. Votes on resolutions in *Journal of the Senate of the State of Missouri*, 15th Assembly, 1848–1849, 175; *Journal of the House of Representatives of the State of Missouri*, 15th Assembly, 1848–1849, 461.

ing issues. A determined group of citizens were intent upon passing resolutions critical of Benton and thus agitated the crowd to do so. Upon discerning this movement, Price intervened and through the force of his presence and his tremendous prestige in the area squelched the anti-Benton movement. Declaring that Benton had not yet been fully heard on all the issues, Price emphatically stated that he would not lend his support to any premature castigation of the Senator. Assuring the assemblage that he knew Benton well and that Old Bullion did not intend to take the issue with the state of national Democracy or to side with the Free-Soilers, Price thus stilled the opposition and obtained resolutions quite favorable to Benton.[23]

While Price made these statements with certainty in public, he, like most of the Boonslick leaders, may have had private doubts. Knowing that if Benton did not side with the Free-Soilers the Missouri Democracy had nothing to fear, the Boonslick leaders could only hope that Missourians would remain uncommitted until Benton arrived in the state to clarify his views. George Penn, aware that Benton's old supporters could determine their course toward the Senator only after he fully outlined his own, hopefully proclaimed: "I most sincerely hope on his account as well as for the success of our party—that we shall have little cause of difference and as heretofore the party will have his valuable services and his old friends can extend him a cordial support—. . . ." Realizing that Benton's hatred of Calhoun might "betray him into a great political blunder," Penn felt that Benton's friends should meet with him upon his arrival in the state to keep him from this. If unsuccessful, they could only prepare to meet the storm that the state must then necessarily encounter.[24] Price and his cohorts could only await Benton's arrival and clarification of his views.

IV

Early in May, 1849, Benton arrived in St. Louis and began a half-year of arduous journeys and speeches throughout the state in defense of his position. On May 9, he began this ordeal with a short statement in which he appealed to the people of the state to allow him to disregard the instructions of the Jackson Resolutions, and he promised to present his reasons for so doing at a later date.[25] This statement shocked the Democrats and greatly pleased the Whigs, who fully recognized the portent of the Wilmot Proviso. A Whig leader advised his party to deal with the issue cautiously, feeling that "let alone by the Whigs, particularly on the subject of the Wilmot Proviso, he [Benton] will upset the Missouri Democracy & leave it

23. Jefferson City (Mo.) *Jefferson Examiner*, April 5, 1853.
24. Penn to M. M. Marmaduke, March 27, 1849, Sappington Papers.
25. *Jefferson Enquirer*, May 19, 1849.

in absolute destruction." The Whigs should "deal with him, therefore, wisely and gingerly."[26] A Whig editor wondered if Jackson and others would "*again* swallow their words [reference to 1844 Texas quarrel] and agree or do battle with the great I am [Benton]."[27] His answer was not long in coming since Benton left for Jefferson City and there forced the issue in a powerful speech.

At Jefferson City Benton castigated Calhoun as the "prime mover and head contriver" of the inflamed slavery issue and condemned the Jackson Resolutions as "copied from those of Mr. Calhoun." Benton then declared that the "design" and ultimate goal of both was to unite all the slave states in "the subversion of the Union." Denying the proslavery group's claim that Congress could not legislate for the territories, Benton exclaimed that Congress very definitely did have the power to either prohibit or admit slavery into the territories. The Senator declared that "if there was no slavery in Missouri today, I should oppose its coming in; if there was none in the United States, I should oppose its coming into the United States; as there is none in New Mexico or California, I am against sending it to those territories." In a final flourish of rhetoric Benton coined a phrase that was to be repeated often in the coming campaign. Referring to Calhoun and the proslavery elements in Missouri—which he equated—Benton cried: "Now I have them, and between them and me, henceforth and forever, *a high wall and a deep ditch!* and no communication, no compromise, no caucus with them."[28] With this statement Benton initiated a war in which he would neither ask nor give quarter.

Following his Jefferson City speech Benton set off on a tour of the surrounding counties. At the same time C. F. Jackson and Benjamin Stringfellow, his most ardent lieutenant, planned a series of county meetings to attack the Senator. Knowing that proslavery sentiment was extremely strong in Chariton County, the two men counted heavily on a meeting in Keytesville to get their anti-Benton campaign established. The two leaders were to meet only frustration at Keytesville—a frustration made all the more galling by the fact that it came at the hands of an old Boonslick ally.

Stringfellow and Jackson mingled with those present at the Chariton County meeting before it convened, with the hopes of building support for their proposed resolutions castigating Benton. They enjoyed a good deal of initial success, but when they introduced their resolutions Price arose and in a blunt speech declared that Benton must be sustained. Once again Price's tremendous personal prestige

26. Charles Daniel Drake to James S. Rollins, February 19, 1849, James S. Rollins Collection. Quoted in John V. Mering, "The Whig Party in Missouri" (Ph.D. diss., 1960), 255.
27. Columbia *Missouri Statesman*, May 18, 1849.
28. *Jefferson Enquirer*, May 26, 1849.

carried the day and he was able to shape the resolutions in accordance with his own thoughts.

As finally passed, the Chariton County resolutions declared that no state or group of states could constitutionally annul a law of Congress, that the Supreme Court should rule on all congressional laws, and that the county was opposed to all armed opposition against the Union except in defense of the Constitution. The final resolution expressed "faith and abiding confidence" in Benton. Price and two others then sent a letter to Benton reiterating the declaration of faith in the Senator and inviting him to speak in their county.[29]

While Price's influence managed to carry the day at Keytesville, the county became more and more inflamed over the slavery issue, the Wilmot Proviso, and Benton. This was reflected by the course of relations between Price and his business partner, Lisbon Applegate. Immediately following the Keytesville meeting Applegate wrote Marmaduke, an adamant supporter of Benton, that Price was "on our side." He continued by expressing his fear that the affairs of Benton would ruin the Democratic party.[30] These were ironic words for less than three weeks later Applegate penned a violent letter to Marmaduke expressing contempt for Benton and the Wilmot Proviso and declaring his violent opposition to "Benton & the whole troop of northern fanitics [*sic*], his new allies." Further, he expressed his belief in the principles of the Jackson Resolutions, holding that even if they were wrong Benton was bound to obey them. His closing remarks indicated the strained relations with his partner resulting from the explosiveness of the slavery issue. Applegate declared that Benton, like Van Buren, was finished in Missouri and that "all prominent men who sustain him in his apostacy will destroy themselves forever."[31]

V

Through the blazing months of June, July, and August Benton carried his heroic appeal to the people of Missouri. His powerful speeches and manifestoes set off a violent newspaper war and counties continued to hold meetings to declare either their allegiance to or their hatred of the Senator. Jackson and others toured the state after Benton carrying their counterappeal to the voters of the state.

Price and his Boonslick associates found themselves caught in the midst of this turmoil. Indicative of the disruption of the state Democracy caused by the slavery issue, the Boonslick group, once the

29. *The* Liberty (Mo.) *Weekly Tribune,* June 22, 1849; *Jefferson Enquirer,* June 16, 1849.
30. Applegate to M. M. Marmaduke, May 30, 1849, Sappington Papers.
31. Applegate to M. M. Marmaduke, June 18, 1849, Sappington Papers.

staunchest supporters of Benton, were now deeply divided among themselves. After Benton's initial speech in St. Louis, Lowry, inferring from the speech that Benton favored the Wilmot Proviso, regretfully stated that "I mourn over him as one of the Democracy's great champions, & a great mind in perfect error." It was with "heart felt" emotions that he abandoned his support of Benton and felt it would cause his "heart to bleed" to see Benton's old friends publicly proscribe him, but that was what must be done.[32] After the Jefferson City speech Lowry became increasingly rabid in his denunciations of the Senator. He viewed the Jefferson City speech as a "text book containing the Pandora's-box of deadly poison, to his old states-rights friends, his Democratic principles, & the integrity of the Union of States!"[33]

George Penn, even after the Jefferson City speech, hoped that Benton would base his objections to the Jackson Resolutions on a personal basis rather than a political one. If this were the case "his friends might still consistently rally in his support." In this Penn reflected the desires of many of the Boonslick group who could not bring themselves to attack their old ally, but neither could they "follow [any] man whatever may be his principles, who is leading [us] from [our] principles." Penn declared that he "had at all times every desire to sustain Col. Benton—not only for his valuable services which he has rendered in the support of true democratic measures & principles but likewise for the valuable services that he can still tender of which the party in Missouri as well as the nation may & likely will greatly need."[34] Penn solved his dilemma by dropping out of active politics.

Price, undergoing the same torment as Penn, remained at Val Verde following his intervention in Benton's behalf at the political rally at Keytesville. He was more and more disturbed by the violent opposition in his neighborhood that was building up against his old friend and mentor. Nonetheless, ever hesitant to express or to commit his views to paper, Price attempted to remain neutral during the summer of 1849. Hoping to be able to follow his characteristic policy of studied silence, which most of his contemporaries believed to be the secret of his political success,[35] Price remained inactive. However, with numerous people invoking his name on both sides of the quarrel, he felt it necessary to put his political views before the people and at the same time to throw his prestige to Benton. This required no little fortitude since Chariton was rabidly opposed to Benton. Thus in abandoning his characteristic silence Price exhibited another of his salient attributes—courage.

Price, in a public letter to the editor of *The Weekly Brunswicker*, outlined his position regarding Benton and the divisive issues of the day.[36] He announced his emphatic opposition to the Wilmot Proviso and to any interference by Congress with slavery in the territories. Continuing, he declared it the right and the duty of a state legislature, responsible to the people, to elect and to instruct a senator. He further declared that had he been in the legislature at the time of the Jackson Resolutions he would have voted for them, however, "not supposing for a moment that a State in the Union would have gone so far as even to threaten nullification or disunion, to both or either of which, (the one is the other) I am opposed." Price continued that it was "the duty of every true patriot in the country, whenever nullification or disunion is agitated, to do all that is in his power to arouse the people and put down that agitation." In Price's mind this was exactly what Benton was then doing and, believing Benton when he claimed that he had not yet said half of what he intended, Price declared: "If I find, when he has said all he wishes to say, that I cannot support him, without abandoning my principles, then I will be 'against Col. Benton' and not until then."

As might have been expected of a republican, Price declared his anxiety regarding Benton's appeal since a legislature's right to instruct a senator was a cardinal tenet of republicanism. He admitted that it "would have been more in accordance with my views of propriety and Democratic usage, for Col. Benton to have resigned his seat in the U.S. Senate, before taking the appeal." However, Price felt that had Benton done this the people of the state would have demanded his re-election. Here Price, whose mind tended to literalness, performed some intellectual gymnastics in order to maintain his ideological consistency by reasoning there to be little difference in resigning and asking to be sustained and not resigning, appealing, and promising to resign if not sustained. With this, Price, the doctrinaire, managed to sustain his loyalty to Benton and to keep his republican principles.

Superficially Price's letter appeared an amalgam, while in reality it represented a position intellectually consistent with the deeper motivating forces of his character. Two counterveiling forces, nationalism and an adherence to the slave system, both existing within the framework of republicanism, guided Price's actions. When he left politics in 1846 to fight in the Mexican War the controlling

36. Price to the Editor of *The* Brunswick (Mo.) *Weekly Brunswicker*, July 22, 1849, reprinted in the *Jefferson Enquirer*, August 4, 1849.

political issues in Missouri and the nation stemmed from the old hard-soft conflict. Price, like Benton and others, never completely abandoned the old issues and could not believe that they were dead. He still viewed politics as a struggle between Republicans and Federalists with its accompanying issues of hard money, banks, and corporations. Therefore, in 1849 he was not willing to lose Benton, who epitomized republican principles and championed Democratic orthodoxy. The belief that this orthodoxy was more in danger than slavery allowed Price's nationalism to gain ascendancy over his devotion to the slave system and, combined with his republicanism, caused him to stand with Benton in the face of strong criticism.

Price also felt a deep personal loyalty to Benton, who had greatly aided him in the past; at the same time he may have been convinced that Benton would win the struggle and that his support at this crucial point would place him in a fine position to further his own political career. Price attended a rally for Benton at Glasgow and there promised to help him in any way possible. With Benton attempting to discredit Jackson's authorship of the resolutions by connecting them to Calhoun through Napton, Price soon had an opportunity to fulfill this promise. Jackson, evidently hoping to gain stature in the anti-Benton movement, repeatedly declared that he was the author of the resolutions he had presented to the legislature. When the question of authorship was put to Napton he denied that he composed them and said the same in a letter to Price. Upon receipt of the letter Price wrote to Benton and informed him of his meeting with Napton the previous winter and that he believed that the resolutions shown him by Napton at that time were the same ones Jackson presented to the assembly.[37]

Benton reached the apogee of his appeal at a great confrontation between the warring factions at Fayette on September 1. Hoping to associate the Jackson Resolutions with Calhoun and thus to nullification, Benton shouted that the resolutions had "a nullification origin—copied from Calhoun, started in a nullification harangue, drawn up by a nullification judge and smuggled into the house under a false paternity. Napton, of the supreme court, drew them—an old nullification correspondent of Calhoun's. . . ." To drive home this point Benton produced and read Price's letter implicating Napton.[38]

After his Fayette speech Benton traveled for six weeks throughout the southwestern part of the state elaborating on his Fayette theme. During this time Benton papers, exploiting Price's prestige within the state, expounded on his letter to Benton. As a result Price, in Benton's

37. Price to Benton, August 8, 1849, printed in the *Jefferson Enquirer*, October 6, 1849.
38. *Jefferson Enquirer*, October 6, 1849.

words, endured "enough cursing to damn a saint."[39] Many of his old Boonslick intimates turned on him with vicious invective. Jackson issued a public letter concerning Price's role, denying that Price had previously seen the resolutions he had presented. He included Price's own resolution of 1841 to show a similarity to his own, pointing out that Price had stated that Missouri would make "common cause" with other slave states, virtually the same point as his resolutions that Missouri would "co-operate" with other slave states.[40] Jackson's intimation of hypocrisy on Price's part was ill-disguised. Price found himself in an ambiguous position as a Benton man espousing anti-Benton principles. Many Benton people distrusted him, while his old intimates, now leading the anti-Benton forces, were perfectly aware of his devotion to the slave system but irritated by his tactics.

VI

In early October both Price and Benton gained a slight respite from the bitter political campaign by attending the National Railroad Convention in St. Louis.[41] Disputes there, though exhibiting overtones of the factional struggle within the state, revolved primarily around the various routes for a transcontinental railroad and resulted in a bitter feud between the supporters of Benton and the Illinois senator, Stephen A. Douglas. When the final votes were taken on several proposed resolutions Douglas' plan gained approval, but no concrete plans had been made for a transcontinental railway. The convention did, however, provide an impetus to the supporters of the Pacific Railroad Company in Missouri, stirring up interest in the state that was to swell to tremendous proportions throughout the 1850's.

The reprieve gained during the railroad convention ended with the adjournment of that gathering. Benton resumed his appeal, not leaving the state until early in November, but his departure did not still the political turmoil. Preparations were already underway throughout the state for the coming state elections and, since Benton would be up for re-election, they were considered crucial by both factions.

The campaign became bitter. David R. Atchison set the tone for the anti-Benton forces when he pledged his services "to this cause soul, and body, with an eye single to the overthrow of the old apostate & Traitor."[42] Benton's forces, just as adamant, took their cue from

39. Benton's speech at Jackson, Missouri, May 25, 1852, *Glasgow* (Mo.) *Weekly Times*, May 27, 1852.
40. *Glasgow Weekly Times*, September 27, 1849.
41. Minutes of this convention published in the *Daily Missouri Republican*, October 16–19, 1849; see also R. S. Cotterill, "The National Railroad Convention in St. Louis, 1849," *Missouri Historical Review*, 12:4 (July, 1915), 203–15.
42. Atchison to J. H. Birch, printed in *Jefferson Enquirer*, April 26, 1851.

Old Bullion's "Scamp Letter." Upon learning of a rumor that there might be some compromise between the forces, Benton declared that he "would sooner sit in council with the six thousand dead who died of cholera in St. Louis, than go into convention with such a gang of scamps. . . ."[43]

As the two factions prepared for the coming campaign they searched for prominent figures to enlist as candidates; inevitably both sides entered Price's name in the canvass. Within a week of one another the editors of the *Jefferson Enquirer* and *The Metropolitan*, the leading Benton and anti-Benton papers respectively, presented Price as a candidate for office representing their faction. The *Enquirer* felt that Price would be the Benton candidate opposing James S. Green for Congress in the Third District.[44] *The Metropolitan* editor, commenting on an editorial in the *Daily Missouri Republican* predicting that Price would be forced to run as a Benton candidate against Green, felt certain that Price would be the anti-Benton candidate representing Chariton County in the state assembly. He anticipated having Price as Speaker to lead the anti-Benton forces in the coming assembly.[45] Once again Price found himself compelled to issue a public pronouncement clarifying his position.

On February 5, 1850, he addressed a letter to the editor of the *Jefferson Enquirer* expressing his gratitude at being considered by so many people for public office.[46] Then, in an effort to unify the party, he dwelt on "those great principles which have ever characterized the Democratic party" and expressed satisfaction, stemming from his years of political experience, "that they are the only true and enlightened principles of governmental policy." Price withheld his name from the canvass "on account of the urgency of my private business, which, in consequence of my prolonged absence from the country, now requires my immediate personal attention." Ever a party man and still obsessed with the party struggles of an earlier day, Price called for every "true Democrat" to rally around the old party policies. In a rhetorical plea he declared that "since we have so successfully battled, as a party, against the formidable array which our political opponents have brought against us from time to time, may we still not entertain the assurance, that with a like action on our part, the combined influence of our common enemy shall not be able to withstand our forces."

Following this call for party unity Price entered a passionate defense of Benton. Reaffirming his faith in the Senator, Price declared

43. *Jefferson Enquirer*, April 6, 1850.
44. *Ibid.*, January 19, 1850.
45. *The Metropolitan*, January 15, 1850.
46. Price to the Editor of the *Jefferson Enquirer*, February 5, 1850, printed in the *Missouri Statesman*, February 22, 1850.

that his confidence in Benton's "honor and integrity and patriotism, remains unshaken." He further expressed the belief that "whenever the vital and absorbing questions of domestic policy, which are now threatening the perpetuity of our government, shall be brought up in our national councils," Benton would be found as always "nobly defending those very doctrines which have cemented our political fabric." Extolling Benton's virtues even further, Price affirmed that "blindness which is the result of the heated enthusiast, or the timid and vacillating statesman, forms no part of his composition." Instead, "with a manliness betokening his dignity, and a penetration which sees quite through the deeds of men, he avows his faith; while with a purpose emanating from the same pure source, and an ability almost unequalled he sustains and defends them."

Again, in this second political testament, Price revealed himself as an orthodox Jacksonian Democrat, fearing that in the turmoil of the slavery issue old Democratic principles would be lost. Price still perceived the danger to Democratic orthodoxy as pre-eminent and feared a division within the party that would throw the state to the Whigs. His nationalism thus remained dominant.

VII

Price's hopes for Democratic party unity were not realized. The state elections resulted in kaleidoscopic patterns of voting in the various counties. In some counties anti-Benton forces joined with Whigs, in others Benton people joined with Whigs. Yet in other counties both Benton and anti-Benton people were sent to the assembly. The lack of unity became glaringly apparent when the assembly met and began balloting for senator. With a divided Boonslick group there was no cohesive force in the assembly and Benton, without his old stalwart supporters, had little chance for victory. Most of those Boonslick men still active in politics had joined the anti-Benton forces. Thus, Old Bullion, who had so long been kept in power by these very men, could now face only defeat. Those issues of orthodox Jacksonianism that had cemented the alliance between Benton and the Boonslick men were now thrust aside by the slavery issue.

Balloting for senator began on January 10, 1851, and continued over eleven days, through forty ballots and constant searching for votes on the part of the involved factions.[47] While the Whigs stood firmly behind their candidate, Henry Geyer, the Benton and anti-Benton leaders attempted unsuccessfully to reach an agreement among themselves. Finally the anti-Benton forces, seeing that they could not elect a man of their choice, threw their support to Geyer,

47. *House Journal*, 16th Assembly, 88–147.

who had earlier given them assurance that he was in agreement with them on the issue of slavery in the territories. Even prior to the election, Carty Wells, a leader in the anti-Benton faction, had confided to a Whig friend that Geyer "was as sound on the slavery subject as he desired."[48] The anti-Benton forces had further extracted an agreement from the Whigs that gave all the positions to be elected by the assembly to anti-Benton men. Thus, in their frenzy to defeat Benton, the anti-Benton leaders were willing to elect a Whig, albeit one who adhered to their position regarding slavery.

Whig leaders soon realized they had been duped. James S. Rollins, reflecting their chagrin, declared that his party was "in a h–ll of a fix."[49] Another Whig leader mourned that his party gained only a Senate seat and nothing else at the expense of "reinstat[ing] a party on the verge of ruin and elec[ting] a Senator who first repudiated us."[50] It would not be long before many Whigs, regretting their shotgun marriage of political expediency, came to a vague realization of the affinity of interests existing between their party and the Benton faction.

VIII

Price, the loyal party man, could not help but be disturbed by Benton's defeat and by the subsequent party disintegration. Following the senatorial election, affairs in both the Whig and Democratic parties remained disrupted by the slavery issue. The Whigs retained a semblance of unity by avoiding the issue and thus would not risk disruption by helping the Bentonites in their unsuccessful attempt to repeal the Jackson Resolutions. The Democrats could not boast even of a shadow of party cohesion, for shortly after Benton's defeat both factions formed separate state central committees and began to organize down to the county level. Thus shattered, Democrats could only look forward to the state convention in 1852, where they would nominate state officers, to restore unity and harmony to the party.

A forecast of the difficulty that would be encountered in the convention was evident when the various county conventions met early in 1852 to elect delegates to the state meeting. Chariton County did not escape this dilemma. The county held its meeting in Keytesville on March 15, 1852, and Price offered a resolution calling for the president of the meeting, a friend of his, to appoint five delegates to the state convention. Benjamin Stringfellow immediately raised the ques-

48. S. T. Glover to Abiel Leonard, September 27, 1850, Leonard Collection.
49. Rollins to Abiel Leonard, February 5, 1851, Leonard Collection.
50. S. T. Glover to Abiel Leonard, January 24, 1851, Leonard Collection.

tion of representation between the two factions. He felt that since the object of the convention was to settle the matters dividing the party it could only be done by fair representation of the two factions. Declaring that the county's congressional vote in 1850 resulted in twice as many anti-Benton votes as Benton ones, Stringfellow called for the delegation to reflect this same ratio. Price immediately protested, denying that there had been an anti-Benton majority in the county in 1850. He objected even more strenuously to any mention of the dispute at all, but did amend his resolution to call for six members, with three drawn from each faction; Stringfellow successfully amended this to call for four anti-Bentonites and two Bentonites. Price gained appointment as a Benton delegate.[51]

The long-awaited convention met in Jefferson City on April 5 and began harmoniously by choosing a Bentonite as president pro tempore.[52] However, when a motion was made for a committee of ten, five drawn from each faction, to report a series of resolutions, a vicious debate followed over who should be appointed to this important committee. Lowry demanded a roll call to see who held qualified credentials before the group was appointed. Benton leaders desired a committee consisting of one man from each electoral district to examine credentials. Soon after this the problem of permanent officers arose to further complicate the dispute. The chairman then declared the motion to appoint a committee of ten out of order. By this time the convention was rapidly approaching a flareup. Recognizing this, several of the older party leaders successfully called for an adjournment.

The following day cooler heads prevailed and the convention decided that a committee of ten, five from each faction, would choose the permanent officers. This resulted in a Bentonite as president, two anti-Bentonites as vice presidents, and two secretaries, one drawn from each faction. A motion by C. F. Jackson to have the president appoint two committees, equally staffed by the two factions, to examine credentials and representation and the mode of voting passed without dissension. Then, also without serious strife, the assemblage chose a committee to report the resolutions expressing the sense of the meeting. Both Jackson and Price were appointed to this crucial committee.

Soon after the appointment of the resolutions committee the convention became the scene of another quarrel. This resulted from a dispute over the badly-split St. Louis delegation's voting power. The

51. Account of this meeting in *Glasgow Weekly Times*, March 25, 1852.
52. Account of the Democratic convention (which voted to keep minutes out of the papers) drawn from reports in *Missouri Statesman*, April 9, 1852; *Glasgow Weekly Times*, April 15, 1852; *Daily Missouri Republican*, April 6–8, 1852.

convention finally decided that the Bentonites would cast two-thirds of the votes to one-third for the anti-Bentonites. Another heated discussion, which never reached a settlement, then arose over voting by proxy. Soon the violent nature of the meeting brought about even another outbreak, this time over the question of whether to nominate candidates for the state office before or after hearing the resolutions. The convention finally decided to hear the resolutions prior to making its nomination.

The resolutions, largely the work of a now reconciled Price and Jackson, pledged Missouri Democrats to the principles of the Baltimore convention, to adhere to the Virginia and Kentucky Resolutions, to abide by the Compromise of 1850, to regard the right of legislative instruction as a vital principle of republicanism, and finally, to express unfaltering devotion to the Union. They concluded with the pledge to "hold no political fellowship with the abolitionists of the North or the Nullifiers of the South."

Lowry, not a member of the resolutions committee, felt that the resolutions conceded too much to the Bentonites and he therefore offered two amendments to rectify this. The first called for the August elections to be conducted with particular attention to the slavery issue and to the equal rights of the states. The second opposed making the Compromise of 1850 a *sine qua non* of the creed of the Democracy. Following a heated discussion Lowry's amendments failed to gain acceptance. C. F. Jackson then offered a successful amendment that the convention would not accept anyone as a nominee who did not subscribe to the principles of the reported resolutions.

John Doxey, a Bentonite from Chariton, moved for the chairman to appoint a committee of fifteen to nominate candidates for the convention. A fight nearly followed this motion. The anti-Bentonites, certain that with a Bentonite as president that faction would have a majority of the committee, would not accept the motion. Seeing that physical violence might erupt, Doxey withdrew his motion and nominations were to come from the floor.

The first gubernatorial nomination, that of Thomas Price, came as no surprise since Benton himself had expressed his desire that he be nominated. The next nomination, coming from the anti-Bentonites, proved the cause of great surprise for many delegates: They nominated Sterling Price.

The first ballot saw Thomas Price hold a lead, but fall short of a majority; the second ballot ended with the same result. Then a violent quarrel broke out over the tallying of the votes. Frank Blair, Sterling's inveterate enemy, claimed that the votes of Pulaski County had not been counted correctly, thus denying Thomas Price the majority he needed. Thomas Shields, an anti-Bentonite, pointed out that Pulaski had been created since 1848, which had been accepted as the election year to be used in deciding the number of votes to be assigned to each county, and its votes should therefore be subtracted from those of the county from which it had been created. When the argument became heated Shields declared that if Blair's position was upheld the anti-Bentonites would walk out. With this Shields' supporters began to cheer and the Bentonites to hiss; Shields, standing near a Bentonite, shouted: "You hiss me, do you! Hiss and be damned, you damned son of a bitch!" The Bentonite replied that he had every intention to continue to hiss. The convention avoided outright violence only by adjourning.

When the meeting took up later in the day both sides had cooled down and desired to work toward compromise. Blair stated that Shields had been correct and Shields apologized to the convention, whereupon Blair declared he would substitute the name of Meredith M. Marmaduke for Thomas Price if Sterling Price's name was also withdrawn. Sterling's supporters, who had gathered more support during the recess, would not bargain and he gained the gubernatorial nomination on the next ballot.

Sterling Price's nomination reflected two aspects of the convention: first, the desire of the majority to compromise and thus smooth the party's quarrels and second, the shrewdness of the anti-Bentonites. Observing the explosive nature of the convention, they realized that only a candidate who could draw votes from both factions could have any hope of being nominated. Price, in the anomolous position of being a Benton man espousing anti-Benton principles, seemed to be the logical choice. Added to his availability was the charisma that was beginning to be attached to his name in Missouri. He could be presented to the people as the man above factions, as the only man suited to unite the warring factions.

While serving with Price on the resolutions committee Jackson, always aware of Price's ardent support of the institution of slavery, became convinced that Price would not deviate from his convictions. Thus Jackson, Stringfellow, and other old members of the Boonslick group began to circulate among the convention delegates creating support for Price, although Price remained as noncommital as necessary.

Price's nomination was secured, although many delegates remained reserved toward him. This doubt became evident when he was escorted to the speaker's stand to accept the nomination. After thanking the convention for its trust, Price pledged himself to unite the state party on the platform that had been adopted. Upon hearing this Lowry shouted out: "General, you say you will attempt to unite the Democracy on our platform. Are you on it yourself?" This remark, drawing a good deal of laughter, reflected doubts about Price that plagued many Missourians. He appeared to be attempting to have the best of two worlds by declaring his loyalty to Benton while adhering to what were definitely anti-Benton principles; to many people he appeared vacillating.

These same doubts were immediately expressed by party newspapers throughout the state. While most editors analyzed the nomination for state officers as consisting of four Bentonites and three anti-Bentonites, one Whig interpreted the results as three Bentonites, three anti-Bentonites, "*and* Sterling Price."[53] The *Daily Missouri Republican* viewed Price as a doubtful politician on the divisive issues of the Democratic party and declared that for some time Price had "been steering between the two factions." The editor continued by forecasting trouble from Benton since his favorite, Thomas Price, had been defeated.[54] The Whig *Missouri Statesman* declared that Price existed in a "state of betweenity, neither fish nor fowl";[55] the *Enquirer*, reflecting the feelings of the majority of Missouri Democrats, felt that the Democracy had been unified by nominating Price, who was best qualified to bridge the gap between the two factions.[56] The extremists in both factions were disappointed and grumbled a good bit, but the bulk of Democrats remained satisfied that the convention and its nomination of Price had saved the unity of the party. Only time would tell whether the *Enquirer's* editor was correct. Many Democrats feared the worst and there was no doubt that Price was to lead the Missouri Democracy during trying times.

53. *Glasgow Weekly Times*, April 15, 1852.
54. *Daily Missouri Republican*, April 8, 1852.
55. *Missouri Statesman*, reprinted in *The Weekly Tribune*, July 23, 1852.
56. *Jefferson Enquirer*, April 17, 1852.

· 7 ·

An Old Republican in the Governor's Mansion

Price's nomination and subsequent election thrust him into the vortex of the storm beginning to convulse the state and nation. Vague and shifting party allegiances resulted from the forces affecting the country in this time of uncertainty, and the tension of being at once a nationalist and a slaveholder increased, but would not reach its apogee during Price's term as governor. Once the Democrats held their convention and it became apparent to the Whigs that there was to be a united Democratic ticket, the Whig gubernatorial nomination lost all its attractiveness. After some discussion the Whigs nominated Alexander Doniphan, who spurned the offer. Finally the party turned to James Winston, its original choice for lieutenant governor.

The Whig platform favored extensive internal improvements by the state and national governments, upward revision of the tariff, and the Compromise of 1850 as the final settlement of the slavery controversy. The Whig campaign, however, consisted mainly of efforts to shatter the fragile Democratic union, which many considered a "flagitious amalgamation."[1] Winston viewed Democrats as "a damned set of knaves after having such a quarrel to unite, without saying anything, or settling anything in relation to the questions which they said were of such paramount importance."[2]

Agitation of the divisive issues of the Democracy did not remain solely a Whig prerogative since Thomas Hart Benton, running for Congress in the First District, set out on a much less strenuous, if not less vitriolic, replica of his great appeal. Prior to his nomination Benton made it clear that union between the warring Democratic factions could take place only through the complete surrender of his opponents. He demanded a complete repudiation of the Jackson Resolutions and of Democratic votes for Henry Geyer, the acceptance of the right of instruction of the people, not according to any legislative sovereignty, and the repudiation of the "new dogma . . . that Congress has no right to legislate upon slavery in the Territories."[3] Once nomi-

1. James Winston to Abiel Leonard, May 18, 1853, Abiel Leonard Papers.
2. *Ibid.*
3. St. Louis *Daily Missouri Republican*, December 15, 1851.

nated, Benton pressed these issues on his tour of the district and set the tone for his supporters throughout the state.

Members of the Benton faction anxiously awaited Old Bullion's opinion of the state Democratic slate of candidates. This was not long in coming, for on May 15, 1852, Benton delivered a speech at Jackson, Missouri, attacking the "union and harmony" convention held at Jefferson City. Benton opposed any unification if it meant loss or compromise of his four principles; dealing explicitly with the gubernatorial nomination, he declared it representative of the fraud practiced by his enemies. He felt that it had been agreed that a Benton man was to receive the gubernatorial nomination and thus, in his mind, Thomas Price's defeat represented "a breach of faith—it was a fraud at the start—was, also, an outrage to the people in trampling their will and their instructions under foot." With regard to Sterling Price, Benton declared that he would "say nothing about the gentleman nominated over him [Thomas Price]—whether as good a friend of Benton, or not" and ended his discussion by repudiating the convention as fraudulent.[4]

The Jackson speech left no one in doubt as to Benton's opinion toward a union with the anti-Benton forces, but his view of the slate of candidates remained obscure. In a revised version of the Jackson speech printed in the newspaper Benton included the then famous Price letter regarding the authorship of the Jackson Resolutions, commenting that Price wrote it to him in the "hottest of the fight," thus providing him with "material aid" in his appeal. He noted that as a result of this aid Price had endured great abuse.[5] Benton's tone seemed sympathetic to Price, but he remained enigmatic.

In a speech at Boonville a month later Benton delivered another powerful address expressing his principles, with special emphasis upon the removal of the Jackson Resolutions, which Benton forces were making the central issue in their campaigns. Once again Benton castigated the Jefferson City convention, but this time qualified his feelings toward the candidates; he now felt that there were several good men on the slate who ought to be elected. Benton maintained that Price had become reconciled to his principles and that he would vote for him for governor.[6]

Benton's statement doubtless gave a great deal of relief to Price— ensuring him of a united Democratic party behind him—but the Whig press would not let it go at that. Many reprinted Price's letter to the editor of *The Weekly Brunswicker*, in which he had explicitly endorsed the Jackson Resolutions, and pointed out that those who had previously cursed Price were now supporting him at the same time

4. *Ibid.*, May 16, 18, 20, 1852.
5. *Glasgow* (Mo.) *Weekly Times*, May 27, 1852.
6. *Ibid.*, June 17, 1852.

Benton was claiming that Price was reconciled to his views. Knowing Price to be in a difficult position, most Whig editors eagerly awaited expression of his views.

The Whigs, realizing Price's predicament, seemed to be following the advice of James Rollins, an emerging party leader, who declared that slavery was "*the* question about which the Democracy have been so much disturbed, and we ought to touch it just far enough to get the state for the Whigs, and no further. . . ."[7] With their own nominee canvassing the state on the various issues of the party platform, Whig editors called for Price to begin his canvass. One newspaperman, desiring Price to speak frankly on the issues and thereby certainly divide the Democracy once again, prodded the Democrats to "Call him out—Call him out."[8] By the first of July a Whig editor posed "A New Question." For him the question was no longer "Who is Pierce?" but "Where is Price?" and he commented that Price much preferred "hunting in the shades of Val Verde" to informing the people of the state about his views on divisive issues.[9] Disregarding Benton's testimony that Price had become reconciled to his principles, Whigs queried: "How is he *now* on the Jackson Resolutions?"[10] After waiting with no results an editor finally asked: "Is Price dead?"[11]

Whig editors and others were to wait in vain: Price did not leave his home, made no speeches, and issued no public letters defining his position. In so doing Price exhibited two of his salient characteristics: those of a gentleman and a shrewd politician. Soon after Price's nomination his wife Martha fell seriously ill with cholera and lingered near death; his son Edwin also contracted the dread disease and Sterling would not leave his family during this time of illness. Rather than make public his family's distress by explaining why he did not leave his farm, Price remained silent and endured the barbs slung at him from all sides. A man less sensitive toward status and honor might have exploited the situation in order to gain the public's sympathy by presenting himself as too distraught even to present his political views in a public letter.

Finally, an acquaintance of the family informed James Lusk, editor of the *Jefferson Enquirer*, of the situation. Lusk immediately expressed his sympathy and informed the state why Price could not leave his home.[12] Upon learning this *The Weekly Brunswicker* announced that due to the "extreme illness of Gen. Sterling Price's lady"

7. Rollins to Abiel Leonard, May 30, 1852, Leonard Papers.
8. *St. Louis Evening News*, reprinted in *Glasgow Weekly Times*, June 24, 1852.
9. *Ibid.*, July 1, 1852.
10. *Ibid.*
11. *Ibid.*, July 15, 1852.
12. Jefferson City (Mo.) *Jefferson Enquirer*, July 24, 1852.

he would not be able to visit "those positions of the State he intended to canvass prior to the election."[13] The Whig editor of the *Glasgow Weekly Times* expressed his sympathy but raised a thorny question when he asked why Price had not spoken out prior to his wife's illness nor written any public letters defining his position since she fell ill. He concluded that Price never intended to do either.[14] Although unknown to him, the editor's partisan accusation was correct.

Price faced a vexatious situation: If he expressed himself on the divisive issues torturing the Democracy he would alienate a faction of the party and very likely lose the election to Winston. Therefore, using his prior political success as a guidepost, he applied his personal political maxim of silence and remained passive. Only through silence could he hope to gain election and maintain a united party, both of which were highly important to him. Although he desired political advancement, Price felt that the Democracy constituted the only institution that could weather the storms of time, maintain the Union, and protect slavery. These were his cardinal desires.

While Price's strategy carried the statewide slate to success by the usual Democratic majority, contests for the congressional and state assembly seats saw the bitter factional struggle intensified.[15] Soon after his election Price could see a portent of what he would face as Missouri's chief executive. On June 10, 1852, Congress granted a liberal portion of the public lands within Missouri to the state to be used to finance railroad construction. To dispose of this land, Governor Austin A. King called the newly-elected legislature into special session late in August. Once the session opened, it became apparent that the Democracy remained divided. The contest for Speaker of the House prompted a violent struggle, for neither faction wanted the other to gain an advantage. After forty-eight ballots, the assembly retained the Speaker Pro Tem as Acting Speaker.[16] When the railroad bills came up for discussion, the old divisions on internal improvements between Whig and Democrat disappeared, being replaced by a shifting kaleidoscope of factional alignments. Finally the legislature did pass bills apportioning land to the Hannibal and St. Joseph Railroad and the Pacific road and its branches.

This session gave indications of the problems that were to plague Price: slavery and railroads—issues that would disrupt the old party lines. Cohesive elements on divisive questions were replaced by shift-

13. *The* Brunswick (Mo.) *Weekly Brunswicker*, reprinted in *Glasgow Weekly Times*, July 22, 1852.
14. *Ibid.*
15. These elections saw the anti-Benton forces double their numbers in the Missouri Assembly at the expense of the Whigs and the Bentonites.
16. *Journal of the House of Representatives of the State of Missouri*, 17th Assembly, extra sess., 6–47.

ing factions responding to varying and multiple motivations. A trying time lay ahead for the new executive, who, like other orthodox Democrats, was perplexed by the new social and political milieu of the 1850's.

II

Price arrived in Jefferson City on December 14, 1852, to confer with old political intimates and his advisers for a week prior to the opening of the legislative session. Any hopes of avoiding an intraparty struggle, however, disappeared almost immediately in a battle over election of a Speaker. Voting lasted through eighteen ballots, with a definite coalition between Whigs and Benton Democrats electing the Speaker.[17] Although this alliance became more pronounced as the session wore on, it would not reach full proportions until the next session of the legislature.

On January 3, 1853, Price presented his inaugural address to the combined session of the assembly.[18] It was a short speech, but full of meaning for those who knew Price well; for those who did not, and thereby lacked an awareness of his extreme literalness of mind and action, the address seemed as innocuous as most inaugurals. Its salient points dealt with the two problems convulsing Missouri and the nation: slavery and railroads. With regard to slavery, Price declared he would stand on the platform of the Jefferson City convention that had nominated him. Few understood what an understatement it was when he declared that "I shall maintain my position on it [the Jefferson City platform], and carry out its principles in good faith." He did go a bit further by expressing his satisfaction with the Compromise of 1850 and especially with the Fugitive Slave Act, which in his mind deserved the people's "respect to a preeminent degree." Price felt that an adherence to the compromise would eliminate agitation over slavery and thus preserve the harmony of the Union at the same time that it protected slavery.

Regarding railroads Price expressed his own interest and anxiety "for the proper development of the resources of the State," and his desire to co-operate cordially in "perfecting such projects as may be of undoubted public benefit." He followed this statement with an important qualification when he declared: "But it will be highly necessary to use great caution and discretion in keeping within proper bounds in the organization of a railroad system." He then warned that the state should be guided by the experiences of other states where "indiscriminent" and "reckless" policies had been followed. Such action could only lead to distrust and finally to "open and violent opposition" to all schemes of internal improvements.

17. *House Journal*, 17th Assembly, 2d sess., 190–203.
18. *Ibid.*, 240–42.

In this succinct address Price laid down guidelines from which he would not deviate during his four years in office. With the extreme literalness of mind and adherence to form that seemed to characterize doctrinaire old republicans, Price set out to pilot Missouri by his own republican chart.

After Price's address the assembly began deliberations on various issues, outstanding among which were railroad bills, but election of bank officers intruded. With these elections it was immediately apparent that the Whig-Bentonite alliance had become more formalized. Many Whigs felt that in previous dealings with anti-Bentonites the latter had co-operated only to their own political advantage, thus most Whigs now "found the Benton men the most liberal."[19] Within this climate of growing accord the Whigs and Bentonites combined to elect Bernard Pratte over James Hughes, choice of the anti-Bentonites, as president of the state bank. This same coalition dominated, although not to the same extent, the filling of the remainder of the bank positions.[20]

Many Whig and Bentonite leaders felt that their newborn alliance would function just as well on railroad legislation and, more importantly, on the repeal of the Jackson Resolutions, thus leaving it "root pig or die" for the "Anties."[21] The coalition plans went according to expectations on the railroad bills with the passage of three bills to aid the Platte County, Lexington and Daviess County, and the Canton and Bloomfield railroad companies. However, much to their surprise and dismay, Price vetoed all three bills. His veto message, delivered to the Senate on January 22, 1853, was a classic example of republican doctrine. After pointing out disasters in other states that had resulted from projects being too far in advance of the needs of a community Price declared that he wished Missouri to keep abreast of her wants and needs, but rather than "to suffer ourselves to be precipitately tempted beyond them, we will place our prosperity upon a solid basis." In his opinion the state's financial backing had already been committed to the major trunk lines. Price thought that the state should therefore be apprehensive lest the value of bonds already issued should decline in their appeal to eastern moneyed men. Moreover, until the main trunk lines were completed, additional mileage would be of little value and, therefore, the state should not hazard its credit until the major projects were finished.

19. Robert Holmes to H. R. Gamble, February 29, 1853, Hamilton R. Gamble Papers.

20. *House Journal*, 17th Assembly, 2d sess., 320–80.

21. George Caleb Bingham to James S. Rollins, January 24, 1853, Rollins Collection, printed in "Letters of George Caleb Bingham to James S. Rollins," C. B. Rollins, ed., *Missouri Historical Review*, XXXII, 1–4; XXXIII, 1–4 (October, 1937–July, 1939).

Price closed his message with a comment on the veto power, which revealed his conception of the role of governor. In his view, the veto power was suspensive rather than absolute, "given to protect the rights of minorities and the safeguards of the constitution, and to check hasty or inconsiderate legislation."[22] Price thus viewed his role not as that of a dynamic innovator or leader, but as a passive guardian of the constitution. His was a negative view of government stemming from his conception, drawn from an earlier era, of government's role in society.

The Whig-Bentonite alliance made an effort to override Price's vetoes, but could not muster the necessary votes after the assembly heard his message. Prior to that effort, however, the issue of the Jackson Resolutions came to a head. Violent arguments raged through January, February, and early March as to whether the Jackson Resolutions should be rescinded. Finally a vote to table the motion to rescind carried 72–49; the anti-Benton forces had carried the measure only with the aid of Whig votes.[23] Tensions within their own party on the slavery issue caused some Whigs to feel they could not afford to have it come up again and so they favored tabling the measure.[24]

Later in the session a vote was taken on an issue that temporarily revived old Democratic-Whig division. This came on a bill to prevent illegal banking in the state. Here the division resembled the old Whig-Democrat splits of the 1830's and 1840's.[25] However, issues were changing and there would rarely be opportunities to revive old rallying cries of orthodox Democracy.

III

The assembly's adjournment in early March left Price in a comfortable position. He had weathered the legislative storm and triumphed on both the slave and railroad issues. Adding to his pleasure, his family arrived in the third week of March and soon were comfortably settled in the Governor's Mansion. Martha and Sterling disliked the manner in which Governor King had furnished the house and as soon as possible Sterling planned to go to St. Louis to buy new furniture. He and his family, fast becoming accustomed to the "gentle" life, intended to redecorate the Governor's Mansion in the luxurious, if somewhat ostentatious, style of Val Verde.[26]

Due to her aunt's delicate health, Sterling's favorite niece "Lizzie"

22. *Journal of the Senate of the State of Missouri*, 17th Assembly, 2d sess., 242–46.
23. *House Journal*, 17th Assembly, 2d sess., 520.
24. John Volmer Mering, *The Whig Party in Missouri*, 185, 194.
25. *House Journal*, 17th Assembly, 2d sess., 650.
26. Lizzie Price to Eliza Davis, April 12, 1853, Missouri History Papers.

accompanied the family to the capital. Since the move seemed to revive Martha's spirits, Lizzie made herself useful by helping care for young Quintus, then about eighteen months old. Sterling found pleasure in the mansion grounds which extended down to the Missouri River and provided ample space for his horses. Price was a superb horseman and immensely enjoyed his leisure moments when he could ride with friends. Occasionally, too, when time allowed, he took his children and their friends jug fishing on the river.

The Price family found social life in Jefferson City much to their liking, especially dinner parties with friends and political associates. Price revelled in his position, for it represented the status for which he had long hungered. Price's halcyon days were short-lived, however. As a result of his political views and an oversight on the part of the adjourned legislature, Price brought down upon himself a storm of criticism and a renewal of factional strife within the Democracy.

The assembly had failed to elect a public printer during its session. Assuming that a vacancy existed, Price proceeded to fill it. Rather than appoint James Lusk, long-time public printer and avid supporter of Benton, Price asked James Tredway, an old friend from Keytesville, to come to the capital to start a new paper; when Tredway arrived Price appointed him public printer. His reasons for doing so stemmed from his literal interpretation of the platform upon which he had gained election and from his personal view of the political situation. He felt that the Bentonites, by continually calling for the repeal of the Jackson Resolutions, were agitating the slavery issue contrary to policies espoused by the Jefferson City platform. Further, his own view on this point differed from that of the Benton faction since, in his mind, the only way to avoid tearing the Democracy apart was to maintain silence on the slavery issue. Feeling that this would best be done by Tredway, Price brought his old friend to Jefferson City to start the *Jefferson Examiner*. The fact that the *Examiner* took the place of the defunct *Metropolitan*, which had been violently anti-Benton, caused Bentonites to view it as that paper's successor.

The Benton faction interpreted Price's action as a deliberate attack on Benton and his followers. This led to a reappraisal of Price's previous appointments, which had caused no prior comment, and the Benton people now decided that these too were decidedly anti-Benton. In late March and early April a trickle, beginning with Lusk stating his admiration for Price as a man but deprecating his position as a politician, soon became a flood of abuse.[27] Lusk soon maintained that Price had made a deal with Claiborne Jackson to obtain the

27. *Jefferson Enquirer*, March 19, 1853.

gubernatorial nomination and was prepared to sell himself again in return for a seat in the United States Senate.[28] In April Lusk claimed that "a wolf in sheep's clothing" had been elected governor of the state.[29] "Chariton" wrote from Keytesville that it would be "a thousand times better to have a decent Whig than a rotten," and went on to say that Price's defection from the Benton ranks elicited only contempt in his district.[30] In a letter to the *Enquirer* an "Old School Democrat" asked: "Will any rational man longer doubt the position of Gov. Sterling Price; he has labored hard to deceive the Democracy of Missouri, by packing water on both shoulders." He felt that Price had tricked the Benton people by his choice of men for membership in his cabinet, as penitentiary officers, as curators of the state university, and by making Tredway state printer.[31]

The state supreme court resolved the Tredway dispute by ruling that the legislature must declare a vacancy in the job of state printer in order for one to exist; thus, Lusk regained his old position. This still did not quiet the discord resulting from the incident, and the *Enquirer* and the *Examiner*, exchanging such epithets as "soft" and "disorganizer," continued a newspaper war long after the court handed down its decision. The Benton faction, looking toward the 1854 state and congressional campaigns, was apprehensive lest their opponents run "pretended friends of Benton." Thomas Price declared that "We have more Sterling Prices *among us* than one. . . ."[32]

During this time the Bentonites and the Whigs moved toward a vague conceptualization of their affinity of interests as it became more and more apparent that a new dichotomy of political interests and thought was arising in Missouri. While many Whigs and Bentonites were beginning to feel that the central concern of government should be internal improvements, the anti-Bentonites single-mindedly felt that government's primary concern should be the protection of the institution of slavery.

IV

Early in November, 1853, Price received the journal of John Woolman and a report from the Society of Friends, which he felt attacked the institution of slavery.[33] His reply necessitated the conceptualiza-

28. *Ibid.*, March 26, 1853.
29. *Ibid.*, April 30, 1853.
30. *Ibid.*
31. *Ibid.*, May 14, 1853.
32. Price to M. M. Marmaduke, October 31, 1853, Sappington Papers.
33. John Woolman (1720–1772) was a leading Quaker critic of slavery whose journal became a prominent tract in the antislavery movement. The work was not a fiery polemic, but simply the journal of the life of a man who viewed slavery in personal terms rather than as an abstraction. Woolman felt a profound sense of guilt for the existence of slavery in America

tion of long-latent attitudes regarding abolitionism and the institution of slavery. In Price's opinion the report and the journal meant to discuss slavery in "an unfair and very partial manner." He stated that the slave states' constitutions protected that institution and that their citizens were those most capable of deciding the important questions growing out of the master-slave relationship. Price declared it "a fact now universally acknowledged by intelligent minds that great and incalculable injury has already resulted to the Slaves of North America, on account of the misguided zeal of those who have undertaken to embrace the whole universe in the sphere of their philanthropy."

Reflecting the slaveowner's dread of slave revolts, Price asserted that half a century had passed since "the seeds of fanaticism," plainly discernible in the report and in Woolman's journal, were sown in London and the first fruits gathered in Santo Domingo. Since that day the spirit of abolitionism had never slept. Price felt that many American citizens opposed the institution of slavery, but were not disposed to agitate the question. The few who did were "exceptions to the law abiding and dutiful citizens, and doubtless to their phrenzied [sic] zeal, may be justly attributed the presumptuous liberties which even *Foreigners* themselves, felt sometimes disposed to take." In closing Price wrote that he was returning the material and requesting that in the future all such efforts "be directed to the improvement and amelioration of the distresses and sufferings of the subjects of the British nation, and especially the inhabitants of the City of London, whence have arisen that false philanthropy, which has cursed the negroes of the West Indies, and which only tends to injure the conditions of the Slaves of this Union."[34]

Price's comments reflected his anxiety over agitation of the slavery issue and his belief that the Negro could not exist in freedom without degrading the rest of society. To Price, Negro freedom was anathema; it would destroy the society he held to be ideal, and with it the status for which he had so long hungered and felt he had at last attained.

V

From January through May, 1854, events in Missouri and Washington ran parallel. In both places the issues of slavery and railroads became intertwined to such an extent that each exerted a tremendous

---

and believed that other Americans should share this guilt. John Woolman, *The Journal of John Woolman.* For sophisticated analyses of Woolman's antislavery thought, see David B. Davis, *The Problem of Slavery in Western Culture,* 483–93, and Winthrop D. Jordan, *White Over Black: American Attitudes Toward the Negro, 1550–1812,* 272–75.

34. Price to Josiah Foster et al., November 22, 1853, printed in the *Jefferson Enquirer,* December 3, 1853.

effect upon the other. During this time the great debates raged over the Kansas-Nebraska Bill. Missourians watched this drama with heightened interest, since it would play a large role in their next assembly where they would elect a senator.

President Franklin Pierce had barely signed the Kansas-Nebraska Bill before rumors began circulating in Missouri concerning the organization of a huge five-million-dollar emigrant aid society in New England to ship abolitionists into Kansas. Many Missourians became firmly convinced that Kansas would be overrun by hordes of abolitionists who would deny them their "natural right" to occupy the territory adjacent to them and would represent a danger to slavery within Missouri itself. Some Missourians moved into Kansas, while others began to steel themselves for a mighty battle. It was in the heat of this situation that the canvass began for the state elections in August.

Railroads and slavery were again of top concern to Missourians. Whigs and Bentonites hoped to focus the elections on the railroad question rather than on slavery. Many Whigs felt that if "niggerism would be thrust aside" they could triumph as the foremost advocates of internal improvements, which they considered to be the true interests of the state.[35] In their opinion the Democrats were using the slavery issue as a smokescreen to remain in power. George R. Smith, a prominent Whig from Pettis County and a leading figure in the struggle for state railroads, reflected his party's interest in transportation when he called for the various counties to choose "railroad" candidates for the coming election. He prompted them to "Catechize your candidates upon this subject, and if both are not for it, and also for legislative aid, run those who will go for it." His concern was such that he declared: "We want the best men, and it matters not whether they are Whigs or Democrats, so long as they are right upon this subject."[36]

During the canvass anti-Bentonites remained dogmatically conscious of the slavery question. C. F. Jackson, exemplifying this single-mindedness, declared to David R. Atchison that if slaves could not be taken to the territories such land might as well be left in possession of the Indians: "They are better neighbors than the abolitionists, *by a damn sight.* If this is to become 'free nigger' territory, Missouri must become so too, for we can hardly keep our negroes here now." Jackson closed his letter with the comment that a certain candidate was "right on the main question."[37]

---

35. Samuel T. Glover to James S. Rollins, "n.d.," Rollins Collection, quoted in Mering, *The Whig Party in Missouri*, 192.

36. Smith to Col. A. K. Longan et al., June 12, 1854, printed in Samuel B. Harding, *Life of George R. Smith*, 187–88.

37. Jackson to Atchison, January 18, 1854, Atchison Papers.

Obviously the "main question" meant something quite different to the opposing forces. This dichotomy of thought reflected demographic changes that Missouri underwent in the late 1840's and continued to experience throughout the 1850's. Immigration into the state no longer came from the upper South, but from the Old Northwest. These new Missourians, like their counterparts in Ohio, Indiana, and Illinois, demanded internal improvements and a government responsive to their needs and demands, rather than one concentrating solely upon the protection of slavery.[38]

The August state elections did not terminate the bitter strife, as plans still had to be made for the coming senatorial election.[39] The issues of slavery, railroads, and the Kansas question became entangled in the anti-Benton and anti-Atchison tirades of the respective political camps; even the Whigs found themselves divided over the slavery issue. James S. Rollins felt that Benton might support a Whig for the senatorial post if unable to win it himself, but Rollins feared that flirtations with Benton might disrupt Whig unity. In his mind, before any party reorganization could take place in the state, Missourians must "*bury* and preach the funeral of Bentonism (that's done now) of Locofocoism, of Achesoniam [*sic*] and then let us rear in their stead, *Genuine* Whiggism."[40] This was an accurate reflection of the Whig determination to maintain party unity by holding fast.

Anti-Bentonites also held mixed views concerning the August election. Atchison wrote in glee to Jefferson Davis that Benton had been "killed" and that many of his "heretofore" friends would be relieved of supporting him and would move to act with the old Democratic party.[41] Although the Benton faction steadily declined while anti-Bentonites increased their power, William Napton believed that Benton had so long epitomized Democracy in the state that only his death would release his hold on many Missourians.[42] John Lowry, more pragmatic than Atchison, felt that the anti-Benton forces would have only enough power to stalemate the election and would have to wait another two years to elect a man fully compatible with their views. Lowry was perfectly willing to wait those two years to defeat Benton.[43]

38. In 1850 there were 15,200 blacks for every 100,000 whites in Missouri. By 1860 there were only 11,143 blacks for every 100,000 whites. Allan Nevins includes several excellent maps portraying the situation of slavery in Missouri, although he exaggerates the extent of free soil doctrines in the state. Nevins, *The Emergence of Lincoln*, I, 164–65; II, 149–51.

39. These elections saw a slight Whig gain at the expense of the Bentonites and the anti-Bentonites.

40. Rollins to Maj. John Dougherty, Reynolds Papers.

41. Atchison to Davis, September 24, 1854, Jefferson Davis Papers.

42. Napton Diary, Missouri Historical Society, 87.

43. Lowry to D. R. Atchison, August 13, 1854, Atchison Papers.

While the various factions immersed themselves in in-fighting, the Kansas situation became greatly inflamed. In July Benjamin and John Stringfellow, acting for Atchison, held a meeting at Weston, Missouri, where they organized the Platte County Self-Protective Association for the purpose of settling Kansas with proslavery men; many other counties followed suit during the summer. After Atchison arrived in the state in August, he and the Stringfellows worked throughout the fall to organize the associations into "blue lodges."

Publicly Atchison defined his mission as an effort to awaken the American people to impending dangers and to suggest means to avoid them. Since the approaching election in the territory of Kansas would decide whether slavery would be permitted there, Atchison urged Missourians to finance a proslavery campaign and to cross over into Kansas for the purpose of voting.[44] Atchison privately revealed to Jefferson Davis how truly rabid and vicious was the nature of his intentions. He boasted of a speech he had delivered in Kansas in which he had urged the settlers to hang all abolitionists without a trial, commenting that "this sentiment met with almost universal applause, and I could with difficulty keep the 'Plebs' from hanging two gentlemen who called a cow, 'Keow.'" Atchison predicted that within six months there would be "the Devil to pay in Kansas and this state; . . . ." He thought that in order to defeat abolitionist organizations: "We will be compelled to shoot, burn & hang, but the thing will soon be over; we intend to 'Mormonize' the Abolitionists."[45]

VI

If any of the "railroad" men, anxiously awaiting the opening of the Missouri General Assembly, expected Price to deviate from his strict interpretation of the state constitution in regard to railroad charters, they were to be sadly disappointed. In April Price again demonstrated his suspicion of corporation leaders when he became involved in a dispute with the board of directors of the North Missouri Railroad. The charter for this road had stated that it must be built as nearly as practicable along the dividing ridge, or watershed, between the Missouri and Mississippi rivers. However, the board preferred a central route, even if it would be more expensive, and for that reason modified the proposed location. Upon learning of this, Price indicated to the board that he would refuse to issue the approved state bonds for the project because the intention of the charter had been violated.[46] After extended discussion with the

44. *Platte* (Mo.) *Argus*, November 6, 1854, reprinted in Harding's *Life of George R. Smith*, 212.
45. Atchison to Davis, September 24, 1854, Jefferson Davis Papers.
46. *Weekly St. Louis Pilot*, April 15, 1854; *The* Liberty (Mo.) *Weekly Tribune*, April 28, 1854.

Governor, the board finally capitulated and adopted the ridge route. This incident demonstrated Price's chronic fear that privileged elites, using underhanded means, would arise at the expense of the public. With characteristic republican dogmatism, Price maintained that only an inflexible adherence to forms prescribed by the state constitution or legislative charters could prevent this and save the public from such a class of men.

The Eighteenth General Assembly convened during the fourth week in December, 1854, and heard Price's first biennial address in joint session on the 25th. In this document, much longer than his inaugural, Price amplified his thoughts and revealed his principles. After noting that the state's finances were in sound condition, Price moved to the question that was beginning to trouble many Missourians. The charter of the Bank of Missouri would expire in February, 1857, and Price wanted the legislature to begin to deal with this problem, since he feared that a system of free banking might be established in the state. He called for renewal of the bank charter and warned of the dire consequences of any change in the direction of free banking and the possible abandonment of the principles of specie redemption of all bank notes.

His next central point dealt with railroads. Price urged either support for the roads then underway or complete abandonment of the system and commented that the latter would bring financial loss to the people of the state. Although he favored internal improvements, and "Anxious as I feel, however, to promote these works, I cannot recommend such legislation as will diminish the securities already held by the State, or involve the Treasury in further expenditures, without ample guarantes," he felt nothing would be more fatal to internal improvements "than the encouragement of a belief, that the follies, imprudences, or misfortunes of those who manage them, will be rectified by legislative clemency." Thus, Price warned the assembly that it must act within the narrow and literal wording of the constitutional provisions; he offered no other solutions.

Price then turned to a justification of his actions in the Tredway incident, announcing his conviction that he had acted properly in that matter in spite of his reversal at the hands of the court. He pointed out that prior to the Tredway appointment he had filled vacancies occurring in state bank offices with nothing being said and that those appointees had functioned well. Continuing, he noted that after the court decision he had declined to appoint men to the state land offices. Although he did not mention it, he had even refused to issue a writ of election in the case of a tie between two candidates for the state assembly. This had obviously resulted from the court's decision, since Price had justified his refusal to act on the grounds that he could not issue a writ until the proper tribunal declared a vacancy.

Price felt that appointments to offices in the state bank, to the state land offices, and to the office of public printer should all have been dealt with in the same manner. Leaving the distinct implication that only partisan interest had created the storm over the appointment of Tredway, Price called for a law to prevent the recurrence of such an embarrassment for the governor.

The final half of Price's message revealed his increasing difficulty in maintaining both his nationalist sentiments and his determination to protect slavery. He reviewed three proposed routes for transcontinental railroads and stated that a central route would "Strengthen the bonds of our Union" and vastly increase national prosperity; because of these benefits Price hoped "that Congress, in whatever it may do to encourage the construction of this great work, will not weaken the bonds of the Union by sectional partiality." Although favoring construction of a great railroad and telegraph line to tie the Union together, and military protection of emigrants in the territories, Price also saw a need to reaffirm the rights of the individual states and to curb the abolitionist menace. Here the prospects, in Price's mind, were not such as to give assurance that the Constitution would be held sacred and the Union perpetuated. In his view, the abolitionists were at the root of the problem. Declaring that over "thirty years ago, emissaries were dispatched into the northern States, and very recently into the southern States, by the enemies of constitutional liberty in Europe, furnished with means to propagate slander and falsehood, and excite the meanest and most degraded prejudices of the human heart," he traced the work of the "agents" and the formation of an abolitionist party, which he considered an open enemy of the Constitution and the harmony of the Union. In his discussion of abolitionist motives, Price revealed an inner fear and suspicion that must have been shared by many slaveholders. He declared that the abolitionists "affect to admit that Congress has no power to interfere with slavery in the State; and yet, if that is not the ultimate object, their whole system of operations is absurd."

Reviewing the pressing problem of slavery in the territories, Price came out firmly against the power of Congress to legislate on territorial matters other than the sale of land. In defense of his position, Price, exhibiting his penchant for literal interpretations, analyzed the motivations of the Founding Fathers: "If it had been their purpose to authorize Congress to organize governments, or to enact municipal regulations for these communities, is it possible to believe that such power would not have been enumerated?" He continued by asking if it was "possible to believe that statesmen, who knew so well the use of accurate language, meant to convey all the powers of government *as an incident* to the power to sell lands?" Price closed by lauding the concept of popular sovereignty and praising the Kansas-Nebraska Act.[47]

The House organized on the day after Price's address and, through a combination of Whig and Benton Democratic votes, elected a Whig, William Newland, speaker on the fifth ballot.[48] Because of the Whig plurality and its apparent alliance with the Bentonites, the anti-Benton forces seemed to be in for a long session, during which Price would face many challenges.

The embryonic Whig-Bentonite alliance failed to materialize during the senatorial election. The nominations of Benton and Atchison were foregone conclusions, but the Whigs did not decide upon a nominee until they conferred after the legislature convened. In this caucus, intraparty differences, submerged during the campaign, could not be suppressed. It became apparent that there were "Benton" and "anti-Benton" factions among the Whigs as well as among the Democrats. When William Newland received the Whig caucus approval for Speaker, he represented the moderate or "Benton" faction. This created an indebtedness to the State-rights wing of the party, which was evened by forcing the nomination of Alexander Doniphan, a proslave Whig, for senator. This compromise among the Whigs proved to be their undoing, for it prevented any alliance with a Democratic faction. Lacking any bargaining material, the Whigs could not deal with the anti-Bentonites.[49]

The balloting for senator began on January 4, 1855, and extended through forty-one ballots and twenty-nine days, when balloting ceased with the seat still unfilled.[50] The monotony of repeated roll calls had caused nerves to wear thin and tempers to flare. B. Gratz Brown, championing Benton's cause with Frank Blair, became so wrought up that he challenged an anti-Bentonite to a duel over a disparaging remark the latter had made about Benton. Although the duel did not take place, the challenge did reflect the tense atmosphere.

As the balloting continued, attempts were made within the various factions to change candidates in hopes of drawing support from another faction. One such effort by the anti-Bentonites saw the old feud between Price and Blair renewed. Prior to the twenty-fourth ballot the anti-Bentonites nominated Price as a compromise. Upon hearing this, Blair, in a violent and abusive speech, disparaged the nomination; declaring that Price's position "was attained by perfidy" and that he was indebted to Benton, who "lifted him from the ground where he grovelled" only to be repaid with treachery, Blair cried out

47. *Senate Journal*, 18th Assembly, 1st sess., 14–26.
48. *House Journal*, 18th Assembly, 1st sess., 8–9.
49. Mering, *Whig Party in Missouri*, 203, 206.
50. *House Journal*, 18th Assembly, 1st sess., 63–202.

that Price "has been faithless to both parties" and "betrayed every party with which he acted." Referring to a recent lithograph of Price, Blair declared that "The subject was worthy of a penitentiary print and the genius of a CONVICT ARTIST."[51]

Blair's diatribe infuriated Price, but his conception of an aristocrat's code of honor prevented a man in public office from demanding satisfaction. Blair himself, although violently hating Price, recognized him as a man of great personal courage. He confided to an acquaintance his belief that Price would have given anything to have been able, without violating his duty, to resign the governorship and challenge him.[52] Tempers eventually cooled, the feud subsided, and the assembly returned to its balloting.

Since the factions continued to support their original candidates the results differed but little from ballot to ballot. Blair declared that Benton would triumph regardless of traitors within Missouri and in spite of "the miserable puppet we call our President!"[53] "Benton or no Senator" became the motto of B. Gratz Brown. It would be better, he insisted, to be totally unrepresented in the Senate than to be misrepresented or "chained to the low-backed car of agitation and negroism, and disunion."[54] Whig tempers also flared; James Rollins and another Whig exchanged the epithets "freesoiler" and "nullifier" in their speeches.[55]

The cessation of balloting on February 1 did not end the controversy, since virtually all other issues had become entangled in the Benton-Atchison conflict. Newspapers complained of the neglect of vital issues, particularly the need of various state railroads for financial aid, but the debate on aid to the Pacific road deteriorated into a Bentonite tirade against Atchison, the Kansas-Nebraska Bill, and the whole Pierce Administration—to which the anti-Bentonites replied in kind.

Although nothing was accomplished regarding the main trunk roads, a bill did pass again calling for aid to the Platte County Railroad. Price sent a veto of this bill to the House on February 17, 1855, for reasons similar to those given in earlier vetoes, the great trunk roads should be completed first. Price also commented on the depression that appeared to be engulfing the state and the nation, and feared lest "Eastern capitalists" grow timid in buying Missouri bonds at par value, which to Price was essential beyond all else. He cau-

51. *Jefferson Enquirer*, January 13, 1855.
52. Thomas C. Reynolds, "General Sterling Price and the Confederacy," 2.
53. St. Louis *Daily Missouri Democrat*, February 1, 1855.
54. *Ibid.*
55. Columbia *Missouri Statesman*, February 9, 1855.

tioned that the state should not overextend itself in this time of "moneyed crisis."[56]

While the Whig-Bentonite coalition failed to elect a senator, it was successful in the election of bank officers; but while the alliance functioned during these elections, it disappeared when another controversial subject arose—a bill to incorporate the Jackson Seminary, a Methodist institution. A violent argument developed on the grounds that one of the incorporators, being a communicant of the Methodist Episcopal Church North, must thereby be an abolitionist. The voting on this bill reflected, to a great degree, the general feeling of Missourians toward abolitionism; while opposing the extreme proslavery position, Missourians supported slavery and violently opposed abolitionism. The bill lost through a combination of anti-Benton and Whig votes.[57]

The Eighteenth General Assembly adjourned in March with the intention of reconvening in special session in November. Price, having recovered from Blair's insults, viewed the session with over-all satisfaction, for again, in the disruption of the assembly over the senatorial election, he had avoided serious challenges to his principles. In the absence of this divisive issue Price could look ahead to greater opposition in the special session that lay ahead. In addition, latent dissension was appearing within his own party, since a slowly widening gap had begun to appear within the ranks of the anti-Benton forces. Price and other conservatives, opposed to the radical behavior of Atchison, Stringfellow, and other proslavery ultras, found themselves in a minority as the party's leadership began to be assumed more and more by the radical proslavery element.

56. *Senate Journal*, 18th Assembly, 1st sess., 188–90.
57. *House Journal*, 18th Assembly, 1st sess., 354–55.

· 8 ·

The Repudiation of the Old Republic

During Price's last two years in office the slavery and railroad issues remained predominant. Affairs in Kansas created a state of anxiety and unrest among many Missourians over what they perceived to be the machinations of the New England Emigrant Aid Society, whose importance they, in their hysteria, exaggerated beyond all bounds of reason. Price's brother Edwin reflected the uneasiness pervading Chariton County. On January 4, 1855, a large proslavery rally met in Keytesville to oppose the emigration societies. Edwin served on the committee that drafted resolutions declaring it the duty of every Missourian to combat these societies and to encourage Missourians to emigrate to Kansas to thwart Northern antislavery purposes.[1]

With the exception of his comments on abolitionism in his first biennial address, Sterling did not take any overt action to place his views before the public on the Kansas issue. However, by July he felt that conditions compelled him to make a public stand that would acquaint Missourians with his views regarding the institution of slavery; at the same time he continued to hope that conservative leadership would prevail within the proslavery camp. Price found himself in the anomalous position of being in sympathy with views of the proslavery radicals but opposed to their methods, which were a possible threat to the harmony of the Union.

During July 12 through 14, 1855, a large proslavery convention met in Lexington, Missouri, with many of the state's leading proslavery advocates present. On the first day the president of the convention, upon being informed of Price's presence, appointed a committee to invite the Governor to a seat within the bar of the convention.[2] Thus, by his presence at such a gathering, Price publicly placed himself with the proslavery forces in the state and lent them his prestige.

Following an impassioned oration by James Shannon, ardent proslavery president of the state university, the convention passed ten resolutions expressing the sense of the meeting. These proclaimed that:

    1 slavery was strictly within the jurisdiction of the states;

1. *The* Brunswick (Mo.) *Weekly Brunswicker*, January 13, 1855.
2. Jefferson City (Mo.) *Jefferson Enquirer*, July 21, 1855.

2 resolutions of several Northern states never to admit another slave state were hostile to the Constitution and implied a threat to slavery in those states where it already existed;

3 diffusion of slaves greatly ameliorated their condition while advancing the prosperity of the owner;

4 the only reliable guarantee the slaveholding minority had was to maintain an equilibrium in government by admitting new slave states;

5 the Kansas-Nebraska Act and the Fugitive Slave Act were commendable;

6 Northern emigration societies represented an attempt to thwart the Constitution;

7 organized emigration would cause hostility and recrimination;

8 Missourians disclaimed all right and any intention to interfere with bona fide settlers but would protect their property against aggression and did not feel it necessary to wait until they were attacked;

9 the eighteen Missouri counties adjacent to or near the Kansas border contained 50,000 slaves worth $25,000,000 that would become worthless and unsafe if Kansas were to fall under the domination of the abolitionists;

10 the convention would appeal to the North to help stop the "agressive fanatics" and would name a committee of five to publish an address to the people of the United States setting forth Missouri's views on the Kansas problem.

Price and William Napton were among those designated for the committee.[3] This appointment offered Price the opportunity to present his views to the people of the state while at the time causing him to further conceptualize his own thoughts upon slavery and its place in American society.

II

The actual drafting of the "Address To The People Of The United States" fell to Price and Napton who, with their affinity of thought regarding slavery, worked well together. Price, not given to reflective analysis, lent the document great prestige, while Napton, the intellectual, was able to translate the views of the two into well-turned phrases. The Address, appearing in October, 1855, reiterated the resolutions of the Lexington meeting within a theme of the threat to private property and social stability posed by abolitionism.[4] The phraseology of the message, with its emphasis upon the protection of private property, revealed the authors' conception of what would

3. *Ibid.*
4. *Ibid.*, October 6, 1855.

appeal to the ethics of what they perceived to be an age of Mammon. Convinced that the North epitomized this lust for gain, Price and Napton felt that Northerners would therefore be especially amenable to a conservative plea based on private property.[5]

While most of the public utterances of Price and his associates, like the Address, dealt with the protection of property, there was something much deeper, much more meaningful to them, than simply the protection of property. Submerged in their thought, perhaps not altogether conscious, was a conception of a separate, somehow unique, society of which they were a part. As the 1850's progressed, the forces of the day were such as to cause Price and his friends to conceptualize their views. It slowly became evident that the protection of the society, with all its implications, was central to Price's thoughts and actions and motivated his and others' behavior in the decade of 1850–1860.

At first Price and his associates seemed aware only that they were protecting private property. Napton reflected this in a letter to Claiborne Jackson; with reference to the perceived threat to property he wrote that "however, unimportant this matter may be to numbers of our friends differently situated, it is vitally important to us individually & all others similarly situated—whose entire property consists in large bodies of land & considerable numbers of slaves."[6] Napton's letter, emphasizing private property and State rights, made use of those shibboleths sanctified by time and usage in American society, but there was something much deeper involved. Napton hinted of this when he wrote that the abolition of slavery would not only divest slaveowners of a great deal of property, but also would "certainly throw us into a state of society novel & uncongenial & distasteful." At nearly the same time, he confided to his diary that he was apprehensive over the "present war" against the South's "social system."[7] Thus the vague conceptualization was gradually changing from the protection of property to the protection of a way of life. Thomas C. Reynolds, a new addition to the Democratic elite in Missouri, born in Virginia and educated in Germany, reflected this attitude when he informed a friend that the effects of time and the abolition of the laws of primogeniture "have not entirely destroyed all vestiges of that gentry which was once so conspicuous a class in the Colonial society."[8]

5. This is clearly seen in Price's second biennial address in the *Journal of the Senate of the State of Missouri*, 19th Assembly, 1st sess., 14–23; and William B. Napton Diary, 305.

6. Napton to Jackson, October 3, 1857, Miscellaneous Manuscripts, Western Historical Manuscripts.

7. Napton Diary, 194.

8. Reynolds to G. T. R. James, June 20, 1853, Reynolds Papers.

Price and his intimate associates believed themselves to be members of a unique society set apart from Northern society, which they equated with Irish workers, rabble, and "the corrupt classes."[9] In their minds the South contained a class of the highest order of intelligence and refinement and, if this aristocracy should fall, America would become a nation of shopkeepers, without the advantage of a "nobility to cultivate some of the higher and more ennobling traits of humanity";[10] materialism would become all-powerful, with consideration for nothing else. The Southerner represented a "race of statesmen, orators, military leaders and gentlemen, equal and probably superior to any now existing on this or the other continent."[11] The South, thus set apart from the North, avoided many of the great evils of society that stemmed from a free, white laboring class.

The institution that set the South apart was Negro slavery; its very existence freed the society from outbursts of emotionalism that stemmed from the ignorance, bigotry, and envy that were products of an oppressed and starving laboring class—a class demagogues could easily exploit to their own advantage. These conditions could not exist in slave states: "Where African slavery exists, we are free from this curse," and from the "[d]esperate politicians and adventurers from all parties and all isms engendered in the corrupt classes of northern society."[12] With slavery, "a certain degree of [in]dependence and a loftiness of sentiment pervades [*sic*] even the poorer and humble classes, which among the idle and higher classes, is united with intelligence, taste, and refinements."[13]

To Price and his intimates the bedrock of their entire social system was slavery. The Missourians thus rationalized their views and believed the prevailing liberal thought of earlier days had influenced the views of their predecessors—Jefferson, Madison, and John Randolph—who had viewed slavery as an evil. Since the formation of abolitionist societies and denunciations from many quarters most Southerners had changed their views. While world opinion might attribute this change to a fanatical loyalty to state sovereignty, indignation at foreign intervention, pride, self-interest or avarice, Price and Napton felt that it came about as a result of a more accurate and enlarged view of slavery.[14]

In this view, Price considered slavery as having arisen from im-

9. Price to William Palm, March 7, 1856, printed in the *Weekly St. Louis Pilot*, March 12, 1856.
10. Napton Diary, 305.
11. *Ibid*, 306.
12. *Ibid.*, 178; Price to Palm, March 7, 1856.
13. Napton Diary, 100–101.
14. Price to Josiah Foster et al., November 22, 1853, printed in the *Jefferson Enquirer*, December 3, 1853.

perfect human nature, but he believed that no society could be perfect and that slavery was thereby entirely compatible with a general condition of good government and a well-regulated society. It therefore became a practical question of whether slavery produced greater suffering than did the poverty of northern and English laborers and Price concluded that the slave was better off.[15] At any rate a master, because slavery was a contributing factor in the elevation and refinement of his social rank, would consequently check any cruelty toward his slaves. Price felt that if the abolition of slavery should become necessary for the stability of government and the happiness of the people, citizens of the slave states would be aware of this and would do something about it. He reasoned that, since the great majority of people in the slave states did not own slaves, if slavery was indeed an incubus on a state's prosperity then the general welfare of such a state would require its abolition. This had not occurred.

Such thought also involved another factor: race. Negro inferiority was vital to slavery, while freedom for the Negro would destroy a perfect society. While continually speaking of the superiority of the white race, most Southerners only rarely admitted the all-pervading influence and powerful grip the fear of Negro freedom had on them; they much preferred to speak of State rights. Napton, however, did confide to his diary that the South was involved in "a contest of races" in which Southerners were faced with choosing between three and one-half million free Negroes or three and one-half million Negro slaves.[16] For the Southerner there could be no choice. Price and his associates desperately hoped they would never be faced with a large free Negro population, which would, in their minds, be incapable intellectually and morally of self-government.

This phobia regarding the Negro in society and the gripping pervasiveness of race motivated many Missourians, but was an especially driving force for Price, who had long hungered for the status denied him in Virginia. By the 1850's he considered himself a member of the Southern aristocracy, but without Negro slavery any status he had gained would be lost. Southern society, with its accompanying personal status for Price, would be completely destroyed by the abolition of slavery and Price was especially sensitive to this. While governor, Price threatened to shoot a free Negro whom he had banished from Missouri if he ever set foot within the state.[17] However, the most revealing expression of his feelings toward the Negro would come after the Civil War when he fled to Mexico rather than live in a so-

15. *Ibid.*
16. Napton Diary, 172–73.
17. Edward Walker to M. M. Marmaduke, January 31, 1855, Sappington Papers.

ciety with free Negroes. He wrote: "I pray to God that my fears for the future of the South may never be realized: but when the right is given to the negro to bring suit, testify before courts, and vote in elections, you had all better be in Mexico."[18]

III

After the Lexington convention Price felt it necessary to go to Washington to clear up a problem of land titles resulting from a federal grant of swamp lands to the state. After a successful session with the commissioner of the General Land Office, Price returned to face the meeting of the adjourned session of the Eighteenth General Assembly. The session was expected to be an exciting one, for the divisive issues previously left unsettled had become inflamed by the activity in Kansas.

The assembly convened in the first week of November, 1855, and heard Price's special message in combined session. Since the assembly had been called to deal primarily with financing state railroad construction, over three-fourths of the Governor's message dealt with that situation.[19] Price began by reviewing the laws that set up the railroad system and the results that had been gained, and then went on to the new propositions for financing such projects. The foremost of these called for the state to release its first lien on the roads and permit the railroads themselves to sell bonds, with a second lien as security. Ever suspicious of capitalists who might try to gain special privilege at public expense, Price opposed such action because he felt the current system whereby the state, holding a lien on the roads and issuing state bonds as the railroads matched each 50,000 dollars, should be continued. He argued that only in this way could the state maintain its credit and ensure that bondholders would not suffer. Operating on the premise that good faith to bondholders and the state treasury was pre-eminent, Price, in words reminiscent of republicans of past eras, declared that "any attempt to release the lien, so far as it stands as a security to the present bondholders, would be such a violation of pledged faith as would essentially degrade our character and impair our credit." In outlining the dire consequences of releasing the lien and allowing the roads to sell bonds, Price dwelt upon the possibility of the state losing control of the railroads to eastern capitalists: "In the present condition of the public mind of the northern States, in respect to our domestic institutions, this would be a result deeply to be deplored. I need not, in view of what is now transpiring along our

18. Price to Dear Sir, December 16, 1865, printed in *The Liberty* (Mo.) *Weekly Tribune*, January 25, 1866.

19. Price's message may be found in the *Journal of the House of Representatives of the State of Missouri*, 18th Assembly, adjourned sess., 1855, 8–18.

western border, dwell upon this aspect of the subject." Thus it became evident that the fear of Northern interference with slavery, ever present in Price's mind, permeated even his thought on railroad construction. With characteristic rigidity, he concluded his remarks on railroads with the comment that he had "no suggestion for a change of system preferable to the one now in force: and if steadily and inflexibly adhered to, will, I have no doubt, secure the final completion."

Although the pending railroad bills were expected to draw the assembly's major attention, an issue that arose early in the session caused tempers to flare and created dissension within the legislature. During the regular session of the Eighteenth General Assembly the House had appointed a committee to investigate the activities of James Shannon, a Christian minister as well as president of the state university, who preached zealous proslavery sermons throughout the state. The outcome of this investigation would be in little doubt, since B. Gratz Brown was its chairman. Shannon, ignoring his critics, had not aided his case by a fiery speech at Lexington where Brown was in attendance. Brown left that meeting determined to get rid of Shannon as university president, but he had an even greater object in mind: He planned to "involve Atchison & Co. along with Shannon."[20] In short, he hoped to reorganize the Democratic party and to purge it of "nullifiers."[21]

Shortly after the opening of the adjourned session Brown delivered a devastating speech against Shannon and the curators of the university, recommending that both the curators and Shannon be dismissed. This precipitated a fiery discussion between Brown and his opponents that reflected the explosiveness of the slavery issue in Missouri. Fearing repercussions throughout the state, the legislature preferred not to entertain a bill specifically dismissing Shannon, and instead passed one stating that no university president, professor, or tutor could exercise the function of a minister of the gospel, or any of the learned professions, while serving in his capacity at the university. This would force Shannon to give up either his preaching or his position with the university. The passage of this bill, aimed directly at Shannon, could have, or should have, been indicative to the radical proslavery element that they did not have the full sympathy of the people. Missourians, while favoring slavery and opposing abolitionism, were distinctly out of sympathy with the radical proslavery element, which included Atchison, Stringfellow, and Shannon. Price, supporting the institution of slavery in a more conservative manner, found himself

20. Brown to James S. Rollins, July 22, 1855, James Sidney Rollins Collection; quoted in Norma L. Peterson, *Freedom and Franchise: The Political Career of B. Gratz Brown*, 50.
21. *Ibid.*

more in the mainstream of political thought in the state. Although Shannon's term of office did not expire until May, 1856, the act did serve to drive him from the university. Convinced that "a combination of Freesoilism, Knownothingism, and the fag-ends of all the various forms of sectarian intolerance" intended to drive him from the university, Shannon declared that he would leave his position in order to continue preaching the defense of "southern rights."[22]

After the Shannon episode the assembly moved to consideration of the state railroads. A combination of Whig and Bentonite leaders introduced a bill combining the needs of the various lines into one bill entitled "An act to secure the completion of certain Railroads in this State." The men, admitting they "had their hands full to electioneer with those who were looked upon as doubtful,"[23] were determined to pass the measure. There was "much quiet work to influence members opposed to the bill" and "noses had been carefully counted in both houses" until it appeared that the railroad advocates could count on a small majority.[24] The instigators of the bill were constantly aware that they needed more than the support of the legislators, as they were certain Price would veto it. They remained apprehensive lest Price, in vetoing the bill, arraign the assemblymen before their constituents for their "wild and extravagant expenditures of public money without any sufficient security for its return." The railroad leaders feared that many legislators with "weak knees" and "faint hearts" might cast a vote in favor of original passage and then buckle beneath the pressure of Price's veto.[25]

After bringing "various influences" to bear on Price to induce him to change his mind, supporters of the bill remained certain that he would not relent. As a last resort they arranged a sumptuous banquet at the City Hotel and invited Price and all the legislators except those considered unalterably opposed to the bill's passage. At the banquet the railroad men's leading orators spoke in support of the measure, thereby hoping to provide any doubters with material to justify a vote in favor of the bill to their constituents.[26]

When the bill came to a vote it passed easily, but there was still some doubt as to Price's course of action. George R. Smith, one of the bill's floor leaders, was confident that prevailing opinion that the bill would pass even over a veto would cause Price to sign it in order to avoid the embarrassment of a legislative repudiation of his views.

22. Shannon to Henry Wise, January 7, 1856, James Shannon Papers.
23. George R. Smith to his wife, November 27, 1855, printed in Samuel B. Harding, *Life of George R. Smith*, 202.
24. Account of J. C. Fagg *ibid.*, 203–4.
25. *Ibid.*
26. *Ibid.*

On December 10, 1855, Smith wrote to his wife that there was "but little doubt but that we will pass the bill."[27] That same day Price sent his veto to the assembly.

Smith's belief that Price would submit to pressure from the legislature indicated either wishful thinking or a complete lack of understanding of the Governor. Price's great personal courage, his inflexible adherence to principle, and his view of the role of governor as an impediment to hasty legislation meant he could not be swayed by external pressures. He vetoed the bill on grounds that it called for the state to assume more than one-half of the financial burden of construction. In his veto message Price reiterated his interest in state construction of railroads, but emphasized that this must take place on the prescribed basis of equal contributions from state and private funds. This was the only way to preserve the integrity of the state and avoid graft at public expense.[28]

The Senate quickly passed the bill over Price's veto, and the House concurred without even listening to a reading of Price's objections. His veto message naturally gave the bill's supporters in the assembly a temporary feeling of anxiety, but their quick and relatively easy victory, according to one assemblyman, led to "the wildest scene[s] . . . ever witnessed in any assembly of men. Members ran across the hall and clasped each other in their arms, and laughed and shouted until they were hoarse."[29]

Shortly after the bill's passage the assembly adjourned and the proponents of increased aid to railroads jubilantly returned to their homes. George Smith took B. Gratz Brown home with him. Smith's daughter, observing how "they were flushed with victory," commented on how "right royally did they recount around our fireside the ways and means that led to its achievement."[30]

IV

It was not long before Brown and Smith discovered their celebration to be premature: Price refused to issue the bonds called for by law to the Pacific Railroad. Exhibiting his literalness of mind and suspicion of moneyed corporations, Price questioned the constitutionality of its passage over his veto on the grounds that there had not been a strict observance of the state constitution.

Soon after enactment of the bill Price went into conference with his attorney general, James B. Gardenhire. Price took the journals of the assembly to Gardenhire's office and asked him to submit an opin-

27. Smith to his wife, December 10, 1855, printed *ibid.*, 206.
28. *Journal of the Senate of the State of Missouri*, 18th Assembly, adjourned sess., 1855, 214–21.
29. Fagg's account in Harding, *George R. Smith*, 206–7.
30. *Ibid.*, 207.

ion on the constitutionality of the legislative action overriding his veto.[31] Price's veto message had not been entered in the House journal until two days after the legislature voted to override him, and the state constitution specifically stated that a bill and the governor's objections to it were to be read and entered on the journal before a vote to override could be taken.

Gardenhire's reply to Price reflected the affinity of thought between the two men; he declared that the veto power was intended to answer two great ends: to prevent hasty, inconsiderate, or fraudulent legislation by securing the combined counsel of two co-ordinated branches of government; and to render the representatives responsible to their constituents. Continuing, he declared himself to be "equally well satisfied that the solemn forms of the Constitution, an observance of which alone can secure these great ends and shield the public from vicious legislation, have been violated in the passage of the bill submitted to my consideration." He then declared it his opinion that the bill was unconstitutional,[32] and both officials maintained explicit faith in strict adherence to "the solemn forms of the Constitution."

On January 31, 1856, the Missouri Supreme Court, stating that the House had not acted so much at variance with the constitution as to make its procedure unconstitutional, ordered Price to issue the bonds to the Pacific road.[33] Learning of the court's decision, Thomas Price, leading Bentonite, wrote George R. Smith that "The country is safe again!" He wanted Smith to "Call a meeting; pass strong resolutions; say what you please about captious opposition, etc., etc., by the Governor; and send to Lusk for publication. Do not fail."[34] The Bentonite-Whig alliance, desirous of castigating Price in order to discredit him before the public, hoped to gain the utmost political advantage from the situation. Price reluctantly issued the bonds.

To say that Price was "captious" deviated greatly from the truth; he was no tool of the anti-Bentonites. Of those remaining in high political office in the Missouri Democracy, Price represented one of the few leaders still adhering to old republican principles. His decisions resulted from his republican heritage and not from any pressure by the anti-Benton faction. Lacking much formal education, not given to intellectual pursuits, and worshipping consistency, Price fell back more and more upon the only guidelines he knew in the difficult position in which he found himself.

Price's veto and subsequent refusal to issue the state bonds led to severe personal criticism by many newspapers and private citizens.

31. Price to Gardenhire, January 7, 1856, printed in *Jefferson Enquirer*, January 12, 1856.
32. Gardenhire to Price, January 7, 1856, printed *ibid.*
33. The opinion of the Supreme Court is printed *ibid.*, February 2, 1856.
34. Price to Smith, January 31, 1856, George R. Smith Papers.

Reacting to one of these critics, Price penned a lengthy exposition of his political creed. In a carefully prepared response to a St. Louis resident who had written him expressing anxiety concerning the railroads and his course toward them, Price agreed with his critic that there was a period in the progress of all communities when works of public improvement became necessary. At such times the legislature had a duty to keep pace with the successive stages of progress of the community—"to neither lag behind nor leap beyond them."[35] He felt that in the earliest stages of a state's economic development the government must by necessity give extensive aid, but that, after a state reached maturity, internal improvements should depend exclusively on private capital and enterprise. In the interval between, there must be a dependence "upon a judicious combination of the two."

Price believed it was neither a question of whether the state should have railroads nor of whether these should be built by private individuals, but of how public and private resources should be combined. He warned of a "class of men" who always appeared when public works were in their inception and, by combinations and machinations that gained them special privileges, reaped the largest advantages. Setting themselves up as "peculiar and almost exclusive friends of the system," they delivered unscrupulous attacks upon all those who did not measure up to their standards, castigating them as enemies of internal improvements. This class of men always insisted that the public pay the greatest share—or the whole of the expense—and planned for certain individuals to reap the entire profit. Price then pointed to experiences in other states to illustrate how these men "have uniformly predominated in the commencement of systems of public improvements and that, in consequence State bankruptcy has ensued—and that, finally, public credit and character had to be rescued by the moderate and conservative masses, who were originally denounced as enemies of the system." Price did not want the failures of many of the eastern and middle western states to be repeated in Missouri. He then reiterated the position he maintained throughout his public career: The original plan of state and private enterprise sharing the cost of construction upon a dollar-for-dollar basis should be maintained. Ironically, later financial disasters resulting from reckless legislative aid to railroads would prove the wisdom of his words.

Following this defense of his railroad policy, Price revealed his conviction that slavery, not railroads, constituted the more urgent problem and should be the focus of the state's undivided attention. Firmly convinced that attacks on slavery threatened to destroy the

35. The following quotations are drawn from Price to Palm, March 7, 1856, printed in the *Weekly Saint Louis Pilot*, March 12, 1856.

Union, Price pointed out duties "more imperative, and responsibilities more serious" than railroad legislation. The duties involved guarding against "organized bands of fanatics and traitors, stimulated by British gold, and animated by the vilest prejudices and passions," who had seized one branch of the federal legislature and from there threatened the Constitution and the Union. Under the auspices of these bands, incorporated societies formed to build up communities on Missouri's western border so as to harbor "reckless and unprincipled kidnappers and felons who openly threaten the destruction of our institutions." These "fanatics" were "enemies of social order, regardless of constitutional and legal duties, [and] open repudiators of religion and morals . . . [who would] hesitate at nothing to accomplish their unholy ends."

In Price's opinion the only institution that could fight these "fanatics" and preserve the Union was the Democratic party. He viewed the Democracy as the "National Guard," fighting for the Constitution and the Union, and believed that "until these are secured, it will cease to weaken its efficiency by quarreling over minor issues." In this great struggle the Democracy of Missouri stood, "by the will of Providence" in the front ranks, and the time was ill-suited to creating minor tests of orthodoxy concerning measures of local policy such as railroad legislation.

V

The months after the end of the special session saw the climax of political developments that had long been taking shape in Missouri. During this period the anti-Bentonites, calling themselves National Democrats, gained complete control of the Missouri Democracy. They smashed the Benton organization and had little to fear from the Old Whigs, who had become badly disorganized. The way was cleared for the formation of new political alignments.

In the late 1855 speculation began concerning the elections that would take place the following year. James S. Rollins, noting the weakness of the Benton faction, felt that "Blair Benton & Co." were not strong enough to keep the Democracy divided and suspected that the Whigs would have to unite with the Bentonites to prevent the election of two "nullifiers" to the Senate. He felt that the nominating of a Benton-Whig candidate for governor might unite all opponents of the anti-Bentonites into a powerful and victorious party.[36] Still considering the possibility of unification, Rollins even felt that Blair and Brown, in order "to accomplish the overthrow of the nullifiers," might accept a Whig. No matter who was nominated, however, he should be a "first rate internal improvements man." Rollins

36. Rollins to George R. Smith, January 30, 1856, George R. Smith Papers.

did not want a repeat of "the trial through which our system has been—by having a Jackass in the Gubernatorial chair."[37]

Benton leaders were of much the same mind. Thomas Price agreed with Rollins' suggestions and was desirous of forming a combination to prevent an "anti-Rail Road" man from being elected.[38] Blair and Brown, fearing that the Benton organization was foundering,[39] courted the Whigs. It became evident that the Whigs and Bentonites, by forming a "Rail Road" party, hoped to sweep the anti-Benton forces and the slavery issue out of state politics.

In February and March, 1856, Blair saw a chance to unite the moderate Whigs and Bentonites behind John C. Frémont, Benton's son-in-law, and thus establish an entirely new and vigorous political organization in Missouri on the basis of free soil. Blair, Brown, and others held secret caucuses with the moderate Whigs to prepare for the state elections and in April, evidently confident they would receive the support of the Bentonites, the Whigs nominated former Bentonite Robert Ewing for governor.[40] However, when the anti-Bentonites and the Bentonites held separate conventions late in April, Brown nominated Benton for governor, thus eliminating any coalition,[41] and the anti-Bentonites nominated Trusten Polk.

After the national Democratic convention the position of Missouri Bentonites became more difficult. Many of them abhorred James Buchanan, the nominee of the national party, preferring to support Frémont, the nominee of the newly-organized Republican party. When Benton came out in support of Buchanan they were placed in an embarrassing position. Frank Blair, reflecting this strain declared, "It is utterly impossible to make any stand in Missouri that would not be ridiculous from its utter uselessness in opposition to Buchanan."[42]

Benton's support of Buchanan, although it greatly miffed Blair and Brown, forced them to declare in favor of the Pennsylvanian. Thus the *Daily Missouri Democrat*, Brown's paper, came out in support of Buchanan. With Brown and Blair "it was a question of meat & bread . . . & a question of the existence or nonexistence of the Benton

37. Rollins to George R. Smith, March 5, 1856, George R. Smith Papers.
38. Price to George R. Smith, March 5, 1856, George R. Smith Papers.
39. Peterson, *Freedom and Franchise*, 52.
40. *Ibid.*, 58.
41. Brown and Blair reversed themselves and nominated Benton because they feared that an alliance with the Whig-Know-Nothing coalition would cause them to lose St. Louis in the coming congressional election. The St. Louis mayoralty race, in which a Know-Nothing had been badly beaten, convinced them that an alliance with the moderate Whigs would lose them the vital German vote in St. Louis. Without the St. Louis City vote, Blair could not be elected to Congress. See Peterson, *Freedom and Franchise*, 58–59.
42. Blair to Montgomery Blair, June 12, 1856, printed in William E. Smith, *The Francis Preston Blair Family in Politics*, I, 344–45.

Democracy in the State."[43] Blair and Brown, to preserve party unity, played along with Benton until the August elections in order to elect Blair to Congress.[44]

The central issue of the campaign in Missouri became the Kansas-Nebraska Act. Benton began a forty-day trip through the state, during which he assailed the "nullifiers" and explained why he had voted against the Kansas-Nebraska Act. He and his candidates accused their opponents of being nullifiers who were agitating the slavery question. P. L. Foy, the Washington correspondent of the *Missouri Democrat* traveling with Benton, even tried to implicate Price in the Kansas debacle by claiming that he had sent cannon and muskets to Atchison and Stringfellow.[45] Those acquainted with Price were familiar with his conservatism and his dislike for Atchison, and so disbelieved the charge. Moreover, James Hackney, quartermaster general of the state, quickly squelched the rumor by publishing a list of where all arms shipments had been sent. The list showed that Price had sent more munitions to St. Louis County than to the rest of the state combined.[46] Throughout the campaign Bentonites called for internal improvements while the National Democrats completely avoided that question, preferring instead to concentrate on the slavery question and adherence to the Kansas-Nebraska Act, which the *Enquirer* referred to as their "golden calf."[47]

The state elections resulted in a resounding victory for the National Democrats; Benton ran a poor third in the gubernatorial contest. The National Democrats elected 73 men to the Missouri House, the Bentonites 28, and the Whigs 29. Shortly after the state elections were over the Benton electoral ticket was removed and all Democratic presidential support went to Buchanan.

Buchanan had evidently been concerned with the Benton ticket since he corresponded with Price about it. Price, somehow certain that the Benton organization would be smashed, guaranteed Buchanan as early as June that there would be only one ticket in the field for the presidential election.[48] The election did shatter the Benton organization, leaving its members to join either the majority Democratic party in the state or to drift into one of the incipient factions forming among the Whigs and some Bentonites.[49]

43. *Ibid.*
44. Peterson, *Freedom and Franchise*, 60–67.
45. Jefferson City (Mo.) *Jefferson Examiner*, July 5, 1856.
46. Hackney to C. J. Corwin, July 1, 1856, printed *ibid.*
47. *Jefferson Enquirer*, July 16, 1856.
48. Buchanan to Howell Cobb, July 10, 1856, in *The Correspondence of Robert Toombs, Alexander H. Stephens, and Howell Cobb*, II, U. B. Phillips, ed.
49. Frank Blair, reflecting the alienation of the Benton people from their leader, wrote to Rollins after the elections, asked him to join the

VI

Price presented his second biennial address to the state legislature on December 29, 1856. After briefly touching upon the railroad situation, he dealt mainly with banking problems. Ever alert for deviations from republican banking principles, Price called for a rechartering of the Bank of Missouri rather than a much-considered amendment to the state constitution to permit free banking. Fearful lest entrenched capitalistic elites, now made even more dangerous because of their abolitionist tendencies, gain control over banking in Missouri, Price called for the legislature to take steps "to secure for the farmer and country merchant, complete independence of mammoth city banks, to be controlled by enemies of our institutions, ready, as in some financial circles of the great Atlantic cities to make his credit with them depend on his political subserviency to their fanatical schemes." The great object of government, "particularly . . . one based on the principles of true republicanism," was to retain control of banking in the legislature.

Price moved on to the political scene by congratulating the people for their election of Buchanan and by castigating Republicans for their complete disregard for the solemn warnings of the Founding Fathers against sectional parties. He felt that a "large debt of gratitude" was due Northern Democrats for their part in defeating "the foes of that Union and Constitution," but his final comment on the issue reflected his own inner fears and anxieties when he expressed the hope "that a conquest gained over such heavy odds will prove to be a durable one."[50]

Price's four years in the Governor's Mansion had been personally rewarding. He had enjoyed the status and prestige of the office, which greatly enhanced his position as one of the most respected men in the state. Although not always in agreement with his political beliefs, Missourians admired him as a man of great personal courage and strength of conviction. His political and military reputation, combined with his striking appearance, would later encourage Missourians to turn to him again when the Union was facing disruption.

Price's years as state executive had been even more pleasant for him because of the good health and happiness of his family. The chronic intestinal disorder he had acquired during the Mexican War moderated in severity; his wife Martha, fully recovered from her

---

Republican party and commented, "I am convinced that some of the things that I have been working for are infirmed *Humbugs* and one of them is the father of *Humbugs* (*not the father-in-law by any means*)." Blair to Rollins, November 24, 1856, Rollins Papers, quoted in Peterson, *Freedom and Franchise*, 67.

50. *Senate Journal*, 19th Assembly, 1st sess., 14–23.

bout with cholera, enjoyed Jefferson City society, and the younger children found ample amusements; his eldest son Edwin married his long-time sweetheart Katherine Bradford in the capital city amid a gala May celebration. Following the wedding, Edwin and his bride returned to Chariton County where he established himself on Farm Place, which he had been improving for some years. In December, 1856, Martha gave birth to their sixth child, a boy named Athol, who became a great favorite in the eyes of his aging parents. Price could indeed be well pleased; while riding on the mansion grounds he could glance down the sloping landscape to the Missouri River and recall his days in Southside Virginia when he lived above the Buffalo River. His years in Missouri had been fruitful.

As Governor, Price displayed the salient features of his character—his strengths and weaknesses. While of only average intelligence and imperfect education when compared to some of the Democratic leadership, Price brought a personal magnetism and strength to the governor's office. He was clear and strong in his perceptions, prompt in his conclusions when promptness became necessary, and an acute judge of men.[51] While he conceived of the governor's role as a passive one to keep the other branches of government in check, rather than as a mandate for initiative and leadership, he was at the same time inflexible. His dogmatic adherence to his republican principles caused neither him nor the state great grief during his term of office, since the issues of the 1850's had not as yet come to a head. However, survival of the Democratic party would within a few years demand a leadership capable of reconciling divergent views and factions. With a population drawn from both North and South, Missouri would need a dynamic governor pressing positive programs to unite all elements of the state's society. Restricted by his conception of the office and by his political ideology, Price could only attempt to ride out the storm by trying to silence the issues—thus leaving them festering for his successors.

In many ways Price represented an anachronism in office. Although economic changes had dissolved the Jeffersonian world that was Price's heritage, he still attempted to resolve the dilemmas of the 1850's with answers drawn from the ideology of old republicans. Missourians envisioned a vast prosperity and did not want to be held back by ideals from an earlier time when the nation was a small, agrarian republic. Aware of the great potential wealth of the state, Missourians shared in the spirit of enterprise permeating the nation. They became restless, speculative, ambitious, and impatient to fulfill the promise of a virgin land. While Price's party, on the eve of his departure from office, stood at the peak of its power, most of his

51. Napton Diary, 293–94.

republican principles were being thrust aside by a new dynamism among the people.

Still upholding the conservative values of an earlier period, Price attempted to thwart the impulse that would reach its boldest peak after the Civil War. What he dreaded most—a land of real-estate developers, railroad and town promoters, and others depending on loose banking, easy money, and rose-colored visions—was already coming into being. Although outdated and trapped by his own rigidity, Price did epitomize the finer qualities of the old republic: adherence to honest, frugal, business practices and protection of the individual from exploitation by capitalistic entrepreneurs adhering to a new business ethic. His anticapitalistic system of values and ethics, however, was lost in the rush of a state and nation desperately pursuing the main chance. The state, just entering the era of the promoter, overrode Price's efforts at a conservative leadership. Missourians had repudiated the old republic.

· 9 ·

A Douglas Democrat

Following his second biennial address to the Missouri Assembly Price made ready to return with his family to Chariton. Shortly after receiving Price's message the Democrats went into caucus to choose nominees for the Senate. When James S. Green received the nomination, many felt Price could have had Green's seat in the House of Representatives, but Price showed no interest and returned to Keytesville. This caused some politicians to believe that Price was readying himself, "in the well known secresy of his habits," to gather strength for a more important post.[1] Such charges would plague Price throughout the remainder of his life. His ambitiousness and vanity, combined with his secretive manner, constantly allowed others to weave power plots around him.

Far from laying schemes for his own personal advancement, Price happily returned to his farm, even refusing a testimonial offered him by the aldermanic council of Jefferson City.[2] Indeed, for the next several years Price engrossed himself in anything but his own political gain. He dropped out of politics to devote time to his tobacco business and plantation and to what became a new and time-consuming task: railroad promotion. Only during the anxious months of late 1860 and early 1861, when Missouri's position in the Union wavered precariously, would Price come forward again to play a political role in the state.

During the year 1857 Chariton and Randolph County leaders pressed for a railroad through their counties to connect with the North Missouri Railroad. In November their efforts succeeded when the newly formed Chariton and Randolph County Railroad Company held its first meeting in Keytesville and, anxious to employ his prestige, elected Price president of its board of directors.[3] From this time until his appointment as state bank commissioner three years later, Price divided his time between his own affairs and strenuous promotion of the Chariton and Randolph. To many this participation might have appeared contradictory to Price's avowed principles, or

1. Thomas C. Reynolds, "Sterling Price and the Confederacy," 8–9.
2. Price to A. Fulkerson, March 31, 1857, printed in Jefferson City (Mo.) *Jefferson Examiner*, June 20, 1857.
3. *The* Huntsville (Mo.) *Randolph Citizen*, December 3, 1857.

even hypocritical after his actions toward railroads during his governorship, but even while involved in this entrepreneurial activity Price's old republican values and principles provided guidelines from which he would not deviate.

The first task before the board was a special election to be held in Chariton County on January 1, 1858, to decide whether the county would subscribe money to the railroad. Price and other county leaders canvassed the county in support of the measure and the voters repaid these efforts by voting in favor of subscribing $150,000 to the Chariton and Randolph. With this accomplished, the board met again to work out a more definite organization of the project. At this meeting Price appointed R. H. Musser to go to St. Louis to present the company's case to the board of the North Missouri line and to obtain their financial support.[4]

Three weeks after this meeting Price suffered a family tragedy when Edwin died of erysipelas. Price, who himself lived with chronic intestinal pains and Martha's constant illness, had little expected his dearest brother to die. As he stood by the grave at the family's burial plot near Brunswick, he could not know that within two years he would revisit that spot to place a tiny casket next to his brother and father.

Beginning February 1, 1858, and extending for little more than a year, the board of directors held its meetings in Keytesville, Huntsville, Roanoke, and Brunswick, in both Chariton and Randolph counties, to arouse support for the line. The meeting in Keytesville on February 1 brought good news from Musser, who reported that the directors of the North Missouri were willing to subscribe $250,000 if the legislature would authorize them to do so. Price then appointed himself, Lisbon Applegate—the old partners had reconciled—and Musser, as a committee to ask the county court for a subscription of $250,000 and to set up another committee to work out the best plan for obtaining private stock subscriptions.[5] Price himself subscribed $500 for five shares.[6]

On March 5, 1858, the board met at the Austin House in Huntsville and appointed a committee, including Price, to ascertain the probable cost of surveying a proposed route.[7] Prior to the meeting of the board in Roanoke on April 2, 1858, the board members attended a huge rally to stimulate support for the road. Price and several others addressed the crowd, expounding on the tremendous prosperity the

4. *Ibid.*, January 23, 1858.
5. *Ibid.*, February 13, 1858.
6. A complete list of stockholders in Chariton County may be found in the *History of Howard and Chariton Counties*, 565–69.
7. *The Randolph Citizen*, March 13, 1858.

project would bring to the area. At the close of the rally the board members accepted private susbscriptions on the understanding that the road would be located near Roanoke.[8]

The Brunswick meeting on August 20 brought good news again from the North Missouri road when its chief engineer presented estimates for various routes and informed the Chariton and Randolph board that his railroad would supply and maintain rolling stock for the proposed line.[9] However, a Brunswick paper voiced what must have been an inner fear of all who were interested in the road's success when it noted that nothing of substance could be done until the legislature met and approved the project. The paper also pointed out that Chariton's own representative had been elected as an antirailroad man opposed to extension of state credit or diversion of bonds by the North Missouri.[10]

Although Price devoted his time primarily to private interests he could not remain completely apolitical while events began to disturb the nation and the Democratic party. Price's loyalty to the Union and his fear of any agitation of the slavery issue made him particularly sensitive to what he perceived to be reckless action in regard to them. The Supreme Court's decision regarding Dred Scott seemed a victory, but events in Kansas soon made it appear a Pyrrhic one. The struggle over a constitution for Kansas caused the eventual defeat of the proslavery element and a seeming victory for the free soil group. In August, 1857, the failure of the New York branch of the Ohio Life Insurance and Trust Company precipitated a financial panic that was to affect the entire nation. Moreover, the Republicans began to acclaim a book, *The Impending Crisis of the South,* written by the North Carolinian Hinton R. Helper, that was filled with disturbing statements about class and slavery. From August 21 through October 15, 1858, Stephen A. Douglas engaged in a series of debates with Abraham Lincoln raising the specter of what might be expected if the dreaded Republicans were ever to gain power. Douglas' opponent had earlier declared that "a house divided against itself cannot stand" and that he did not believe the nation could continue to endure half slave and half free.

In early October, 1858, John Lowry sponsored a rally of Missouri Democrats in Fayette.[11] Their object was to discuss the disturbing events of the day and to oppose what Missourians perceived to be an invasion of "Black Republicans," whom most believed to be responsible for the calamitous affairs that shook the nation. Price presented

8. *Ibid.,* April 10, 1858.
9. *Ibid.,* September 4, 1858.
10. *Ibid.,* September 11, 1858.
11. Account of meeting taken from *ibid.,* October 22, 1858.

the opening address, emphasizing the threat the Republican party posed to the institutions of Missouri and the peace and harmony of the nation. Reflecting his republican heritage, he expressed his abhorrence of sectional parties as threats to the very existence of the Union.

After the speakers had finished, Price, as chairman of the committee on resolutions, delivered its report. The preamble enunciated a deep interest in the permanency of the state's institutions and expressed a desire to co-operate with the nonslave states in preserving the Union against disruption by nullifiers and abolitionists. The resolutions, rejoicing in the defeat of Republicans in Cole County and St. Louis, stated a will to "heartily cooperate" with the "liberal and unprejudiced" of all parties to wage a war of extermination on the Republican party. They gave a renewed endorsement to President James Buchanan and commended Missouri's congressional delegation, "always excepting Francis P. Blair." These resolutions, strongly reflecting the views of their chairman, may well have been composed by Price.

Soon after the political rally Price returned to his railroad duties. Early in April, 1859, the board met at Brunswick and instructed Price and two others to draft a circular address to the people of Chariton and Randolph counties to bolster their enthusiasm for the road.[12] The directors also agreed to hold regular board meetings the first Tuesday of each month beginning in May. In an effort to gain popular support the board planned a large barbecue for April 20 at Brunswick. Price and Applegate, anxious for this "breaking dirt" ceremony to be a success, sent an invitation to Price's old antagonist James S. Rollins. The letter reflected Price's republican principles in its intimation that the people of the county and the board meant to build the road "whether aided by the state or not" and that nearly $500,000 of a projected $800,000 had already been subscribed.[13] Price reiterated his conviction that roads could be built without state funds when he spoke at a Ray County railroad convention, which formed the Missouri Valley Railroad.[14]

At a rally in Huntsville in November Price's republicanism again provided the guidelines for the resolutions that were adopted. The first resolution declared that no state aid should be granted to any railroad except according to the dollar-for-dollar procedure previously established by the legislature;[15] the second declared that a portion of the remaining thirty million that the state could constitu-

12. *Ibid.*, April 8, 1859.
13. Price and Applegate to Rollins, April 14, 1859, Rollins Collection.
14. *The Randolph Citizen*, May 27, 1859.
15. *Ibid.*, November 28, 1859.

tionally loan should go to the Missouri Valley road.[16] Such aid to the road, which would pass through the old, established, rich agricultural counties of the state, would make it a financially solvent line immediately upon completion. Through the increased traffic the Missouri Valley line would give the North Missouri, the latter would be able to pay the interest on its state bonds and ultimately cancel its debt, to the benefit of the state. This illustrated the concept of railroad construction in which Price always believed.

In March, 1860, the "English Bill," which included much of the state's railroad legislation, passed both houses of the assembly only to be vetoed by Governor Robert Stewart on grounds of economy. The Governor's veto did not deter the people of Chariton and Randolph counties, who remained determined to build their railroad, and Price and others still felt it could and should be done without state support. The Chariton County Court gave 33,000 acres of swamp land to the company and this, added to what had already been subscribed, provided the company sufficient money to grade and tie the road. Once this had been completed the company intended to mortgage the line to obtain capital for rails; the North Missouri would then supply the rolling stock. Thus, supporters of the company remained sanguine in their expectations of success. Their hopes were to be disrupted by the outbreak of the Civil War.

II

By 1860 Price found himself unable to continue as president of the board of directors of the Chariton and Randolph. The financial crisis of 1857 had damaged his businesses, and by 1860 he was in financial difficulty. In May, 1860, Price resigned his position on the board to become state bank commissioner, although, with Missouri and the nation in increasing turmoil, he felt compelled to re-enter politics by attending the state nominating convention as a delegate from Chariton County.

The Democratic party, coalescing around the issues of slavery and opposition to the Republican party, had at last healed the wound of the old Benton-anti-Benton factional discord, but there were cracks in this unity. Even before Price left the governor's office, signs of latent antagonism had appeared between the ultra and the more moderate proslavery people. While in office Price refused to lend aid to Atchison and Stringfellow. Though a slaveholder and an ardent supporter of the institution, Price's nationalism and conservatism precluded his condoning such activity. An open antagonism, dating from the 1830's, existed between Price and Atchison, and the issues of the 1850's

16. The Chariton and Randolph Railroad was to merge with the Missouri Valley Railroad.

greatly exaggerated it.[17] Thus, when Price left office certain ultras viewed him, because of his conservatism, as a "trimmer" on the issue of slavery.[18]

By 1860 this division in the Missouri Democracy paralleled that of the national party; both involved the issue of slavery in the territories and focused on the candidacy of Stephen A. Douglas. The anti-Douglas position was being conceptualized in Congress where Albert G. Brown, Mississippi senator, demanded a plank in the national Democratic party platform endorsing protection of slavery in the territories until a territory became a state, contrary to Douglas' popular sovereignty. This was expanded, although in less radical form, when Jefferson Davis introduced a series of resolutions in the Senate on February 2, 1860. In a direct effort to stop Douglas, Davis proclaimed that neither Congress nor a territorial legislature could annul or impair, either directly or indirectly, the constitutional right of a citizen to take slave property into the territories. Only when a state constitution was being formed for immediate statehood could slavery be prohibited or inhibited. This removed the ambiguity of Douglas' position and went further by calling for Congress to protect slave property in the territories. Assuming this same position, the anti-Douglas forces in Missouri prepared to meet the supporters of Douglas head-on in the state nominating convention, which met in Jefferson City April 9–12.

Factional infighting began shortly after Claiborne Jackson, chairman of the state central committee, called the meeting to order in the hall of the House of Representatives.[19] James N. Burnes, a leading anti-Douglas man, nominated Judge Charles Rowland for temporary convention chairman. Thomas Hudson, knowing that Rowland virulently opposed the nomination of Douglas, nominated E. D. Brevitte, a conservative and reliable Douglas supporter. These nominations precipitated a round of fiery speeches. Finally James Young, desiring harmony, nominated Price as a compromise candidate and moved that he be accepted by acclamation. Young's action prompted a vehement protest from Burnes, who condemned Young's action as a deceitful trick to gain control of the convention for the Douglas faction. The Douglas group, finding itself greatly outnumbered, capitulated and Rowland gained election.

17. This antagonism dated from the Mormon problems in the 1830's when Atchison was a legal representative for the Mormons. The struggles of the 1840's over centralism also contributed to the bad feelings between the two men.

18. Reynolds, "Price and the Confederacy," 8.

19. Except where otherwise noted the following account of the Democratic convention is drawn from the St. Louis *Daily Missouri Democrat*, April 11–13, 1860, and the St. Louis *Daily Missouri Republican*, April 10–13, 1860.

A new storm arose over a motion to instruct the chairman to appoint a committee for the purpose of choosing permanent officers. Once again the anti-Douglas faction emerged victorious, with only John B. Henderson, staunch conservative and Douglas supporter from Pike County, gaining appointment to the committee. As a result the officers of the convention came almost wholly from the anti-Douglas faction.

Following a heated debate over the basis of county representation, the convention named a resolutions committee with the delicate task of formulating resolutions acceptable to all. Only John B. Henderson, the committee's chairman, and Price stood as bulwarks against the radical anti-Douglas men. Price's personal ambivalence became painfully evident in the twenty-four hours during which the committee fought over resolutions. A member of the committee commented that Price occupied the "unsatisfactory position of favoring both sides."[20] This delineated Price's long-time tension resulting from his nationalism and adherence to slavery; his sympathies lay with the society and institutions of the ultra proslavery group, but he remained eminently conservative and an ardent nationalist. As always he viewed the Democratic party as the "national guard" and feared for the Union if the party's harmony should be seriously disrupted.

As a result of his personal beliefs Price attempted to assume the role of peacemaker between Henderson and the majority of the committee, but he had little success since neither side wished to compromise. In the end, he and Henderson were overwhelmed when the various resolutions passed individually by a majority vote. To preserve party harmony Price passively accepted the resolutions; Henderson refused his consent but, also attempting to avoid discord, did not submit a minority report. He did, however, refuse to read the resolutions to the convention—his duty as chairman—and Price reluctantly consented to present them in the interest of party unity.

The measures evoked mixed feelings from Price. The first resolution, endorsing the principles adopted at the Democratic national convention of 1856, elicited his earnest support. As a disciple of Douglas, however, he ardently opposed the second resolution, which denied both Congress and territorial legislatures the power to prohibit or inhibit slavery in the territories. He staunchly upheld the view that the Fugitive Slave Act should commend unimpeachable respect and that acts by Northern states to nullify it subverted the Constitution. The calls for annexing Cuba and constructing a transcontinental railroad from Missouri's western border found Price a willing adherent. The sixth resolution reflected Price's own thoughts and may even have been composed by him, since it referred to the

20. John F. Snyder, "Missouri Democratic Convention of 1860," in the *St. Louis Globe-Democrat*, February 13, 1898, 37.

"treasonable invasion" of Virginia by "lawless desparadoes" [the John Brown raid] as another proof of the "legitimate consequences of the teachings of the Republican party" and additional evidence of the wisdom of refraining from all interference with the domestic institutions of individual states. He also supported the party's indignant repudiation of the charge of disunion made by its opponents, declaring that nothing tended toward disunion so much as the "irrepressible conflict" doctrine of the Republicans who drew support from the "Opposition" in Missouri. The final resolutions also bore the stamp of Price's thought. One declared that state aid to the railroads should not become a test of Democracy and that the votes of the people on the subject as expressed by their representatives in the assembly should be respected "when not in conflict with the constitution of the State." Another called for the Democratic party to guard against all "fraud and extravagance on the part of Railroad corporations." The final measure called for redemption in coin by all banks of issue created by the legislature and that they and other corporations under the control of the legislature should be "restrained from the wholesale importation and circulation in our midst of the depreciated currency of other States." Price still could not abandon his Democratic orthodoxy.

From its inception the convention was the scene of unreasonable confusion and riotous disorder resulting from violent invectives exchanged by the struggling factions. The chairman, Robert Acock—old, physically weak, and feeble of voice—frequently could not control the turbulence. Completely exhausted when the time came to ballot for nominations, Acock stepped down and Price was immediately called to take the chair, but even Price, despite his commanding presence and stentorian voice, found it difficult to keep order and had to use the gavel constantly.

The balloting for candidates went better than anticipated, since they were not asked to state their views on the divisive issues. The convention nominated Claiborne F. Jackson for governor on the fourth ballot, and Price then left the chair to nominate Thomas C. Reynolds for lieutenant governor; the remaining nominations went smoothly.

Discord broke loose again after the convention had nominated its delegates to the national convention. An anti-Douglas man moved that the delegation be instructed to vote for Daniel Dickinson, an ardent opponent of Douglas. When this met a storm of disapproval from the Douglas men, another anti-Douglas delegate offered a substitute asking for no instructions except to vote against any man who did not enthusiastically endorse the first, second, third, and fourth resolutions passed by the convention. Either motion would have bound the Missouri delegation to an anti-Douglas course of action at

Charleston; a violent debate ensued. Acock's feebleness proved to be a blessing to the Douglas faction, since his resignation enabled Price to guide the debate in favor of supporters of the Illinois senator. After the partisan dialogue ended, the convention tabled the motions and allowed the delegates to proceed to Charleston uninstructed—the conservatives' only real victory during the convention.

The convention finished its work by appointing men to the state central committee, including Price as a representative of his congressional district. The appointment thrust him into the vortex of the coming campaign strife.

III

Dissension at the Charleston and Baltimore national Democratic conventions created unrest among the Missouri Democracy. When the Democratic national party split, giving factional support to both Douglas and John C. Breckinridge, the division affected both the leadership of the Missouri Democracy and its individual members. Leaders of both factions began to exert pressure on the state nominees. Prominent Breckinridge Democrats in St. Louis urged Claiborne Jackson to state his choice for President, asking if he did not feel that Breckinridge best embodied the principles of the Jackson Resolutions. They further warned that an unfavorable response would force them to nominate another candidate.[21] In July, Jackson, delivered a speech at Fayette declaring that, although personally favoring Breckinridge, he considered Douglas the regular nominee of the Democratic party. This was the first of a series of fence-straddling tactics that were to characterize Jackson in the coming months. This particular effort failed, however, for the Breckinridge men held a meeting in St. Louis on July 2 and, with the endorsement of Senator James Green, decided that since neither Douglas nor Breckinridge had been nominated by regular means they were free to select the candidate most pleasing to them. They endorsed Breckinridge and nominated Hancock Jackson for governor and Monroe M. Parsons for lieutenant governor.[22]

On July 7 the leaders of the revolting faction met in Jefferson City where they completed their ticket by endorsing the remainder of the regular state ticket. This action prompted a large number of county meetings to endorse candidates. These gatherings demonstrated that the populace was confused as to who was the regular Democratic candidate for President. Claiborne Jackson won the state gubernatorial election with over 46 per cent of the vote; Sample Orr, the Opposition candidate, received nearly 42 per cent; Hancock Jack-

21. James Bowlin et al., to C. F. Jackson, June 27, 1860, Sappington Papers.
22. *Daily Missouri Republican*, July 6, 1860.

son and James Gardenhire, the Republican candidate, did poorly.[23] It was obvious what an immense appeal a regular nomination had for a Democrat in Missouri. The races for the state assembly, where Democrats did not run against one another, resulted in 47 Breckinridge Democrats being elected to 37 who favored Douglas. Thus, Jackson's victory did not represent a Douglas victory in Missouri.

IV

With the state elections completed, the leaders of the two factions began to canvass for Douglas and Breckinridge. Observing the perplexity of the voters concerning the nominees, Price felt he must intervene on behalf of Douglas. During the presidential campaign Douglas supporters had formed Douglas clubs throughout the state. On August 28, at an organizational meeting in Jefferson City, Price delivered an hour-long keynote speech.[24] Not an able speaker, but an impressive and respected leader in the state, Price admitted he had not made an extended speech in some time, but asserted that the time had arrived for every patriotic man to work for preservation of the Union. He expressed his conviction that the secessions at Charleston and Baltimore were premeditated and that William L. Yancey had associated himself with the Democratic party only to break it up and thereby achieve a dissolution of the Union. Price claimed that if the seceders had remained in the convention Douglas could not have been nominated, and declared that if a "bargain and sale" had not been made among those who bolted that it was certainly something that closely resembled it. Price felt that the "disorganizers" in Missouri, by bringing out Hancock Jackson, had enabled Frank Blair and others to trade votes with the Union party, thereby succeeding in electing Blair to Congress and thirteen "black Republicans" to the state legislature. Price ended with an emphatic assertion that Douglas was the regular nominee of the party and warned of the dire consequences of a split in the Democratic party.

Price's address to the Douglas club exhibited great moral conviction since Chariton County and its leaders were supporting Breckinridge and feelings were running perilously high throughout the state. Prior to his address, Price had faced a situation in which he displayed his personal courage and fairmindedness—traits that were winning Missourians to his support. Following the Republican's nomination of Lincoln, bands of ruffians roamed throughout Chariton and neighboring counties threatening all who even hinted at supporting the

23. Gardenhire, Price's Attorney General, ran on the Republican ticket in 1860. His decision to become a Republican is illustrative both of the political confusion of the period and of the intellectual dilemma faced by many individuals adhering to old republican doctrines.

24. Jefferson City (Mo.) *Jefferson Enquirer*, September 1, 1860.

Republican. R. C. Vaughn, a staunch unionist, prevented a mob from destroying the press of an editor in Lexington who had come out in favor of Lincoln. Vaughn later sheltered a German in his home to prevent his being killed by an enraged mob because of his intention to support Lincoln. When the mob discovered that the German had taken refuge in Vaughn's home they approached the house with every intention of ridding the community of two "black Republicans."

Fortunately Price, who was visiting Lexington on business, came upon the scene and confronted the emotion-charged mob. Little caring for the German's political views himself, Price nonetheless faced down and disbanded the milling, angry, hotheads.[25]

As time passed Price's political intimates and friends in the Boonslick area began to turn against him. Lowry called a meeting at Fayette that castigated Douglas as a "disrupter and [a] disorganizer" of the Democratic party.[26] In the face of this antagonism Price disregarded his usual policy of silence, because he was firmly convinced that the Union and the Democratic party—to him they were synonomous—were in danger. He spoke forcefully in favor of Douglas, thus lending him his personal prestige within the state.

Breckinridge editors began to agitate for a more thorough organization of their faction and called for a convention. Senators James Green and Trusten Polk, who had equivocated during the state elections, favored such a step and began to take the leadership in organizing it. As a result a Breckinridge convention met in Jefferson City on September 20, 1860. John F. Snyder, who served on the resolutions committee for both state conventions, commented that the task of writing resolutions became a mere formality, "as neither Gen. Henderson nor Gen. Price were present to interpose objections or offer suggestions."[27] Harmony prevailed throughout the meeting and no problems arose in appointing new electors or reorganizing the state central committee.

During the convention both Green and Polk delivered speeches in favor of Breckinridge. Much to the surprise and dismay of the Douglas people Governor-elect Jackson also appeared at the convention and declared his preference for Breckinridge. The convention issued an address to the state blaming party divisions on the Douglas people and urging faithful, old-line Democrats to vote for Breckinridge.

Prior to and during the Breckinridge convention the regular state Democratic central committee supported Douglas. The committee scheduled a meeting for September 18 but, lacking a quorum, could

25. R. C. Vaughan to James O. Broadhead, May 8, 1863, James O. Broadhead Papers.
26. *Glasgow* (Mo.) *Weekly Times*, September 6, 1860.
27. Snyder, "Democratic Convention of 1860."

not meet. When a quorum was still lacking the following day, those present scheduled a meeting for September 26; on that date a quorum finally appeared but, on convening, Thomas Hudson resigned and had to be replaced.[28] Following this transaction the committee appointed Price and Gustavus St. Gem to prepare an address to the Democracy of the state. Price offered a preamble and resolutions, which the committee adopted. In his preamble Price traced the formation of a new organization and party—the Breckinridge group—devoted to dividing the Democracy in the nation as well as in Missouri. Their actions in the August elections had caused Frank Blair and James S. Rollins to be elected to Congress and would divide the Democracy by setting up new and proscriptive tests. They were supporting a candidate who had received no party sanction except that of the "disunionists" at Richmond, in opposition to Douglas and the "regular and only Democratic nominees." Price's resolutions called for the central committee to fill vacancies created by desertion of any electors and committee members to the Breckinridge faction. He also urged "all who value party integrity, fidelity and honor, to adhere faithfully to party pledges and principles," and to support the regular nominees. The committee followed Price's advice by filling vacancies in its membership and naming him chairman of the central committee.

The following day the central committee's public announcement appeared.[29] Bearing the heavy imprint of Price's thought, it attempted to disprove the contention of the Breckinridge faction that Douglas' nomination was not in accordance with party usage and therefore that a Democrat could vote for someone else without violating party allegiance.

Instead, Price stated that "true fidelity to party interests requires that irregularities should always be disregarded in favor of the substantial ends to be accomplished"—strange words for one as rigid regarding form as Price. The Address maintained that there was no irregularity in Douglas' nomination; it pointed out that Douglas received the votes of two-thirds of those present at the Baltimore convention, just as Lewis Cass had in 1848. Going even further, it maintained that Douglas had actually received the votes of two-thirds of a full convention, since there were 424 delegates present when he was nominated. His nomination had been approved by acclamation and, whether many of those present conceived of themselves as spectators or otherwise, their actual presence made them delegates. Once again Price's literal mind became apparent.

More important than irregularities, however, "Principles of the

28. Minutes of the meeting of the Democratic state central committee published in the *Daily Missouri Republican*, September 27, 1860.
29. *Ibid.*

deepest import to the Democratic party [were] at stake." The seceding delegates had demanded the right to shape the party platform, thus grossly deviating from the Democratic practice of following the wishes of the majority of convention delegates. Yielding to the seceders would mean certain destruction of the party, which must not think of sacrificing its national platform and party doctrines to a dissatisfied minority. The address called for complete noninterference by Congress, whether favorable or unfavorable to slavery in the territories, and ended by defending Douglas' position on popular sovereignty. Here it made a telling point regarding the inconsistency of those who held that territorial legislatures could not rule on slavery by asking why, if these people felt that a territorial legislature could not rule on slavery, they rushed into Kansas to vote in the first election. The address left the distinct implication that since the ultras had been defeated in their purposes in Kansas they now took a different position.[30]

C. F. Jackson's enigmatic stand on the presidential election created unrest among Douglas supporters, because it allowed the Breckinridge leaders to play on the confusion existing among the Democratic electorate. Being intimately acquainted with Jackson and his principles, Price knew that pressure would have to be brought to bear on the Governor-elect to compel him to speak out for Douglas. As chairman of the state central committee Price accomplished this at a mass rally at Democratic party headquarters in St. Louis. There he arranged for the passage of two important resolutions: The first stated that Jackson's action in speaking to the Breckinridge convention "admits of an interpretation we think unjust to that gentleman, as inducing the belief that it is his purpose to support the candidate of the Richmond Secession Convention"; the second appointed a committee to present a card in the *Daily Missouri Republican* and the *Daily Morning Herald* asking Jackson to answer by the same means if he intended to use his efforts in behalf of the regular Democratic nominee.[31] The committee's tactfully phrased letter requested Jackson to define his position, not because of any doubts the committee or party leaders held concerning his position, but simply to aid the populace in making a choice, since "unscrupulous politicians" might take advantage of the uncertainty as to who was the regular Democratic nominee.[32]

30. It is interesting to note that Benjamin Stringfellow, writing in 1842 prior to the time when the issue of slavery in the territories had arisen, declared that if the states lost any more of their rights they should "resolve [themselves] again into territories, and openly acknowledge the right of Congress to legislate for us." Stringfellow to Thomas Reynolds, September 20, 1842, Reynolds Papers.
31. *Daily Missouri Republican*, October 1, 1860.
32. *Ibid.*

Realizing he must respond, Jackson declared in a speech at Boonville that, although Breckinridge remained his personal preference, he would support Douglas as the party nominee.[33] He maintained that he had never stated that Douglas was not the party's regular nominee. Although he spoke the truth, Jackson did all the hedging possible in his attempt to gain the best of two political worlds.

The efforts of Price and other Democratic leaders paid off locally when Douglas carried Missouri in the November election, but New Jersey was the only other state to give the Little Giant its electoral votes. Lincoln's election was a tremendous disappointment to Price. His dejection was all the more keen because his wife and son Athol had become ill in October; their fate and that of the nation were beyond his ability to control. He could only hope that providence would restore his family and that the state legislature, soon to convene, would act wisely. Athol, who had been a joy to Sterling and Martha in their middle age, did not recover from the illness, but the blow was somewhat softened by Martha's return to good health.

33. *Ibid.*, October 3 ,1860.

· 10 ·

A Time of Trial

The Twenty-first Missouri General Assembly convened at Jefferson City on December 30, 1860, in an atmosphere fraught with uncertainty. South Carolina had seceded from the Union on December 20. Five days after convening, the two Missouri houses met in joint session to witness the inauguration of C. F. Jackson. Jackson's inaugural address began with a lament over the state of the Union and then blamed the Republican party for creating the dissension that existed.[1] He claimed that from its inception, by "emissaries from the headquarters of fanaticism in London," to its triumph in the November election, the Republican party had adhered to only one principle: hostility to slavery. Its ultimate object was "to strike down [slavery's] existence everywhere—to sap its foundation in public sentiment—to annoy and harass, and gradually destroy its vitality, by every means, direct or indirect, physical and moral, which human ingenuity could devise." Jackson felt that the Republican victory represented the triumph not of a political party, but of a section, and asked: "Is there nothing alarming in the fact that the whole power of the Federal Executive is pledged in advance for the subversion of the constitutional rights of nearly one-half of the Republic?"

After tracing South Carolina's course to secession he lauded that state's courage and warned against coercion by the federal government. Jackson felt that if efforts to reconcile conflicting issues failed the interests and sympathies of all the slave states would combine to unite their fortunes, and he declared that Missouri's, "honor, her interests, and her sympathies point alike in one direction, and determine her *to stand by the South*." In order to terminate sectional conflict Jackson suggested that the slave states call a convention, draw up needed constitutional amendments, and deliver an ultimatum to the North. To prepare Missouri for the months ahead Jackson called for a state convention to determine Missouri's position within the Union and asked for legislation to strengthen the state militia. While expressing a desire for reconciliation in his public address, Jackson

1. *Journal of the Senate of the State of Missouri*, 21st Assembly, 1st sess., 46–54.

privately hoped for secession while the state could still capture sufficient arms to defend itself.[2]

The day after Jackson's inaugural address his supporters introduced measures to give him extraordinary powers in marshaling the forces of the state, but legislators were hesitant either to approve these or to rush passage of a bill calling for a convention. While they meditated, Mississippi, Florida, and Alabama left the Union. On January 9, 1861, South Carolinians fired on the *Star of the West*, a ship sent by President James Buchanan to reinforce Fort Sumter. Finally, on January 18, the legislature passed a bill calling for a convention to consider the position of Missouri within the Union, but the bill passed only after being amended to state that if the convention passed an ordinance of secession it must be submitted to a popular vote. When the legislature adjourned only one of Jackson's emergency bills had passed.[3]

The act calling for a convention created no great alarm throughout the state since many editors had already been calling for such action as a means of having the state's course of action thoroughly discussed and settled. The bill provided for election of three delegates from each state senatorial district, thus precipitating immediate canvasses throughout the state. Since the bill designated February 18 as election day, the candidates had little time to present their views to the people.

Price, Jonathan Davis, and Thomas H. Price became candidates for election to the convention from Chariton County. Both Sterling and Thomas Price spoke at a meeting on February 2 at Brunswick, with Thomas leading off with a carefully prepared speech lasting nearly two hours.[4] He claimed to support the Union, but hedged his position by demanding so many conditions as to clearly indicate he held strong reservations about Missouri remaining within the Union. He bitterly denounced the North and classed with Northerners all those who favored preservation of the Union by any compromise.

Tremendous applause greeted Sterling when he rose to speak, but he found himself in a difficult position because he had just finished his official report as bank commissioner and had not had time to prepare a formal address. Knowing him to be a poor speaker, his audience must have been apprehensive, but his deep feelings about the Union shaped his extemporaneous words so eloquently that many listeners considered it his finest speech. He began by expressing his belief that designing and ambitious office seekers were responsible for the difficulty and that remedies had not been applied where and

2. Jackson to J. W. Tucker, April 28, 1861, James O. Broadhead Papers.
3. This bill took control of law enforcement in St. Louis out of the hands of local officials and gave it to a board appointed by the Governor.
4. St. Louis *Tri-Weekly Missouri Republican*, February 11, 1861.

when necessary. Since the free states had trampled with impunity on the laws of Congress, he believed, the people of Missouri and the South should not permit any act of coercion by the federal government. At the same time Price took issue with Jackson's inaugural address by deprecating the idea of a Southern convention or any ultimatum being presented by the South or Missouri to the North. Price believed it would be an insult to Northern people to demand of them a signed apology prepared by Missouri without first meeting with them and giving them an opportunity to redress the wrongs they had committed. He suggested calling a general convention of all the states to consider the constitutional measures most likely to effect the desired result. This convention should receive and consider whatever concessions the North was disposed to make and, if all else failed, the South should present an ultimatum and act upon it immediately. If the Southern states would follow this procedure Price pledged them his support. After stating all this, he quickly assured his listeners of his belief that the North would not drive Missouri and the South to that extremity and cited as evidence the submission of monster petitions by Northerners to their congressmen asking them to accept the Crittenden Compromise.[5] He further felt that there were many other acts indicative of a conciliatory feeling on the part of the North.

In his peroration Price departed from his usually constrained style to passionately declare his devotion to the Union. He announced, to tumultous applause and even some tears, his determination to stand by the flag under which he had fought the battles of his country as long as there was a star left or a shred to flutter in the breeze. In this short, heartfelt speech Price revealed himself as a nationalist, and he remained so because of his conviction that the North would accept Crittenden's proposals, which he vigorously supported, and under which Missouri's institutions, especially slavery, would be protected. He also left the implication that if such a course of action failed he would have serious doubts as to the value of preserving the Union.

During the remainder of his canvass Price elaborated upon this theme. In republican style he felt that the secession of a state was utterly subversive of the rights of government and could not be tolerated, but he also believed the inherent right of revolution, as maintained by the Founding Fathers, existed as long as the people

5. John C. Crittenden introduced his compromise measures in Congress on December 18, 1860. The most essential provisions were that the Missouri Compromise line be drawn to the Pacific, and that Congress could not abolish slavery in the states or in the District of Columbia nor could it prohibit the interstate slave trade where slavery was recognized. The Fugitive Slave Act would also be improved and enforced. While bearing Crittenden's name, these measures represented the views of the majority of Democrats in Congress.

maintained their rights of self-government. He declared that if the Northern states invaded the rights of the South and attempted to subvert her institutions, the Southern states should assert their God-given right of revolution and he in turn would be ready to co-operate to the best of his ability.[6]

By the second week in February the newspapers in Howard, Chariton, and Randolph counties, comprising the sixteenth senatorial district, were presenting the names of Price, Thomas Shackelford of Howard, and W. A. Hall of Randolph at the head of their columns as either the "constitutional union" ticket or the "union" ticket. These candidates were to address a rally on February 9 at Glasgow to culminate their canvasses.

At that meeting Price expressed his most carefully considered views in a formal address. He began by stating his conviction that the slave states had been unjustly treated. Nevertheless, Missouri, trusting that it would receive the justice it demanded, still remained loyal to the Union. He proclaimed his support of the Union as long as there was hope of preserving it under the laws of the Constitution, and that he would fight to maintain it so long as such hope existed. Price considered election by one section of the country of a President opposed to the institutions of another as a severe test of patriotism and forbearance by the minority. Notwithstanding this ill-advised impediment to the harmony of the country, he did not regard the election of Lincoln as a cause for dissolution of the Union. Pointing out that the South still had sufficient security in both houses of Congress against any aggressive act by Lincoln, Price felt that it became the duty of the South to avail itself of this fact and not desert the Union. If the antislavery party increased its strength and was able to carry out its purposes through the use of the federal government, the South had strength to resist and therefore there was no need to be hasty. He regarded the Republican claim that the territories must be free as unjust and unconstitutional, a claim that a free people jealous of their rights would resist. Laws of the free states nullifying or impairing the operations of the Fugitive Slave Act were unconstitutional and he demanded their repeal. Price viewed the Constitution as a compact, not to be broken at the will of each state but subject to dissolution only by the common consent of all or by revolution. He closed by recommending passage of the Crittenden Compromise and the calling of a constitutional convention. Indicative of his republican heritage, he deplored the existence of a Union held together by the sword, with laws enforced by a standing army. This would prove to be a presage of his future actions.[7]

6. Thomas Shackelford, "A Chapter of the Unwritten History of Missouri, General Sterling Price," Price Family Papers.
7. *Glasgow* (Mo.) *Weekly Times*, February 14, 1861.

Price's Glasgow oration, while not as passionate as his Brunswick speech, did contain all the rudiments of his thought and reflected the views of many Missourians. It represented one of the rare times that Price deserted his policy of passivity and assumed a dynamic position by suggesting measures that should be taken. He remained firmly convinced that a compromise protecting the all-important institution of slavery would be achieved, thereby permitting him to retain his unionism, although the tension of being at once a slaveholder and a unionist noticeably increased for Price as the crisis deepened.

Missourians went to the polls on February 18, the same day that Jefferson Davis was inaugurated President of the Confederate States of America in Montgomery, Alabama. The result in Price's district reflected that of the entire state; with only rare exceptions the "union" ticket was successful. Price, Shackelford, and Hall were the near-unanimous choice of their constituents. Missourians now looked forward to the meeting of the convention ten days in the future.

II

The convention assembled in the Cole County courthouse in Jefferson City on February 28 and the following day elected Price presiding officer; his prepossessing stature and the respect he commanded seemed to make him a perfect choice. Unfortunately, in his opinion this post demanded the assumption of a stance of impartial passivity rather than a continuance of the dynamic position maintained during the canvass. Shortly after electing Price, the convention delegates voted to move to the more spacious quarters of the Mercantile Library Association in St. Louis.

On March 4, with the focus of the nation on the inauguration of Abraham Lincoln, the convention reconvened amid the patriotic surroundings of the chamber prepared for it in the Mercantile Library. The hall exuded all the atmosphere of a patriotic rally, with great amounts of red, white, and blue bunting in evidence and oversized American flags hung on opposite sides of the chamber. Following opening preliminaries Hamilton R. Gamble, a prominent St. Louis lawyer and long-time Whig leader, introduced a resolution calling for a committee on federal relations to draft a report dealing with Missouri's position in the Union.[8] After a short debate on the number to comprise this committee, the convention settled on thirteen and proceeded to elect its members. Gamble received a unanimous vote for chairman and soon became the dominant figure in the conven-

8. *Journal and Proceedings of the Missouri State Convention Held at Jefferson City and St. Louis, March, 1861,* 18–19. Since the above work is divided into two parts and numbered separately, the writer will hereinafter cite *Journal* or *Proceedings* to indicate which section is used.

tion; he was determined to have both the convention and the committee declare for the Union in unequivocal terms.

On March 16 Gamble presented the resolutions of the federal relations committee, which stated that no adequate cause existed at the moment to compel Missouri to dissolve her connection with the Union; instead she should labor for peace. Moreover, they held that the people of Missouri wanted a fair and amicable adjustment of all causes of disagreement; that the Crittenden proposals offered a basis for adjustment of sectional differences; that a national convention should be called to propose amendments to the Constitution; that coercion would plunge the nation into civil war; that when the convention adjourned it should meet again in Jefferson City on the third Monday of December, 1861; and finally that a standing committee should be named by the convention to gather at an earlier date if public exigencies so required.[9] Gamble began debate on the resolutions with a strong plea for their adoption and during the following ten days adroitly managed to have all of them confirmed.

Price took no part in the debate on the report, but his votes on several amendments reflected his position. James Moss introduced an amendment stating that Missouri would "never countenance or aid a seceding State in making war on the general Government, nor will she furnish men or money in any attempt to coerce a seceding State."[10] Price voted against this motion but supported a substitute maintaining that Missouri would "not countenance or aid a seceding State in making war on the Federal Government, nor will she countenance or aid the General Government in any attempt to coerce the submission of a seceding State by military force."[11] Once again Price exhibited his literalness of mind and the doctrinaire's penchant for exact form. The original amendment did not specifically state that Missouri opposed coercion by the federal government; without an explicit declaration to that effect there remained room for doubt. Regardless of form, this was one principle upon which Missourians were nearly unanimous: There must be no coercion of a seceded state by the central government.[12]

On March 19 the convention, by a vote of 89–1, adopted the first resolution of Gamble's committee to the effect that no adequate cause existed for Missouri to dissolve its ties with the Union; only George Bast, wealthy Montgomery County slaveholder, voted against it.[13] The second resolution, calling for a fair and amicable adjustment

9. *Journal*, 36–37.
10. *Ibid.*, 40.
11. *Ibid.*, 41.
12. *Ibid.*, 16–45.
13. *Ibid.*, 46.

of the conflict, passed by a vote of 90–1.[14] However, when the third resolution supporting the Crittenden Compromise came up for vote, Bast offered an amendment that, should the North refuse to settle the slavery question justly and should the states of the Upper South secede, Missouri should "not hesitate to take a firm and decided stand in favor of her sister slave states of the South."[15] This prompted a heated and passionate debate, most delegates feeling compelled to explain their vote.[16] When the Bast Amendment came to a vote it caused Price to come to grips with the issue that had remained latent for thirty years: the conflict between loyalty to the Union or to Southern society and slavery. When it came time for his vote Price unhesitatingly joined a minority of twenty-three voting in favor of the amendment.[17]

That night, upon returning to the Planter's Hotel, Price drew Shackelford aside and asked if he was surprised at his vote on the Bast Amendment. When Shackelford replied that he was, Price declared: "You know that during the canvass while I opposed secession I favored revolution when our rights were invaded. Now I see that war is inevitable. I am a military man and can't fight against the South. This is a revolution."[18] Price was and would remain a unionist only so long as he could be certain that slavery would be protected, thus ensuring his place in his idealized Southern society.

The next day the fourth resolution gained adoption without significant change, but the fifth, dealing with coercion, was discussed at length.[19] Thomas Shackelford called for removal of federal troops from the seceded states where there was danger of collision between federal and state forces. Price voted with the majority to pass the amendment,[20] and the sixth and seventh resolutions passed without incident.[21]

The adoption of the seven point report of the Committee on Federal Relations completed the major task of the convention. Following the election of the seven-man standing committee, with Price as chairman, the convention adjourned March 22 to meet again on the third Monday in December, unless convened earlier by the committee. All Missourians could do was wait and watch anxiously while the storm developed around them.

14. *Ibid.*
15. *Ibid.*
16. Debates given in *Proceedings,* 217–30.
17. *Journal,* 47.
18. Shackelford, "Unwritten Chapter."
19. *Journal,* 48.
20. *Ibid.,* 48–49.
21. *Ibid.,* 49–51.

III

After adjournment of the convention, Price returned to Chariton and, with other Missourians, began a period of tense expectancy. These anxious weeks came to an abrupt end when, on April 12, Confederate batteries fired on Fort Sumter in Charleston harbor and secured its surrender. On April 15 President Lincoln issued a proclamation calling for 75,000 volunteers to enforce federal law in the seceded states. Secretary of War Simon Cameron immediately telegraphed a call for troops to the governors of all the states still in the Union, including 3,123 officers and men from Missouri.[22]

On April 17 Governor Jackson issued a stinging reply, refusing to supply troops on the grounds that the request was "illegal, unconstitutional, and revolutionary in its object, inhuman and diabolical, and cannot be complied with." The Governor continued by saying that not "one man will the state of Missouri furnish to carry on such an unholy crusade."[23] That same day Jackson conferred with leading secessionists in St. Louis; at this meeting it was decided to have Major General Daniel Frost, commander of the state militia for the St. Louis district, make plans to capture the massive federal arsenal in St. Louis. In order to do this, however, the militia needed more arms and Jackson dispatched two militia officers to Jefferson Davis in Montgomery with a request for siege guns and mortars. Jackson followed this several days later with a proclamation calling the general assembly into special session early in May "to place the State in a proper attitude of defense."[24] At the same time he ordered the state militia to assemble in their respective military districts.

Lincoln's call for troops following Sumter's fall stirred up partisans of both sides in Missouri. A group of Southern sympathizers in Chariton County held a meeting at Keytesville to pass a resolution calling for the legislature to ignore the convention and pass an ordinance of secession.[25] They also passed a resolution complimenting Price for his vote on the Bast Amendment and censuring Hall and Shackelford for their votes against it. Edwin, Price's eldest son, told the meeting that his father would not be flattered with the resolution and declared that he considered Hall and Shackelford true and loyal sons of Missouri and her institutions. Sterling, acutely apprehensive over the

22. Cameron to Governor Jackson and others, April 15, 1861, *The War of the Rebellion: A Compilation of the Official Records of the Union and Confederate Armies,* Series III, Volume I, 69. Hereinafter this will be cited as *O. R.* Unless otherwise indicated, all subsequent citations are to Series I.

23. Jackson to Cameron, April 17, 1861, *O. R.,* Series III, Volume I, 82–83.

24. *Messages and Proclamations of the Governors of the State of Missouri,* II, Buel Leopard and Floyd Shoemaker, eds., 384.

25. *Glasgow Weekly Times,* May 9, 1861.

rapidly moving affairs, still hoped that Missouri could remain within the Union.

Prior to the firing on Fort Sumter, Frank Blair had been busy in St. Louis organizing the Home Guards, or Wide Awakes. On February 6 a company of regular United States troops commanded by Captain Nathaniel Lyon arrived in St. Louis from Fort Riley, Kansas. Lyon supported Blair's efforts to prevent Missouri's secession and to provide military strength to keep the state in the Union if it should be needed. Lyon immediately began attempts to gain control of the St. Louis arsenal from its commandant, whom he believed to be a Southern sympathizer.

On the day that Jackson refused Lincoln's call for troops Blair arrived in St. Louis from Washington with an order for 5,000 arms to be taken from the arsenal and given to loyal troops. By this time Lyon had gained control of the arsenal and quickly issued these arms to Blair's Wide Awakes. When rumors began to circulate that the secessionists planned to capture the arsenal Blair and Lyon took steps to prevent this. They thought Major General William Harney, commander of the Department of the West at St. Louis, was too cautious and lenient toward the secessionists and so took action to have him removed. Blair dispatched a special emissary to Washington to accomplish this and implored his brother, Montgomery, Lincoln's postmaster general, to aid the cause.[26] Action came quickly: In April the War Department issued an order relieving Harney of his post and calling him to Washington for consultation; at the same time Lyon, who assumed temporary command of the troops around St. Louis, was authorized to muster into United States service the four regiments the Governor had refused to furnish. With the departure of Harney, Lyon and Blair mustered the Home Guards, marched them to the arsenal, and distributed arms to them. Shortly before midnight on April 25 Lyon and Blair ordered the remaining munitions at the arsenal to be loaded on a steamboat and taken to Illinois.

On April 30 Lyon dispatched a message to Washington informing the War Department that he expected an attack on the arsenal and was taking steps to defend it.[27] That same day, urged by a President who fully realized the importance of holding Missouri, the War Department issued orders to Lyon to enlist under his personal command up to 10,000 men "for the protection of the peaceable inhabitants of Missouri." The orders also permitted Lyon to proclaim martial law in St. Louis if he deemed it necessary.[28] General Winfield Scott endorsed this unusual order with the terse comment "It is revolutionary

26. Blair to Simon Cameron, April 18, 1861, and Frank Blair to Montgomery Blair, April 19, 1861, Gist Blair Papers.
27. Lyon to Col. L. Thomas, April 30, 1861, *O. R.*, I, 675–76.
28. Simon Cameron to Captain Nathaniel Lyon, April 30, 1861, *ibid.*

times, and therefore I do not object to the irregularity of this."[29] Union leaders, from Lincoln through the local commanders in Missouri, realized the urgency of the situation and took the necessary steps regardless of their propriety while the Confederate and state officials remained stifled by a self-imposed rigidity resulting from their inflexible adherence to form and principles.

Jackson's stinging rebuke of Lincoln's call met almost universal favor in Missouri, not because Missourians favored secession, but because they adamantly opposed coercion by force of arms. While the people approved Jackson's call to put the state in an armed position of defense, they completely misread the Governor's intentions, for Jackson had long favored secession.[30]

During this period Price went to Jefferson City to confer with Jackson about calling the convention. Jackson and Price held a short conference, during which the Governor, distrusting Price's unionism, said little except to intimate that he intended to pursue a peace policy. He further counseled Price to delay his plans to call the convention into session until the legislature could meet and thus enable him and Price to consult with members from all sections of the state.[31]

After this conference Price proceeded to St. Louis to consult with the editors of the *Daily Missouri Republican*, who issued an editorial stating: "The sober sense of the people is beginning to react upon those who have been mainly instrumental in getting up an excitement by which this State was to be taken out of the Union." After thus alluding to the Governor, the editorial commented that during Price's interview with him, the latter had declared himself in favor of a peace policy. The editor then rejoiced that peace would result for Missouri.[32]

The editorial evoked no public response from Jackson, but he privately vented his feelings in a letter to an acquaintance: "If it be the purpose of Paschal [a *Republican* editor] and Price to make me endorse the position of Gov. Price's submission convention, then they are woefully mistaken." Jackson felt that Price had been driven by his constituents from a position of unconditional unionism to one of armed neutrality and revealed that "I do not think Missouri should secede today or tomorrow, but I do not think that I should *publicly so declare*, I want a little time to arm the state, and I am assuming every responsibility to do it with all possible dispatch." He then confided that, "She [Missouri] ought to have gone out last winter when

29. Scott's endorsement *ibid.*

30. C. F. Jackson to David Walker, April 19, 1861, Miscellaneous Manuscripts, folder 1786, Western Historical Manuscripts.

31. Jackson to J. W. Tucker, April 28, 1861, James O. Broadhead Papers.

32. *Daily Missouri Republican*, April 27, 1861.

she could have seized the public arms and public property and defended herself. This she had failed to do, and must now wait a little while."[33]

The actions of Governor Jackson and President Davis exemplified the problems that were to plague the Confederacy throughout the war. When Basil Duke and Colton Greene, two militia officers dispatched by Jackson to Davis, arrived in Montgomery they found only Judah Benjamin interested in the problems of Missouri. According to Duke, Davis and the others were inclined to take a roseate view of the problem and did not recognize the importance of holding Missouri.[34] While Davis did send four pieces of artillery to Jackson to aid in the capture of the St. Louis arsenal and wrote that he looked forward anxiously and hopefully to the day when Missouri would join the Confederacy, the Confederate president never, like his counterpart Lincoln, realized the strategic value of Missouri and the West.[35]

Soon after this Davis sent a message to Jackson asking for a regiment from Missouri to join the Confederate service. Being restricted by a rigid adherence to form that permeated many Southern officials throughout the war, Jackson refused on the grounds that he had no legal authority to do so since Missouri had not yet seceded. Once the legislature gave him the proper authority and the Confederacy supplied the arms, Jackson expressed confidence that Missouri could put 100,000 men in the field. However, until that time Jackson maintained that he "must move cautiously."[36] When he discovered that Lyon and Blair had removed the munitions from the St. Louis arsenal he took steps to procure arms from other places. He obtained several thousand private arms in St. Louis and added these to the artillery and other munitions confiscated when the state militia captured a small federal arensal at Liberty, Missouri. With these arms the state militia went into camp south of the St. Louis arsenal.

Camp Jackson, as this bivouac came to be called, caused great consternation for Blair and Lyon. They finally became convinced that the Camp Jackson inhabitants were Confederate sympathizers and on May 10 moved with 10,000 men to capture its 700 state militiamen. When General Frost found himself surrounded by this force, he had no choice but to capitulate. The Union leaders placed the militia under arrest and began to march them out of the camp; a crowd that had gathered to jeer the Union soldiers soon became unmanageable. Rocks and brickbats began to fly, accompanied by cheers for Davis

33. Jackson to David Walker, April 28, 1861, Broadhead Papers.
34. Basil W. Duke, *Reminiscences of General Basil W. Duke*, 44.
35. Davis to Jackson, April 23, 1861, *O. R.*, I, 677.
36. Jackson to L. P. Walker, May 5, 1861, *O. R.*, I, 690.

and the Confederacy. Someone in the crowd fired a shot and a soldier fell dead. In the ensuing melee, the troops fired into the crowd, killing twenty-eight and wounding many others.

The Camp Jackson incident spread terror through St. Louis and alarmed residents in the outstate areas. The legislature, convening on May 2, had been reluctant to pass legislation giving Jackson virtually absolute power over the state militia. There seemed little prospect of such action until the Governor rushed into the chamber early in the evening of May 10 with the news of Camp Jackson; within fifteen minutes a militia bill passed both houses, along with other emergency measures. At an extraordinary midnight meeting of the legislature the members, many of whom came armed, expressed fear that Blair was marching on the capital. For that reason they passed an extraordinary act giving Jackson authorization "to take such measures as in his judgement he may deem necessary or proper to repel such invasion or put down such rebellion."[37] That same night panic-stricken state militiamen burned part of the bridges over the Osage and Gasconade rivers. A diffuse fear and unrest permeated the state.

IV

Since the adjournment of the convention, Price had remained apprehensive regarding the movements of both North and South. If civil war came, what would be the consequences for slavery? Camp Jackson aroused his fears to a fever pitch since Frank Blair's and B. Gratz Brown's evident influence with the Union forces boded ill for slavery. Deciding that the time had come for him to act, Price left for Jefferson City to offer his services as commander of the state militia.

When he arrived in the capital Price found Jackson, evidently still suspicious of his conservative views, hesitant to appoint him to command the troops, but Lieutenant Governor Thomas Reynolds and others urged his appointment.[38] Jackson, knowing that Price's addition to the state forces would lend great prestige to its cause, could little afford to lose a man of such state-wide influence. Therefore the Governor appointed Price to command the state troops with the rank of major general.

In his first action Price issued General Order Number Two calling for all brigadier generals in the state militia to organize their men and hold them in readiness. He specifically ordered his generals to use every lawful means to protect persons and property without reference to political opinions, carefully pointing out that the object of the militia's organization was simply to protect the people in their constitutional rights. The orders further cautioned all officers and

37. *Laws of the State of Missouri*, 21st Assembly, 1861, 48.
38. Thomas R. Reynolds, "General Sterling Price and the Confederacy," 14.

men to be careful to avoid collision with any armed bodies, unless in an emergency it should be necessary to protect the lives, liberty, and property of the people, and that only the state flag was to be flown.[39] Thus, Price, considering armed neutrality the only course that would keep the state in the Union and at the same time protect its institutions, assumed that stance.

Despite the inflamed situation, many people felt that peace could be maintained, especially upon learning that Price had been appointed to command the state forces. One state senator, believing that those in charge previous to Price would "carry us to the devil," expressed his relief when informed of Price's appointment.[40] The *Daily Missouri Republican*, also encouraged by Price's appointment, considered him a conservative and discreet man who would not precipitate Missouri into antagonism with the Union. The *Republican* editor expressed relief that Harney, who had been reinstated in command, was back in St. Louis, for he considered Harney to be as conservative and careful as Price.[41]

Price did attempt to act prudently. He rebuked some of his troops for molesting a federal mail carrier and gave assurances that mail agents would have safe conduct throughout the state.[42] He still remained agitated over possible action by the Union forces and when confronted with a rumor that federal forces might oust the Governor and legislature became terribly upset, for he had felt certain that they had no such intention.[43] In a state of mental torment, Price desperately wanted Missouri to remain in the Union, but would fight for this only if he could be certain of the preservation of slavery. At a time when he might have acted boldly with Jackson in an attempt to arm the state and take it out of the Union, his unionism prevented him. Now, still torn by contradictory motivations, he could only support armed neutrality. Price's republican principles, never dynamic, always essentially negative, left him in a passive position. His future depended not upon his own actions but on those of others. Ironically Lyon, Brown, and his old antagonist, Blair, suffered from no such restrictive ambivalence.

39. *The* Huntsville (Mo.) *Randolph Citizen*, May 23, 1861.
40. Reynolds, "Price and the Confederacy," 15–16.
41. *Daily Missouri Republican*, May 16, 1861.
42. A. P. Richardson to James O. Broadhead, May 20, 1861, Broadhead Papers.
43. *Ibid.*

· 11 ·

Civil War Comes to Missouri

As the month of May passed, affairs in Missouri became more inflamed. Sporadic violence erupted throughout the state and both the federal and state authorities attempted to calm the populace. Price and General William Harney, representing the conservative elements in the state, struggled to keep Missouri free from the hostilities that appeared imminent throughout the nation.

Harney's return to command in St. Louis in May, 1861, calmed some people while disturbing others. Nathaniel Lyon, the ardent unionist, felt that Harney's authority greatly embarrassed his efforts to guarantee control by the federal government within the state.[1] Soon after returning to his command, Harney issued a proclamation to the people of Missouri warning them of the secessionist tendencies of the Jackson Administration and defending Lyon's actions at Camp Jackson; he did, however, pledge himself not to interfere with state prerogative while upholding the Constitution and the federal government.[2]

Harney's proclamation elicited varying responses among Missourians. One agitated slaveowner expressed his thanks to Harney for the tranquilizing tone of his message. Moreover, he stated that he had assured an anxious friend that the federal government had no intention of interfering with slavery in the state. Reflecting the concern of most Missourians, he did want Harney's assurance that he had been correct in believing the institution of slavery to be safe.[3] Harney replied that while he had received no official word regarding slavery he was astonished that any doubts concerning its safety could even arise.[4]

Price and Jackson, dubious regarding the meaning of Harney's proclamation, desired him to be more explicit. On May 20, at the request of Harney and with the consent of Governor Jackson, Price traveled to St. Louis to discuss Harney's motives. The Union leader's conservative views on both slavery and the power of the federal gov-

1. Lyon to Col. L. Thomas, May 12, 1861, *O. R.*, III, 9.
2. *O. R.*, III, 371–72.
3. Thomas T. Gantt to Brig. Gen. W. S. Harney, May 14, 1861, *ibid.*, 372–73.
4. Harney to Thomas T. Gantt, May 14, 1861, *ibid.*

The Civil War in Missouri

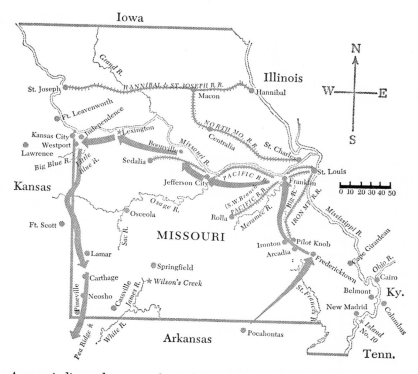

Arrows indicate the route of Price's invasion of 1864. Other locations that figured prominently in the war are shown, along with strategically important railroads and rivers.

ernment within the state reassured Price as to the wisdom of his position of armed neutrality. Price and Harney reached an agreement that they immediately publicized. The bargain declared that the state government would assume responsibility for maintaining order within the state and that so long as order prevailed Harney would have no occasion to take any military action that might create excitement and distrust between state and federal forces.[5] Thus did the two conservative military leaders, so alike in their desires, easily come to an agreement that they felt would keep Missouri within the Union, protect its institutions, and avoid the hostilities that were spreading throughout the nation.[6]

5. *Ibid.*, 374–75.
6. The Price-Harney agreement and the motivations of the major figures involved in the struggle for Missouri during the summer of 1860 are sources of tremendous disagreement among historians. In *The War for the Union*, 119–29, Allan Nevins views both Price and Harney as honorable men intent upon preserving Missouri's neutrality. He considers Claiborne F. Jackson a hotheaded secessionist and feels that the machinations of

The Price-Harney agreement prompted various responses from the two opposing camps. Blair, Lyon, and other ardent unionists were disgusted by it and suspected Harney of being too long exposed to slaveowning friends; they immediately began working for his removal from command.[7] At the same time, Governor Jackson saw the agreement as a means of gaining time to arm the state in preparation for taking it out of the Union. He dispatched Colonel Colton Greene to ask the Confederate commander in Arkansas for aid and sent E. C. Cabell to Richmond to confer with President Jefferson Davis and seek support from the Confederate government. At the same time Lieutenant Governor Thomas C. Reynolds wrote to Davis soliciting support and soon left for Richmond to present his pleas in person.[8]

Following their meeting in St. Louis, both Price and Harney worked arduously to uphold their agreement, both being convinced that it was the best way to keep Missouri in the Union. Harney was continually receiving reports from citizens throughout the state that state troops were not protecting unionists against depredations at the hands of Southern sympathizers; he in turn notified Price of such incidents

---

Nathaniel Lyon and Frank Blair undercut Price and Harney. William H. Lyon maintains, in "Claiborne Fox Jackson and the Secession Crisis in Missouri," *Missouri Historical Review,* 58 (July, 1964), 422–41, that both Jackson and Price sincerely desired neutrality. Just the opposite view emerges in Arthur Roy Kirkpatrick's article, "Missouri in the Early Months of the Civil War," *Missouri Historical Review,* 55 (January, 1961), 235–66. Kirkpatrick feels that both Price and Jackson were dishonest with Harney and Price signed the agreement only to stall for time in order to arm the state for the Confederacy. The most careful recent analysis appears in Albert Castel, *General Sterling Price and the Civil War in the West,* 14–22, where Castel takes issue with Nevins' interpretation of Price, Harney, Blair, and Lyon. He feels that both Price and Jackson were secessionists stalling for time, that Harney was honest and sincere, and that Blair and Lyon took the only action possible given the extant conditions. This interpretation of Lyon and Blair is astute, but it is extremely difficult to accept Castel's coupling of Jackson and Price and his belief in Price's dissemblance both in signing the agreement with Harney and in his consequent efforts to enforce that agreement. Clearly Jackson was a secessionist stalling for time, but it seems far more reasonable to assume that Price was sincere in his actions. Given his penchant for honor and his attachment to republican principles, it is difficult to conceive of Price acting in the devious manner described by Castel. To have behaved in that manner would have totally contradicted Price's motivations and life up to that time. It should be noted that Castel deals with Price's Civil War career and thus is not familiar with Price's life prior to the war. It is also of importance to note that Castel is a judicious scholar and that the manuscripts that could provide a definitive statement regarding Price's motives are no longer in existence.

7. Blair to Hon. Simon Cameron, May 24, 1861, *O. R.,* III, 375–76.
8. Reynolds to Davis, June 3, 1861, *O. R.,* LIII, 692–94.

and left them for him to handle.[9] In turn, Price informed Harney that he was investigating these rumors, that he was returning his troops from Jefferson City to their own districts to better maintain peace, and that he would "carry out [their] agreement faithfully."[10]

Harney gradually came under pressure from Washington regarding his position. Adjutant General Lorenzo Thomas wrote him, intimating that his agreement was unwise and that President Lincoln felt concerned about the loyal citizens in the state. The President considered it immaterial whether outrages on these people occurred from inability or indisposition on the part of state authorities. It was Harney's duty to stop them. Thomas warned Harney against relying upon professions of loyalty by the state authorities since they had falsified their position too often and were too far committed to secession to be entitled to his confidence.[11]

Harney informed Price that he did not want him to be misled by rumors of measures that might become necessary on Harney's part to meet a threatened invasion of the state from Arkansas and to prevent depredations on loyal citizens within the state. Harney maintained that their recent agreement had not covered the contingency of an invasion and that Price could hardly be expected to assume the responsibility for repelling such an action. Further, the exigencies of depredations upon unionists in the state might cause him to extend authorization to various counties to organize home guards, "unless you can give me assurances that such a measure is unnecessary." Harney further assumed that raising such a force would not violate their agreement.[12]

Price responded to Harney's letters by assuring him that if any Confederate troops entered Missouri he would "cause them to return *instanter*." He also felt that calling out the home guards would bring about the very thing they were trying to avoid: hostilities between state and federal forces. Price assured Harney that he had looked into the various complaints the latter had brought to his attention and that they were untrue. He would thus consider the actions proposed by Harney as violating their agreement and assured Harney once again that it was his "unchanged and honest intention" to faithfully adhere to their agreement and that he assumed Harney's honor would impel him to uphold his word.[13]

Trusting Price implicitly, Harney considered their agreement the

---

9. See *ibid.*, 378–83, for correspondence regarding depredations in Missouri.
10. Price to Harney, May 24, 1861, *ibid.*, 379.
11. Thomas to Harney, May 27, 1861, *ibid.*, 376.
12. Harney to Price, May 27, 1861, *ibid.*, 379–80.
13. Price to Harney, May 28 and 29, 1861, *ibid.*, 379–81.

only method of maintaining peace and order in the state without creating a violent situation, but he feared his program would suffer interference from "unauthorized parties."[14] In this he had good reason, for on May 30 Frank Blair informed him that he had been replaced in command by Nathaniel Lyon. Following his dismissal, Harney wrote to The Adjutant General defending his position and maintaining that his confidence "in the honor and integrity of General Price, in the purity of his motives, and in his loyalty to the Government," remained unimpaired. He felt that Price had worked to calm discordant elements and that the Price-Harney agreement had secured Missouri for the Union without bloodshed, although "those who clamored for blood had not ceased to impugn" his motives.[15] Regardless of Harney's protests, Lyon and Blair were now in control of the federal cause in Missouri.

Responding to the apprehensions created by Harney's dismissal, Price issued a proclamation hoping to calm local unrest by announcing that he would adhere to the agreement made with Harney despite the latter's removal.[16] In a letter to his brigade commanders Price attempted to correct any misrepresentations that might have arisen regarding his position. He stated that he had always exerted himself to prevent war from coming to Missouri and he wanted the people of the state to be able to choose their own position without military interference from either side. Price felt that even though Harney had been removed the federal government would adhere to the previous agreement.[17]

With Blair and Lyon now in control of federal forces in the state, Price and Jackson became increasingly apprehensive. Neither Lyon nor Blair displayed the conservatism of Harney and both were determined that federal power should dominate the state. Following a series of exchanges regarding a conference, Lyon announced that Price and Jackson would be given passage into St. Louis until midnight of June 12. Early in the morning of June 11 they left Jefferson City in a private railroad car to confer with federal officials in St. Louis, although they went with different intentions in mind. Jackson hoped to stall for time to prepare the state for secession, while Price was unwilling to turn against the federal government without one last effort at reconciliation; Price, thoroughly acquainted with Blair and knowing that Lyon was his ardent ally, could not have maintained much hope of this.[18]

14. Harney to Lieut. Col. E. D. Townsend, May 29, 1861, *ibid.*, 377.
15. Harney to Thomas, June 5, 1861, *ibid.*, 383.
16. *The* Liberty (Mo.) *Weekly Tribune,* June 7, 1861.
17. Columbia *Missouri Statesman,* June 14, 1861.
18. Jackson to David Walker, April 28, 1861, James O. Broadhead Papers.

When Jackson and Price reached the city they registered at the Planter's House and notified Lyon of their presence the following morning. Lyon sent a note saying he would send a carriage to take them to the arsenal where the conference would be held. Already piqued that a governor should have to come to see an army general, Jackson angrily refused to go to the arsenal and demanded the conference take place in his room; Lyon consented.[19] Shortly after 11 A.M. Lyon, accompanied by Frank Blair and Major Horace Conant, entered the Planter's Hotel and proceeded to the Governor's suite. There Lyon, resplendent in his brigadier general's dress uniform complete with sash and gold-trimmed epaulets, confronted the state group. Governor Jackson and Thomas Snead, his adjutant, had worn civilian clothes while Price was dressed in his Mexican War uniform, replete with cocked and plumed hat, curved sword, and high cavalry boots.

After the group was seated around a massive oval mahogany table Jackson declared his willingness to disband the state guard, disarm the companies being recruited by the state, and to pledge himself not to attempt to organize the militia under the powers granted to him. No arms or munitions would be brought into the state and the state authorities would protect all citizens in their rights regardless of their political sympathies. He continued that he would repel all attempts to invade the state from whatever quarter they might come and thus maintain strict neutrality in the current conflict. He further proposed that if necessary he would invoke the assistance of United States troops to carry out his pledges. All this would be dependent upon an agreement by the federal representatives to disarm all existing home guards and a pledge not to occupy any localities in the state not already held by federal troops.

For his part Price maintained that he was in perfect harmony with the concepts of the Price-Harney agreement and felt that both sides should adhere to it. He saw no reason why that pact should not be acceptable to Harney's successor. Blair stated the Union position and commented only infrequently when Jackson spoke and scarcely at all while Price made his remarks.

As the discussion progressed, Lyon began to dominate the argument. After the state's position had been clarified, he began to question Jackson sharply as to exactly how he intended to protect the rights of Missourians without a state guard if he could not do so with one in existence. It became evident that Lyon was far too shrewd to be taken in by the Governor's duplicity. After four hours of heated discussion it was painfully clear that no agreement could be reached

19. The following account is drawn from Thomas L. Snead, *The Fight for Missouri*, 187–201.

that would satisfy both sides. Finally, Lyon, seated at first and speaking slowly and deliberately to emphasize each point, but rising and pointing at those present as he reached a climax, declared that before he could concede to the state authorities the power and privilege to limit his government's prerogatives within Missouri he would see each man present and "every man, woman, and child in the State, dead and buried." Lyon then turned to Jackson and declared that a state of war now existed between the state government and the United States and that within an hour he would send an officer to escort the state authorities through the Union lines. Without uttering another word Lyon turned on his heel and marched from the room.

With the conference thus ended and war indeed begun, the state group could only make ready to depart. They boarded their special train and hurried back toward Jefferson City.

II

Aboard the train Price and Jackson began to formulate plans. By the time they reached the capital, shortly after 2:00 A.M., June 12, they had decided upon a course of action. Jackson would issue a proclamation calling for militia volunteers, Price would take command of all state troops that could be put in the field, and the Confederate government would be asked to send a co-operating army into Missouri as quickly as possible.

Jackson's proclamation, appearing later in the day, was printed and sent to all parts of the state. The Governor declared that a "series of unprovoked and unparalleled" outrages had been inflicted on the state. After outlining the course of the meeting at the Planter's House, he called for 50,000 men to join the state militia. He cautioned that the state was still in the Union and that as chief executive he would not disturb that relationship; instead, the question would be left to a convention to decide. However, he did declare that the public's first duty was to the state and that Missourians were under no obligation to obey the "unconstitutional edicts of the military despotism at Washington."[20]

Realizing that Jefferson City could not be easily defended and wishing to take advantage of the manpower of the pro-Southern counties north of the Missouri River, Price advised that a stand be made at Boonville. The plan adopted, state officials began to pack state records and make ready to abandon the capital; haste was of the utmost importance since Lyon was already on his way toward Jefferson City. Price had earlier ordered the railroad bridges over the Gasconade and Osage rivers destroyed, but this would only temporarily check Lyon's advance.

Lyon, following his usual astute course of action, began an advance

20. *O. R.*, LIII, 696–98.

along two axes. He led a force up the Missouri River, hoping to gain control of the river and thus shut Price off from a reservoir of Southern sympathizers. He also ordered a force under Colonel Franz Sigel to proceed from Rolla toward the southwestern part of the state to cut off any possible aid from Arkansas and at the same time be in position to attack the state forces should they retreat to the southwest.

On Thursday, July 13, the state forces abandoned Jefferson City and fell back toward Boonville. When they reached that city they were joined by state militia under Brigadier General John B. Clark, and men continued to come in as each day passed. On June 16 Price became seriously ill and decided it best to take a steamer upriver to his home to recover, after which he would proceed to Lexington to rally forces in that part of the state. Price turned over command of the force at Boonville to Clark and ordered him to hold that position as long as possible.

On June 14 Lyon arrived at Boonville and after a brief skirmish defeated the state force, which began a retreat to the southwest. Price, still weak from his illness, arrived at Lexington to gather troops but, upon learning of Lyon's victory at Boonville, had no alternative except to withdraw. Lyon had been successful in depriving Price of the great bulk of support that would have come from the river counties. Price ordered Brigadier General John Rains to take command of the forces gathering at Lexington and to move toward the southwest to effect a junction with the retreating militia under Clark and Jackson. Price rode ahead to seek out Brigadier General Benjamin McCulloch, commander of the Confederate troops in northwestern Arkansas, to ask his aid. Accompanied by his staff and a small escort he began a difficult journey toward Arkansas. Riding swiftly and gathering men as he went, Price had over 1,000 men with him when he reached Cowskin Prairie in the extreme southwestern part of Missouri.

On July 1 Price left his force at Cowskin Prairie for a meeting with Brigadier General N. B. Pearce, commanding Arkansas state troops at Maysville, Arkansas. There, Pearce informed Price that McCulloch and his Confederate troops were on their way from Fort Scott, Arkansas, and would reach Maysville the next day. Price returned to his troops with over 600 muskets, which Pearce had loaned him, to begin the difficult task of attempting to arm and organize his men while awaiting McCulloch's arrival.

III

Early in June, 1861, a dialogue began between those favoring taking and holding Missouri for the Confederacy and the Davis Administration, which throughout the war never appeared to realize the potential strategic importance of the state to the Confederate cause.

This lack of realization of Missouri's strategic value, combined with a developing personal antagonism on Davis' part toward Missourians and others who continually agitated the issue, was to greatly affect Price's relations with the Confederate command system.[21]

On June 14, following a conference with Governor Jackson's emissary, Colton Greene, McCulloch wrote Confederate Secretary of War L. P. Walker suggesting that Jackson's request for Confederate aid was of great importance to the Confederacy and hoped it would meet with favorable attention. He also suggested that he be permitted to capture Fort Scott, Kansas, thus fulfilling his orders to protect Indian Territory, while at the same time giving encouragement to Southern sympathizers in Missouri.[22] Within a week the governor of Arkansas also urged the Confederate Secretary of War to aid Missouri, since he could not do so under state authority. The Governor hinted at what Davis and others never realized: "It is suggested that an active campaign in Missouri would aid Virginia."[23] A week later Gideon J. Pillow, commanding Confederate troops in Tennessee, wrote to Walker that Tennesseans were anxious to aid Missouri and that he could recruit 20,000 men for that purpose if President Davis would issue orders for him to do so.[24] Pillow, however, had overlooked another consideration that would plague the Confederacy throughout its existence, when he believed that Tennessee would place its troops under unrestricted Confederate command. Three days after his suggestion, the Secretary of War informed him that Tennessee's governor objected to any of his troops being taken out of the state.[25]

McCulloch's requests brought only further restrictive orders from the Confederate high command. Samuel Cooper, Adjutant and Inspector General, informed him that he could capture Fort Scott and

21. The strategic importance of Missouri, while overlooked for a long period of time by historians and denigrated by most Confederates in high command positions, is fully recognized in recent historical writing. Allan Nevins considers Missouri of "cardinal importance" in *The War for the Union*, I, 119–29. In his *Turning Points of the Civil War*, James Rawley clearly delineates the grave strategic threat Missouri posed for the Union, 11–45. Two of the most prominent recent works recognizing Missouri's importance are Albert Castel, *General Sterling Price*, and Robert G. Hartje, *Van Dorn: The Life and Times of a Confederate General*.
22. McCulloch to Walker, June 14, 1861, *O. R.*, III, 594–95.
23. H. M. Rector to L. P. Walker, June 21, 1861, *ibid.*, 595.
24. Pillow to Hon. L. P. Walker, June 28, 1861, *O. R.*, LII, 703–4.
25. L. P. Walker to Pillow, July 1, 1861, *ibid.* The failure of the movement of Tennessee troops to Missouri was actually more complex than Walker indicated. It involved bitter quarreling between Gideon Pillow and Leonidas Polk and finally broke down completely. Thomas Lawrence Connelly, *Army of the Heartland: The Army of Tennessee, 1861–1862*, 40–45, 48–49.

"give such assistance to Missouri as will subserve the main purpose of your command."[26] Since the "main purpose" of his command was to protect Indian Territory, McCulloch was being ordered to hold Indian Territory and consider Missouri as only of secondary importance. Walker also wrote McCulloch to keep steadily in mind "the great object of your command," and to aid Missouri only if the right opportunity presented itself. Walker's closing comment reflected the attitude of the Confederate high command and its restrictive principles: "The position of Missouri as a Southern State still in the Union requires, as you will readily perceive, much prudence and circumspection, and it should only be when necessity and propriety unite that active and direct assistance should be afforded by crossing the boundary and entering the State before communicating with this Department."[27]

E. C. Cabell, Jackson's personal emissary, reached Richmond early in June but made no headway with the President; nor did Thomas C. Reynolds' arrival to aid Cabell in the quest for Confederate aid seem to lessen President Davis' distrust of Governor Jackson. Davis resented the Price-Harney agreement and Jackson's later proclamation announcing his intention to oppose troops trying to invade Missouri, no matter what their source. Jackson's devious stall for time had thus created a distrust in President Davis' mind that greatly impaired the state's relations with the Confederate government.

Cabell, acting as Missouri's gadfly in Richmond and often behaving as if President Davis had no problems to contend with except the state of Missouri, requested that troops be sent to the northern border of Arkansas under William Hardee and to Leonidas Polk in Tennessee. He advised that both commanders be "distinctly authorized to enter the State of Missouri." Cabell also requested that McCulloch be authorized to enter the state, assuring Davis that only enemies of the Confederacy would protest such a move and that he made the request "because I have reason to know that the instructions to these officers are of so guarded a character as to produce doubt as to their authority and embarrassment as to their movements."[28]

Cabell continued to argue that Confederate military control of Missouri would assure the safety of Arkansas, Tennessee, and the whole Mississippi Valley. With this accomplished, Lincoln could not send a force down the Mississippi for fear of a flank attack from Missouri.[29] In another letter to Davis, Cabell announced that he would not leave Richmond until the Confederate Congress met,

26. Cooper to McCulloch, June 26, 1861, *O. R.*, III, 599.
27. L. P. Walker to McCulloch, July 4, 1861, *ibid.*, 603.
28. Cabell to Davis, July 6, 1861, *ibid.*, 603–5.
29. *Ibid.*

which he hoped would "authorize you to do what you do not now consider within the scope of your constitutional powers."[30]

Such letters as Cabell's served only to irritate Davis. While President Davis was burdened with problems at this time, the incident did reveal that he preferred not to exceed his constitutional powers even when his nation was fighting for its very existence.[31] The President curtly wrote Cabell that he would not discuss troop movements and that he had no time for "discussing with you the question of the constitutional power of the Executive."[32] Thus began an antagonism between those favoring an invasion of Missouri and those who supported Davis; this antagonism was to grow with the passage of time.

IV

On July 2, 1861, McCulloch arrived at Maysville and continued on to Cowskin Prairie to meet with Price. When he reached Price's camp, the latter informed him that Jackson and Rains were trying to effect a junction of their forces north of Carthage, Missouri, and were being closely pursued by Lyon. To add to their difficulties, Sigel, who had been unsuccessful in capturing Price on his ride south, was advancing on Jackson from the south and threatened to cut him off from McCulloch and Price. Upon learning of Jackson's predicament, McCulloch, acting on his own initiative and anxious to aid the Missourians, decided to support Price and also persuaded Pearce to join the effort with his Arkansas troops.[33]

30. Cabell to Davis, July 6, 1861, *ibid.*, 605.
31. Historians vary in their evaluation of Jefferson Davis as President of the Confederacy. Rembert Patrick's *Jefferson Davis and His Cabinet*, and Hudson Strode's *Jefferson Davis: Confederate President*, are extremely sympathetic toward their subject. Less sympathetic, but far from critical, portraits emerge in Clement Eaton, *A History of the Southern Confederacy*, and E. Merton Coulter, *The Confederate States of America, 1861–1865*. Extremely critical views of Davis are presented in *Inside the Confederate Government*, Edward Younger, ed.; Bell Wiley, *The Road to Appomattox*; and Frank Vandiver, *Rebel Brass: The Confederate Command System*. Davis' political and military capabilities appear quite inadequate when contrasted with those of his counterpart Abraham Lincoln. The most sophisticated comparative studies are T. Harry Williams, *Americans at War: The Development of the American Military System*, 45–81; T. Harry Williams, "The Military Leadership of North and South," in *Why the North Won the Civil War*, David Donald, ed., 33–54; David Donald, "Refighting the Civil War," in *Lincoln Reconsidered: Essays in the Civil War Era*, David Donald, ed., 103–27; Allan Nevins, *The Statesmanship of the Civil War*; and David Potter, "Jefferson Davis and the Political Factors in the Confederate Defeat," in *Why the North Won the Civil War*, David Donald, ed., 91–112. The picture that emerges from Davis' relationship with Price, while reflecting no credit on the latter, elucidates and confirms the extremely critical views mentioned previously.
32. Davis to Cabell, July 8, 1861, *O. R.*, III, 605–6.
33. Ben. McCulloch to Hon. L. P. Walker, July 9, 1861, *ibid.*, 606–8.

On July 4 the combined force, each under its respective commander, moved north to aid Governor Jackson in his desperate attempt to avoid both Lyon and Sigel; leaving their infantry behind, they pressed on with their mounted troops. On July 5 their advance units captured some of Sigel's troops and also some badly needed arms, and on July 6 McCulloch, Price, and Pearce learned that the Missouri state troops under Jackson had defeated Sigel in a pitched battle north of Carthage. Later that same day the two Southern forces met, much to the relief of the hard-pressed men under Jackson.

After the juncture of forces McCulloch, Price, Pearce, and Jackson reviewed the Missouri troops. At the sight of McCulloch and his staff the Missourians broke into loud huzzas; one soldier recalled how they "were all young then and full of hope, and looked with delighted eyes on the first Confederate soldiers we had even seen, the men all dressed in sober gray, and their officer resplendent with gilded braid and stars of gold." Confident that the Confederate troops had come to help them regain their state, the Missourians were jubilant.[34]

McCulloch, on the other hand, was not impressed by the Missourians. Proud of his well-drilled and well-equipped force, he could only be amazed at the ragtag Missouri state forces. They had only a scattering of uniforms and officers could be distinguished from the ranks only by bits of red flannel or pieces of cotton cloth fastened to their shoulders or tied about their arms. Many Missourians had no arms and those who did carried common hunting rifles, shotguns, or even old flintlock weapons. None knew of a manual of arms or even suspected what military discipline entailed.

Since the Missouri state force was now temporarily safe, McCulloch and Pearce led their troops back to Arkansas and Price's troops returned to Cowskin Prairie where he began the task of whipping them into an army. McCulloch reported to the Confederate secretary of war that he had made his move into Missouri without authority and had fallen back to organize a force for future operations. He felt that Lyon should be attacked before he could build up a sufficient concentration of troops for a move into Arkansas or Indian Territory. McCulloch, still anxious to aid the Missouri cause, suggested that he and Pearce be authorized to co-operate with Price in an attack on the federal force at Springfield to prevent this from happening.[35] Such an action would necessitate the building up of an effective fighting force of Missourians—the task being undertaken by Price at Cowskin Prairie. Prior to their movement southward, recruits had reported to their respective brigade commanders, drifted into companies, and aggregated into regiments under the controlling influence of county

34. Snead, *Fight for Missouri*, 238.
35. McCulloch to L. P. Walker, July 9, 1861, *O. R.*, III, 606–8.

lines and local pride. They then selected their officers, most of whom were strangers to war. The vast majority of recruits, however, had to flee north Missouri so quickly that they were not even organized into regiments when they reached Cowskin Prairie. Organization thus became the first necessity, although Price was anxious to move ahead with the problem of arming and equipping the men. For the latter purpose he had only eight cannon, no shells, and only a few rounds of solid shot, grape and cannister. Price thus had to rely on such crude devices as trace-chains, iron rods, hard pebbles, and smooth stones for shot, and had to produce shell casings in an equally primitive manner. Nonetheless, before the end of July, 1861, Price considered his army ready to take the field. He estimated that he had an effective force of 5,000 men and an additional 2,000 unarmed men ready to make use of weapons that might be acquired from dead or wounded soldiers in battle.[36]

Thus, at the very outset of the Civil War, Price began to display what would become a salient characteristic: a nearly complete lack of an understanding of, or concern for, logistics. His fabulous success during the Mexican War, when he completely disregarded logistical restraints in wild dashes after the enemy, was to exert a determining influence upon him. His Mexican War experience also greatly inflated Price's view of his personal military prowess; throughout the Civil War, he would display a romantic attitude toward warfare.[37]

V

While Price attempted to create an effective fighting force, McCulloch remained unimpressed, hesitating to join with the Missouri troops in the field for fear they would prove undependable and through their complete lack of discipline destroy the morale of his own men. Finally, at Price's urging and with the belief that Pillow was advancing into Missouri at New Madrid, McCulloch consented to a joint attack on Lyon's troops, but he did this only after gaining assurances from Price that he would leave his unarmed men behind.[38] The three commands under Price, Pearce, and McCulloch were to rendezvous at Cassville, Missouri. By July 20 Price and McCulloch had reached that village and Pearce was within ten miles of them. Price's force of 7,000 Missourians still included the 2,000 unarmed

36. Price to Claiborne F. Jackson, August 12, 1861, *ibid.*, 98–102.

37. In an attempt to reach a greater understanding of Price my emphasis during the Civil War years will be upon Price the general as a projection of Price the man. More attention will therefore be devoted to those aspects of his military career that shed light upon his personality than to detailing campaigns and battles in which he participated. For an excellent narrative of these campaigns, see Albert Castel, *General Sterling Price.*

38. McCulloch to J. P. Benjamin, December 22, 1861, ibid., 743–49.

troops, but McCulloch's 3,000 soldiers were well-armed, as were the 2,500 commanded by Pearce. After McCulloch remonstrated again with Price about the presence of his unarmed men, Price agreed to leave them behind and to permit McCulloch to draw up the line of march.[39] McCulloch led the advance on July 31, with Price and Pearce moving out during the next two days.

By August 1 McCulloch was encamped at Crane Creek, halfway between Cassville and Springfield, and the following day he learned that Lyon was in the vicinity. Rains and his Missouri militia encountered an advance unit of Lyon's force and McCulloch sent Colonel James McIntosh to evaluate the situation. McIntosh and Rains decided that the Federals were not in force and McIntosh left Rains to keep watch on the Union troops. Because of Rains' lack of vigilance part of Lyon's force routed him at a skirmish at Dug Springs and, although not a serious setback, this defeat confirmed McCulloch's reservations regarding the Missouri troops. Convinced that the two armies were facing one another, Price pleaded with McCulloch to attack, but McCulloch did not wish to co-operate with the Missourians unless Price would be willing for him to have direct command of all the troops.

Price knew he must have the support of McCulloch and his men if he hoped to defeat Lyon, but disliked the idea of subordinating himself to another. On Sunday, August 4, he attempted to persuade McCulloch to change his mind. Finding this in vain, Price at last exclaimed that he was McCulloch's senior in years, rank, and experience and that he had been a brigadier general in the Mexican War with an independent command when McCulloch was only a captain. In a pompous tone Price continued that he had fought and won more battles than McCulloch had ever witnessed, that his force was nearly twice as large as the Texan's, and that they would be operating on Missouri soil.[40] He nevertheless found it necessary to yield to McCulloch's demands, since the professional soldier was not willing to endanger his own force by co-operating with the Missourians unless he was in command of the entire operation. Finally Price submitted, because he knew he could not rid Missouri of Lyon's force without the aid of McCulloch. Although the Texan finally agreed to attack Lyon, he was not pleased with Price's overbearing nature, which would gradually temper McCulloch's desire to aid the Missourian.

McCulloch's doubts about the Missouri troops soon received additional confirmation. Hoping to surprise the enemy, McCulloch advanced his army at midnight to be in position to attack at dawn. To his chagrin, faulty intelligence reports from the Missourians kept

39. *Ibid.*
40. Snead, *Fight for Missouri*, 256–57.

him from knowing that Lyon had already retreated to Springfield. He had marched his men all night and now faced an additional long, hot march with fatigued troops. In blistering weather the Southern forces set out after Lyon and finally encamped along Wilson's Creek in the Oak Hills southwest of Springfield on August 6.

VI

Wilson's Creek, rising near Springfield, flows southwestwardly some fifteen miles before emptying into the James River, a tributary of the White River. Tyrel's Creek flows into Wilson's Creek from the west about a mile above its mouth, and a mile and a half farther north Skegg's Branch also flows into Wilson's Creek from the west. The road from Cassville, on which McCulloch was advancing toward Springfield, crossed both Tyrel's Creek and Skegg's Branch just above their mouths. After crossing the latter the road ran north along the west bank of Wilson's Creek for nearly a mile, crossing the creek at a ford, and then turned northeast toward Springfield, nine miles beyond. Between Tyrel's Creek and Skegg's Branch was an expansive valley, partly wooded, lying between the Springfield Road and Wilson's Creek. It was in this valley that the Southern force encamped.

Price's Missourians bivouacked on Skegg's Meadow near the base of Oak Hill, which rose some five-hundred feet above Wilson's Creek. This hill was deeply seamed with ravines, pitted here and there with sinkholes, and covered with dense undergrowth interspersed with scrub oaks. Pearce's men camped farther south and Rains' brigade of Missourians was several miles north. With his army encamped, McCulloch daily reconnoitered, contemplating whether to attack Springfield but fearing to do so without exact information.

On August 8 Price received information that Lyon was preparing to abandon Springfield. He pressed McCulloch to attack and the Confederate commander promised he would consider the matter carefully and let Price know his decision that evening. Once again McCulloch rode out and returned late without communicating his purpose to Price. When Price awoke on August 9, he sent his adjutant Thomas Snead to McCulloch to ask about his plans. Just after Snead arrived at McCulloch's camp, Price, unable to control his impatience any longer, rode up and dismounted. Price insisted that McCulloch keep his promise made at Crane Creek and lead the army against Lyon.[41] McCulloch consented to meet with his generals in council at Price's headquarters. At this conference McCulloch expressed great unwillingness to attack, but Price declared emphatically that if orders were not issued forthwith for a forward movement he would resume command of the Missouri troops and lead them against Lyon.

41. *Ibid.*, 262.

Battle of Wilson's Creek
August 10, 1861

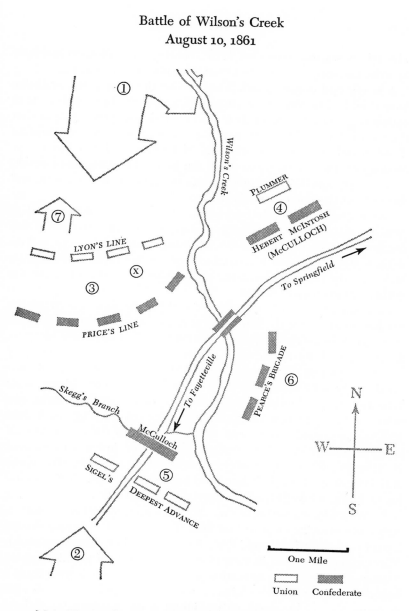

1. Main Union advance under Lyon at 5:30 A.M.
2. Secondary Union advance under Sigel begins when he hears Lyon's fire.
3. Price confronts main Union force about 6:30. Continuous contact until 10:30 when Lyon killed at x. Price reinforced between 10:00 and 11:00 by McCulloch from 5 and Pearce from 6.
4. Union left wing repulsed at 7:30. Confederate counterattack fails.
5. McCulloch, with part of Hebert's regiment, scatters Sigel by 10:00.
6. Pearce moves to join Price at 10:30.
7. Union forces withdraw, 11:00 A.M.

The others warmly seconded Price, causing McCulloch reluctantly to order the army to be ready to move by nine that night.[42]

A heavy rain began to fall. Since few of the troops had cartridge boxes and had to carry their ammunition loose in their pockets or in cotton bags strung around their necks, there was great danger that the vast majority of the men would be without effective ammunition if the march began; consequently, McCulloch ordered the troops to sleep on their arms throughout the night. Thinking there would be a march, most of the commanders brought in their pickets, and did not put them out again in the morning.

When Lyon returned to Springfield he found himself in a difficult position; it would be hard to retreat with the Southern troops massed nearby. Thus he decided to attack, doing so by sending Sigel with slightly over 1,000 men to march around the Southern army and attack from the south at the same time that he drove them in from the north with over 4,000 troops.

As a consequence of failing to put out pickets, Rains' men on the northernmost part of the Southern encampment were caught unaware by Lyon's advancing troops at the same time that Sigel and his men, managing to keep undercover, gained a position from which they could completely surprise several of McCulloch's brigades. At approximately 6:00 A.M. Price, McCulloch, and other officers were breakfasting at Price's headquarters when a breathless rider dismounted to report that Lyon was attacking from the north. At first McCulloch considered it only another of Rains' false alarms and thought nothing of it, but another rider arrived just at the moment that the thunder of Sigel's artillery broke out to the south. McCulloch and Price leaped on their horses to rally their troops. Price headed for Oak Hill while McCulloch sped down the valley.

Price could see swarms of men, some on foot and others mounted, streaming over the crest of Oak Hill. These were Rains' men fleeing from Lyon's surprise attack. Price immediately began to summon his Missourians encamped in a meadow near the base of the hill, hoping to stem the tide of the retreating men and at the same time form a battle line to repulse the Union attack. He galloped up the hill with as many men as he could gather, intent upon checking the federal advance until the rest of his troops could come up; his raw, undisciplined men wheeled into line with remarkable speed and calmness. In short order he had established a battle line and checked the panic-stricken troops who had been pushed in by Lyon's surprise attack. When the opposing lines formed they were not more than three hundred yards apart, but entirely concealed from one another by the dense undergrowth and heavy foliage. Since Price's men were armed

42. Account of the Battle of Wilson's Creek drawn from the reports in *O. R.*, III, 53–129.

almost exclusively with shotguns and common rifles it was imperative for him, near as the two forces already were to each other, either to advance closer to the Union line or wait for it to attack. Price chose the latter alternative.

He did not have to wait long for the Union commander's shouts of "forward!" and the accompanying crash of thousands of men breaking through the underbrush disrupted the silence of the morning. When the Northern force came within easy range Price's men fired volley after volley into them. Missourians were truly locked in civil war on the slopes of what was to become known as "Bloody Hill," for the majority of men on both sides were from Missouri. The battle raged for hours, with each side advancing and retreating after delivering and receiving a withering fire from within a few paces. While Price desperately attempted to stem Lyon's onslaught, McCulloch rushed to the east side of the creek and attempted to rally his forces there. Sigel's initial attack had been a success, and the Southerners had been driven from their camps in a complete rout; but, rather than follow up his advantage, Sigel allowed his men to wander leisurely through the abandoned camps picking up booty.

The fleeing Southerners, running into Pearce's troops, rallied and McCulloch gradually had a battle line drawn up to advance toward the unsuspecting federal troops. Shielded by thick woods and ravines, he was able to move toward Sigel unnoticed. When McCulloch had his artillery and troops in position they delivered a withering fire into Sigel's surprised soldiers, who became demoralized and fled from the field. Sigel's rout left this part of the field to McCulloch who quickly ordered part of his force to support Price, who was bearing the brunt of the Union attack.

By this time it was after nine in the morning and Price had been riding up and down his battle line rallying his men where they seemed to be faltering, and exhorting them to hold firm. Wherever it seemed a portion of his troops might break he appeared and bolstered them by personally urging them on, to the accompanying pleas from his soldiers that he take cover. He displayed a reckless courage that was to endear him to his men and that seemed to get the utmost out of volunteer troops. Several times bullets ripped his linen duster and finally he suffered a painful, but not serious, flesh wound in the side. Although Price escaped serious injury, many of his officers and men fell mortally wounded.

Lyon, becoming aware of Sigel's failure and that Price was receiving reinforcements from that part of the field, tried to rally his men for a final effort, but fell mortally wounded while leading the charge. His men, unaware of his death, fought on under the command of Major Samuel Sturgis. Sturgis soon realized that with Sigel routed, the Confederates massing in his front, and his troops dangerously low on ammunition, he must withdraw. The federal troops retired in good order, leaving the Southerners in possession of the battlefield.

The fighting had been intense. The Southern forces suffered 10 per cent casualties and the Northerners nearly 20 per cent. More important to the Southerners was their capture of large numbers of arms and several artillery pieces, but to the annoyance of McCulloch, most of the arms went to Price's unarmed soldiers who had appeared and picked up guns from the wounded to continue the fight.

Price urged McCulloch to pursue the retreating federal troops, but McCulloch knew that his ammunition was virtually exhausted and he still distrusted the Missouri troops. Although admiring them for their gallantry in battle, he decided that it was best to consolidate his victory rather than pursue the enemy. Price, who fought more from impulse than from thoughtful consideration of military propriety, continued to urge McCulloch to pursue Sturgis, insisting that the federal troops must be equally as low on ammunition as the Confederates and that they outnumbered Sturgis by nearly two to one. McCulloch remained adamant and the Southern forces remained at Oak Hills. Thus had the amateur and the professional again clashed in what was to become a bitter feud.

· 12 ·

Hero of Lexington

The day following the fighting at Wilson's Creek, Benjamin Mc-Culloch still stubbornly refused to pursue the Federals in their flight toward Rolla. Price moved his troops into Springfield and continued agitating for a movement into north Missouri. It became evident that the two generals held irreconcilable opinions and that a personal antagonism was developing between them.

A variety of motivations compelled McCulloch to withdraw into Arkansas. Perhaps the strongest was his mistrust of the Missourians, whom he blamed for the complete surprise at Wilson's Creek, and his growing dislike for their overbearing leader. He feared that his troops, if constantly exposed to the Missourians' lack of discipline, would become completely demoralized. McCulloch also faced an added problem since terms of enlistment for the Arkansas troops were expiring and they were preparing to disband.[1] Had these circumstances not been present, he still faced the restrictive orders from the high command. An invasion might upset the Davis Administration, which was committed to a defensive policy and remained cautious in its dealings with a state that had not yet seceded.

At the same time Price remained extremely anxious to recapture Missouri. He felt that the quicker he returned to the Missouri River the more recruits he could muster, and with Union forces scattered, this seemed an opportune time to invade the state. Price also worried about the movement within the state to establish a provisional government, depose Claiborne Jackson, elect a new assembly, and establish control of the state for the Union. Deepest of all, however, was Price's controlling desire to free Missouri from federal control, because his whole life was committed to the state. Seeing that Mc-Culloch would not relent, Price resumed command of his army on August 14 and made preparations to move north. He sent James Rains with a mounted force to clear the western counties of Missouri from marauding bands operating out of Kansas. On August 25 Price's army headed north.

The day before Price left, McCulloch, who desired Price to remain in Springfield and fortify the city, gave vent to his feelings toward

1. McCulloch to J. P. Benjamin, December 22, 1861, *O.R.*, III, 743–49.

Price in letters to General William Hardee and President Davis.[2] Reflecting the bitter antagonism he had developed toward Price, Mc-Culloch wrote Hardee that little could be expected of the people of Missouri since their force in the field was "undisciplined and led by men who are mere politicians; not a soldier among them to control and organize this mass of humanity." McCulloch felt that Price's troops were in no condition to meet an organized army and would not be if they remained under their current leadership. Repeating his old charge that he dared not join them for fear of demoralizing his own troops, McCulloch continued by lamenting the fact that Price's unarmed soldiers had taken weapons from his wounded and that Price had not returned the muskets loaned to him by the Arkansas commander. In addition, Price's men had stolen tents and other equipment McCulloch's men put aside to facilitate marching and fighting: "In a word, they are not making friends where they go, and from all I can see we had as well be in Boston as far as the friendly feelings of the inhabitants are concerned."[3] McCulloch's letter to Davis, although dealing more with problems of supply, did state that little could be expected of Missouri since the state "had no military leader or arms."[4]

II

Shortly after Price and his army left Springfield, Rains reported that he had met the enemy in such force that he could not deal with them. Therefore, Price decided to march toward Fort Scott, Kansas, to attack the "Jayhawkers" and "abolitionists" under James Lane.[5] On September 2 Price's advance troopers ran into a Union force at Dry Wood Creek, Missouri. Following a sharp encounter the federal troops withdrew, with slight casualties on both sides. The Union troops did not retreat to Fort Scott, but rather withdrew toward northern Missouri. Price, not wishing to enter Kansas unless he had to, was thereby relieved of that task. He was determined to remain in Missouri unless border ruffians renewed depredations in Missouri, in which case he intended to enter Kansas and lay waste to it.[6]

As Price moved northward he gathered a great number of recruits; whole companies who had been able to elude the Union forces in north Missouri came into his camp. On September 10 Price learned that a detachment of federal troops and home guards was marching from Lexington to Warrensburg to bring in money from a bank

2. *Ibid.*
3. McCulloch to Hardee, August 24, 1861, *ibid.*, 672.
4. McCulloch to Davis, August 24, 1861, *ibid.*, 671.
5. J. T. Hughes to Col. R. H. Miller, September 4, 1861, M. M. Parson Papers.
6. Price to C. F. Jackson, September 4, 1861, *O. R.*, LIII, 435–36.

there.[7] Although his men were greatly fatigued from several days' continuous marching, Price was determined to press forward and to surprise the enemy at Warrensburg. After allowing his men to rest for several hours, Price resumed his advance at sunset and marched until 2:00 A.M. Realizing his infantry had not eaten for nearly twenty-four hours and could march no farther, he ordered them into camp and proceeded with his mounted men. They reached Warrensburg at daybreak and saw that the enemy had fled that city. Price called a halt to await his foot soldiers.

A violent rainstorm delayed the army's march on September 12 until mid-morning. At that time, having been joined by the infantry and artillery, it pushed forward rapidly, thereby hoping to overtake the enemy. Finding this impossible if accompanied by his infantry, Price again went ahead with a detachment of cavalry until he was within several miles of Lexington, where he learned that the enemy had already reached the haven of the town. With his men utterly exhausted by their rapid marches, Price halted for the night. Early the next morning a sharp skirmish, which threatened to become general, broke out between Price's pickets and the enemy's outposts. Unwilling to bring on a doubtful engagement when he could delay and be certain of success, Price withdrew his forces several miles to await the arrival of his infantry and artillery. When these troops arrived Price advanced toward the town, easily driving in the enemy's pickets. On the outskirts of Lexington the enemy attempted to take a stand, but were driven into positions around the Masonic College on the northern edge of the city. By sunset Price's weary and hungry troops were nearly out of ammunition, forcing him to withdraw and await the arrival of his supply train.

While Price's troops surrounded the town and were awaiting their supplies, Colonel James A. Mulligan prepared his troops to defend themselves.[8] The Union forces were in an advantageous defensive position, for the Masonic College was located on a broad, open meadow several hundred feet above the Missouri River. Throughout a drenching rain on Friday the thirteenth most of Mulligan's men struggled to throw up entrenchments around the building, while some worked in the basement of the college casting and preparing 150 rounds of grape and cannister for each of their seven pieces of artillery and their two brass mortars.

The much-needed material arrived after a four-day wait and early

7. Account of campaign against Lexington drawn primarily from Price's report, *O. R.*, III, 185–88.
8. An excellent account of the Union situation is in Colonel James A. Mulligan's "The Siege of Lexington, Mo.," in *Battles and Leaders of the Civil War*, I, Robert Underwood Johnson and Clarence Clough Buel, eds., 307–13.

on the morning of September 18 Price's forces again moved forward through the city. After reconnoitering the Union fortifications, Price deployed his troops, completely encircling the Union position and placing his six batteries at strategic locations. Shortly thereafter a tremendous fire commenced from both sides. Early in the action Price's men successfully stormed the Anderson House, which overlooked the Missouri River. From the upper floors of the house their sharpshooters poured a deadly fire into the Union trenches. Seeing this danger, Mulligan sent a part of his Irish Brigade to retake the position, which they did, but Price massed an assault and recaptured the strategic position after stiff fighting.

On the morning of the nineteenth Price intercepted a messenger from Major General Samuel Sturgis informing Mulligan that he was on his way with over 1,000 men. Price promptly dispatched Brigadier General M. M. Parsons with over 3,000 men to repel this advance. When Sturgis learned of Mulligan's situation he returned to Leavenworth, leaving Mulligan to face a force outnumbering him nearly six to one. Mulligan's men were also low on food and water and whenever one of them dashed outside his lines toward a well one of Price's sharpshooters would pick him off.

As the day wore on it became obvious to Price that something more should be done. He could easily starve Mulligan into capitulation, but only at the risk of giving the federal forces in the state time to mass against him. At the same time it would mean a terrific loss of life to attempt to storm the Union position. While he greatly outnumbered Mulligan, the latter was in a strong position and Price's men would have to cross a wide expanse of open ground to reach the Union trenches.

Early on the morning of the twentieth Price employed a new tactic. His troops had captured several boats tied at the wharf and also a large number of hemp bales ready for shipment. Price ordered his men to bring these bales up the bluff to positions on either side of the Anderson House, to soak the bales with water, and then to station three men behind each one. Once in position, these bales constituted moveable breastworks behind which Price's men could advance without being harmed. The Union gunners fired roundshot and bullets into the advancing line with little effect, except to rock an occasional bale. The exasperated federal gunners then fired heated shot into the bales, but to no avail. When Price's troops advanced to within one hundred yards of the Union position, a white flag appeared above the Union trenches. Mulligan and his men, after resisting gallantly for three days without food and water, greatly outnumbered and running low on ammunition, accepted Price's terms of unconditional surrender.

Price and his staff entered the Union position where Price refused

Mulligan's sword. However, Price could make excellent use of the over 3,000 stand of arms, the artillery, and the mass of ordnance he had captured. In addition he obtained over $900,000 in gold and paper that had been gathered up to prevent it from falling into his hands. Price returned this money to the proper banks.

III

Following Mulligan's surrender, Price continued his effort to improve the organization of his army while Governor Jackson, who had joined Price at Warrensburg prior to the siege of Lexington, issued a call for the Missouri General Assembly to convene in Neosho on October 21. On the same day he issued this proclamation, Jackson appointed E. C. Cabell and Thomas Snead as commissioners to negotiate an offensive-defensive treaty with the Confederacy and ratified in advance any action they might take in accordance with their instructions. Snead, leaving at once, went by way of McCulloch's camp in Arkansas to ask him to either join Price or send him much-needed percussion caps; McCulloch would do neither.

Price remained in Lexington for ten days following Mulligan's surrender. During this time a great number of recruits came in. Price's force, now well in excess of 18,000, was composed largely of raw and undisciplined men, eager, but in great need of training. Few of Price's captains could even drill their companies. Indeed, one colonel recalled watching the only well-trained company in the army—it having been one of the regular city companies in St. Louis prior to the war—going through its maneuvers. The colonel became fascinated with the way the troops could, with two steps, go from "front face" in two lines, to marching four abreast at the command of "right face." He had the drill captain repeat this maneuver until he got it into his head and then rushed off to attempt it with his own regiment, having with infinite trouble also obtained a copy of "Gilham's Manual."[9] Regardless of the rawness of his troops, Price had managed to overcome Lyon's initial advantage by quickly capturing control of the Missouri River. If he could remain at Lexington for any length of time he could recruit a great number of men. While Union forces still made it difficult to cross the river, many men came over in flatboats and one company even captured a steamboat.

Price could have sorely used McCulloch and his regulars to help instill discipline in his own army, which was really little more than a mob, coming and going as it pleased. Without weapons to give his unarmed recruits, Price had difficulty retaining them. The war was too young and the personal consequences too remote for these men to organize, drill, and discipline themselves preparatory to receiving

9. R. S. Bevier, *History of the First and Second Missouri Confederate Brigades*, 307.

arms at a future time. When Price found himself forced to move south upon learning that General John C. Frémont, commanding Union forces in Missouri, was massing more than 40,000 men to attack him, he had to send many of his recruits away with a promise to return to Missouri at a later date. Nevertheless, Price withdrew from Lexington with nearly 50 per cent more troops than when he left Springfield.

As Price began his withdrawal, word of his capture of Lexington spread, making him a public hero throughout the South. His name began to appear in Southern newspapers, which printed laudatory biographical sketches of him to enlighten their readers regarding this new Confederate hero.[10] The *Daily Richmond Whig* rated the "Brilliant Success in Missouri," second only to Manassas, as the greatest victory of the war. The same article commented on the unfortunate discord between Price and McCulloch and hoped that the latter would still advance to aid the Missourian. Already beginning to attack the Davis Administration's policies, the *Whig* editor used Price's success to prove a point. Referring to Price as one of the "coming men" and the "Man for the Times," the editor claimed that Price was the only one of the South's generals who appreciated the character of his volunteer troops and knew how to make the best use of them. Using Price's success to attack Davis' defensive policy, he claimed that by going on the offensive Price "set an example worthy of universal imitation."[11]

Cabell wrote Price from Richmond congratulating him on his accomplishments and expressing certainty that Davis would appoint him a major general in the Confederate army as soon as the Missouri troops were transferred to Confederate service.[12] Writing in October, Cabell had no way to know what a storm would arise over the appointment of a major general to command troops in the West.

IV

Aware that Frémont could soon surround and overpower him if he remained unsupported in north Missouri, Price began to withdraw in slow easy marches; this enabled him to escape with his wagon train of captured supplies, although he lost many men who did not want to leave north Missouri. His object was to get close enough to McCulloch to enable the two forces to effect a juncture and turn on Frémont. As he neared Springfield, Price realized that Frémont had

10. *Natchez* (Miss.) *Daily Courier*, September 18, 1861; *Daily Richmond* (Va.) *Whig*, October 3, 1861; *Memphis Avalanche*, reprinted in *Daily Richmond Whig*, October 12, 1861; *Richmond Daily* (Va.) *Examiner*, October 11, 1861.
11. *Daily Richmond Whig*, September 30, October 9, 1861.
12. Cabell to Price, October 18, 1861, *O. R.*, LIII, 749–50.

concentrated the bulk of Union forces in the state to pursue him, thus leaving St. Louis comparatively unguarded. Although impulsive in battle and a poor tactician, for he eschewed reading the tactical manuals of the day, Price had a fine grasp of strategy. On October 16 he informed General Albert S. Johnston, commander of the western department, that Frémont, by drawing a large number of troops out of St. Louis to pursue him, left "that city almost defenseless, . . . which may have an important bearing on your operations."[13]

At the same time, Price began to correspond with McCulloch, who suggested that he continue to withdraw, destroying forage as he went, and thus draw Frémont farther from his base of supplies. McCulloch suggested that if Frémont did not proceed beyond Springfield they might advance into Kansas and lay waste to the state.[14] Holding genteel concepts of warfare, Price refused to destroy subsistence needed by local inhabitants. In regard to McCulloch's suggestion of an advance into Kansas, Price shrewdly noted that it would be far wiser to first drive north into Missouri and cut the Hannibal and St. Joseph Railroad line. This would prevent Union reinforcements from reaching Kansas and thereby allow Price and McCulloch to move into that state without danger of being attacked from the rear. Price further maintained that a move back to the Missouri River in force would bring out vast numbers of recruits, thus enabling the Confederacy to secure Missouri and thereby establish Southern independence in the Mississippi Valley.[15] Here Price exhibited the interrelationship between his realization of the strategic importance of Missouri to the Confederacy and his personal desire to keep control of the state. The ideas were in perfect accord, with each influencing the other.[16]

13. Price to Johnston, October 16, 1861, *O. R.*, III, 719–20.
14. McCulloch to Price, October 12, 1861, *ibid.*, 721.
15. Price to McCulloch, October 23, 1861, *ibid.*, 722.
16. While Price remained intensely committed to regaining Missouri for personal reasons, this study stresses that the strategy involved remained sound. Albert Castel disagrees and thus forms a different opinion of Price's abilities as a strategist. While fully recognizing the initial strategic value of Missouri, Castel contends that once the state fell to federal troops, it was impractical to attempt to regain it. Castel feels that Missourians did not support the Confederacy and would not enlist in the Confederate cause (pages 27, 284). Picturing Price as unable, or unwilling, to recognize this, Castel therefore approves of Davis' decision to drain troops away from Missouri to fight east of the Mississippi River (page 83). *General Sterling Price and the Civil War in the West.*

Ascertaining whether Missourians would or would not support the Confederacy will always involve tenuous judgments, but the simple fact is that they never had the opportunity. The rapid Union sweep up the Missouri in 1861 effectually shut off Missouri's Confederate supporters for the duration of the war. Jefferson Davis' conscious decision to subordinate the West to the East led him to withdraw the Army of the West in a futile effort

Late in October the remnants of the Missouri General Assembly met at Neosho and then Cassville under the protection of Price's army. They passed an ordinance of secession and appointed delegates to the Confederate Congress, and Jackson sent the ordinance to Richmond with the recommendation that Price be appointed major general to command Confederate troops in Missouri and Arkansas.[17] By the end of November, Missouri had been accepted into the Confederacy and state troops could be transferred to Confederate service.

During this period Price retreated deeper into the southwestern part of the state, closely pursued by Frémont. While on the march he received a letter from General Albert Johnston congratulating him for his "brilliant success at Lexington" and expressing his high admiration for the "very skillful manner in which you have conducted your operations since."[18] As much as Price enjoyed such praise from the high command, he could not help but be chagrined by Johnston's unwillingness to co-operate in a movement against St. Louis. Johnston did, however, send Price some artillery.

Still unwilling to abandon an attack on St. Louis, Price urged Johnston to move on that city. Johnston's threat to the city would cause Frémont to withdraw to defend St. Louis and in turn free McCulloch

---

to concentrate forces in Mississippi. (It is for just such strategic moves that historians have been most critical of Davis.) Thus, in the crucial first years of the war, Missouri was written off to the Union. Even in the absence of Confederate troops, vast numbers of Missourians resisted and kept the state in turmoil throughout the war. See William E. Parrish, *Turbulent Partnership: Missouri and the Union, 1861–1865*; Richard Brownlee, *Gray Ghosts of the Confederacy: Guerilla Warfare in the West, 1861–1865*; and W. Wayne Smith, "An Experiment in Counterinsurgency: The Assessment of Confederate Sympathizers in Missouri," *Journal of Southern History*, 25: 3 (August, 1969), 361–80.

While it involves dealing with the counterfactual, a case can be made for Price's judgment that Missouri was lost because Confederate troops were not made available. A strong force (the Army of the West) was in Arkansas but was drawn away to the East. It is impossible to conjecture as to what would have happened to this army had it remained near Missouri, but it can be stated with certainty that once this force went to Mississippi, Missouri was lost. It should come as no surprise that Missourians did not leave their homes and travel hundreds of miles to join a regular Confederate force that showed no inclination to fight in Missouri.

While Castel, like Jefferson Davis, fails to see the continuing strategic value of Missouri, the same cannot be said of Abraham Lincoln and his commanders. The evidence is overwhelming that these men considered Missouri of the utmost strategic value throughout the war. (See Chap. 13, note 29, and Chap. 15, note 64, for examples of their thought on this question.) Given the Union commitment to the state and the willingness of Lincoln's commanders to draw troops away from other areas to protect it, Price's desire to return to Missouri appears to be good strategic thinking.

17. Jackson to Jefferson Davis, October 12, 1861, *O. R.*, III, 717–18.
18. Johnston to Price, October 31, 1861, *ibid.*, 729.

and Price to follow him; Frémont would thus be trapped between Johnston and Price.[19] About the same time that Price wrote this letter, David Hunter replaced Frémont and was cautioned by Lincoln against overextending himself in a futile chase after Price.[20] While Hunter planned his course of action, McCulloch advised Price to fall back into Arkansas and to burn mills, grain, and forage in his path.[21] Price asked several times for an interview with McCulloch to coordinate plans, since Price neither wanted to retreat into Arkansas nor to destroy subsistence. In an imperious tone he wrote to McCulloch that if "upon more mature reflection you should determine to aid me . . . we will adopt such line of action as will compel the enemy to attack us in a short time."[22] McCulloch replied that he felt it best for Price to continue to retreat, since even a defeat of the Federals would only cause them to withdraw to Springfield without serious losses. Even though busily preparing for an attack, McCulloch, by this time thoroughly exasperated with the pompous Missourian, agreed to meet him on the Bentonville Road ten miles from Price's camp at Pineville.[23] The relationship between the two men had degenerated to such an extent that the refusal of each to go to the other's headquarters forced them to meet halfway between.

Prior to this meeting Hunter divided his force and withdrew to Sedalia with 15,000 men, while Franz Sigel pulled back toward Rolla with 12,000, and James Lane with 4,000 men moved westward. At their meeting Price urged McCulloch to accompany him in pursuit of Lane and then on a drive northward into Missouri. McCulloch adamantly refused to do so, claiming that their force was inadequate to achieve any important objectives, and also too large for joint action because of the scarcity of forage in the country through which they would have to pass. He felt that they could never maintain a position on the Missouri River for any length of time because of its distance from their line of supplies.[24] Once again Price, oblivious to logistics, chose to invade Missouri without McCulloch's assistance.

V

Prior to advancing northward, Price informed President Davis of the situation in Missouri and asked for his aid. His communication displayed bitterness at the policy the Union element in Missouri had pursued prior to the outbreak of hostilities. He spoke of the "venal

19. Price to Johnston, November 7, 1861, *ibid.*, 731–32.
20. Abraham Lincoln to David Hunter, November 8, 1861, quoted in Allan Nevins, *Frémont: The West's Greatest Adventurer*, 617.
21. McCulloch to Price, November 10, 1861, *O. R.*, III, 736–37.
22. Price to McCulloch, November 10, 1861, *ibid.*, 737.
23. McCulloch to Price, November 11, 1861, *ibid.*, 738.
24. McCulloch to J. P. Benjamin, December 22, 1861, *ibid.*, 743–49.

and treacherous" public press that had deluded and misled the people of Missouri into believing there was a strong possibility of compromise. Expressing the belief that the people had also been betrayed and deceived by the agents and officers of the federal government, Price's statements revealed as much his own sense of betrayal as of the public at large. He then mentioned the hardships his army had endured and how loyal the people of the state were to the Confederacy. After noting that he had advised Johnston to attack St. Louis, he requested a force of Confederate troops large enough to cut its way to the Missouri River. Price pledged Missouri's ability to defend the northern and western lines of its territory if this force could remain on the river for just two months. Claiming that he had been compelled to leave nearly 10,000 men on or near the river for want of time to join him, he declared that as soon as he could be placed in a position to make this strength available he could have 50,000 to 100,000 men in his command. In a patronizing manner Price closed by stating: "Allow me, therefore, as one who, at the age of fifty-one years, has placed home and comfort and property and family and life on the altar of my country's safety and well-being, to ask aid to move back to the river."[25]

Davis' answer was a disappointment. Stating, perhaps a bit peevishly, that Price need not have written him of "the difficulties and embarassments" under which he had struggled, Davis claimed to be aware of these and sympathetic toward Price. Davis said that he looked forward to the time when he could extend aid to Price, but this could come only after Missouri troops had been tendered to the Confederacy to be organized into brigades and divisions.[26]

Without aid Price moved north once again. At the same time McCulloch informed Adjutant General Samuel Cooper that Price's action could only end in disaster and that he was putting his troops into winter quarters in Arkansas.[27] Price's advance threw the Union forces in Missouri into complete confusion. Rather than advancing in one force, he split his troops into many groups to ease the problem of obtaining forage, and sent detachments ahead to recruit. Consequently, whenever a Union commander encountered one of these detachments or received a report of one, he believed Price to be in the vicinity. If Union reports were to be believed, Price had 30,000 to 50,000 men with him, whereas, in reality, he had barely 12,000.[28]

25. Price to Davis, November 10, 1861, *ibid.*, 735–36. Price's revelation of his sense of betrayal (which he had no reason to fabricate at this time) lends credence to the judgment that he was sincere in his dealings with General William Harney in the summer of 1861. See Chap. 11, note 6.

26. Davis to Price, December 20, 1861, Confederate Museum, Richmond, Virginia.

27. McCulloch to Cooper, November 19, 1861, *O. R.*, III, 742–43.

28. For confused and conflicting Union reports, see *ibid.*, 395–400.

When he reached Marshall, Missouri, Price issued a bombastic proclamation calling for 50,000 volunteers and stating that if this number had turned out at Jackson's original request there "would not now be a Federal hireling in the State to pollute our soil." He spoke of the hardships his men had suffered, wondered where their fellow citizens were while this was happening, and asked: "Are we a generation of driveling, sniveling, degraded slaves?"[29]

While H. W. Halleck, Union commander of the newly created Department of Missouri, reported that his department was in complete chaos, Price went into winter camp near Osceola on the Osage River and sent recruiting parties into north Missouri—adding to the confusion of the Union officers.[30] At the same time, Price's presence in the area prompted insurrections in the pro-Southern counties north of the Missouri River. Halleck made the incredible report that "no doubt the enemy was moving north with a large force." He also warned that rebels were organizing in many counties and committing depredations on Union sympathizers.[31] While the latter was certainly true, Price's army itself was melting away. To enable him to sustain himself at Osceola, Price furloughed a great number of men and many others drifted away to their homes to await the spring campaigns.

Even while suffering in the December cold, Price felt that conditions north of the Missouri River necessitated advancing once again to the river. Predatory bands from Kansas were committing outrages in the western river counties and at the same time effectually closing the roads to recruits that might join Price. Price again asked McCulloch for aid and informed him that he was transferring state troops to Confederate service as rapidly as possible.[32] He also wrote Davis, pleading for Confederate forces to be sent to him and saying that under the circumstances all he could do was to occupy the most threatening position possible, thereby hoping to hold in check the greatest possible number of the enemy to prevent their use elsewhere. He claimed that the only obstacle in the way of complete success was the want of co-operation by Confederate forces.[33] By this time such a plea was futile, since Davis was embroiled in a furious debate with those calling for Price's appointment as a major general, to which Davis was bitterly opposed.

Price's request to McCulloch also went unheeded since McCul-

29. *Missouri Army Argus*, Extra, November 23, 1861, Dr. James A. Gaines Papers.

30. Halleck to Maj. Gen. George B. McClellan, November 27, 1861, *O. R.*, VIII, 382.

31. Halleck to Maj. Gen. George B. McClellan, November 29, 1861, *ibid.*, 395.

32. Price to McCulloch, December 6, 1861, *ibid.*, 702–3.

33. Sterling Price to Davis, December 16, 1861, *ibid.*, 714–15.

loch had gone to Richmond to defend himself against charges of not aiding Price when he should have; he left Colonel James Mc-Intosh in charge in Arkansas. Upon receiving Price's call for aid, McIntosh, disdainful of all operations west of the Mississippi River,[34] wrote Adjutant General Cooper that "such a project at this season of the year is almost madness."[35] Rather than dispatching troops to Price's assistance, McIntosh sent several regiments to aid in putting down a minor uprising of the Cherokees in Indian Territory.

When Leonidas Polk, commanding Confederate troops in Tennessee, sent a message to acquaint himself with affairs in Missouri, Price wrote him a letter revealing his bitterness toward McCulloch. He felt that two obstacles stood in the way of a successful prosecution of the war in Missouri and that both were attributable to McCulloch. The first, federal control of the state which prevented recruits from joining Price, could have been ended with McCulloch's aid. McCulloch's constant refusal to co-operate led to the second obstacle—a feeling of futility among Missourians who felt deserted and doubted whether the Confederate government sympathized with them and ever intended to extend aid. Had McCulloch co-operated with him they could have destroyed the railroads, driven the Federals into St. Louis, and consequently created a diversion in favor of the Confederates in Kentucky. Price's troops, aware of this, developed "the greatest dissatisfaction with and distrust of the Confederate Government." Price declared that this "feeling grows daily, and will do us incalculable harm if not speedily quieted" and that Polk and he could still make the winter campaign a success by co-operating in a movement against St. Louis. Price felt that regardless of whether they succeeded in gaining their main object—St. Louis—the people of Missouri would see that the Confederate government desired to help them and that Missourians would be free to join Price's army when the Federals withdrew into St. Louis.[36]

At the same time, Davis and his Administration remained blind to the advantage of having a large Confederate force in Missouri, even though military commanders on both sides recognized the potentialities of such a move. General Pillow, attempting to hold Columbus, Kentucky, a key point in the Confederate first line of defense, felt that the threat posed by Price in Missouri had caused the Union commanders to recall forces sent to Kentucky to build up strength for an attack.[37] Even the meager force Price had in Missouri in the winter of 1861 forced the Union commanders to maintain troops in

34. McIntosh to Cooper, December 15, 1861, *ibid.*, 713–14.
35. McIntosh to Cooper, December 14, 1861, *ibid.*, 712–13.
36. Price to Polk, December 23, 1861, *ibid.*, 729–31.
37. Pillow to Governor [Isham] Harris, November 25, 1861, *O. R.*, LII, Pt. 2, 221.

the state. General Halleck had received a suggestion from Lincoln that he act in concert with commanders east of the Mississippi against Pillow and Polk, but wrote that he could not withdraw troops from Missouri because of Price and the insurrectionary nature of the state, due in large measure to Price's presence.[38] Even such an obvious object lesson as this went unheeded in the fury of a controversy that had arisen involving Price.

VI

The Price-McCulloch feud assumed larger proportions following McCulloch's refusal to move north with Price in November, 1861; it soon even spread to Richmond where it involved many persons in the command system. Prior to Price's move north, McCulloch wrote Judah P. Benjamin, then acting secretary of war, complaining that the Missouri troops were completely without discipline and should be taken into the Confederate service to be reorganized during the winter. The force was, in McCulloch's mind, "under the control of politicians, who know not the value of discipline, and consequently can never make an army that would be better than a city mob." Mc-Culloch felt that there was excellent potential with which to make an army and advised that a general who had not been involved in the previous quarrels be sent west, and recommended Braxton Bragg. McCulloch excluded himself because he had made enemies of the Missourians by his continual reprimands regarding their lack of discipline.[39]

In response to the adverse publicity he was receiving for his failure to aid Price, McCulloch requested permission to go to Richmond to defend himself.[40] This became more imperative for him upon receipt of a telegram from Benjamin expressing concern as to why McCulloch had not supported Price and closing curtly with: "Send an explanation."[41] McCulloch penned a long letter attempting to explain why he had acted as he did and expressing indignation at charges that he had not aided the Missourians.[42] It galled McCulloch to find himself the goat after Price's brash, yet spectacular, success.

When the controversy finally reached official channels, McCulloch received the worst of it. Cooper, commenting on a letter from McIntosh explaining why he had not moved to aid Price, declared that this force should not have gone into winter quarters, but rather to "where it would render good service to the cause."[43] By January, 1862, the

38. Halleck to Lincoln, January 6, 1862, *O. R.*, VII, 532–33.
39. McCulloch to Benjamin, November 8, 1861, *O. R.*, III, 733–34.
40. McCulloch to Benjamin, November 19, 1861, *O. R.*, VIII, 686.
41. Benjamin to McCulloch, November 30, 1861, *O. R.*, III, 699.
42. McCulloch to Benjamin, December 22, 1861, *ibid.*, 743–49.
43. McIntosh to Cooper, December 7, 1861, *ibid.*

issue had entered Congress. On January 3, 1862, the secretary of the Confederate Congress sent a resolution to Davis requesting him to transmit all information, including correspondence within his control or possession, in regard to the reason troops under McCulloch had not and were not co-operating with Price. The resolution also asked if any immediate steps were being taken or contemplated by the War Department to reinforce or sustain Price in his advance on the enemy.[44] Major General Leonidas Polk, having investigated the feud, reached the conclusion that McCulloch was at fault and that his force should be controlled by someone "who would co-operate freely and vigorously with General Price, and that this should be done as early as practicable." Polk stated that as long as Halleck's troops were kept occupied by Price in Missouri they could not co-operate with Union forces east of the Mississippi against Johnston or himself. Polk closed with the recommendation that the Confederate high command send all available resources at their command to aid Price.[45]

VII

These words of advice to Davis did not cause him to lessen concentration on the eastern theater of action or to heed those who felt that the security of the Confederacy could best be served by taking advantage of the flanking position Missouri occupied. Davis, bothered by the feud between Price and McCulloch, had decided to take measures to end it. Late in November he sent for Colonel Henry Heth, a West Point graduate, and informed him that since "Price and McCulloch are fighting each other over there harder than they are fighting the enemy," he would put him in command of the Trans-Mississippi District of the Western Department.[46]

While en route to Richmond, the Missouri congressional delegation heard a rumor that Davis intended to appoint someone other than Price to command the Trans-Mississippi District and, upon reaching Richmond, they went to speak with him about this.[47] Davis informed the delegation that from conversations and correspondence with informed people he was convinced that the public interest required that a general be sent to Arkansas and Missouri who had not been previously connected with any troops there. He further informed them that he had chosen Heth to bring the two commanders into harmony.

44. J. J. Hooper to Davis, January 3, 1862, *O. R.*, LIII, 765.
45. Polk to Davis, January 3, 1862, *ibid.*, 728–29.
46. "Memoirs of Major General Henry Heth, C.S.A.," typescript in the Heth-Selden Manuscripts, 133.
47. Account of this meeting drawn from Congressional Delegation to Price, December 13, 1861, *O. R.*, LIII, 761–63.

Upon hearing this the Missourians warned Davis that such a step would paralyze Missouri and expose the whole Mississippi Valley to the enemy. Then, in stronger language, the delegation urged that the services performed by the Missouri troops deserved some recognition and that utter ruin to this army would result if Price should be replaced.[48]

Davis remained firm in his opposition to these views. While granting that Price had performed well, and expressing the kindest feelings for him, Davis was determined not to appoint any man as a major general to command the Trans-Mississippi who was a resident of Missouri, Arkansas, or Texas, and alluded to the difficulties between Price and McCulloch as the principal reason for his decision. Davis then intimated that the "guerilla" fighting in Missouri must give way to a regular systematized style of warfare. With this the conference ended.

Davis' reference to "guerilla" warfare in Missouri reflected his desire to employ West Point-trained commanders. The President again referred to "irregular warfare" in Missouri in response to a letter from an Arkansas congressman who had derisively referred to Heth as a "West Point Cadet." Davis declared that federal forces in Missouri were no longer to be commanded by "pathfinders and holiday soldiers, but by men of military education and experience in war." The contest there was going to be on a scale of very different proportions than "that of the partisan warfare witnessed during the past summer and fall." By thus deprecating Price's success, he indicated that he had no use for such a person as Price, but preferred using West Point men. In his letter Davis adhered to the position that he maintained throughout the dispute: He had no constitutional power to appoint Price a major general because he had not received muster rolls showing that Missouri troops had been incorporated into Confederate service; therefore, he could not appoint a man as major general before he had troops to command.[49]

When word of Davis' decision was made public it met with considerable indignation within the Confederacy. Price had won the hearts of many people by his brash actions and they were determined that he should not be outranked by a new man simply because of his military training. When the Confederate Congress heard the first rumors of Davis' decision, it unanimously passed a resolution tendering thanks to Price. Commenting on this action, the *Daily Richmond Whig* wrote that Price was "the soul of the cause in Missouri"

48. According to Thomas C. Reynolds, the Missouri delegation was overbearing in its conference with Davis. Reynolds, "General Sterling Price and the Confederacy," 34.

49. Davis to W. P. Hariss, December 3, 1861, *O. R.*, VIII, 701.

and that "considering his means, he has accomplished more than any one man since the war began, and deserves hearty thanks and liberal encouragement from Government and people."[50]

Newspapers throughout the South ran editorials deprecating Davis' decision.[51] The *Memphis Appeal* even stated that it could not believe the Davis Administration "guilty of such reckless imbecility as this change would indicate."[52] While all the papers lauded Price and deplored Davis' action, some also used the affair to attack Administration policies. The *New Orleans Delta* felt that Price should have been supported in his move into Missouri to prevent Union troops from the Northwest being used in an invasion of the Confederacy elsewhere. The *Delta's* editor closed with the biting comment that "there are a great many people who think Price's strategy is preferable to the defensive and entrenching strategy of some of our leaders."[53] This reflected a growing disenchantment among Southerners with Davis' penchant for West Pointers and defensive tactics.[54] Even the *Daily Richmond Enquirer*, an Administration paper, hoped that nothing would be done to "obstruct" or "hinder" Price's energies.[55]

Aroused by the public outburst against his judgment, Davis sent a telegram to Memphis stating that the rumor that Price was to be superseded was false, "if not malignant," and that he had "not received a tender of Missouri troops, and consequently have no power to make appointments for them, or to control their organization."[56] To this the *Daily Richmond Whig* pointedly commented that it could not understand why, "if there are no troops in Missouri, and Price cannot therefore be appointed a Major-General, anybody else can."[57] Heth, realizing the unpopularity he would suffer in the West and fearing that Congress would not ratify his appointment, informed

50. *Daily Richmond Whig*, December 6, 1861.

51. *Memphis Appeal, Nashville Banner, Nashville American and Union*, reprinted in *Daily Richmond Whig*, December 11, 1861; *Montgomery Advertiser*, December 5, 1861, reprinted in *Daily Richmond Whig*, December 12, 1861; New Orleans *Daily Picayune*, December 10, 1861; *Memphis Argus*, December 5, 1861, reprinted in the Little Rock *Arkansas State Gazette*, December 14, 1861.

52. Reprinted in *Daily Richmond Whig*, December 11, 1861.

53. *New Orleans Delta*, reprinted in *Daily Richmond Whig*, December 11, 1861.

54. For an excellent running commentary of the irritation with Davis' bias in favor of West Pointers, see the *Richmond Daily Examiner*, March 13 and 26, and May 29, 30, and 31, 1862.

55. *Daily Richmond Enquirer*, December 4, 1861.

56. Davis to Major W. A. Broadwell, December 9, 1861, printed in *Memphis Avalanche*, December 10, 1861, reprinted in the *Daily Richmond Whig*, December 14, 1861.

57. *Daily Richmond Whig*, December 17, 1861.

Davis that he would not accept the post.[58] Davis and Benjamin then attempted to persuade Bragg to assume command of the district, stating that the Missouri army needed a "master mind to control and reduce it into order and convert it into a real army."[59]

While Davis searched for a general for the West, Governor Jackson became involved in a violent exchange of letters with the President that injured Price's cause even more. Jackson informed Davis that he fully concurred with the President's opinion that Missouri troops should be transferred to Confederate service for the duration of the war, but went on to relate the hardships Missourians had endured. After the discouragement and disheartenment of Missouri soldiers resulting from "having been abandoned by every Confederate soldier from the other states," and thus having been left alone to fight against overwhelming odds, Davis could not expect great success from attempts to incorporate these men into the Confederate army, especially if Price was superseded in command. Jackson advised Davis that confidence in the Confederate cause, which had been so shaken in Missouri, could be restored immediately by appointing Price to command the western district.[60]

Davis sent Jackson a scathing reply, castigating him for mentioning only "what others have not done," and placing the blame for Missouri's situation on the Governor. Davis declared that while the Confederacy needed muster rolls, all Jackson sent were reasons why Missourians would be unwilling to contribute to a Confederate army needed to defend Missouri. Still infuriated by Jackson's comments and what he felt to be the Governor's past duplicity, Davis criticized Jackson for finding fault with him for not having an organized army in Missouri when Missouri had not furnished him a single regiment. Davis had become irritated with the constant agitation from Missourians regarding their troubles and how many men they could raise if only they were given some assistance.[61]

Thus did the two Southern officials, both straitjacketed by their particularist political principles, destroy any chance of saving Missouri for the Confederacy. Davis, unwilling even under the extraordinary circumstances of a nation fighting for its very existence, would not disregard his rigid constitutionalism; at the same time, the Governor could have offered troops to the Confederacy even before the state officially seceded, but he, too, remained dogmatically inflexible.[62]

58. Heth, "Memoirs," 133.
59. Benjamin to Bragg, December 27, 1861, Civil War Papers.
60. Jackson to Davis, December 30, 1861, *O. R.*, VIII, 724–25.
61. Davis to Jackson, January 8, 1862, *ibid.*, 733–34.
62. Not all Southerners were so doctrinaire. The editor of the *Richmond Daily Examiner*, with reference to the Missouri situation, declared: "Those

Price found himself in a difficult position with respect to President Davis. The unwise and overbearing course of his friends gave his claims the aspect of a personal controversy between the two. Any argument that he might advance regarding the importance of Missouri to the Confederacy would be disregarded as a plot for personal gain or ignored as another amateurish scheme for retaking Missouri. Price's relationship with Davis was ill-starred from the beginning.[63]

---

who demand more exactitude and ceremony forget the nature of the times. Constitutional hair-splitting is now unreasonable and irrational. We cannot throw away the kernel for the shell, the reality for the appearance and sacrifice the independence of a sovereign state to save its theoretical rights." The editor felt that while Virginia controlled the East, Missouri controlled the West and should be saved for the Confederacy. *Richmond Daily Examiner*, August 19, 1861.

63. The observations of John Beauchamp Jones, a clerk in the Confederate war department throughout the war, indicate that Price's relationship with Davis was indeed ill-starred. Throughout his diary Jones makes repeated references to the "red-tape West Point gentry" (I, page 87) that surrounded Davis. Hoping that these men would not prevent the appointment of Lee to the command of the army of Northern Virginia, Jones commented: "I trust the President will see through the mist generated around him" (I, page 107). On October 26, 1861, Jones noted: "Gen. Price, of Missouri, is too popular, and there is a determination on the part of the West Pointers to 'kill him off.' I feel he will gain no more victories" (I, page 88). Five months later he recorded their success: "Price, Beauregard, Walker, Bonham, Toombs, Wise, Floyd, and others of the brightest lights of the South have been somehow successively obscured" (I, page 116). J. B. Jones, *A Rebel War Clerk's Diary at the Confederate States Capital*.

13

Pea Ridge

As the new year began, the issue of a command for the West remained agitated. Finally, on January 10, 1862, Adjutant General Samuel Cooper issued Special Order Eight establishing the Trans-Mississippi District of Department Number Two and placing Major General Earl Van Dorn in command.[1] Hopefully, Van Dorn's appointment would quiet the disturbance.

While there was little opposition to Van Dorn, many people remained concerned over Price's position and desired that Davis appoint him a major general, not to command the district, but to lead Missouri troops when they became Confederate soldiers. At the same time a feeling spread throughout Arkansas and Missouri that the Confederate government was not doing all that it could for the West. Many felt that Davis drained troops from the West to aid the East and they wanted more attention paid to Missouri and Arkansas and less to Kentucky and Virginia.[2] Price became a focal point for this feeling since the manner in which the Davis Administration treated him reflected upon the West.

Content with Van Dorn, but still anxious regarding Price, the Confederate Congress, the press, and private individuals continued to agitate for Price's appointment as a major general. Congress passed a bill to recruit and organize troops for the Confederacy in Missouri and asked Davis to commission officers to lead them.[3] Davis vetoed this on grounds that it discriminated in favor of Missouri because it called for the President to commission officers in advance of receiving muster rolls of troops. He further stated that he did not want to deprive state troops of their officers while being mustered into Confederate service.[4]

Davis pursued this same policy with respect to Price. Judah P. Benjamin informed Price that he and the President had considered commissioning him a brigadier general to command the Missouri brigade already formed, as a preliminary to further nomination to

1. *O. R.*, VIII, 734.
2. Little Rock *Arkansas State Gazette*, March 1, 1862; *Washington* (Ark.) *Telegraph*, January 15, 1862.
3. *O. R.*, LIII, 771–72.
4. *Ibid.*

command a division when it was formed. However, the two men had decided against this for fear that Price's removal from command of the state troops might break up that force before the new command was organized. Perhaps to keep Price contented, Benjamin did write that every effort was being made to raise troops in the West for a vigorous campaign in the near future. Although not stating it, he left the impression that this campaign meant a drive into Missouri.[5]

While Davis and Benjamin made these plans, Thomas C. Reynolds wrote Davis expressing the hope that the President would appoint Price to command the troops in Missouri and Arkansas within the Trans-Mississippi District. Playing up to Davis' penchant for West Pointers and regularized warfare, Reynolds stressed the idea that Price, under a man of the experience and training of Van Dorn, could render efficient service. Reynolds expressed the belief that Davis, by placing Price in command of the Missouri-Arkansas area, could make the fullest advantage of the Missourian's popularity with both his soldiers and the citizens of the country.[6]

Public expressions of favor toward Price continued to appear: A Nashville editor declared that he could not "be deterred from an expression of indignant chagrin and mortification at continual and protracted neglect by the administration at Richmond of the claims of Gen. Price" and expressed his conviction that Price's cause was endorsed by "one unanimous sentiment" throughout the Confederacy.[7] Coinciding with such expressions the Tennessee legislature passed resolutions complimentary to Price. It was becoming evident that public opinion would not allow Davis to shunt Price aside, if such was his purpose.

II

During this time Price and his army, now reduced to less than 7,000, encamped in reasonably comfortable winter quarters in Springfield, Missouri. By late December conditions at Osceola had become unbearable and, with no sign of assistance, Price had withdrawn to Springfield and sent recruiting detachments into northern Missouri to enlist additional men. While at Osceola, Price exerted every effort to transfer men from the state guard into the regular Confederate service. Not wishing to commit themselves to service out of the state, many men still enlisted in an attempt to ensure Price's appointment as a major general. They felt it necessary to fill up a Confederate brigade in order for Price to be appointed their commander.[8]

5. Benjamin to Price, February 5, 1862, *O. R.*, VIII, 747–48.

6. Reynolds to Davis, January 30, 1862, Jefferson Davis Papers.

7. *Nashville Banner*, reprinted in *Washington Telegraph*, February 5, 1862.

8. Ephraim Anderson, *Memoirs*, 1868, 138.

While in Springfield, Price had mixed reactions toward the course of events then taking place. Van Dorn's appointment gave him hope that vigorous measures would be taken in the West, since he received communications from the new commander indicating that he meant to move into Missouri and capture St. Louis,[9] but the aid he had been promised never appeared. While secure for the moment in Springfield, Price remained apprehensive regarding federal movements within the state, believing that the existing situation would soon change greatly.

Price's apprehensions proved to be well-grounded, since changes were being made in Union strategy. Generals Henry Halleck, who had earlier taken over the Department of Missouri, and Samuel Curtis, who had replaced David Hunter, were determined to rid the state of Confederates. Early in February Curtis set out from Rolla with a force of slightly over 12,000 men and fifty pieces of artillery. By the second week in February he was approaching Price's position in Springfield. Determined to wait for expected reinforcements, Price nearly tarried too long. On February 12 Curtis' advance units attacked Price's pickets and he was barely able to avoid being engulfed by the superior forces descending upon him.

After Price abandoned Springfield, the two armies fought a continuous series of running skirmishes with Price withdrawing toward the Boston Mountains of Arkansas, where he expected to rendezvous with McCulloch. While Curtis did stay close to Price's retreating army, he followed cautiously, for Halleck had warned him to be careful not to split his force or let Price lure him into a trap. The departmental commander remained only too aware of how disastrous Sigel's detour had been at Wilson's Creek and warned Curtis not to let Price entice him into the same error.[10]

Price's retreating soldiers endured the forced march through bitter cold and blowing snow without adequate provisions. Weary, footsore, and physically drained, the men held onto the dogged hope that any day they would meet McCulloch's men, but, after repeated disappointments, declared that they would believe McCulloch was coming only when they saw him.[11] By the time they reached Cross Hollows, Arkansas, they had marched six days and seven nights, during which time they had eaten only six meals and had slept less than twenty-four hours. Many of them could gain a little sleep by leaning against a companion when the line of march temporarily halted.

Although Price attempted to rally the lagging morale of his men he himself was dispirited. His son Edwin, serving as a brigadier in the state guard, had been captured while on his way to his father

9. Van Dorn to Price, February 7, 14, 1862, *O. R.*, VIII, 748–52.
10. Halleck to Curtis, February 15, 1862, *ibid.*, 556.
11. Anderson, *Memoirs*, 148.

with recruits gathered in north Missouri, and General Halleck had paroled him on the condition that he leave the state. While Price may have been revived by the cheers of his men as he passed along the line of march, he had every reason to feel disheartened.

III

When Earl Van Dorn, a headstrong and daring soldier, set out for the West he entertained grandiose plans of sweeping into Missouri and capturing St. Louis.[12] The calculations on his scratch pad appeared impressive enough to make this seem feasible without aid from east of the Mississippi. He assumed that by March 1, 1862, he would have 18,000 men gathered at Jacksonport, Arkansas, to which he could add the 10,000 he expected from Price, the 5,000 from McCulloch, and 8,000 Indians under Albert Pike from Indian Territory. He could then leave 20,000 men to defend Arkansas while uniting another 20,000, by secret and rapid marches, west of Ironton, Missouri. From there he would move on to St. Louis, thus capturing Missouri and relieving Union pressure on Albert S. Johnston east of the Mississippi.[13]

Upon his arrival in Arkansas, Van Dorn was to have a rude awakening. His forces were already being united, but neither where he desired nor of their own volition. Price, instead of having 10,000 eager, fresh recruits, had less than 7,000 fatigued and battle-weary men. Undaunted, Van Dorn set out to assume command of the forces gathering in the Boston Mountains. After a long ride through bitter wintry weather, Van Dorn reached the combined forces of McCulloch and Price on March 3 at Cove Creek south of Bentonville. There the new commander met his two subordinates and must have been struck by the glaring contrast between the two men. Price, the romantic amateur who surrounded himself with a gigantic staff of like-minded young men, offered Van Dorn and his aides the luxuries of large wall-tents carpeted with thick buffalo robes, a breakfast of kidneys stewed in sherry served in a silver chalice, and the music of his regimental band. McCulloch, stoop-shouldered and wiry, remained undemonstrative, reticent, even cautious. His staff, limited to five or six men, bespoke, in the eyes of Van Dorn's aide D. H. Maury, "the stern seriousness of soldiers trained to arms."[14]

Upon his arrival at Cove Creek, Van Dorn learned that Curtis was

12. Van Dorn's biographer describes him as a "rash young commander with a one-dimensional mind" who was extremely proud and ambitious. These characteristics were to shape his actions during the Civil War. Robert G. Hartje, *Van Dorn: The Life and Times of a Confederate General*, 12–13, 92–93.

13. Van Dorn to Price, February 14, 1862, *O. R.*, VIII, 750–52.

14. D. H. Maury, "Recollections of the Elkhorn Campaign," in *Southern Historical Papers*, 2 (July to December, 1876), 184–85.

camped at Sugar Creek where he was awaiting reinforcements. Van Dorn decided to attempt to destroy him and thus open the way to St. Louis, and he dispatched orders for Pike to join his army near Elm Springs. The Missourians and McCulloch's men prepared rations and readied themselves for the march on the following day.

Early on the morning of March 4 the Southern force moved out of camp with Price's Missourians in the lead. Van Dorn, having contracted a severe fever during his ride to join the army, was reduced to traveling in an ambulance. Price rode alongside him to identify passing commands and to relay orders from the commander. On March 6 they reached Bentonville just as Sigel's force was withdrawing. The Confederates pressed Sigel closely for the remainder of the day and by that evening were close to the Union position on Sugar Creek, where they came to a halt. That night Price, McCulloch, and Pike, who had joined the army with 2,000 Indians, went into conference with Van Dorn to determine their strategy for the following day.

Curtis was simultaneously readying his forces, now a little over 10,000 strong, for the coming battle. His position extended in an east-west line along Sugar Creek, with Pea Ridge rising abruptly from the level land three miles north and to his rear. The tiny hamlet of Leetown, consisting of a dozen cabins clustered around a store and a blacksmith shop, stood a little past the midway point between the two positions. Pea Ridge extended westward for some two miles and then it gave way to a narrow north-south valley. The Springfield-Fayetteville Road, known locally as the Telegraph Road, passed through this defile and extended on south through Curtis' position, crossed Sugar Creek, and stretched on through the rebel army just filing in and kindling campfires in the dusk. Just south of the point where the narrow gorge gave way to an open meadow stood a two-story frame house, the southern terminus of the telegraph line. Since the telegrapher took in overnight lodgers, the house had become known as the Elkhorn Tavern.

IV

Early on the evening of March 6 the Confederate commanders formulated their plans for action on the following day. Not given to intricate tactical planning, Price favored a frontal attack to come from the south and west on Curtis' right flank; McCulloch and McIntosh favored swinging around the Union army and attacking down the Telegraph Road from the north. The audacious Van Dorn approved this daring plan and later that evening put the army on the road.[15] Van Dorn accompanied Price and his troops, who were to lead the march during the night along the Bentonville and Keetsville Road

15. Van Dorn to Braxton Bragg, March 27, 1862, *O. R.*, VIII, 283; Maury, "Elkhorn Campaign," 182–83.

to the west and rear of the federal troops, screened from their view by darkness and Pea Ridge. McCulloch and Pike were to move their troops up the same road, thus leaving only 1,000 men under Brigadier General Martin Green to protect the wagon train and keep dummy campfires going to deceive Curtis into believing that the bulk of the Confederate army was still camped south of Sugar Creek.

Curtis, nonetheless, was not completely surprised by the night marches of the Confederates, for he had sent out reconnaissance forces that reported troop movements along the Bentonville and Keetsville Road. Knowing that the Rebels were on the move Curtis considered several alternatives. He could wheel his forces and fight with his back to his entrenchments along Sugar Creek or he could attempt to escape the trap. The latter would prove difficult because he could not pass through Cross Hollow along Telegraph Road without encountering the Southern force, and if he moved south he would have the Rebels at his back across his supply line, leaving him in a wintry vacuum. Deciding to take a stand, Curtis adjusted his troop placements to meet the anticipated assault. He placed two divisions, commanded by Colonel Jefferson Davis and Colonel Peter Osterhaus, in a north-south line extending from the base of Big Mountain through Leetown. He then sent a division under Colonel Eugene Carr to take up a position near Elkhorn Tavern and to block an attack from the north, leaving only one division under Brigadier General Alexander Asboth along the original line near Sugar Creek. In this manner he hoped to be able to meet an attack from whatever direction it might come.[16]

Price's men, having marched more than fifty miles in the past three days through wet, driving snow, ran into unexpected trouble. Curtis had ordered trees felled on the Bentonville and Keetsville Road, which slowed the Confederates considerably. This, added to their fatigue and hunger—their rations having run out the previous day—caused extreme distress. Some of the Missourians found army crackers, evidently from passing sutler's wagons, and ate them out of the wagon ruts, but most knew that if they were to eat they would have to capture their food from the enemy. These obstacles slowed Price's march so much that his troops reached the Telegraph Road at 10:30 A. M. rather than at dawn when they could have had some element of surprise on their side. Because of their delay Carr had ample warning of their coming. To compound the Confederate attempt to carry out the enveloping movement was the fact that Van Dorn had made no arrangement to cross Sugar Creek; this slowed the progress of the army so much that McCulloch, realizing he could not get his division

16. Curtis' report, *O. R.*, VIII, 198–99; Franz Sigel, "The Pea Ridge Campaign," in *Battles and Leaders of the Civil War*, I, Robert Underwood Johnson and Clarence Clough Buel, eds., 320–24.

Battle of Pea Ridge, March 7, 1862 (First Day)

1. McCulloch assaults Union left. After initial advance, he falls. His command is flanked and routed in Union counterattack.
2. Price and Van Dorn advance steadily to S. W. By nightfall have secured tavern and crossroads.

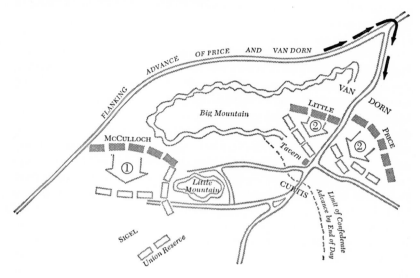

Battle of Pea Ridge, March 8, 1862 (Second Day)

1. Rout of McCulloch previous day permits Sigel to reinforce compact Union line on high ground.
2. Remnants of McCulloch's command have joined Price.
3. Sigel successfully attacks Van Dorn's right, turns Confederate line.

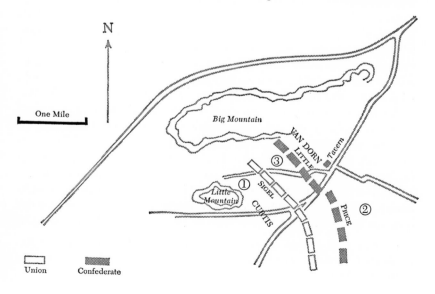

into position in time, requested and received permission from Van Dorn to turn off the Bentonville Road and attack west of Pea Ridge. Consequently, the two wings of the Confederate army were separated by nearly three miles and were unable to see one another because of the intervening bulk of Pea Ridge.

Price was greatly concerned since he knew that Curtis, occupying interior lines, could encounter the Confederate wings separately.[17] Nonetheless Price's men, weary but keyed up for the attack, crashed through the underbrush on either side of the Telegraph Road and came on hard into Carr's position. The latter had prepared his position in depth by staggering batteries along the road to support lines of infantry posted alongside. Price's initial attack captured the forward battery and forced the infantry supporting it to retreat. Heavy artillery fire now ensued on both sides, throwing cannister into the opposing ranks. The Union troops managed to mass along their second perimeter of defense and to repel two limited charges by Price's troops.

While Carr was attempting to check the Missourian's thrust, Curtis became concerned about his west flank from which he could hear the bloodcurdling screams of Pike's Indians and McCulloch's men. Although Davis' men had steeled themselves against an attack by the Indians, they were shaken by the sight that greeted them. In full regalia, Pike's Indians attacked savagely with tomahawks and arrows and enjoyed an initial success by breaking through the first line of the Union defense, but Pike could not get his Indians back into line to support McCulloch who had run into trouble. Instead, they fell to scalping the wounded or prancing around the captured "Yankee wagon-gun."[18]

As the day progressed it became increasingly evident that Van Dorn had erred grievously in allowing his army to attack in separate wings. Being so far apart they could not judge how well the over-all strategy was working out. This proved disastrous because the Confederate force on the Union west flank soon became a leaderless mob, while Price and his Missourians carried the day in their attack. McCulloch, seeing that his men were meeting stiff resistance, rallied them for a charge but was killed while in advance of his force. Colonel James McIntosh was also killed and Colonel Louis Hebert was surrounded and captured, leaving McCulloch's troops without a leader. Ironically, Price's Missourians had stood firm while McCulloch's veteran regulars became demoralized by the deaths of their leaders. By late afternoon the Confederate attack on the west flank had disintegrated. Fortunately for the Confederates, Davis and Os-

17. Col. R. H. Musser's account, printed in St. Louis *Daily Missouri Republican*, November 21, 1885.
18. Anderson, *Memoirs*, 174.

terhaus had had enough fighting for the day and allowed the Confederates on their front to drift away.

When the Missourians began to falter after their initial success, Price rode up and down his line to rally his men. In so doing he suffered a painful wound in his arm, but he refused to have it dressed. Instead he threw a sling around the injured arm and continued to urge his men on. Drawing courage from Price's example the Missourians steeled themselves for another attack.

The declining noise of battle on his west flank made Van Dorn aware of what was happening there. When he learned of the loss of his commanders in that section he ordered a final, desperate charge on the front facing Elkhorn Tavern. To the command of "Forward Missourians," Price's exhausted troops swept down upon the Union position and pushed it back, capturing the tavern and the Union camps surrounding it. Carr withdrew his men as the sun was setting. With his fatigued men short of ammunition and darkness falling, Price called a halt to the action and his men settled down around the tavern for the night.

During the evening of March 7, the opposing commanders held conferences with their staffs to decide upon the next day's action. During the night Pike straggled in with a portion of the troops that remained from the Confederate right. From 11,000 men when the fighting began they were down to an effective fighting force of less than 6,000. Van Dorn found himself in a difficult position as most of his troops had been without food since the morning of the sixth and were nearly out of ammunition. Further, they could not replenish their supply because the ammunition train had disappeared in the night and the supply train, which had been left on the Bentonville and Keetsville Road, had moved south to avoid capture after the Confederate right gave way. Consequently, after counseling with Price and Pike, Van Dorn, now repentant that he had not followed Price's advice regarding a frontal assault, decided to assume a defensive position and to await Curtis' action the next day. The men slept on their arms, eating only what they could find in captured enemy knapsacks.[19]

Curtis, on the other hand, found himself in a comparatively strong position. The opposing armies were now more nearly equal in numbers and Curtis still had fresh troops to throw into the fight, since Sigel's men had seen little action on the seventh. Thus, Curtis decided to give battle the following morning.

When the sun rose on the eighth, Curtis sent Sigel against the Confederate right, following a cannonade against the remnants of McCulloch's army. Van Dorn had lined up his men to feel out the enemy but

19. Maury, "Elkhorn Campaign," 188; Green's report, *O. R.*, VIII, 317; Price's report, *O. R.*, 306.

began to withdraw them once Curtis made a determined effort. Price and his Missourians, holding the center and left, protected the withdrawal and then retreated in good order to the southeast. Not being closely followed by federal troops, the Southerners were able to carry off much of their captured supplies and artillery. Regardless of this, Van Dorn's plans had been seriously, if not fatally, blunted.

V

Both during and after the battle Price displayed his unique ability to handle volunteer troops. His bearing on the battlefield instilled confidence among even lagging troops while his actions during the retreat toward Van Buren, Arkansas, displayed a feeling for his men that greatly endeared him to his soldiers. Riding in an ambulance because of weakness caused by his loss of blood, Price was cheered whenever he passed a group of his soldiers. Repeatedly along the march cries of "General, I am wounded!" were heard and Price would stop a vehicle and have the fallen man placed on it.[20] This slowed the retreat but he was determined to leave no wounded man behind, even if it meant endangering his whole army. Fortunately for Price, ruled more by his heart than his head, the federal troops were not following closely.

After marching some seven miles, the Missourians crossed the White River and camped beyond, sending back details to bury the dead. The following day they pushed on toward Van Buren, traveling through heavy rains that made quagmires of the roads and flooded streams that had to be forded. Still encouraged by the sight of Price, the men managed to muster a cheer for their beloved leader whenever he passed. On the second evening of the march some of the Missourians camped on a hillside covered with large, flat, white rocks. Using them to cook their corn pone, the men discovered that the rocks exploded with a loud report, scattering corn pone in all directions without doing any serious damage. With obvious reference to Van Dorn's braggadocio, the men referred to the rocks as "Van Dorn Skillets."[21] Many of them by this time had become convinced that Price rather than Van Dorn should have supreme command.[22]

When the army reached Van Buren, Price received intelligence of his appointment as major general. This was welcome and gratifying news to the men, whose attachment for him had steadily grown be-

20. R. S. Bevier, *History of the First and Second Missouri Confederate Brigades*, 107.
21. *Ibid.*, 320–21. While not laudatory of Price, Hartje is quite critical of Van Dorn's leadership at Pea Ridge. Hartje, *Van Dorn*, 117, 132–34, 157–58.
22. P. R. Smith to Col. J. R. Eakin, published in the *Washington Telegraph*, April 2, 1862.

cause of his kindness and paternal regard for them and because they felt confident with "Old Pap," as he was now affectionately known, in the field. Moreover, Price's appointment pleased others who had been supporting his advancement. The editor of the *Richmond Whig* declared it had been "gloriously won and grudgingly bestowed," and noted that the Senate had unanimously approved it without even the formality of consideration by a committee. Continuing his attack on the Davis Administration, the editor felt that earlier action on the matter might have roused Missouri and created a favorable diversion, thus saving the Confederacy from disasters in Tennessee. He hoped that it was not yet too late to achieve great results.[23] Later, in devoting two and one-half columns to Price, the editor hoped that those in authority would learn a lesson from Price, who did not tie himself to a single policy.[24]

While at Van Buren the Missourians received orders to march to Des Arc, Arkansas, on the White River where they would embark for Memphis.[25] Van Dorn had written Albert Johnston that he intended to regroup his forces for a push toward New Madrid or Cape Girardeau, Missouri, as a means of relieving Johnston who was being hard-pressed in Tennessee. If successful in this, he might then move on St. Louis.[26] Soon, however, Van Dorn received orders to join Johnston's force east of the Mississippi River as soon as possible.[27] Thus, on March 9, 1862, Price, commanding the first division of the Army of the West, as Van Dorn's force had come to be designated, received orders to ready his men for the march to Des Arc.

On April 8 at Des Arc, Price tendered his resignation from the Missouri State Guard and addressed his troops. In a flowery farewell speech to his state guard troops he urged them to join the Confederate service and follow him and 5,000 others who had already done so. He closed dramatically: "Soldiers! I go but to mark a pathway to our homes. Follow me!"[28] These were stirring words, but Price himself had serious misgivings about the wisdom of taking his troops across the Mississippi. His own compelling personal desire was to hold Missouri for the Confederacy, while at the same time he was convinced that the state's flanking position made it an urgent military necessity for the South to defend the state. While he had remained in Missouri, Halleck had kept large numbers of soldiers west of the river. When Price left the state, Halleck was free to mass vast numbers of troops

---

23. *Daily Richmond* (Va.) *Whig*, March 7, 1862.
24. *Ibid.*, April 10, 1862.
25. *O. R.*, VIII, 793.
26. Van Dorn to Johnston, March 18, 1862, *ibid.*, 789–90.
27. Beauregard to Van Dorn, March 19, 1862, *ibid.*, 791.
28. General Order 79, April 8, 1862, *ibid.*, 814.

east of the Mississippi, where Confederate bastions had already begun to crumble with the fall of Forts Henry, Donelson and Island Number Ten.[29]

On April 8 Price and his men boarded steamboats at Des Arc to descend the swollen White River to its juncture with the Mississippi and to travel up that river to Memphis. Price's boat pulled up to the wharf at Memphis in the late afternoon of April 11. A large crowd that had gathered at the wharf inquired as to the identity of the regiment aboard; when it learned that Price was the commander, immediate chants of "Price!" "Price!" "Price!" rang out and in a moment he appeared on the hurricane deck attired in a handsome dress uniform of a Confederate major general, complete with sash and sword belt. He was greeted with shouts from both his soldiers and the crowd on the wharf, and a band struck up "Dixie" while Price, bareheaded, bowed in acknowledgment of the cheers.[30]

Price was escorted ashore by several gentlemen and given his choice among several cabs for the trip to his hotel; once there, he was greeted by still another assemblage. That evening the hotel gave a gala reception in his honor, and its galleries were filled with elegantly attired ladies and well-dressed gentlemen to do him honor. Such acclaim by the aristocracy of Memphis pleased him greatly.

In response to a call, Price delivered a martial speech, expressing his gratitude for the complimentary demonstration, but he claimed he would much prefer demonstrating his gratitude on the battlefield. To the accompaniment of cheers from the galleries Price continued by declaring that the time for speeches had ended and the time for action had arrived. Saying that he had begun service without men, money, or arms, Price declared that he now had a large army, unsurpassed in valor and zeal, who would stand by him and he by them to the end. Exuding confidence, he announced that he expected to be heard from in the thundering tones of cannon, the roar of muskets, and the clash of bayonets.[31]

While Price was being feted at the hotel his men marched to the

29. For Northern opinions, both military and political, regarding the extreme importance of holding Missouri and controlling the upper Mississippi River valley, see Governor Oliver P. Morton to Abraham Lincoln, October 27, 1862, quoted in Ludwell H. Johnson, *Red River Campaign: Politics and Cotton in the Civil War*, 22–23; John A. McClernand to Abraham Lincoln, November 10, 1862; S. Treat to David Davis, November 20, 1862; William J. Allen to Edwin Stanton, November 20, 1862; Oliver P. Morton to Abraham Lincoln, February 8, 1863; John A. McClernand to Abraham Lincoln, February 14, 1863; John A. McClernand to Governor Richard Yates, February 16, 1863, Abraham Lincoln Papers, Library of Congress.

30. Anderson, *Memoirs*, 191.

31. *New Orleans Delta*, reprinted in Columbia *Missouri Statesman*, May 9, 1862.

Memphis and Charleston Railroad depot and prepared to embark for Corinth, Mississippi, to aid General P. G. T. Beauregard. Price was to have his opportunity on the field of battle, but he was also to become involved in another dispute with President Davis. This affair with the President would be brought on by Price himself, whose ego, greatly enhanced by his Memphis reception, was swelling to tremendous proportions.

14

A Thorn in Davis' Side

Immediately upon his arrival in Memphis Price telegraphed P. G. T. Beauregard, commander of the Western Department upon Johnston's death at Shiloh, that all of his troops that had reached there were being sent to join Beauregard at Corinth, Mississippi, the great rail junction where Beauregard was massing his forces to meet Henry Halleck's threat.[1] Price himself remained in Memphis until the remainder of his men arrived there and then hastened to Corinth.

Within two weeks the entire Confederate Army of the West had joined Beauregard, increasing his force to nearly 70,000 men. Beauregard began to throw up entrenchments in and around Corinth to meet the expected attack of Halleck's army of over 100,000 troops. While Beauregard's men were thus occupied they became seriously afflicted with dysentery and other diseases common in the low-lying area around Corinth. By mid-May Beauregard had 18,000 soldiers on the sick list, while Halleck continued to build up a tremendous force.[2] On May 25 Beauregard called a conference of his generals—Braxton Bragg, Leonidas Polk, Earl Van Dorn, John C. Breckinridge, William Hardee, and Price—to consider the alternatives of attacking, awaiting an attack, or evacuating. Hardee, the tactician, strongly recommended withdrawal down the Mobile and Ohio railroad line to Tupelo, Mississippi. The others, given the situation at Corinth, agreed and began to plan evacuation procedures.[3]

A master of deception, Beauregard began plotting ruses to confuse the Union commanders as to his real intentions. He sent out "deserters" to inform their captors that Beauregard was being reinforced. While withdrawing on the evening of May 29 Beauregard shuttled railroad cars in and out of Corinth with squads of men cheering the arrival of each to convince the enemy that heavy reinforcements were coming in. It worked to perfection. The cautious Halleck received word that the area was heavy fortified, for Beauregard had stationed dummy guns and gunners at every point; thus, when Halleck eventually advanced he found only an abandoned town. During this time

1. Price to Beauregard, April 11, 1862; April 14, 1862, P. G. T. Beauregard Papers.
2. O. R., X, Pt. 1, 776.
3. Ibid., 775.

the Confederates withdrew to Tupelo, fifty miles south of Corinth. Both armies then settled down to organize and discipline themselves, causing Price to fret at the prospect of his men being inactive while Missouri remained completely unprotected.

II

Soon after the departure of the Army of the West for Memphis a great many people west of the Mississippi began to agitate against the policy of the Richmond government of draining troops from their area to fight in the East. The Arkansas congressional delegation requested Davis to establish a separate department west of the Mississippi and to place either Price or Bragg in command. They also asked that Van Dorn be removed as commander of the Trans-Mississippi District.[4] Thomas Moore, governor of Louisiana, also requested Van Dorn's replacement by either Price or Bragg.[5]

Aware of the unrest in the West, Davis decided to take steps to calm it. To counter the prevailing impression among Westerners that they had been abandoned by the Confederate government, Davis instructed Van Dorn, as district commander, to issue a proclamation denying that the transfer of the Army of the West meant any such thing. Davis carefully outlined what Van Dorn should say: The people should be told that the Army of the West would soon return, having been withdrawn by the commander of the western department, not by Davis, for an urgent and special service. This involved defeating Halleck in Tennessee, which would constitute the most effective way of protecting areas west of the river. Van Dorn should admit that he had been detained longer than anticipated but should announce his hopes of returning very soon for an active campaign with at least as many troops as had been temporarily withdrawn. In the meantime the people should prepare for his return by raising a home guard to oppose the small enemy force being sent into Arkansas. Davis wanted Van Dorn to consult with Price and to issue the proclamation under their joint signatures, with the public to understand that it came from them and not Davis.[6]

When Price learned of Davis' letter to Van Dorn he would have no part of it. In his opinion Davis was practicing subterfuge on the people of the Trans-Mississippi area and he meant to discover exactly what course Davis did intend to follow regarding the West. Since there seemed to be little possibility of immediate action in Mississippi, Price decided to go to Richmond to discuss the situation with Davis personally.

Upon Price's departure for Richmond in the first week of June, Van

4. Arkansas delegation to Davis, April 15, 1862, *O. R.*, XIII, 814–16.
5. Moore to Davis, May 8, 1862, *O. R.*, LIII, 806.
6. Davis to Van Dorn, May 20, 1862, *O. R.*, XIII, 828–32.

Dorn informed Davis that, since Price had refused to join him in the proclamation suggested by the President, he had sent Major General Thomas C. Hindman to Arkansas in hopes of quieting the people in the West. Having heard that Davis had appointed Major General John Magruder to command the Trans-Mississippi District, Van Dorn advised him not to send anyone immediately "as it would have a bad effect." He was certain that Price would soon arrive in Richmond to discuss the subject. Van Dorn continued that "since the love of the people of Missouri is so great" for Price, "wisdom would seem to dictate that he be put at the head of affairs in the West." While claiming that he would relish the glory of capturing St. Louis and Missouri, Van Dorn wrote that he considered it to be in the interests of the Confederacy for Price to take command and concluded that no one was more worthy to wear the crown of glory than Price.[7] Van Dorn neglected to mention his desire, as a native Mississippian, to remain east of the Mississippi.

Crowds along Price's route to Richmond feted and honored him, although not all Southerners, even in the West, favored his appointment to command the Trans-Mississippi District. When Price's plans for going to Richmond became known, the general impression was that he would demand command of the Trans-Mississippi District and would resign if Davis refused. According to the *Arkansas State Gazette*, Price's friends were continually commenting on what he was "*going to do.*" The editor felt that all who favored the necessary order and discipline to protect life, property, and even the army itself against destruction should protest against Price being made commander in the West: "His want of qualification as a disciplinarian and his lawless cortege of loose unorganized stragglers would make him a scourge to our people."[8] The *Washington Telegraph* criticized the *Gazette* for being too harsh on Price, saying that he and Stonewall Jackson had been the most outstanding generals of the war and that had it not been for Price's efforts Arkansas would have been overrun by the Union army. Nevertheless, the *Telegraph's* editor felt that candor compelled him to admit that he did "not accord him [Price] credit for sufficient military knowledge or experience, to command the Trans-Mississippi department." Moreover, if Price had any intention of demanding this appointment in return for remaining in the service "he evinces thereby arrogance, and want of patriotism, and should be rebuked by having his resignation promptly accepted."[9] The *Gazette* agreed that no one could question Price's exploits and personal courage, but added that his "want of qualification as a dis-

7. Van Dorn to Davis, June 9, 1862, *ibid.*, 831–32.
8. Little Rock *Arkansas State Gazette*, June 28, 1862.
9. *Washington* (Ark.) *Telegraph*, July 2, 1862.

ciplinarian, his pruriency of fame, his demagoguism, and his general lack of endorsement as a leading military man, unfit him for a separate command, and would make him one of the worst, if not the very worst appointment for the command of the Trans-Mississippi District."[10]

Price's reception in Richmond was a far cry from the views expressed by the Arkansas newspapers. The *Daily Richmond Whig*, upon noting his presence in town, exclaimed: "The Washington of the West is now in Richmond—All hail!"[11] Even in the midst of the great anxiety caused by General George B. McClellan's closing in on the city, the Virginia General Assembly gave Price a formal reception and Richmond citizens went out of their way to acknowledge their respect and admiration for him. With such a reception, Price's already high opinion of his own military prowess and importance increased. This was all the more exaggerated since he had returned so triumphantly to his native state.

Price's wild welcome by the populace did nothing to reduce President Davis' reservations regarding him. During a brief interview, Davis told Price to submit his views regarding the West in writing to the Secretary of War. Accordingly, Price wrote to George W. Randolph on June 19, stating that the increasing difficulty of communication between the Trans-Mississippi District and the East made it imperative for the Trans-Mississippi area to be set up as a separate department under the command of a general who would be left untrammeled by specific instructions. Price felt that the territorial boundaries of such a command should encompass only those vitally interested in it and suggested that it include Missouri, Arkansas, and those parts of Louisiana and Texas not interested in some other theater of the war.

Price further felt than an immediate advance into Missouri would force the enemy to divert a great number of troops to that state, thus relieving pressure upon other hard-pressed points of the Confederacy. Price proposed to raise the large number of soldiers necessary for the invasion of Missouri by using those already there, transferring others from Beauregard's command, and gaining a great many recruits in Missouri. If Davis should establish the new department and make Price its commander, the Missourian wanted to put the proposed plan of action into operation.[12]

Four days later Randolph submitted Price's letter to Davis, noting that the order placing Magruder in command of the Trans-Mississippi District had not been rescinded. He suggested appointing Price

10. *Arkansas State Gazette*, July 12, 1862.
11. *Daily Richmond* (Va.) *Whig*, June 16, 1862.
12. Price to Randolph, June 19, 1862, *O. R.*, XIII, 838–39.

second in command, with the additional promise that he could with-draw his own division to the district as soon as was feasible.[13]

The day after Randolph submitted his letter to Davis, Price wrote to the Secretary inquiring as to what action had been taken on his recent communication.[14] Randolph replied that before hearing of Price's visit to Richmond he had issued orders assigning Magruder to command the Trans-Mississippi and that Magruder would like to have Price's assistance. Randolph hoped that Price would agree to this and assured him that his own division would be ordered west as soon as it could be spared.[15]

President Davis considered Price's military knowledge inadequate for the post to which he aspired and also disliked the imperious man-ner in which he insisted upon having his own way. Moreover, with the Union army threatening to engulf Richmond and many people displeased with Davis, there had been comments, consisting mostly of loose talk among the Missouri congressional delegation, that Davis should be deposed and Price put in his place. While it was incredible for anyone to give credence to such a scheme, Price's presence in Richmond at the height of the emotion was taken by some as more than mere coincidence.[16]

Davis summoned Price to his office for a final interview regarding Price's assignment, at which time he promised his eventual transfer to the West but would make no commitment concerning troops un-der his command.[17] To receive so little after so long a wait infuriated Price. Certain that he was supported by public opinion, Price de-clared that if Davis did not want his services he would resign and return to Missouri to raise another army without the President's as-sistance. Fighting once more under the state flag of Missouri, he would win new victories for the South in spite of Davis' government.

Unruffled, but speaking in contemptuous tones, Davis expressed a willingness to promptly accept Price's resignation. If he did return to Missouri, raise an army, and win new victories, the President declared that no one would be more happy than he, "or more surprised." To this Price, his ego greatly injured, declared that he had every inten-tion of surprising Davis, adding emphasis to his statement by pound-ing his fist so vehemently on the President's desk as to make the ink-stands dance about. He then stormed out of Davis' office and returned

13. Randolph to Davis, June 23, 1862, *ibid.*, 837.
14. Price to Randolph, June 24, 1862, *ibid.*, 840–41.
15. Randolph to Price, June 24, 1862, *ibid.*
16. Thomas C. Reynolds Papers, Letter Book 4468 (unpaginated mem-orandum on the appointing of a Confederate senator written in 1864).
17. Account of this interview is drawn from Colonel Thomas L. Snead, "With Price East of the Mississippi," in *Battles and Leaders of the Civil War*, II, Robert Underwood Johnson and Clarence Clough Buel, eds., 717–34.

to his hotel to write out his resignation. When he reached the Spottswood Hotel he declared, in a stormy scene, that he was going to return to Missouri to resume fighting under the state flag. This prompted his aide Thomas Snead to rip off his Confederate insignia and to declare that he, too, would no longer fight for the Confederacy, but for Missouri.[18]

The following day calmer attitudes prevailed. Davis informed Price that he would not accept his resignation and that he would instruct Bragg to transfer Price and his Missourians to the Trans-Mississippi District as soon as it could be safely accomplished. Davis endorsed Randolph's previous letter on the matter by stating that it had never been his intention to have the Missouri troops permanently withdrawn from operation west of the Mississippi and that they had been stationed elsewhere longer than he had anticipated.[19]

Somewhat mollified, Price left Richmond to rejoin his army. Arriving at Tupelo on July 2, 1862, he assumed command of the Army of the West, Van Dorn having been ordered to take command of troops in and around Vicksburg. When Price showed Bragg his authority from the War Department that would allow him and his troops to return west of the Mississippi at Bragg's discretion, Bragg said that he could not be spared at the moment.[20] Price remained satisfied, however, confident that his transfer would soon be approved.

Price's satisfaction could not have lasted long. On July 16, 1862, the War Department created the Trans-Mississippi Department along the geographic lines suggested by Price, but promoted Theophilus Holmes to lieutenant general and placed him in command of the newly-created department. Shortly afterwards Price received a letter from Missouri Senator John B. Clark, a leader in the charade to depose Davis, that typified the prompting Price continually received. Clark commented that Magruder had been recalled and replaced by Holmes without the knowledge of anyone outside the War Department. In Clark's mind this demonstrated how "determined and persistent" Davis was in disregarding the interests and wishes of the West and the entire Confederacy and also "his continued neglect and insult" to Price. Still, Clark hesitated to advise Price to resign, because he felt that the whole Confederacy preferred him over Davis: "No man in public position in the Confederacy is so odious as President Davis, while no one is so popular as yourself. . . ." Since the Confederacy faced imminent peril and "you are one of the men, if not the only man, looked to to save us," Clark expressed concern for

18. Thomas C. Reynolds, "General Sterling Price and the Confederacy," 36–37.

19. Davis' endorsement on Randolph to Davis, June 23, 1862, *O. R.*, XIII, 837.

20. Bragg to Samuel Cooper, July 12, 1862, *O. R.*, XVII, Pt. 2, 644–46.

the cause if Price should resign, even though his self-respect would have to be sacrificed if he did not.[21] Constantly receiving such letters, Price maintained a sustained sense of importance and prestige.

During this time some of Price's officers were stimulating unrest among his troops concerning the manner in which Missourians had been treated by the Davis Administration. E. C. Cabell informed President Davis of the dissatisfaction among Price's troops and of his disappointment that Price, who was committed to driving the Federals out of Missouri, had not been chosen to command the Trans-Mississippi Department. Warning that the season for operations in Missouri was fast passing away, Cabell requested that Price be sent west and explained how oppressed Price felt at his inability to fulfill his pledge to his troops to lead them home and how restless and dissatisfied they were at their disappointment.[22] Circumstances beyond Davis' control made it necessary for Price and his Missourians to be used in operations east of the Mississippi.

III

During the months of June and July, 1862, strategy changes, both Union and Confederate, began to take place in the western theater of operations.[23] After the great confrontation at Corinth both Henry Halleck and Braxton Bragg, who had replaced Beauregard as commander of the Western Department, shifted their attention away from that rail depot. In June, Halleck began to disperse his tremendous army by sending Don Carlos Buell with over 30,000 men toward Chattanooga, William T. Sherman to Memphis with 7,000 men, and shifting one division west of the Mississippi to reinforce Union forces in Arkansas, thus leaving John Pope with 30,000 men to hold Corinth. In July, President Lincoln called Halleck to Washington to become his general in chief. Prior to his departure he split his force into two separate commands: one under Buell, to attempt to capture Chattanooga, and one under Ulysses S. Grant, who was to disperse approximately 67,000 men over western Tennessee to protect railway lines.

For his part Bragg shifted the bulk of his forces eastward to defend

21. Clark to Price, July 17, 1862, *O. R.*, LIII, 816–17.
22. Cabell to Davis, July 28, 1862, Jefferson Davis Papers.
23. An excellent conception of these movements may be drawn from *The West Point Atlas of American Wars*, I, Colonel Vincent J. Esposito, ed., Maps 74–83, 100–101. For an analysis of the over-all Confederate strategy in the West, see Archer Jones, *Confederate Strategy from Shiloh to Vicksburg*, 70–88. More detailed accounts of Bragg's movements are found in Grady McWhiney, *Braxton Bragg and Confederate Defeat*, I, 253–92; and Thomas Lawrence Connelly, *Army of the Heartland: The Army of Tennessee, 1861–1862*, 187–242. For Union strategy, see Bruce Catton, *Grant Moves South*, 285–323.

Chattanooga, thus leaving Price and Van Dorn to defend Mississippi. Van Dorn, with approximately 16,000 men, spread his forces from Port Hudson to Vicksburg and northeastward to Holly Springs near the Tennessee border, while Price concentrated another 16,000 men at Tupelo.

After his successful defense of Chattanooga throughout late July and August, Bragg moved northward in conjunction with Edmund Kirby Smith to invade Kentucky. He planned to cut Buell's line of communication, defeat him, and then turn on Grant. During this time Van Dorn and Price were to co-operate to prevent Grant from reinforcing Buell and, if possible, to move to the aid of Bragg. Bragg had begun the execution of his plan on July 21 by placing Price in command of all Confederate troops in Mississippi not included in the districts of Mississippi and the Gulf. Two days later, just prior to his departure from Tupelo for Chattanooga, Bragg wrote Van Dorn, commanding the district of South Mississippi and East Louisiana, informing him that it was his wish that Van Dorn should consult and co-operate with Price. Bragg expected Van Dorn to do "all things deemed needful" without awaiting instruction from him as departmental commander.[24] Events were to demonstrate that this was wishful thinking on Bragg's part. In addition, they would exemplify the lack of co-ordination among commanders in the West and between the Western Department and the War Department that plagued the Confederate war effort.

Price received a precursory hint of what was to come just prior to Bragg's departure. General Hardee, about to leave with Bragg, warned Price's chief of staff Thomas Snead to caution Price regarding Van Dorn's overzealous actions. Hardee informed him that he had learned of Van Dorn's expedition against Baton Rouge and expressed the fear that this would necessitate other movements that would greatly overtax Van Dorn's strength and thus necessitate a call on Price for assistance.[25] Hardee advised Snead that when this happened, as he was certain that it would, Snead should inform Price that the success of Bragg's movements into Tennessee and Kentucky depended greatly upon Price's ability to keep Grant from reinforcing Buell. Consequently, Bragg would sternly disapprove sending reinforcements to Van Dorn. Hardee recommended that Snead say to Price that Bragg expected him to keep his men well in hand and ready to move northward at a moment's notice.[26]

Shortly after Bragg's departure Price formulated his own strategy, which he suggested to both Bragg and Van Dorn. Price felt that

24. Thomas Jordan to Van Dorn, July 23, 1862, *O. R.*, XVII, Pt. 2, 656.
25. Van Dorn was involved at this time in a campaign to thwart the attempts of Admiral David Farragut to capture Vicksburg.
26. Snead, "With Price East of the Mississippi," 726–27.

Mississippi could best be defended by an offensive into western Tennessee and Kentucky in conjunction with Bragg's movement into middle Tennessee. Since Grant had scattered his forces Price felt that Corinth should be recaptured prior to any invasion of Tennessee.[27] Price's plan reflected his usual desire to take the offensive, but it also involved excellent strategy. He assumed that his advance, simultaneous with that of Bragg, must end in Confederate victory on one of two fronts. If the Union troops moved against him, then Bragg would be successful, and vice versa; ultimately the Union forces would be trapped between a pincers. When notifying Van Dorn of his plans Price volunteered to place himself under Van Dorn's command. Bragg approved the plan since it coincided nicely with his own movements, and notified Van Dorn to co-operate with Price in its execution.[28]

In preparation for his proposed advance, Price began to gather his forces in Tupelo, including regiments that had been scattered over Mississippi and Alabama to guard various outposts. In so doing he informed the governors of these states that he could not wait for state troops to relieve these men and was withdrawing them immediately.[29] It was ironic that Price, so jealous regarding the protection of Missouri, would treat these state executives so brusquely when involved in a campaign affecting the entire Confederacy. He never realized that President Davis was forced to do this very thing on a larger scale.

By early August Price found himself facing a difficult decision. Bragg informed him that the road into western Tennessee was open,[30] but word arrived from Van Dorn that John C. Breckinridge was in trouble at Baton Rouge and needed assistance.[31] It soon became evident that because Van Dorn did not intend to co-operate with Bragg, Price was involved in a conflict between two commanders working at cross-purposes. Bragg, unaware of the problem, advised Van Dorn to press the enemy closely in west Tennessee. Success in such a move would enable Van Dorn to swing behind the Union force in Kentucky and join Bragg. However, the departmental commander did not insist on this course of action, instead suggested that Van Dorn follow Price's idea of moving on Corinth and then into Tennessee.[32]

On August 4 Price wrote Van Dorn that dispatches from Bragg

27. Price to Van Dorn, July 31, 1862, *O. R.*, XVII, Pt. 2, 665.
28. Bragg to Price, August 10, 1862, *ibid.*, 675.
29. Price to Governor John Pettus, July 31, 1862, *ibid.*, 666; Price to Governor John Pettus, August 4, 1862, *ibid.*, 664–65; Price to Governor of Alabama, August 9, 1862, *ibid.*, 674.
30. Price to Van Dorn, August 4, 1862, *ibid.*, 663–64.
31. Van Dorn to Price, *ibid.*
32. Bragg to Van Dorn, August 11, 1862, *ibid.*, 675–76.

made it inadvisable for him to reinforce Breckinridge. Instead, the Confederate forces should move quickly against Corinth while Union forces were being reduced at that point.[33] Van Dorn continued to urge Price to send at least a brigade to reinforce Breckinridge, declaring that he could not hope to join Price in a move on Corinth for at least another two weeks.[34] Concurrently, Bragg urged Price to support him with at least a division in west Tennessee and also cautioned him to avoid any danger of having his army defeated because of its diversionary value to him.[35]

On August 19 Bragg reported that he was moving into middle Tennessee and that the enemy must weaken itself on Price's front, thereby leaving west Tennessee open to invasion. Bragg insisted that Price should not depend too much on Van Dorn since the latter already had his hands full.[36] Price, still attempting to find a way out of his dilemma, wrote Van Dorn that before any move could be made into western Tennessee, as recommended by the departmental commander, Corinth must be taken. Since his own force was insufficient to accomplish this he urged Van Dorn to join him near Corinth "straightaway" to prevent reinforcements from reaching Buell, and before any more Union troops could be sent to Corinth. Success, he stressed, depended upon the rapidity of their movements.[37]

On August 27 Bragg informed Price that he was moving out of Chattanooga, leaving the Union forces in and around Corinth to Price and Van Dorn. In what must have been encouraging to Price, Bragg confidently wrote that he expected to meet him on the Ohio River and there open a way into Missouri.[38] Two days later Price received a dispatch from Bragg stating that Buell was in full retreat upon Nashville and that Price must watch William Rosecrans, Grant's new commander in northern Mississippi upon Pope's transfer to the East, to prevent him from moving to join Buell.[39] Price immediately wrote Van Dorn that this called for rapid action and that he would have his whole command ready to move in three days. He further expressed the hope that nothing would prevent Van Dorn from coming without delay.[40]

33. Price to Van Dorn, August 4, 1862, *ibid.*, 663–64.
34. Van Dorn to Price, August 11, 1862, *ibid.*, 675.
35. Bragg to Price, August 12, 1862, *ibid.*, 677.
36. Bragg to Price, August 19, 1862, *ibid.*, 682.
37. Price to Van Dorn, August 27, 1862, *ibid.*, 687.
38. Bragg to Price, August 27, 1862, *ibid.*, 688. Bragg may well have been playing on Price's desire to return to Missouri, since Bragg had nothing but disdain for the Trans-Mississippi area and had advised President Davis to abandon Missouri in favor of holding areas east of the Mississippi River. McWhiney, *Braxton Bragg*, 197–99.
39. Bragg to Price, August 29, 1862, *O. R.*, XVII, Pt. 2, 690.
40. Price to Van Dorn, September 2, 1862, *ibid.*

Van Dorn replied that he could not move for two weeks and that if Rosecrans continued to remain in Corinth Price and Van Dorn should join forces west of that point and maneuver the Union commander out of that city. Van Dorn, looking toward his own strategy of moving into Kentucky rather than to preventing reinforcements from reaching Buell, wanted Price to move west to meet him.[41]

Price, frustrated with Van Dorn's reluctance to join forces with him to move against Corinth, felt that he should not move west to effect a juncture with Van Dorn. In his mind Bragg's orders compelled him to stay where he was to keep a close watch on Rosecrans, who was at Iuka and supposedly crossing the Tennessee River at Eastport, so Price intended to move his army forward slowly toward Iuka.[42] Price soon received another message from Bragg informing him that the enemy had evacuated Alabama and all points in middle Tennessee, thereby causing Rosecrans to move to the northeast and necessitating a rapid movement by Price toward Nashville to join Bragg.[43] Responding to this, Price informed Van Dorn that he was definitely moving against Iuka.[44]

By now Van Dorn had become fully aware that Price was responding to Bragg's wishes rather than to his own and so wrote to the Secretary of War to request that he be given command of Price's army as a means of gaining concerted action;[45] he received little clarification for his efforts. Secretary Randolph "supposed" that Bragg, as departmental commander, should have control over such matters, and Davis merely stated that, when acting in concert with Price, Van Dorn's seniority gave him command.[46] The problem remained unchanged, since Van Dorn and Price were not as yet acting in concert.

On September 9 Price informed Van Dorn that he felt that Bragg's letter calling on him to move toward Nashville and contain Rosecrans

41. Van Dorn to Price, September 3, 1862, *ibid.*, 691.
42. Price to Van Dorn, September 5, 1862, *ibid.*, 692–93.
43. Sam. Jones to Price, September 6, 1862, *ibid.*, 694.
44. Thos. L. Snead to Maj. M. M. Kimmel, September 8, 1862, *ibid.*, 695–96.
45. Van Dorn to Randolph, September 9, 1862, *ibid.*, 697.
46. Randolph's and Davis' endorsements, *ibid.* It is difficult to assess the problem developing between Price and Van Dorn without being highly critical of Van Dorn, who was apparently determined to follow his own course of action without regard for the wishes of Bragg. Castel reaches this same conclusion in *General Sterling Price and the Civil War in the West*, 93–100. McWhiney notes that Bragg was extremely critical of Van Dorn and indicates that Price acted responsibly in this affair (McWhiney, *Braxton Bragg*, pages 267–70, 281–82, 295). Bragg described Van Dorn as being "self-willed, rather weak minded & totally deficient in organization and system. He never knows the state of his command and wields it only in fragments" (quoted in McWhiney, *Braxton Bragg*, 295).

prevented him from delaying his movements any longer. He was moving on Iuka and keeping 4,000 exchanged prisoners of war, now returned to duty, that Van Dorn had requested be sent to him.[47] This caused Van Dorn to turn again to the Secretary of War, and he informed Randolph that, since Price intended to follow Rosecrans and he intended to clear west Tennessee, there could be no co-operation between them; therefore, he wanted Price ordered to turn over the exchanged men to him.[48] Randolph answered that because of his distance from the field of action he could not instruct him as to his line of operations, but that co-operation with Price was indispensable to success and had been contemplated by Bragg.[49]

Rosecrans' movements caused a change in both Price and Van Dorn's plans. Realizing that Rosecrans was moving westward toward Corinth with 10,000 men, instead of eastward across the Tennessee River, Price felt that he and Van Dorn should jointly move against Corinth to destroy the Union force that would soon be there.[50] Van Dorn, in an abrupt about-face, replied that he was readying his men for a march toward Corinth and that, since Rosecrans was moving rapidly, he and Price must do likewise.[51] Anxious to get his campaign underway, Price was already moving toward Iuka when Van Dorn penned his reply. Catching the enemy force at that point completely by surprise, Price encountered only minimal resistance in capturing Iuka and its tremendous supply depot. Despite this victory Price found himself still in the quandary of being torn between two commanders—Bragg never having countermanded the order for him to move toward Nashville. While Price remained in Iuka in a state of indecision, Grant plotted his destruction.

IV

Even prior to Price's capture of Iuka, Grant began to set in motion a plan to destroy him, although Rosecrans warned that Price, being "an old woodpecker," would be hard to trap.[52] Assuming that if Price remained in Iuka long enough he could be defeated, Grant sent Rosecrans with 9,000 men southeastward to approach Iuka from the south and dispatched Major General E. O. C. Ord down the Memphis and Charleston Railroad toward Iuka with another 7,000 men. Together they should be able to trap Price and recover the lost supplies. Upon reaching Burnsville on the Memphis and Charleston, Ord was to swing northeastward to descend upon Price from the north. Once

47. Price to Van Dorn, September 9, 1862, *ibid.*, 698.
48. Van Dorn to Randolph, September 11, 1862, *ibid.*, 701.
49. Randolph to Van Dorn, September 16, 1862, *ibid.*, 704.
50. Price to Van Dorn, September 14, 1862, *ibid.*, 702.
51. Van Dorn to Price, September 16, 1862, *ibid.*, 703–4.
52. Rosecrans to Grant, September 17, 1862, *ibid.*, 224.

Price fixed his attention on Ord and moved to meet him Rosecrans was to fall on him from the rear.[53]

Ord and Rosecrans moved out on September 17 to be in position to attack on the morning of the nineteenth, but Rosecrans could not get into position in time. Nevertheless, Ord proceeded on schedule and his advance contacted Price's cavalry outposts. Grant ordered Ord to advance and halt four miles from town and await the sounds of battle, indicating that Rosecrans had attacked, and then move in from the north.[54] By 6:00 P.M. Ord's forward commanders reported smoke coming from the direction of Iuka and concluded that Price was evacuating the city and burning the captured supplies.[55] Ord timidly pushed forward, halting his troops and putting them into camp with a strong northwest wind blowing at his back. This wind may well have saved Price, for the smoke that Ord observed came from the battle between Price and Rosecrans. The strong wind out of the northwest prevented Grant and Ord from hearing the sounds of battle and thus they assumed that Rosecrans had not as yet gotten into position.[56]

While Grant's forces were moving in on him Price remained undecided in Iuka. With Rosecrans to the west there was little danger of his aiding Buell, and Price had received word from Van Dorn that Davis had authorized the Mississippian to take command when their armies acted together. Price therefore decided to join Van Dorn and deal with Rosecrans rather than proceed to Bragg. He ordered the captured supplies loaded on wagons and his troops readied to move the next morning toward Baldwyn on the Mobile and Ohio Railroad.

While these plans were being consummated Price kept Brigadier General Henry Little and his division stationed north of Iuka to confront Ord's advance. By 2:00 P.M. September 19, Price learned that his pickets had been driven in on the Jacinto Road and that Rosecrans was advancing from the south with his entire force. Price immediately ordered Little to send Louis Hebert's brigade to him; it came forward and Price took it with him to the front. By this time Brigadier General Charles Hamilton's division of Rosecrans' army was within a mile and a half of the center of town and Price saw that he was badly outnumbered on his southern flank. He ordered Little to send up another brigade. The fight now became severe and Price, taking the chance that Ord would not move on him from the north, ordered Little to come up with his entire division. After starting his men toward Price, Little himself rushed forward and met with Price and his staff in the thickest of the fight. While they consulted, a Minié ball crashed

53. *O. R.*, XVII, Pt. 1, 117–19.
54. *Ibid.*
55. *Ibid.*
56. Ulysses S. Grant, *Personal Memoirs of U. S. Grant*, I, 412.

through Little's forehead, killing him instantly. Dazed by the loss of his favorite subordinate, Price nonetheless pushed still more men forward. With the bulk of his force now facing Hamilton, Price drove him from the field, capturing nine pieces of artillery. Both commanders soon had full divisions on the field, but nightfall interrupted the battle.[57]

Although Grant was disturbed upon learning that his convergence of troops had worked exactly as planned while producing only a costly repulse, he now had Price where he wanted him: His two columns were in the desired position and Grant was ready to put the squeeze on the boxed-in Price. On the morning of September 20, Grant ordered his two columns to converge on the town, only to discover that it had been abandoned and was barren of supplies. Price, having been convinced by his subordinates not to fight,[58] had slipped away in the night with all his captured supplies down a southeast road left unguarded by Rosecrans. Grant vainly sent Rosecrans after Price, hoping to capture the stores, but the chase was abandoned after the troops ran into an ambush eight miles out of town. The old woodpecker had gotten away.

V

Following his narrow escape from the Union forces, Price circled Rosecrans' army to the south and headed for a rendezvous with Van Dorn at Ripley, Mississippi, just west of the Hatchie River. When the two forces reached that point on September 28, Van Dorn outlined his scheme. They would move northward, as if heading for Bolivar, Tennessee, until they reached the Memphis and Charleston Railroad at Pocahontas. At that point they would turn sharply eastward and drive toward Corinth, twenty miles away. Van Dorn would have a combined force of 22,000 against Rosecrans' estimated concentration of 15,000. Such odds would now give Van Dorn every chance of success.[59]

Van Dorn and Price started their march toward Pocahontas, thirty miles from Ripley, and reached that point on October 1. From there the army swung down the railroad line toward Corinth and encountered enemy cavalry and infantry along their march. Van Dorn knew that whatever element of surprise he had had was lost, but moved on. By October 3 his men ran into a heavy line of federal infantry

57. Captain Frank Von Phul, "General Little's Burial," *New Orleans Daily Picayune*, August 11, 1901; Snead, "With Price East of the Mississippi"; Price's report, *O. R.*, XVII, Pt. 1, 117–19.

58. Von Phul, "General Little's Burial"; Snead, "With Price East of the Mississippi"; Dabney H. Maury, "Recollections of Campaign against Grant in North Mississippi in 1862–1863," *Southern Historical Society Papers*, 13 (January–December, 1885), 290.

59. *O. R.*, XVII, Pt. 1, 376–77.

in the entrenchments that Beauregard had dug to defend against Halleck in May. Van Dorn did not hesitate in sending his soldiers crashing into the federal line. Unfortunately, instead of attacking outnumbered forces, Van Dorn was weaker than the defenders. Rather than reacting as Van Dorn expected, Rosecrans had called in his troops from the surrounding area and was preparing to march to Bolivar, where he expected the Southern attack. Therefore, Van Dorn was assaulting a strongly entrenched army that outnumbered him by 1,000 men.

At first the Southerners had good fortune. They drove the Federals from their outer positions and continued to advance, capturing several pieces of artillery. However, by the end of the day they had managed to fight only to the outskirts of Corinth and still faced the strongest Union entrenchments. Van Dorn halted his men, determined to deliver the fatal blow the following day.

On the morning of October 4 Van Dorn, following a tremendous artillery duel, threw his entire force at the Union trenches. Price's two divisions began the attack and met a blast of cannonfire. The left elements met a sudden and bloody repulse, but three regiments in the center achieved a breakthrough when the Union artillerymen fell back from their guns in a panic that spread to the supporting infantry. Price's screaming men swept forward and burst into the streets of Corinth, driving snipers from the houses, sweeping past Rosecrans' headquarters, and reaching the depot beyond the railroad crossing. At that point, however, they discovered that they were unsupported and had to turn and fight their way out. Price, deeply touched by the slaughter of his gallant troops, wept as they streamed back from Corinth.[60]

The remainder of the attackers had hugged whatever cover they could find from the intense Union fire. While occasionally rising to charge an emplacement, none could gain appreciable ground against the impregnable defenses. Before noon Van Dorn realized that his gamble had failed and he began to pull his troops back. By 1:00 P.M. the Confederate army was in full retreat. Its loss had been terrific: 4,233 men to the Federals' 2,520. This was a high price for no rewards.

Still, the impetuous Van Dorn would not give up. Halting the retreat at Chewalla, short of the Tuscumbia River, Van Dorn issued orders for his troops to move against Rienze the following day. He meant to attack Corinth from the south. Price, characteristically loath to avoid combat, was shocked by this incredible order. He rushed to Van Dorn's headquarters, where he discovered the general asleep in his ambulance. Awakening him, Price declared that any attempt to

60. R. S. Bevier, *History of the First and Second Missouri Confederate Brigades, 1861–1865,* 155; Maury, "Campaign against Grant," 299.

capture Corinth was sheer madness and advised Van Dorn to cross the Hatchie River as soon as possible. Van Dorn finally assented and ordered his army to move southward toward the Hatchie.[61] This came none too soon, for the army had to fight for its very life to escape before it encamped safely at Holly Springs.

VI

At Holly Springs Price received a visit from his son Edwin, who had been exchanged and had come south to see his father. Price's pleasure at seeing his son changed to anguish when Edwin announced his determination to return home, and did so even after long hours of urging by his father against it.[62]

Following great outbursts of criticism against Van Dorn over his management of the Corinth campaign, which prompted a court of inquiry, Davis replaced him with John C. Pemberton. On assuming command, Pemberton, evidently under the impression that Price's men were poor troops, requested Randolph to transfer Price and his men west of the Mississippi.[63] Following a review of the troops, however, Pemberton changed his mind and withdrew his request.[64]

It was not long before Price and Pemberton, both strong personalities, clashed. Pemberton, a pompous martinet, took great pride in his military abilities, especially the entrenchments he was creating around Vicksburg, while Price disdained trench warfare and made no effort to hide his feelings.[65] This, added to Price's desire to return to Missouri, led him once again to begin agitating for permission to move his troops to the Trans-Mississippi Department.

During the second week of November, Price reminded Randolph that five months had passed since the secretary had "promised" him that his command would be transferred as soon as possible. Price declared that he and his men wanted to retake Missouri to protect their families and property and that they greatly feared that a peace treaty might be made between the Union and the Confederacy before this could be accomplished. With Missouri in the possession of the

61. John Tyler to William Lowndes Yancey, October 5, 1862, Western Historical Collection; Celsus Price, "Gens. Price and Van Dorn," St. Louis *Daily Missouri Republican*, June 5, 1886 (paper read by Price before the Southern Historical Society of St. Louis, June 3, 1886).

62. Reynolds, "Price and the Confederacy," 38–39.

63. Pemberton to Randolph, October 31, 1862, O. R., XVII, Pt. 2, 739.

64. Pemberton to Cooper, November 3, 1862, *ibid.*

65. Upon his arrival at Corinth Price reputedly commented that he had captured the only entrenchments that he had ever encountered. Evidently he showed even more disdain for Pemberton's efforts. Th. H. Holmes to General T. C. Hindman, October 18, 1862, O. R., XIII, 888–89; Thomas C. Reynolds to Col. W. P. Johnston, April 13, 1863, Thomas C. Reynolds Papers, Letter Book 4470; Columbia *Missouri Statesman*, June 27, 1863.

North, any treaty written would be forced to accept Missouri's presence within the old Union. Therefore Price felt it was not fair to say that soldiers of other states had as much right to be sent to their own state, since a Mississippian knew that wherever he fought he was fighting for his state, and a Missourian did not. Since his troops, anxious to return to Missouri, did not agree that the Confederacy had a right to conscript them and would claim their discharge, Price believed it would be best to order him and his troops back to Missouri in "accordance with your and the President's promises."[66]

James A. Seddon, having replaced Randolph as Secretary of War, wrote to Pemberton, enclosed Price's letter, and stated that the War Department would grant Price's wishes if possible, leaving the time for doing so up to Pemberton. Pemberton was free to act on the matter without further instructions and might work out an exchange of troops with Theophilus Holmes.[67]

Pemberton had no intention of releasing some of his best troops. On December 7 his forces were designated as the Army of the Department of Mississippi and East Louisiana and were divided into two corps, with Van Dorn commanding the first and Price the second.[68] By this time Price's soldiers had become greatly discontented. On December 14, 1862, Price issued Special Order Eighty-Two to deal with this. Knowing that some of his troops were greatly disturbed at being kept east of the Mississippi and at being detained in service beyond their original enlistment period, Price declared that he had been informed that some of them were considering deserting. Although believing that this feeling had been aroused by and "artfully intensified by designing men," Price admitted that there was seemingly much cause for this discontent since they had enlisted under his assurance that they would not be taken from the state and had received promises in good faith that they would be returned home. Price declared that if he felt the government had acted badly he would lead them back to Missouri personally, but that he did not believe this. Announcing that he was working for their return, he asked for their patience, called on them to uphold the honor of the old state guard, and declared that they could only thwart his efforts by mutinous behavior. Price claimed the right to speak to them in such a manner since he had never deserted them and would not do so now.[69] Being so deeply concerned for his men and personally anxious to return to Missouri, Price came into further conflict with Pemberton, who would not approve their return. Instead, Pemberton ordered

66. Price to Randolph, November 15, 1862, *O. R.,* XVII, Pt. 1, 759–61.
67. Seddon to Pemberton, November 26, 1862, *ibid.,* 759.
68. General Order No. 17, December 7, 1862, *ibid.,* 787.
69. *Ibid.,* 794–96.

Price to hold his troops in readiness to move into the trenches around Vicksburg.[70]

At the same time Price suffered another disappointment when Edwin accepted a full pardon from President Lincoln. This caused rumors to circulate that Price himself was unhappy with the Confederacy and might be considering quitting because of the treatment he and his men had received.[71] A story also circulated that Edwin had returned home in connection with the Copperhead movement to lay groundwork for his father's return to establish an independent confederacy of the old northwestern states; they would then rejoin the Union under a guarantee of the protection of slavery.[72] Another rumor spread that Price was the supreme commander of the army of the Order of American Knights, a Copperhead organization.[73] Price's known discontent with the Confederate Administration, combined with his characteristic habit of silence, did nothing to still these speculations. Price himself inadvertently added to the existing suspicions by his explanation of Edwin's return home. Rather than admit that his son had abandoned the Confederate cause, he informed several people in confidence that he had sent Edwin back to Missouri to stir up support for the South and to organize troops in order for Price himself to have several thousand men available upon his return.[74]

Relations between Price and Pemberton worsened, reaching a climax when Pemberton told Price and Van Dorn that 100,000 men could not take Vicksburg and that he could spare as many as 8,000 men to Bragg if necessary. That Pemberton could make such a statement and still not allow Price and his 3,000 Missourians to be ex-

70. Pemberton to Major General Loring, December 27, 1862, *ibid.*, 759.

71. Wm. H. C. Bartlett to James S. Rollins, November 9, 1862, James S. Rollins Collection; *Daily Richmond Whig*, November 5, 1862; *Missouri Statesman*, December 5, 1862; *Washington Telegraph*, December 17, 1862.

72. Thomas C. Reynolds firmly believed this. See Reynolds, "Price and the Confederacy," 38–39, 57.

73. As commander of the Department of Missouri, General William S. Rosecrans and his provost marshal, Colonel John P. Sanderson, were convinced of this. See Sanderson's report of the activity of the Order of American Knights in Missouri, *O. R.*, II, Pt. 7, 228–314. It is interesting to note that this rumor was so firmly held by many people that an encyclopedia published in 1895 stated, in its biographical sketch of Price, that he was the grand commander of the Knights of the Golden Circle. *Johnson's Universal Cyclopedia*, VI, 774. The best account of the Copperhead movement in the Midwest is Frank Klement, *The Copperheads in the Middle West*. Klement exposes the myths of the Knights of the Golden Circle and shows that Sanderson's report is nothing more than a witch hunt.

74. Reynolds, "Price and the Confederacy," 54–55; Thomas C. Reynolds Papers, Letter Book 4468.

changed for a like number from the West was too much for Price to bear. Making a note of Pemberton's statement and having Van Dorn endorse it, Price was determined to seek justice by another personal visit to Richmond.[75] On January 23, 1863, he turned over the command of his corps to Brigadier General John Bowen and left for Montgomery to obtain transportation to Richmond. Pemberton telegraphed Price at Montgomery that his troops were being ordered to Jackson, Mississippi, and would probably move from there to Vicksburg, where Pemberton would be in immediate command and Price next in seniority. Pemberton declared that unless urgent necessity prevented Price from joining his troops, he should do so at once.[76] Disregarding Pemberton's notes, Price departed for Richmond.

VII

Even before Price decided to go to Richmond, steps had been taken in that city to aid his cause. Lieutenant Governor Thomas C. Reynolds had assumed the governorship of the Missouri Confederate government-in-exile upon Jackson's death in December, 1862, and had arrived in Richmond in January, 1863.[77] Shortly thereafter, E. C. Cabell informed Reynolds of Price's dissatisfaction with his situation under Pemberton and his eagerness to lead an invasion of Missouri. With characteristic vanity, Reynolds responded that if he had been handling Price's affairs from the beginning, dissatisfaction would never have developed, but he nonetheless informed Cabell that he was not familiar enough with affairs in Richmond as yet to state whether Price would be moved west.[78] Upon hearing of Price's Special Order Eighty-Two, Reynolds himself seriously doubted whether Price should be transferred.[79]

Soon after Reynolds' arrival in Richmond, Price telegraphed him that he was on his way to the capital, and the Governor began to sound out officials as to whether Price's transfer could be ready for him when he arrived in the last week of January. It became obvious that Price had not lost his popularity, since the Confederate senate unanimously voted to invite him to a seat in that chamber during his stay in the city.[80]

75. *O. R.*, XXIV, Pt. 3, 596–97.
76. Pemberton to Price, January 26, 1863, *ibid.*, 605–6.
77. For an excellent survey of the Missouri government-in-exile, see Arthur Roy Kirkpatrick, "Missouri, The Twelfth Confederate State" (Ph.D. diss., 1954).
78. Reynolds, "Price and the Confederacy," 41; Reynolds to Cabell, January 14, 1863, Thomas C. Reynolds Papers, Letter Book 4463.
79. Reynolds to Seddon, January 22, 1863, Thomas C. Reynolds Papers, Letter Book 4463.
80. *Daily Richmond Whig*, February 6, 1863.

On his arrival, Price, Snead, and Reynolds immediately went into conference regarding Price's status.[81] At this meeting Reynolds expressed his desire for the Confederacy to send an army into Missouri, but recognized that many obstacles stood in the way of Price commanding it. Primary among these were the supposed counter-revolutionary plot of the summer of 1862 and the rumors regarding Price's connection with a Northwest confederacy. Upon hearing that his name had been mentioned in connection with such plots, Price expressed surprise. He said that he had been aware of Senator John B. Clark's wild talk and had written him to stop it, but knew nothing of his name being used. However, he felt that this did clarify a discussion with Davis earlier in the year when the President had visited forces in Mississippi. Davis had commented that the gigantic efforts being made by the federal government to crush the Confederacy made it necessary to avoid internal dissension and had asked Price if he agreed. When Price assured Davis that he did the President had remarked that he was delighted to hear him say so. This had puzzled Price at the time, but he understood it now. Reynolds also asked Price about the stormy meeting with the President in June, 1862, but Price would not comment any more than to say that he had "skinned" the President. He did point out that when Davis visited Mississippi cordial relations existed between them.

Shortly after his conference with Price, Reynolds received a visit from Cabell, who broached the subject of Reynolds' appointing Price to command the Missouri State Guard if he resigned from the Confederate service; he also intimated that Price was so upset with Pemberton that he might do so. Reynolds felt that Cabell's visit was intended to obtain a promise that he would appoint Price to command the state guard if he resigned, thereby giving him more leeway in his dealing with Davis. Reynolds told Cabell that it was not necessary to discuss this matter until Davis decided on Price's transfer.[82]

However much Reynolds might claim to be working for Price's cause, he always maintained a reserve toward him because of distrust. Ever since the 1850's, when Reynolds had considered Price a "trimmer," the Governor continually suspected Price of hatching secret schemes for his own benefit. Even now Reynolds felt that there was an intrigue between Price and his son Edwin, and the Governor did not want Price to resign for fear he might go to Missouri to raise troops on his own. Reynolds suspected that Price, with his "known facility for change," might even join the Union side or leave the service to return to Missouri to set himself up as an independent leader

81. Account of this conference taken from Reynolds, "Price and the Confederacy," 42–44.
82. *Ibid.*, 53.

or as a revolutionary governor.[83] Knowing Price's popularity within the state, Reynolds felt that such developments were not beyond the realm of possibility and this attitude crept into his discussion with Confederate leaders. He suggested to Judah P. Benjamin that if Price was given a command he should have subordinates who were loyal to the Confederacy.[84]

When Reynolds finally obtained an interview with Davis, he sounded him out on the "skinning" that Price had given him. Davis would not enter into details beyond saying that he considered Price the vainest man he had ever met. He also blamed the friction between Price and Pemberton on Price's open disdain for Pemberton's fortifications, and spoke of Price's alleged connection with the Northwest confederacy scheme. The President knew that a woman had come through the lines from Ohio and that she was staying at the Spottswood Hotel where Price was also residing.[85] This came at a time when there was much agitation, especially among opposition newspapers, for steps to be taken to conciliate the old Northwest in the hope that it would break away from the Union and join the Confederacy.[86] Davis remained cool toward this idea and since Price's name had been so often linked to it he was naturally suspicious.

When Reynolds next saw Price, he raised the question of the Northwest conspiracy with him, quite frankly stating that the connection of his name with that movement had done him great harm. Reynolds continued that no executive, especially one leading a revolution, could look without jealousy upon a military officer who connected himself while in its service with another revolution within the enemy's territory. Price disclaimed any connection with the movement other than a sympathy for it. He had indeed recommended the woman who had come to Richmond, a Mrs. Clark, whose mission was the termination of the war by incorporation of the old Northwest into the Confederacy. However, he agreed with Reynolds that this matter should be handled by Davis.[87]

Following his conference with Price, Reynolds felt confident that he could and should support Price's transfer. In doing so he would also be helping himself since he, too, wished to return to Missouri and realized that without Price's support this would be difficult.[88]

83. *Ibid.*, 57.
84. *Ibid.*, 59–60.
85. *Ibid.*, 44.
86. See the *Daily Richmond Whig*, March 6, 7, 16, 25, April 2, May 19, June 8, 13, 1863.
87. Thomas L. Snead to John B. Clark, *O. R.*, LII, Pt. 2, 408; Reynolds, "Price and the Confederacy," 44–45.
88. A close reading of the Reynolds Papers and his manuscript "Price and the Confederacy" reveals that while Reynolds mistrusted and often denigrated Price, he was using Price to return to Missouri where he wanted

Price did not make his task easier and, under the already trying circumstances of the connection of his name with various schemes, he insisted not only upon his transfer, but that of his troops as well.

Reynolds began a series of conferences with Confederate officials to attempt to obtain Price's transfer. Dealing primarily with Seddon, Reynolds' main argument was that Price's name would attract large numbers of volunteers in Arkansas and Missouri. Seddon maintained an open mind on the subject and, when Reynolds inquired about the alleged "promise" to which Price constantly referred, Seddon—who had not been secretary when it was supposedly made—asked Davis about it. He reported that the President flatly denied that such a promise had been made and became so agitated that Seddon dropped the entire matter. The Secretary claimed that Davis viewed such inquiries as doubting his veracity and advised that Reynolds urge Price to drop any further mention of the promise lest another quarrel prevent any arrangement to gratify his wishes.[89] Reynolds believed the whole trouble arose from Price's habit of considering a superior's intimation of an intention as a promise to be fulfilled at every sacrifice.[90]

By the first week in February others joined in the agitation for Price's transfer. The Arkansas congressional delegation wrote Davis requesting, among other things, that Price be placed in command of Arkansas and Missouri.[91] The agitation finally bore fruit when Seddon wrote to Edmund Kirby Smith, commander of the Trans-Mississippi Department following Holmes' appointment to command the District of Missouri and Arkansas, on February 3, 1863, to see if he could arrange with Pemberton to transfer Price and his command west of the Mississippi.[92] In this way they could afford to move Price west of the river, as he would be subordinate to two men trusted by the President and the War Department.

In a longer letter to Kirby Smith, Seddon revealed much of the thought of the President and the War Department regarding Price and the situation in the West. He stated that the department had long been contemplating the transfer of Price and his command and would have done so except for various exigencies. This had caused much dissatisfaction and some distrust among Missouri troops and Seddon feared that "General Price himself has conceived the idea of an injustice done him." This had been the subject of complaint and misrepresentation on both sides of the river among those disaffected toward the government. Since Davis was becoming ap-

---

to hold the key political position. Once Price's army accomplished this, Reynolds would attempt to deal with Price's prestige and power.

89. Reynolds, "Price and the Confederacy," 50.
90. *Ibid.*
91. Arkansas delegation to Davis, February 2, 1863, Davis Papers.
92. Seddon to Kirby Smith, February 3, 1863, *O. R.*, XXII, Pt. 2, 781.

prehensive regarding the western areas breaking away from the Confederacy, he felt Price's transfer might aid in extinguishing this unrest.

Seddon also felt that Price's influence and reputation would be most valuable to the government in the Trans-Mississippi Department. When the time arrived, as Seddon trusted it soon would, for an advance into Missouri, Price, "more speedily and effectually than any one else, might arouse the Missouri people to a united and energetic movement to relieve themselves from the thraldom of their present tyrants."[93] At Reynolds' request the Secretary informed Pemberton that it would be "very gratifying" to the War Department if Pemberton would arrange Price's transfer as soon as possible.[94]

On February 10, 1863—the eve of his departure for Mississippi— Price was serenaded at the Spottswood Hotel by a band and a large throng of citizens. In response to this demonstration, Price appeared at a window and expressed his gratitude to the crowd, who complimented him in the capital of his native state. He added that he believed the governmental authorities were now inclined to give him a fair chance in the field, where his friends would soon hear from him. With this he withdrew amid great applause and Senator Clark and several others appeared for short speeches.[95]

Price, anxious to return to Mississippi, wanted to proceed across the Mississippi River to Arkansas, where he hoped he would be able to drive into Missouri to free the state from federal control. At the same time, Davis must have believed himself finally rid of the thorn in his side that had so agitated him by becoming a focal point for those dissatisfied with his administration.

93. Seddon to Kirby Smith, February 5, 1863, *ibid.*, 781–82.
94. Seddon to Pemberton, February 6, 1863, *ibid.*, 618.
95. *Daily Richmond Whig*, February 11, 1863.

· 15 ·

Return to the Trans-Mississippi

On February 27, 1863, Pemberton issued orders relieving Price of duty in the Department of Mississippi and East Louisiana and ordered him to report to Lieutenant General Edmund Kirby Smith in the Trans-Mississippi Department. His troops would follow when they could be replaced with a like number from west of the Mississippi.[1] Price, pleased with this arrangement, hoped his troops could join him soon, for he was anxious to return to Missouri as soon as practicable. This desire was greatly heightened by the receipt of many letters from Missourians lamenting their treatment at the hands of the Federals and lauding him as their savior.[2]

At the same time prospects for a harmonious relationship west of the river seemed promising since Theophilus Holmes, while still in command of the department, had informed President Davis that Price was much loved by the inhabitants of the department and that he would like to have Price with him if he decided to invade Missouri.[3]

II

Price arrived at Little Rock on April 1, 1863, and assumed command of a division under Holmes, who now commanded the District of Arkansas and Missouri. The Missourian's arrival prompted Major General Samuel Curtis, Union commander of the Department of Missouri, to warn that Price would "move Heaven and earth to raise or mass forces in Arkansas" and that Union commanders should therefore attack Helena, Arkansas, on the Mississippi River before Price could set his plans in motion. Curtis urged dispatch since Price's "popularity in Arkansas and Missouri will enable him to do much mischief."[4] Henry Halleck, now Union general in chief, concurred and Helena was soon captured and fortified.

Indeed, Price did exert every effort to promote recruiting and to shaping up his division. He spent much time trying to improve the

1. *O. R.*, XXIV, Pt. 3, 646.
2. *Jackson* (Miss.) *Argus and Crisis*, reprinted in the *Daily Richmond* (Va.) *Whig*, March 12, 1863.
3. Holmes to Davis, March 6, 1863, *O. R.*, XXII, Pt. 2, 796–97.
4. Curtis' endorsement of John F. Tyler to Col. J. M. Glover, April 6, 1863, *ibid.*, 203.

living conditions of his men since troop strength in Arkansas had been falling off, in great part, because of their neglect by the former district commander, Thomas C. Hindman.[5] When Price assumed command of the division, men began to return, thereby replenishing the skeletal regiments. In a little over a month after Price assumed command General Kirby Smith informed President Davis that there was a rapidly improving condition in the area that he attributed to the removal of Hindman and the arrival of Price.[6]

While Price was establishing his usual excellent rapport with his troops he was, just as characteristically, to become embroiled in disputes with his superiors. Governor Thomas C. Reynolds arrived during the second week in May in Camden, Arkansas, where he remained in order to put the affairs of the exiled Missouri state government in order. He corresponded with Holmes, Kirby Smith, and Price regarding military, political, and other matters. The Governor instructed Price to submit regularly numbered correspondence to him[7] and informed Holmes, in a rather vain manner, that the Missouri government would make every effort to promote military objectives.[8] Reynolds, holding an extremely high opinion of his own abilities and priding himself on his great experience and training in executive functions, was intent upon establishing civil authority.

Within two weeks after Reynolds' arrival in Arkansas he became involved in a dispute with Price which, given their vanity, ambition, and headstrong personalities, was nearly inevitable. Price engaged himself with the military problems necessary for an invasion of Missouri and he could not understand why Reynolds remained in Camden rather than proceeding to Little Rock to facilitate this program. Reynolds, an officious bureaucrat, felt that before anything else the state government machinery should be set in order and remained determined that civil matters would come first.

The immediate cause of their quarrel stemmed from Reynolds' decision to defer payment of Price's soldiers until state records were in order and Price's consequent accusation that Reynolds intended to remain in Camden as a means of deferring payment to his soldiers indefinitely.[9] Always suspicious of Price, Reynolds believed he was trying to undermine him by exciting the state's creditors and others to expect impossibilities from their governor, only to raise a cry

5. For an excellent description of the condition of the men under Hindman's treatment, see the Journal of Dr. Henry Dye, Josiah Trent Collection, 13, 14, 83, 89.

6. Kirby Smith to Davis, June 16, 1863, *O. R.*, XXII, Pt. 2, 871–73.

7. Reynolds to Price, May 18, 1863, Thomas C. Reynolds Papers, Letter Book 4463.

8. Reynolds to Holmes, May 19, 1863, Thomas C. Reynolds Papers, Letter Book 4463.

9. Reynolds to Price, May 25, 1863, Letter Book 4463.

against him when he could not perform the impossible.[10] Once again Price's known vanity and ambition, combined with his secretiveness, allowed another to believe the worst of him. In this case, Reynolds, himself tremendously ambitious, was quick to see this trait in others and to interpret their actions as being self-seeking.

Reynolds, still hoping to avoid a quarrel with so powerful a figure as Price, wrote to E. C. Cabell, who had returned from Richmond to serve with Price, that his relationship with the latter since their first meeting over ten years previously had been one of mutual services and that he had always sustained Price. He claimed to have smoothed the way for Price's appointment as state bank commissioner after Price had canvassed for him as lieutenant governor in 1861. Since that time Reynolds claimed that he had worked to get Price his commission and that he had "almost unaided" smoothed relations between Price and Davis. He claimed that he had tried to preserve cordial relations with Price and had not stood on etiquette, "although occasionally pained by his [Price] entire neglect to notice the reception of my frequent messages & letters."

Reynolds also attempted to explain the financial problems besetting the state government. Prior to his arrival state debts had been paid, in Reynolds' opinion, in a slipshod manner, which had resulted in graft and loss of public funds. Further, his plans for establishing state solvency would be ruined if this continued. He intimated that formerly state officers had been advised to usurp powers belonging to others in order to strip the state of its funds and that his efforts to rectify this situation might lead to charges that he planned to repudiate financial obligations. This could only incite the public against him and make it impossible for him to achieve fiscal stability. The latter objective required him to halt all payments until state records were organized.

Reynolds had been further offended by Price's adjutant, Thomas Snead, who had written the accusing letter concerning nonpayment of troops, since it addressed him as "Governor" without the customary additions. Reynolds saw in this the possible beginning of a series of semi-official letters intended to picture him as a tyrant and Price as the people's friend and guardian. Reynolds complimented Price for being as kind-hearted and magnanimous as he was brave and therefore suggested that perhaps his scheming subordinate Snead had penned the letter without Price's careful perusal. Nonetheless, knowing Price to be "shrewd, quick, adroit, and far seeing . . .," the Governor suspected that Price or his friends might be attempting to destroy his influence because he stood as an obstacle to Price's assumption of power in Missouri. Reynolds closed his letter to Cabell

10. Thomas C. Reynolds, "General Sterling Price and the Confederacy," 63, 69.

by declaring that he intended to get the affairs of the state in order and did not want to be made odious in so doing, and asked for the support of Cabell and Price.[11]

Evidently Cabell replied that Price was satisfied with Reynolds' explanation and called for a consultation, since Reynolds sent still another letter stating that he would be glad to meet with Price at all times to discuss any subject. Still projecting his own motives upon Price, he declared that Price would be *"our leading military figure in the picture of Missouri's redemption . . .,"* but that any invasion of the state must wait until he had put financial affairs in order. Reynolds assured Cabell that once Missouri had been reconquered, Price and other impatient Missourians would consider the delay occasioned by his work in Camden to have been time well spent. The Governor wanted a fully functioning government to be ready when they retook the state, rather than military anarchy.[12]

In the last week of May, Price moved his division to Jacksonport, Arkansas, in order to superintend recruiting in northern Arkansas and southern Missouri. Reynolds met with him late in June. Price sent the divisional band to serenade him, thus impressing Reynolds most favorably.[13] The two men met and talked in a cordial manner, but points of difference still remained. Reynolds, ever distrustful of Snead, felt confirmed in his earlier suspicions when the latter told him that Price *"was* the State of Missouri."[14] While in camp Reynolds was also taken aback by Price's loose discipline; he witnessed Price excuse an officer arrested for raising a command for himself in northern Arkansas and impressing supplies for his recruits. The officer had acted without orders and thus had violated a congressional edict. Price excused the man on the grounds that he had been unaware of acting improperly.[15] Reynolds and Price also held different views regarding the handling of volunteers—the Governor favoring iron discipline and Price, from experience, considering this impossible.[16] Although Price's treatment of his troops gained their affection and devotion, his methods were unpopular with Arkansas residents who resented depredations suffered at the hands of Price's men.

Reynolds left Jacksonport satisfied that he had Price's cordial cooperation. He informed long-time Price associate J. W. Tucker, editor of the Jackson, Mississippi, *Argus and Crisis*, of his confidence that

11. Reynolds to Cabell, May 27, 1863, Thomas C. Reynolds Papers, Letter Book 4470.
12. Reynolds to Cabell, May 31, 1863, Thomas C. Reynolds Papers, Letter Book 4463.
13. Reynolds, "Price and the Confederacy," 75.
14. *Ibid.*, 72.
15. *Ibid.*, 85–86.
16. Reynolds to Waldo P. Johnson, December 24, 1863, Thomas C. Reynolds Papers, Letter Book 4464.

the military would remain subject to civilian authority and would invade Missouri as order-loving men when the time came. Reynolds commented that Missouri's "best men," including Price, agreed with him. The Governor further indicated that relations between Price, Holmes, and the Confederate command system were finally harmonious.[17]

The indomitable Tucker, in his hard-hitting style, was already blasting Holmes and Davis for their treatment of Price. Tucker felt that when Price and Kirby Smith were ordered west it was universally understood that Kirby Smith would command the department and that Price would be assigned to active, untrammeled command in the field. However, in Tucker's opinion, the public had been sadly deceived, for Price's return to Arkansas had attracted thousands of men back to the service, but despite repeated pleading he had not been given an independent command. Tucker also blasted Holmes personally for failing to prevent Grant from being supplied from the Northwest. Moreover, the "old imbecile" Holmes had "thwarted" the best efforts of others to do so and had left Price chafing with inactivity. According to Tucker, Holmes could not find his way out of Arkansas unaided.[18]

Tucker's blasts were echoed by the *Richmond Whig*, its editor declaring that when Price was sent west it was generally believed that the bitter feeling of the Davis Administration against him had disappeared. Now Tucker's letters disproved this: "It is not the first time in the history of this war that the people of the Southwest have been duped and trifled with."[19] Once again it appeared as if Price's "friends" were fomenting a quarrel between him and his district commander. Indeed, Holmes was beginning to have second thoughts about the man he had so eagerly sought as a subordinate. Moreover, Price was not blameless for this transformation in Holmes' opinion. In his usual headstrong manner he continually urged Holmes to move against the fortified city of Helena as a diversion to relieve pressure on Vicksburg. Dissatisfied with Holmes, who remained cautious and refused to move, Price found the situation much to his dislike and was not hesitant to expound upon what he would do if he were district commander.[20]

Ironically, in this instance Price and the War Department were in perfect accord. Secretary of War Seddon had written Joseph John-

17. Reynolds to Tucker, June 29, 1863, Thomas C. Reynolds Papers, Letter Book 4463.

18. Tucker to Editor, June 19, 1863, printed in the Jackson *Mississippian*, reprinted in the *Daily Richmond Whig*, June 29, 1863.

19. *Daily Richmond Whig*, June 29, 1863.

20. Reynolds to Snead, June 2, 1863, Thomas C. Reynolds Papers, Letter Book 4463.

ston, commander of the Western Department, to suggest that he contact Price or Holmes and have them move against Helena, commenting that this "policy is so apparent that it is hoped it will be voluntarily embraced and executed."[21] When this letter was forwarded to Holmes, there was an amazing transformation of his indecision. He immediately informed Kirby Smith that he felt he could take Helena and requested permission to attempt it,[22] to which the department commander readily assented.[23]

Holmes, nevertheless, remained apprehensive with regard to the undertaking, and felt he had been forced into it by his brash subordinate. Further, he had become resentful of Price's great popularity with the troops in the district. Holmes believed he was risking his military reputation on the Helena campaign and informed Price that he expected him to publicly sustain the propriety of the venture if it should fail.[24] By this time Holmes may well have become, like Reynolds, suspicious that Price acted only for his own well-being and reputation and would like to see Holmes disgraced. Thus was the Helena campaign inaugurated.

III

Holmes set his troops in motion so as to converge on Helena and surprise that post, but extremely heavy rains and swollen streams in his line of march prevented Price from reaching the point of rendezvous on schedule.[25] Holmes, beside himself with anxiety lest the element of surprise be lost, urged Price on, ordering him to move as rapidly as good order and efficiency would permit.[26]

By the morning of July 3, Holmes had all his troops in position five miles from Helena, but to his dismay the Union fortifications were much stronger than anticipated. In the center of town Fort Curtis, a formidable defensive position, dominated the surrounding area and the town was surrounded by trenches supported by three batteries that could enfilade the entire line. In addition the Union gunboat *Tyler*, with its giant eight-inch guns, rode at anchor in the river and could sweep the entire low-lying area surrounding the town. While Holmes had over 7,600 troops as against the defenders' 4,126, the enemy's tremendous firepower gave them the edge.[27] Ironically, the

21. Seddon to Johnston, May 25, 1863, *O. R.*, XXII, Pt. 1, 407.
22. Holmes to Kirby Smith, June 15, 1863, *ibid.*
23. Kirby Smith to Holmes, June 16, 1863, *ibid.*
24. Thomas C. Reynolds to E. C. Cabell, July 4, 1863, Thomas C. Reynolds Papers, Letter Book 4470.
25. For the difficulties that Price's troops underwent, see Price to Holmes, June 27, July 1, 1863; John Mhoon to Snead, June 27, 1863, *O. R.*, XXII, Pt. 2, 887–91.
26. Holmes to Price, July 1, 1863, *ibid.*, 899–90.
27. *O. R.*, XXII, Pt. 1, 386; Colonel Thomas L. Snead, "The Conquest

Union troops were commanded by Brigadier General Benjamin Prentiss, who had been exchanged for Price's son Edwin.

Holmes' battle plan called for Price, leading two brigades, to attack the Union center at Graveyard Hill. Brigadier General J. F. Fagan would move against Hindman Hill to the south and Brigadier General J. S. Marmaduke, supported by Brigadier General L. M. Walker on his left flank, would strike Rightor Hill on Price's left. All these actions were to begin simultaneously at sunrise. After formulating this plan, the Confederate commanders put their troops into motion to gain their respective positions during the night. Poor reconnaissance on their part became immediately apparent. The terrain surrounding Helena was extremely rough, with deep ravines and dense timber and underbrush made even more impassable by Union obstructions. The terrain was such that a co-ordinated attack such as planned by Holmes would be extremely difficult to initiate successfully. To make matters worse several of the separate forces lost their guides and stumbled around in the dense underbrush before they could find their way.[28]

Nevertheless, at early daylight on the morning of July 4, Fagan and Marmaduke attacked. Marmaduke met stiff resistance against Rightor Hill and was attacked on his left because Walker never came to his support; this forced Marmaduke's men to halt their advance, take cover, and absorb high casualties. In the meantime, Fagan's men drove in the Union pickets before them and fought their way under heavy fire through five lines of trenches. They suffered from a violent enfilading fire from Graveyard Hill, which was supposed to be under siege by Price's force. Fagan's men, exhausted by their efforts, nevertheless made an attempt to take the gun emplacements on Hindman Hill to await the aid from Price that would never come.[29]

Price had moved his men into position early in the morning, but when he found that he would arrive in position prematurely, he called a halt and conferred with Holmes, who was accompanying him. Darkness, the rugged terrain, and obstructions in his path had compelled Price to leave his artillery behind. Instead, he armed his artillerymen with carbines and brought them along to man the guns he hoped to capture.[30]

Nearly an hour and a half after Fagan had moved forward Price sent his two brigades into action. Unfortunately, the terrain caused

---

of Arkansas," in *Battles and Leaders of the Civil War*, III, Robert Underwood Johnson and Clarence Clough Buel, eds., 454–56.

28. Reports of Holmes, Price, Fagan, Marmaduke, *O. R.*, XXII, Pt. 1, 408–27.

29. *Ibid.*, 427–32; "The Attack on Helena," *Southern Historical Papers* (Richmond, 1896), 24:197–200.

30. *O. R.*, XXII, Pt. 1, 413–17.

them even further delay. Price had instructed his brigade commanders to attack simultaneously when both columns had moved into adjacent positions, but they found themselves separated by a high ridge, and thus unable to co-ordinate their efforts. Consequently, they remained inactive, each waiting for the other to come into line. Holmes rushed up to Price to inquire why he was not attacking and Price, explaining the situation, sent forward a staff officer to order the brigades to charge. When they finally attacked they came on hard through a hail of Minié balls and artillery fire; they also suffered from the enfilading fire from the hills on either side. They persevered, however, and rushed into the fort on Graveyard Hill. Price sent up his artillerymen to turn the captured guns on the Union positions, only to find that they had been shot-wedged and were useless. Price dispatched his chief of artillery to bring forward his artillery, but it was too late.

Price found himself in a difficult position: Many of his men, in their eagerness once they captured the fort on Graveyard Hill, continued on into the town and were captured; all the Confederate positions were suffering from heavy fire, made even more deadly by the rain of shot from the *Tyler*. Price realized that the only way to save the day was to send reinforcements to Fagan on his right, but by the time he had issued the order, his troops had suffered too many casualties to be able to execute it.[31] By 10:30 A. M., after nearly six hours of brutal fighting, Holmes saw that he had been defeated and ordered his men to retreat. Many found themselves pinned down by such heavy fire that they were unable to withdraw and were forced to surrender. Prentiss did not have sufficient forces to pursue and so let the Confederates slip away.

It had been a disastrous day for the Confederates, their losses approaching 20 per cent as against less than 6 per cent for the enemy. The battered Southerners straggled back toward Jacksonport, their efforts thwarted perhaps less by the powerful Union entrenchments than by their own poorly co-ordinated attack. Holmes, as commanding officer, would bear the blame for ordering an attack of the sort attempted under the physical conditions at Helena, and Price and the other subordinates, who took their cues from the Missourian, would have to bear a heavy responsibility for urging the cautious Holmes to attack without having made a careful reconnaissance. Price compounded this by his romantic conceptions of warfare. He felt that a rush by gallant troops would carry the day and so did not bother to force his artillery through the obstructions. Fagan and Marmaduke also faced such obstructions, but managed to get their artillery through. It was indeed unrealistic to suppose that any cap-

31. *Ibid.*

tured guns would not be spiked. Thus, once again the admirable courage of Price's troops went for naught.

IV

The aftermath of Helena brought bitter recriminations among the Confederate officers involved and relations between Price and Holmes deteriorated completely.[32] Holmes suffered from severe headaches, which were not ameliorated by Price's vanity. Sick, and becoming frenzied in his hatred of Price, Holmes blamed him for the failure at Helena. He wrote President Davis that while he had good troops he had been "singularly unfortunate" in the generals sent to him. Then, commenting that perhaps he should not say more about individuals "than should be said to one who like you can make or unmake at discretion," Holmes proceeded to declare that Price was "utterly and entirely worthless, in the field an imbecile, in the [councils?] without resources and everywhere thinking of nothing and caring for nothing but some sound that will echo and recho [*sic*] Sterling Price."[33]

Holmes was not alone in complaining of Price, since Hindman, upon reaching Richmond after being removed from command in the West, wanted to return there with a command independent of both Holmes and Price. He degraded Holmes and said of Price: "I apprehend that no officer can serve where he is without lending himself to factious schemes and losing sight of discipline, or else becoming involved in endless disputes."[34]

Nonetheless, Price had his defenders. At the same time that Davis was receiving these reports, Reynolds defended Price against savage attacks coming from the *Arkansas State Gazette,* and informed Secretary of War Seddon that he could look forward with complete confidence to harmonious action between Price and himself due to an alteration in Price's attitude.[35] Soon a system of counterpoises among the military "politicians" and civilian authority would be established.[36] News of the dispute even reached South Carolina where former Governor Francis Pickens, evidently under the power of the Price image pervading much of the South, wrote Senator L. T. Wigfall of Texas that in the current state of affairs west of the Mississippi it would be disastrous to retain Holmes in command, since there was no earthly doubt that he was totally unfit. Pickens felt that the posi-

32. *Ibid.,* 406–42.
33. Holmes to Davis, July 14, 1863, Theophilus Holmes Papers.
34. Hindman to S. Cooper, June 30, 1863, *O. R.,* XXII, Pt. 2, 895–96.
35. Reynolds to A. Leay, July 11, 1863, Thomas C. Reynolds Papers, Letter Book 4463.
36. Reynolds to Seddon, July 20, 1863, Thomas C. Reynolds Papers, Letter Book 4470.

tion of commander in the area required statesmanship as well as generalship and believed that "Price combines more of the qualities necessary to combine & command the country west of the Miss. than any other. . . ."[37]

Also making reference to the Helena debacle, the editor of the *Daily Richmond Whig* bitterly attacked Davis' war policy and his appointment of incompetent officers. To emphasize this last point, the editor pointed to Davis' first having placed Heth, then Van Dorn, and finally Holmes over Price.[38] If Davis felt that by transferring Price he had terminated dissatisfaction in the West, stilled the rumors of a plot to secede from the Confederacy, and quieted the disputes and controversies that seemed to develop wherever Price was stationed, he was sadly disappointed.

V

With the capture of Vicksburg and Port Hudson during the first two weeks in July, the Union forces succeeded in splitting the Confederacy, and their commanders began to consider additional action. Halleck wrote to Grant that as long as Price remained where he was he could threaten Missouri and thus require the retention of large Union forces in that state. If Little Rock and the line along the Arkansas River could be secured by Union forces, all of Arkansas north of the river would soon be cleared and Missouri could be protected solely by militia, thus releasing a great number of troops to Grant.[39] Grant replied that he was sending troops to Helena to destroy Price.[40] Halleck urged Grant to employ all the men he could spare from Vicksburg, and thus Grant sent Brigadier General Frederick Steele with a division to drive Price out of Little Rock.[41] At virtually the same time, Brigadier General James G. Blunt was readying his Union troops for a drive through Indian Territory to take Fort Smith, Arkansas, less than 150 miles up the Arkansas River from Little Rock.

As early as July 23, 1863, Price had warned Kirby Smith that troops in the Arkansas District should be combined on the Arkansas River.[42] On that same day he took temporary command of the district due to Holmes' illness. Price left Des Arc with his division and ordered his commanders to combine their troops around Little Rock. He ordered Marmaduke and Walker to have their cavalry stationed between Helena and Little Rock to slow the expected Union advance.

37. Pickens to Wigfall, July 28, 1863, Wigfall Papers.
38. *Daily Richmond Whig*, July 18, 1863.
39. Halleck to Grant, July 11, 1863, *O. R.*, XXIV, Pt. 3, 497–98.
40. Grant to Halleck, July 21, 1863, *ibid.*, 539.
41. Grant to Halleck, July 24, 1863, *ibid.*, 546–47.
42. Price to Kirby Smith, July 23, 1863, *O. R.*, XXII, Pt. 1, 941–42.

By July 27 Price was in Little Rock, where he took charge of fortifications and began work on a line of rifle pits and other defenses on the north side of the Arkansas River about two and a half miles in front of the city. He connected these fortifications with the city on the south side of the river by three pontoon bridges. At the same time he informed Kirby Smith that he did not feel he could hold the city with his current force. To oppose Steele, who had over 12,000 troops, Price had only 8,000 men scattered throughout the district.[43]

On August 1 Steele slowly began to advance, taking a position at Devall's Bluff, twelve miles northwest of Helena. On September 1 he began his push toward Little Rock, fifty miles away. By that time Blunt had captured Fort Smith. Price pulled his infantry back into his fortifications, which he continued to strengthen, but he kept Walker and Marmaduke's cavalry between the Union forces and himself, where they maintained constant skirmishing. Price was ready to fight Steele if the latter would attack against his fortifications, but he was fully aware of the weakness of his position. Since the Arkansas River was fordable at a dozen places within as many miles of Little Rock, Steele could send men across the river and easily turn Price's position. Realizing this, Price ordered all his supplies and stores removed to Arkadelphia to be certain that they would not fall into enemy hands.

Through the last days of August and the first of September, Price's cavalry engaged in constant skirmishing with the advancing forces.[44] On August 31 Price moved Walker and all of his cavalry south of the Arkansas River and began to construct defenses on that side of the river. By September 9 Steele was within fifteen miles of Little Rock and was putting pontoon bridges across the river. On the next day Brigadier General John Davidson crossed the river with nearly 6,000 troops and he and Steele advanced on opposite sides of the river toward Little Rock.[45]

Realizing his position was untenable and about to be turned, Price sent Marmaduke to the south side of the river and began to pull his troops and artillery out of the trenches. His infantry began to leave their positions at 11:00 A.M., September 10, and the city was fully evacuated by 5:00 P.M. After his men were across the river, Price burned his pontoon bridges. Using Marmaduke's cavalry to screen his withdrawal, Price moved his army toward Arkadelphia, where he arrived on September 14.[46]

The evacuation was a bitter experience for Price. Being an aggres-

43. Price to Brig. Gen. W. R. Boggs, July 27, 1863, *O. R.*, LIII, 884.
44. *O. R.*, XXII, Pt. 1, 468–544.
45. *Ibid.*, 483–86.
46. *Ibid.*, 520–22.

sive and impulsive fighter, he was chagrined at having to abandon the city without a fight, although he had displayed tactical wisdom in withdrawing rather than allowing himself to be trapped in a hopeless situation. Realizing this, Kirby Smith telegraphed Price that he understood the latter's temptation to give battle, but against such superior force he "did wisely in saving and keeping together your little army."[47] This was little solace for Price, who was being criticized in the newspapers and ridiculed by Holmes, who had resumed command of the district on September 25.[48]

VI

In the months following Holmes' resumption of command the Price-Holmes imbroglio became greatly inflamed and there was also a growing questioning of administration strategy regarding the Trans-Mississippi Department. Early in November, 1863, Reynolds learned of the death of Robert L. Y. Peyton, one of Missouri's senators, and was faced with naming a successor. He had earlier considered Price an excellent man for the Senate, but now felt otherwise. Reynolds feared Price's abilities as a party manager and, knowing his dislike for Davis, was apprehensive lest he should become the center of dangerous agitation against the President. There were more personal reasons for his not appointing Price. Desirous of returning to Missouri, Reynolds wanted Price to lead the expedition, since he felt that if he appointed Price to the Senate and the expedition failed he would be blamed for naming Price to the Senate at the expense of the Missouri venture. Moreover, should Price be defeated while leading an invasion of Missouri, his defeat would greatly enhance Reynolds' position as the Confederate leader of the state. Reynolds also recalled Price's delay in earlier years in opposing Thomas Hart Benton, his delay in joining the secession movement, and the connection of his name with the rumored plot against Davis in 1862 and the Northwestern conspiracy of 1862–1863. The use of Price's name in connection with these movements, in Reynolds' opinion, had aroused distrust of him in the minds of cotton-state politicians, whose support Missouri greatly needed.[49]

Missouri's senatorial vacancy afforded Holmes' supporters an excellent chance to rid themselves of Price, and many pressed Reynolds to appoint him as a means of getting him out of the district.[50] Holmes,

47. Kirby Smith to Price, September 12, 1863, *O. R.*, XXII, Pt. 2, 1014.
48. Price to R. W. Johnson, September 27, 1863, *O. R.*, LIII, 897–98.
49. Thomas C. Reynolds Papers, Letter Book 4468 (unpaginated memorandum regarding the appointment of a senator, written in 1864).
50. Reynolds to Price, December 4, 1863, Thomas C. Reynolds Papers, Letter Books 4463 and 4468.

laughing at the seriousness with which Reynolds regarded the appointment of a Missouri Senator, declared: "Price is your biggest man, why not appoint him?"[51] Finally, however, Reynolds appointed Waldo P. Johnson.

Holmes and his intimates, by suggesting that Price be appointed to the Senate, demonstrated the extent to which the feud had grown. The district commander and his closest friend, his adjutant John Hinsdale, believed that Price was motivated solely by a desire for fame. Hinsdale felt that he could have more respect for Price if he "was fighting more for the glorious cause and less for his precious self."[52] Kirby Smith grew increasingly apprehensive with regard to the dispute. He considered Holmes' military abilities to be superior to Price's, but he felt that Price had the confidence and love of the troops. The departmental commander, realizing that the situation could be solved only by separating the two men, felt that one or the other must be transferred out of the district.[53]

For his part, President Davis refused to assess blame because of his distance from the scene, but he did suggest that Price might be directed to campaign in the direction of Kansas and western Missouri.[54] In the meantime he continued to receive reports from the area describing conditions in the Arkansas-Missouri District. One officer wrote from Camp Bragg, Arkansas, that horrible conditions prevailed in Arkansas, where Jo Shelby's Missouri cavalry engaged in stealing in sight of both Holmes and Price. He considered Holmes a poor commander, declaring that nearly everyone had lost respect for him and that the prevalent feeling in the army was that he was a drunkard, played favorites, and had not the slightest capacity to organize or command an army. At the same time the writer referred to Price as our "indomitable old hero," still as pleasant as ever. Noting that as long as Holmes was over Price the people and soldiers would view the latter as an object of governmental oppression, the correspondent closed by stating that Arkansas needed a strategist and an organizing brain.[55]

By January, 1864, Kirby Smith wrote Davis that while he considered Holmes a true patriot his memory was failing, he lacked confidence in himself, and had no fixity of purpose. A younger man should replace him, although Price was not equal to the job. He would con-

51. Thomas C. Reynolds Papers, Letter Book 4468.
52. Hinsdale to Mrs. Wright, August 9, 1864, Holmes Papers.
53. Kirby Smith to Col. R. W. Johnson, October 8, 1863, *O. R.*, XXII, Pt. 2, 1035–36.
54. Davis to Kirby Smith, November 19, 1863, *ibid.*, 1071–72.
55. Cyrus Franklin to Thomas A. Harris, November 30, 1863, Jefferson Davis Papers.

sider it unfortunate if Price were to replace Holmes, for, while he respected Price's fighting abilities, he seriously questioned his administrative capabilities.[56]

In February, 1864, the Confederate Inspector General visited Arkansas to investigate existing conditions. He reported that Holmes was temperate in his habits and true to the cause, but that dissatisfaction with him both in the army and among the people was very great and had become so firmly implanted that his usefulness as commander of the district was greatly impaired. His only comment regarding Price was that he was attentive to his duties and his division was in good order.[57]

The Price-Holmes feud also stimulated much thought regarding the Trans-Mississippi area's relationship to the rest of the Confederacy. Following a conference held in Marshall, Texas, in August, 1863, to discuss the problems of the department, Reynolds wrote Davis that the "real" cause for dissatisfaction in the department was the continual draining of troops from the West to the East. This, plus other difficulties, created the impression among residents of the department that they were the "step children of the Government."[58] Holmes' remaining over Price, their hero, added to the feeling of the West being slighted.

Even stronger criticism of the Davis Administration came from other sources. The *Mobile Register*, commenting on the condition of Missouri, felt that Missourians had stood the test of patriotism more than any other people in the Confederacy, as they had been deserted by their government. The *Register's* editor cited the late General Albert S. Johnston's comment that Price's capture of Lexington and his diversion of Frémont's army had saved the Mississippi Valley for a year. When Price, after a year of marching, fighting, and masterly strategy, had been forced to withdraw because of lack of support from McCulloch, the federal forces were thus relieved of Price's presence in Missouri. Once this occurred, "that resistless march of the *anaconda* began." Forts Henry and Donelson had fallen, Bowling Green had been abandoned, Nashville was captured, Island Number Ten had fallen, as had Memphis and New Orleans. Then Price and his veterans had appeared at Corinth to save what was left. Missouri fought on even after Price withdrew from the state *"for want of support*, which support was always accessible, had the order from Richmond been given." In the editor's opinion, Missouri must not be

---

56. Kirby Smith to R. W. Johnson, January 15, 1864; Kirby Smith to Davis, January 20, 1864, *O. R.* XXXIV, Pt. 2, 868–70, 895–96.

57. *O. R.*, XXII, Pt. 2, 1128–33.

58. Reynolds to W. P. Johnson, August 27, 1863, Thomas C. Reynolds Papers, Letter Book 4471.

abandoned because it was the key to the Mississippi Valley and the entire West.[59]

General Joseph E. Johnston had also come to this conclusion. He felt that if the efforts wasted in Kentucky in 1861 had been made in Missouri, the Confederacy would have gained at least 60,000 troops in that state and so prevented the invasion of the Mississippi Valley by pinning down Grant's army in Missouri or on its borders.[60] However, this was after the fact and Johnston was in no position to send aid to Missouri.

Even Thomas C. Reynolds, a pro-Davis man, maintained doubts about the manner in which the war was being fought. He felt that the Confederate government had always regarded the Trans-Mississippi area as of minor importance and had stripped it of troops to protect the eastern portions of the Confederacy. He could not help but think that future historians would relate with wonder the fact that the Confederate government bent all its energies towards an invasion of hostile Pennsylvania and doubtful Kentucky, while neglecting "the road through friendly Missouri to the Copperhead district of Illinois." Missouri teemed "with men & means, *flanking* the discontented North West, yet we have *systematically* neglected to seize this great advantage."[61] Reynolds like many others, gave great credence to the rumors of discontent within the North centering on the Copperhead movement. Under the impression that the war would go on for five or six more years and would not close without the recovery of Missouri, Reynolds felt that the war's end would come through a union of conservatives in Missouri, Kentucky, and the Northwest, which would bring that section into the Confederacy.[62]

Reynolds believed that the Confederacy had blundered in concentrating forces east of the Mississippi, that Davis had at one time fully appreciated the advantages of an attack into Missouri, and that the transfer of troops east had been without his knowledge. However, he realized that the President continued to sanction withdrawal of troops from the Trans-Mississippi Department and it was now hard for the Governor to say when the error would be rectified.[63]

It was ironic that now, when the opportunity was past and could

59. *Mobile Register*, reprinted in the *Daily Richmond Whig*, November 20, 1863.

60. Undated and unsigned letter in Joseph Johnston's handwriting, Wigfall Papers.

61. Reynolds to E. T. Merrick, November 2, 1863, Thomas C. Reynolds Papers, Letter Book 4463.

62. Reynolds to Col. C. S. Stone, February 20, 1864, Thomas C. Reynolds Papers, Letter Book 4464.

63. Reynolds to Hon. E. T. Merrick, February 25, 1864, Thomas C. Reynolds Papers, Letter Book 4464.

not be recovered, that so many men were coming around to the strategy that Price had persistently pressed since the first days of the conflict.[64] It was even more ironic that Price and his friends, through their vain and headstrong actions in promoting Missouri's cause, may have been instrumental in closing administration minds to Missouri's strategic value.

VII

Shortly after Holmes resumed command of the Arkansas-Missouri District Price went on an extended furlough to Washington, Texas. There he visited with Martha and his family who had fled Missouri in 1862 after the battle of Lexington. Events occuring prior to and during his furlough demonstrated how truly misunderstood he was in both the North and South. This stemmed as much from his own characteristics and actions as anything; while no more ardent Southerner could be found—his entire life style was bound up in the Confederacy—his habits of secrecy, combined with his vanity and ambition, caused many to view him as entirely devoid of principles and motivated solely by his own self-interest.

This misunderstanding was exemplified when news of Price's furlough passed beyond Confederate lines. A Fort Smith, Arkansas, newspaper claimed that Price, "like a rat deserting a sinking ship," had gone to Mexico on a furlough which he meant to prolong into a "French Leave."[65] General Frederick Steele, also under this impression, reported to Major General N. P. Banks that Price and his staff had gone on a sixty-day leave of absence and he had it on good grounds that they "have deserted the sinking ship and gone to Europe."[66] Steele had no doubt that this report was true and anxiously anticipated the desertion of Missouri troops upon learning of Price's disappearance.[67] Steele wrote these letters a day before Price returned to camp to take command of his division.

A conviction that Price was weakening in his allegiance to the Confederacy as early as July, 1863, helped shape events in Missouri that culminated in President Lincoln's efforts to win him over to the Union cause. In July, the *Missouri Republican* reported that Edwin Price had been circulating a petition in southwestern Missouri asking Lincoln to pardon his father. The *Republican* editor also referred to an article in the *Saint Louis Union* stating that Price was penitent

64. It is interesting to note that in late 1862 Abraham Lincoln wrote Judge Samuel Treat of St. Louis that there could be no move in force down the Mississippi River as long as such cities as Louisville, Cincinnati, and St. Louis were endangered by Confederate troops. Lincoln to Treat, November 19, 1862, Abraham Lincoln Papers, Missouri Historical Society.
65. *Fort Smith* (Ark.) *Weekly New Era*, February 20, 1864.
66. Steele to Banks, March 7, 1864, *O. R.*, XXXIV, Pt. 2, 519.
67. *Ibid.*

and wanted to abandon the Confederate cause.[68] These reports caused Edwin to state that he had neither corresponded with his father nor circulated a petition, since he wanted to be left alone to lead the life of a private citizen.[69]

During this same time James S. Rollins, Price's old Whig adversary, also got the impression that Price might be weakening in his resolve and wrote to President Lincoln regarding the situation. Stating that Price was "no smarter that he ought to be, or he never would have been caught in this rebellion against the Government," Rollins declared that Price began as a Union man and that Rollins had "every reason to believe his vanity and his ignorance induced him into the whirlpool of treason." Relying on reports he had received from some of Price's old friends, Rollins felt that with the status of Missouri fixed, Price would be glad to quit, lay down his arms, and return home. Since Price was so prestigious in the state Lincoln could rest "assured (altho' I have no respect for the intellect or the intelligence of this man) it would be a great point gained to get him back." Rollins felt that his return might cause a great many others to desert the Confederacy, and thus asked that Lincoln offer Price a pardon if he returned. Rollins further wanted Lincoln to permit him to enter into negotiations with some of Price's friends who might go south to try to persuade him to return.[70] Lincoln approved Rollins' scheme, saying that if Price voluntarily returned and took the oath of allegiance before the next meeting of Congress he would be pardoned.[71]

When Rollins learned that Edwin Price had applied for a passport to go to Texas to visit his mother he was quick to take advantage of this opportunity to further his scheme. Rollins told Edwin that he was looking for a prominent Southerner whose original sympathies had not been with the rebellion to "rise above the prejudices of the hour and strike for his country" and that he felt Edwin's father to be just that man. Appealing to Sterling's vanity, Rollins stated that this would require moral courage of a high order, and it "would be a magnanimous and Godlike act of which few men are capable," that it would excel in glory any victory on the battlefield, and it would emblazon and consecrate the name of him who did it upon the most sacred page of history; if Price so acted most Missourians would hail him for his heroism.

Since Missouri was already securely in the Union, Rollins could

68. Articles of both papers reprinted in *The* Liberty (Mo.) *Weekly Tribune*, August 7, 1863.

69. Price to the Editor of the St. Louis *Daily Missouri Republican*, July 23, 1863, reprinted *ibid.*

70. Rollins to Lincoln, July 26, 1863, Abraham Lincoln Papers, Vol. 118, Library of Congress.

71. Lincoln to Rollins, August, 1863, *The Collected Works of Abraham Lincoln*, VI, Roy P. Basler, ed., 360.

see no reason why Price should hesitate. Still appealing to Price's vanity, Rollins closed by stating: "The question is, is he equal to the task, and to the occasion? Can he rise above the ordinary actions of ordinary men? Will he attempt this sublime achievement?"[72] Rollins enclosed a passport for Edwin that he had procured from Lincoln and informed him that if he needed anything further it would be granted by General John M. Schofield. After receiving Rollins' letter Edwin wrote that he would like to meet with him in St. Louis to discuss the project.[73] The two did meet in Barnum's Hotel in St. Louis, but nothing more came of the project, since Jefferson Davis refused to allow Edwin to pass through Confederate lines.

Edwin had written Davis asking permission to visit his mother. After meeting with several members of his cabinet and some of the Missouri congressional delegation, Davis denied the request because of the ever-present rumor that Price and his son planned to form a Northwest alliance and to break away from the Confederacy.[74] When Governor Reynolds saw Davis in the early months of 1864 he remarked that Davis had acted wisely in vetoing Edwin's visit to his mother in Texas since his father had been there at the time and "was known to have been very doubtful last fall of our independence." In Reynolds' opinion, the conjunction of their visits might have stirred suspicions of the Northwest plot—a reflection of Reynolds' chronic doubts about Price.[75] Thus were Price's motives constantly in question by his superiors.[76]

72. Rollins to Price, October 28, 1863, James S. Rollins Collection, printed in *The Columbia Missourian*, May 15, 1924, 8.

73. Price to Rollins, November 8, 1863, Rollins Collection, printed *ibid*.

74. Thomas C. Reynolds Papers, Letter Book 4468.

75. *Ibid.*

76. Albert Castel reaches essentially the same conclusion regarding Price's innocence of conspiracy and his desire to avoid having it known that his son had abandoned the Confederate cause. *General Sterling Price and the Civil War in the West*, 195–96.

· 16 ·

District Commander

On the same day that Price resumed command of his division in March, 1864, he wrote General Kirby Smith to offer suggestions for the coming campaign. Feeling that Union strategy would involve a thrust by Frederick Steele from Little Rock, Price suggested that they mass their forces against him. This would render Union strategy useless and at the same time open Missouri to recruiting officers. After taking Little Rock either he or Kirby Smith could lead an invasion into Missouri and could, with a large force, maintain themselves and attract tens of thousands of recruits. Hoping to win support from those who considered the area east of the Mississippi to be of pre-eminent importance, Price declared that he "need not point out to you the immense relief which the presence of an army in Missouri would give our overtasked armies beyond the Mississippi, and for whose relief it is our duty to dare much."[1]

A sudden and unexpected request by Holmes for a transfer put Price in an excellent position to attempt to execute his plan, but it created a dilemma for Kirby Smith.[2] The departmental commander wished to be rid of Holmes, but did not want Price to become district commander, and Price, being the senior major general in the department, could not be easily shunted aside. If Kirby Smith did not appoint him to the position, he would face a storm of abuse from Price's followers. While admiring Price's fighting abilities, Kirby Smith had serious doubts as to his administrative ability and worried over depredations continually attributed to his cavalrymen. Since circumstances did not allow a general to be brought from another department, Kirby Smith had no alternative except to appoint Price to command the district; this he did on March 14, 1864.[3]

Several days after making the appointment, Kirby Smith received Price's letter offering suggestions for the campaign, which involved an attack upon Arkansas and Missouri. Kirby Smith replied that he did not have enough forces to do this; moreover, not wishing to lose

1. *O. R.*, XXXIV, Pt. 2, 1028–29.
2. Holmes requested to be relieved of duty in the Trans-Mississippi Department in February, 1864, upon learning that Kirby Smith no longer felt him capable.
3. Kirby Smith to Price, March 14, 1864, *O. R.*, XXXIV, Pt. 2, 1041.

an opportunity to stress the need for discipline, he told Price to dismount any excess cavalry, instill discipline in the rest, and to dismount immediately any cavalry company to which depredations were traced.[4]

On March 16 Price assumed command of the district and made ready for the ensuing campaign. It would not be long before he had the opportunity to earn the plaudits heaped upon him by his supporters, once they learned that he had at last become commander of the Arkansas-Missouri District.[5] Union strategy called for Nathaniel Banks to advance up Bayou Teche in Louisiana with 17,000 men to rendezvous with 10,000 sent by Major General William T. Sherman from Vicksburg, under Major General A. J. Smith. At the same time Steele was to advance south from Little Rock with 15,000 men to join the other force somewhere near Alexandria, Natchitoches, or Shreveport. From there the entire force would advance up the Red River toward the fertile heartland of the Trans-Mississippi area.[6]

To meet this force Kirby Smith ordered Major General Richard Taylor to oppose A. J. Smith while he commanded the troops against Banks. Price was to slow Steele's advance until Taylor and Kirby Smith had disposed of Banks' Red River expedition. Above all, Price was to keep Steele from joining the bulk of the Union force.

On March 18, 1864, Kirby Smith ordered Price's old division sent to Shreveport immediately.[7] Responding with alacrity, Price had his troops on the march to Kirby Smith on the twentieth. At this same time he notified the departmental commander that he had received communications from St. Louis that affairs in Missouri, Illinois, and Indiana were such that it would be advisable to send a man to contact the Copperhead organizations and to arrange for them to report on an opportune time to move northward.[8] Kirby Smith refused to provide the key to the departmental code to Price's man so he could arrange for the receipt of such information, but did say that if timely notice of any general movement in the North could be gained he would send Price and all his cavalry into Missouri—conditions permitting. If possible, Kirby Smith would support Price in such a move with all of his troops, but circumstances prevented either man from undertaking such a mission, since both were soon hard-pressed on their respective fronts.[9]

4. Kirby Smith to Price, March 15, 1864, *ibid.*, 1043–44.
5. See the *Daily Richmond* (Va.) *Whig*, March 18, 1864.
6. For an excellent analysis of the Red River Campaign, see Ludwell H. Johnson, *Red River Campaign: Politics and Cotton in the Civil War.*
7. S. S. Anderson to Price, March 18, 1864, *O. R.*, XXXIV, Pt. 2, 1056.
8. Reference to this letter in E. Cunningham to Price, *ibid.*, 1077.
9. *Ibid.*

II

Steele began to move from Little Rock toward Arkadelphia on March 23, 1864. By this time Price had dispatched all of his infantry to Kirby Smith. Having only cavalry, all he could do was harass Steele's advance. He received orders from Kirby Smith to retard the enemy and to avoid a general engagement unless extremly advantageous conditions presented themselves. Kirby Smith, perhaps anxious regarding Price's impetuousness, counseled him to fall back whenever advisable since he would withdraw toward reinforcements.[10] Replying that Kirby Smith's instruction had been received and was being carried out, Price wrote that Steele's cavalry was in miserable condition and would thus place the Union commander in a precarious position the deeper he penetrated into the forage-stripped countryside. Moreover, since Price had consumed or destroyed everything around and near the enemy, it would be impossible for him to obtain further supplies or forage.[11]

With Marmaduke and Shelby harassing him all the way Steele continued to advance, and on April 15 Price left Camden to take personal command of his own cavalry. Prior to leaving Camden, Price ordered all supplies removed, leaving only a small detachment there with orders to destroy the pontoon bridges across the Ouachita River if the enemy advanced to that point. Upon taking direct command, Price adopted the practice of forming his men into line of battle from time to time, thus forcing Steele to concentrate his forces for an attack, only to see Price withdraw. At the same time, Price's cavalry disrupted supplies and communications in Steele's rear.

With only 5,000 men Price struggled to slow Steele's force of over 12,000. Reporting to Kirby Smith, Price declared that "I shall endeavor to draw him on slowly, confident that, removed so far from his base, when reinforcements reach us (which I trust you will soon be able to spare) his destruction is certain."[12] To slow Steele, Price had his men fell trees in the enemy's path, continually forced him to deploy for battle, and disrupted his communications and supply lines with cavalry thrusts to his rear. Given the lack of foliage and supplies in the area, Price's tactics were masterful. Not only did he slow the enemy advance, but he forced Steele to continually concentrate his force, thus depriving him of a desperately needed wide forage front.[13] Years of fighting had wrought changes in Price's conception

10. Kirby Smith to Price, March 27, 1864, *ibid.*, 1095.
11. Price to Kirby Smith, April 8, 1864, *O. R.*, XXXIV, Pt. 3, 751–52.
12. Price to Brig. Gen. W. R. Boggs, April 11, 1864, *O. R.*, XXXIV, Pt. 1, 532.
13. For a perceptive analysis of the problems involved in foraging dur-

of warfare; he now ordered his troops to destroy anything the enemy might be able to use. Three years earlier he had ignored McCulloch's counsel to do this very thing.

Kirby Smith continued to implore Price to slow Steele as much as possible. He wanted to dispose of Banks and have Steele drawn far enough into Arkansas to be able to turn on him and destroy him completely. Kirby Smith ordered Price, above all else, to prevent communications between Banks and Steele, since if Steele was to hear of a repulse of Banks he would retreat beyond reach.[14] On April 14 Kirby Smith ordered Price to destroy all supplies in the area of Camden and to keep Steele out of that town if possible, advising that three infantry divisions would soon reach him.[15] On April 15 he repeated his orders to Price, saying that reinforcements should reach him within a week. Aware that he could not give definite orders since he was so far distant from the action, Kirby Smith left the defense of Camden to Price's discretion, although he did caution Price not to place any portion of his force in Camden if this would involve sacrificing it.[16] On April 15 Steele marched into Camden. Price, not knowing when, or if, reinforcements would reach him, felt that he could not risk placing his army in a defense of the town. Much as he hated to retreat, he could not afford to jeopardize his small force.

By the time that Steele entered Camden, Bank's Red River expedition had already been thwarted by Taylor and Kirby Smith and the departmental commander was imploring Taylor to send troops to Price. The two generals disagreed on the necessity for so doing: Taylor, convinced that Price had thwarted Steele's advance, wanted to pursue the withdrawing Federals on his front;[17] Kirby Smith felt that if they moved rapidly they could completely destroy Steele's army and wrote Taylor that the "patient and uncomplaining spirit manifested by Arkansas, the prompt and unselfish behavior of Price in pushing on his whole infantry force to your support, merit a return." Further, Kirby Smith believed that greater results would come from Steele's destruction, as this would save Arkansas politically, gain control of the Arkansas Valley, relieve the whole department from trouble on its northern frontier, and open the road into Missouri. The departmental commander felt that the latter was im-

ing the Civil War, see John G. Moore, "Mobility and Strategy in the Civil War," *Military Affairs*, 24 (Summer, 1960), 68–77. See especially 74–75 for the problems involved in maintaining a wide forage front while at the same time being forced to concentrate for battle.

14. S. S. Anderson to Price, April 12, 1864, *O. R.*, XXXIV, Pt. 3, 761.
15. Kirby Smith to Price, April 14, 1864, *ibid.*, 766.
16. E. Cunningham to Price, April 15, 1864, *ibid.*, 767.
17. Taylor to Kirby Smith, April 28, 1864, Edmund Kirby Smith Papers.

portant since successes east of the Mississippi now warranted an advance. Since Steele was being bold to the point of rashness, Kirby Smith felt that he could be destroyed and that continuing the campaign in Louisiana did not offer the permanent results that would follow a defeat of Steele.[18]

Taylor finally released Brigadier General James Fagan's brigade, which marched north to join Price. On April 25 Fagan completely surprised a Union wagon train at Mark's Mills, Arkansas. His surprise was so complete that he captured all the wagons, six pieces of artillery, and over 1,000 enemy soldiers. This was disastrous for Steele, since a week previously he had lost large amounts of supplies when Price had given Marmaduke extra troopers in order to attack the Union supply line and the latter had captured a wagon train at Poison Springs.[19]

On April 26 Kirby Smith joined Price with a division of infantry and took command of the army, with Price assuming command of two divisions of infantry. That same evening Steele, by this time desperate for supplies, evacuated Camden and began withdrawing toward Little Rock. The following day the Confederate force entered Camden. Kirby Smith pushed his army on a forced march of forty-two miles, finally overtaking Steele in the Saline Bottoms near Jenkins Ferry on the morning of April 30. The Confederate troops, having marched through rain and deep mud the previous night, were at a great disadvantage when thrown against the Federals. They were fatigued and forced to attack through mud and water up to their knees and in places up to their waists.[20]

Marmaduke's dismounted cavalry began the engagement and fought until Price could bring up his infantry. The nature of the ground—swampy, with dense undergrowth and woods—rendered the troop movements difficult, and the falling rain created even more discomforts. The very lay of the land also worked against the Confederates since they were forced to maneuver within an extremely restricted area and had to attack against an enemy barricaded behind fallen timbers.

By the time Price's men were ready Steele had sent back more of his troops to meet them and the battle raged in the swamp for several hours. Price had difficulty getting his artillery into place and never was able to generate an effective fire. Price's troops then began to run low on ammunition, and Kirby Smith sent in another supporting division as Steele was concentrating nearly his entire force to hold

18. Kirby Smith to Taylor, April 12, 1864, Kirby Smith Papers.
19. *O. R.*, XXXIV, Pt. 1, 743–57, 779–82, 788–800.
20. *Ibid.*, 677, 782, 799–800, 802, 809, 815, 817; John M. Harrell, "Arkansas," in *Confederate Military History*, X, Clement A. Evans, ed., 265.

off the Confederate attack so that he could escape across the pontoon bridges thrown across the rampaging Saline River. The Union troops, fighting under the same handicaps as the Confederates, held their ground stubbornly as Steele's men attempted under heavy fire to get their wagons across the Saline.[21]

Steele succeeded in getting his army across the river and destroyed his pontoons after he crossed. Although the Confederates claimed a victory at Jenkins' Ferry, Steele had held them at bay while he crossed his army and thus escaped their grasp, leaving them only his wounded men and several pieces of artillery captured during the battle. Kirby Smith and Price, in their anxiety to pin Steele against the river and prevent his escape, had acted impetuously and had thus aided the Union general in his escape. Had they carefully reconnoitered the field of battle before throwing their troops against Steele's position, they might have been able to seek out the enemy's weak left flank. Instead, they threw their troops in piecemeal as they came up and forced them to endure an enfilading fire.

Once Steele was across the Saline, he was free to retreat toward Little Rock unimpeded, since the swollen condition of the river would prevent pursuit by the Confederates. Nevertheless, the combined Camden and Red River campaign of Kirby Smith, Taylor, and Price had skillfully thwarted the grand strategy of the Union commanders. In turn, Steele had escaped the Confederate attempt to crush him and to regain the Arkansas Valley. The status quo was restored and little else.

III

With the campaign ended, Price and Reynolds, the two leaders most interested in Missouri's future, began to consider a movement into that state. When Price first arrived in the department early in 1863, he had not rashly pressed for an immediate advance into Missouri. Instead, he demonstrated a moderate and sound policy regarding the state, knowing that first things had to come first. Nonetheless, while Price had lost his impetuousness regarding Missouri, he never abandoned his desire to conquer the state for the Confederacy. In a reply to several Missourians who called for an immediate invasion he revealed his deepest motivation for securing the state. Urging Missourians to come to him so that he could retake the state, Price warned of what would happen if Missouri remained in the Union. He believed that if the Confederacy signed a peace treaty with the North while Missouri remained under Northern control, Missourians of "Southern birth and blood," forming a "distinct and superior class," would be shut out by their conquerors from all political privileges. They would be oppressed and impoverished by their

21. *O. R.*, XXXIV, Pt. 1, 782–83, 801–20.

"greedy masters" and "the fate of the Irish and the Poles will be theirs." To him nothing could be more "wretched."[22]

For his part, Governor Reynolds did not maintain a consistent policy regarding an invasion of Missouri. When he became governor he opposed sending an army into the state unless it had a good chance of remaining.[23] In order to give an invasion an aura of permanence he felt that it should be led by the commander of the department and be accompanied by the governor of the state. If Price should go alone, his invasion would be viewed as ancillary to the defense of Arkansas, a mere repetition of the Lexington campaign. Unless the governor accompanied the troops Reynolds felt that Missourians would expect them to withdraw again and would not cooperate to the fullest for fear of reprisals when the army left. Of course, a regular military man must lead the movement to instill discipline,[24] since Reynolds continually objected to the vicious guerilla warfare in Missouri and the lack of discipline among Price's troops.[25] At the same time he felt that Southern sentiment in Missouri was strong, especially after Lincoln's Emancipation Proclamation of January, 1863. Reynolds believed that the population of Missouri was "not so much *pro-slavery* as *anti-free negro*" in its sympathies and opinions.[26]

In February, 1864, Reynolds corresponded with President Davis concerning a move into Missouri. All intelligence from the state confirmed his belief that intense dissatisfaction with federal control existed there, but he again noted that his friends in the state frankly declared that they would not rise unless "they see a *decided* chance of success." Reynolds was in no hurry, since he believed that the war would last at least four or five years longer and therefore no army should enter Missouri until it had sufficient strength to remain.[27]

Price and Reynolds began to correspond with one another on the subject in early June, 1864. Reynolds asked Price to furnish him copies of his letters to Kirby Smith regarding his plans for a campaign.[28] Price, with his usual regard for secrecy, replied that he did not feel "at liberty" to furnish these, but would if Kirby Smith autho-

22. Price to Col. John H. Winston and John C. C. Thornton, January 3, 1864, *O. R.*, XXXIV, Pt. 2, 817–18.

23. Reynolds to Gen. M. J. Thompson, April 13, 1863, Thomas C. Reynolds Papers, Letter Book 4463.

24. Reynolds to Col. W. P. Johnston, May 26, 1863, Thomas C. Reynolds Papers, Letter Book 4470.

25. Reynolds to J. A. Seddon, January 31, 1863, Thomas C. Reynolds Papers, Letter Book 4463.

26. Reynolds to my dear Garesche, June 28, 1863, *ibid.*

27. Reynolds to Davis, February 20, 1864, Thomas C. Reynolds Papers, Letter Book 4464.

28. Reference to this letter in Price to Reynolds, *O. R.*, LIII, 999–1000.

rized it. Then, in a rare expression of personal feelings, Price confessed his dejection resulting from repeated rejections of his plans for a Missouri campaign. He informed the Governor that he had "but little encouragement to form opinions or plans for our future military movements" since none had been adopted. Declaring that he could only hope to gain the approbation of his country, he still maintained that a concentration of troops in Missouri would greatly aid and relieve the whole of the Trans-Mississippi Department.[29]

Reynolds, aware that when Price first assumed command of the district he would have preferred an independent command and authorization to enter Missouri, realized that now Price was growing sensitive regarding his military reputation. In thwarting Steele, Price had been forced to retreat continually without giving battle and to abandon Camden, all of which left him on edge. Now he would consider being replaced as commander of the district as a slur on his reputation. Although Reynolds felt that Price's administrative shortcoming made it advisable for an outsider to command the district, he was changing his opinion regarding Price as a military commander. As an officious bureaucrat, Reynolds felt that Price gave satisfaction in all matters except those in which "as of old his goodness of heart" made him too lenient, but even Reynolds was now willing to grant that "even in these it may be that he is right and others too rigid."[30]

Relations between Price and Reynolds had never been so cordial. The Governor attempted to cheer Price by informing him that Kirby Smith had paid him high compliments for his handling of the Camden campaign. He also informed Price that he refused to believe the harsh interpretations that had been placed on Edwin's desertion and would not accept his resignation from the state guard, since it had never been signed.[31] However, the Governor could never quite rid himself of his suspicion of Price and remained apprehensive regarding his "popularity and tact of management."[32]

By July Reynolds' opinion regarding an expedition had also changed. No longer did he demand a force able to remain in Missouri, since he felt that Davis and others wanted only a diversionary effort. Feeling that a strong diversion in favor of the hard-pressed troops in Georgia and Virginia should be made, he now wanted Price to command it, since he felt that Price's name would gather recruits in Missouri. Price had earlier informed him that the recovery

29. *Ibid.*
30. Reynolds to Waldo P. Johnson, July 14, 1864, Thomas C. Reynolds Papers, Letter Book 4471.
31. Reynolds to Price, May 17, 1864, *ibid.*
32. Reynolds to Davis, May 10, 1864, *ibid.*

of the Arkansas Valley was necessary in order to reoccupy Missouri, but Reynolds felt that a strong diversion could be made without retaking Little Rock, since there would be no intention of occupying Missouri. He presented these thoughts to Price and asked him if he would lead the expedition.[33]

In his reply Price considered Reynolds' suggestion practicable only if Kirby Smith did not want to concentrate troops to take the Arkansas Valley. Price wanted to lead an expedition if it was made and felt that Missourians were ready for a general uprising, the time never having been more propitious than now. He felt that Confederate sympathizers in Missouri should be encouraged and supported promptly, since delay would be dangerous. If not supported, Missourians might become dispirited and apathetic concerning their fate.[34]

Price expressed these same thoughts to Kirby Smith, declaring that accumulating evidence drawn from private letters and contacts in Missouri indicated that federal troops in the state were scattered and the state militia was untrustworthy. Nearly all the principal towns of north Missouri were controlled by Southern sympathizers, and large guerrilla parties were operating in the southern part of the state. Once again he expressed his fear that an increasing desire for peace in the North, combined with late Confederate successes, might bring about a cessation of hostilities and that negotiations for boundaries would take place while Missouri was still in the possession of the Union.[35]

Two days later Reynolds also wrote to Kirby Smith, saying that General Joseph Johnston seemed to be in great peril in Georgia and that a powerful diversion in Missouri might aid him. He also reported that the state was nearly stripped of federal troops and ripe for an uprising. An invasion, even an unsuccessful one, might save Johnston; if successful, it could be reinforced. He claimed that only five to six thousand men under Price would be needed. As governor, he would join the expedition only if it proved to be successful in permanently recovering the state.[36]

Brigadier General Jo Shelby also corresponded with Kirby Smith's headquarters, stating that the entire Missouri department had been stripped of regulars to send to Grant and Sherman, that Southern victories had inflamed the populace of the state, and that uprisings had occurred in over twenty counties. The rebels and the militia

33. Reynolds to Price, July 18, 1864, Thomas C. Reynolds Papers, Letter Book 4464.
34. Price to Reynolds, July 22, 1864, *O. R.*, XLI, Pt. 2, 1020.
35. Price to Kirby Smith, July 23, 1864, *ibid.*, 1023–24.
36. Reynolds to Kirby Smith, July 25, 1864, Thomas C. Reynolds Papers, Letter Book 4464.

alike were calling for organized help from the South. Shelby felt that with a little encouragement over 20,000 men would join the Confederate ranks.[37]

The departmental commander kept an open mind regarding these repeated entreaties on behalf of Missouri. Indeed, as early as June he had ordered Price, through his friends and agents in the state, to obtain accurate information respecting the prospective state of affairs in Missouri during the coming months.[38] Finally, Kirby Smith summoned Price to Shreveport to discuss plans for a raid and on August 4, 1864, ordered him to make immediate arrangements to move into Missouri. Kirby Smith expressly ordered him to avoid all wanton acts of destruction and to rally all loyal Southerners to his cause. Price was to remember that his great need in the state was men and that his primary object, should he not be able to maintain himself within the state, was to bring out as large an accession as possible to his force. He was to make St. Louis the objective of his raid; if compelled to withdraw he could retreat through Kansas and Indian Territory, sweeping them clear of mules, cattle, and military supplies of all kinds.[39]

Upon learning of the proposed expedition, Reynolds decided to accompany it, even though he had earlier stated that he would not go along on a diversionary raid. In a letter to Secretary Seddon, Reynolds indicated that he may have accompanied the raid with the sanction of the War Department to keep an eye on Price and the Copperhead movement in Missouri. While mentioning that the risk was necessary to relieve troops in the East, Reynolds wrote that he would remember Seddon's suggestions about the Northwest but apprehended embarrassments in carrying them out because of Price's propensity for assuming authority. However, Reynolds felt that by gratifying Price's love of fame in the proceedings to be taken, harmony might be secured. Reynolds claimed to be indifferent to everything except success by "proper means," but was not sanguine, since the Copperheads were, in his mind, "very singular people." Evidently Seddon wanted Reynolds to gain control of the Copperhead movement in Missouri and the Northwest for the Confederacy.[40]

While Reynolds may have had governmental sanction to accompany the raid he also had personal reasons for so doing. He revealed these when he mentioned to Seddon a "singular movement" that he believed to be on foot among Missouri exiles, whose watchword and

37. Shelby to Lieut. Col. J. P. Belton, July 27, 1864, *O. R.*, XLI, Pt. 2, 1027–28.

38. W. R. Boggs to Price, June 3, 1864, *O. R.*, XXXIV, Pt. 4, 642.

39. W. R. Boggs to Price, August 4, 1864, *O. R.*, XLI, Pt. 2, 1040–41.

40. Reynolds to Seddon, August 6, 1864, Thomas C. Reynolds Papers, Letter Book 4471.

cardinal principle called for "justice to Genl. Price." Reynolds felt that his appointment of two senators of his own choice, especially his exclusion of John B. Clark,[41] had "evidently blocked some gain or other, designed by Major Snead and Gen. Price's friends." Reynolds felt certain that Price intended to hold a general election once his army was within the state and he feared that an attempt would be made to substitute an army council with Price at its head for his own administration. Constantly anxious regarding his own status, since according to the Missouri Constitution he should have called a gubernatorial election after Governor Jackson's death, Reynolds feared what might happen once Price and his friends reached Missouri.[42] Reynolds thus decided to accompany the raid to protect his own political position.

While many Missourians were sanguine in their expectations for the raid, Trusten Polk, ex-United States senator, former Missouri governor and now an intimate of Price, was apprehensive regarding the expedition once he learned that Reynolds was to accompany it. Immediately upon learning of this Polk wrote Snead, who had gone to Richmond as a congressman, that they were going into "our dear old State under the leadership of the old hero" and were anxious for Snead to accompany them. He wanted Snead to go along to watch out for Reynolds, since he "likely to be a marplot, assumes to possess and wield autocratic powers, and in all probability will at least interfere with, impede, and embarrass the operations of General Price and the army, if indeed, he does not absolutely check or counteract them." Aware of Reynolds' "notions about his duty and mission to protect the people there," Polk feared that Reynolds, in his desire to restore a regular government and his opposition to the style of warfare that had arisen in Missouri, might seriously handicap Price.[43]

On August 26 Price received a letter from a member of a secret order calling itself the Order of the American Knights in Missouri, informing him that he could expect the full co-operation of the society once he entered Missouri. The Knights felt that there had never been a better time to redeem Missouri, since the state militia was fully armed and for the most part under the control of officers who were knights in the O.A.K. He was fully satisfied that thousands would flock to join Price once he entered the state and several thousand additional might even come from Iowa and Illinois to join him.[44]

41. Reynolds chose Waldo P. Johnson to replace Robert Peyton upon the latter's death and when John B. Clark's term in the Senate expired, Reynolds did not reappoint him. Clark was an intimate of Price.
42. Reynolds to Seddon, August 6, 1864, Thomas C. Reynolds Papers, Letter Book 4471.
43. Polk to Snead, August 11, 1864, *O. R.*, XLI, Pt. 1, 1060–62.
44. B. P. Van Court to Price, August 26, 1864, *ibid.*, 1085–86.

This report and others like it convinced Price and his group that Missourians would swarm to their colors. The exiled Missourians were to be sadly disappointed once in the state, for they had not taken into consideration the effect of four years of bitter partisan warfare on the Missouri populace.[45]

On August 27, 1864, Price issued General Order Forty, turning over command of the Arkansas-Missouri District to John Magruder.[46] Price was finally to lead an expedition into Missouri with the sanction of the Confederate government; he was going, however, for different reasons than simply the military diversion desired by the Confederate command, who had little expectation of his remaining in the state.[47] Price hoped to gain enough support in the state to allow him to occupy it and keep it within the Confederacy. He was also motivated by another consideration. The United States presidential election was due in November and, believing the rumors of Northern dissatisfaction with the war and the tremendously exaggerated reports of the influence of the Copperhead movement, Price and others felt that a successful raid at the time of the election might be a powerful prod to the people of the North to defeat Lincoln and sue for peace. If Price could hold Missouri until this happened it would become a part of the Confederacy, thus ensuring the continued existence of his position in a Southern slave society.[48]

45. For an excellent description of guerrilla warfare in Missouri, see Richard S. Brownlee, *Gray Ghosts of the Confederacy: Guerrilla Warfare in the West, 1861–1865.*

46. *O. R.*, XLI, Pt. 2, 1087–88.

47. Smith to his mother, November 16, 1864, Smith to Davis, March 11, 1865, Kirby Smith Papers.

48. Price to Col. John H. Winston and John C. C. Thornton, January 3, 1864, *O. R.*, XXXIV, Pt. 2, 817–18; Price to Kirby Smith, July 23, 1864, *O. R.*, XLI, Pt. 2, 1023–24. Albert Castel, while recognizing that Price's motives differed from those of Kirby Smith, feels that he desired to set up a Confederate government within the state. It appears that Castel has given too much credence to the suspicions of Thomas Snead and Thomas Reynolds, each of whom distrusted the other. It is appropriate to recall that Price and Reynolds were on the best of terms prior to the raid and while Price might have been willing to set up a government if the opportunity arose, it is far more likely that he desired the larger object of affecting the election and securing a truce while he was in control of the state. This squares with his stated beliefs throughout the war and does not depend upon the suspicions of either Snead or Reynolds. Castel, *General Sterling Price and the Civil War in the West*, 202. Castel's opinion of Price's motives appears to affect his interpretation of the raid. See Chap. 17, note 13.

The Last Great Effort

Upon receipt of Kirby Smith's order to lead an expedition into Missouri, Price began to make preparations and gather his forces. He ordered Brigadier General Joseph Shelby to attack DeVall's Bluff, Arkansas, and the railroad line between Little Rock and the White River to divert the enemy's attention, thus enabling Price to cross his troops on the lower Arkansas River. In response to this order Shelby began to create havoc in northeastern Arkansas. During this time Price was forced to wait for necessary ordnance stores, delaying him over a week. He was finally able to leave Camden on August 28, 1864, and arrived in Princeton, Arkansas, on the twenty-ninth, where he assumed command of Brigadier General John S. Marmaduke's and Major General James F. Fagan's cavalry.[1] Since he had been so long delayed, Price determined to cross the Arkansas River above Little Rock and south of Fort Smith, rather than below the capital city.

Price reached Dardanelle, Arkansas, on September 6, where he crossed the Arkansas River and proceeded on to Dover. Then beginning a northeasterly march, he moved toward Batesville, Arkansas, where he had instructed Shelby to meet him. On September 12 he reached the White River a little above Batesville, where he learned that Shelby was at Powhatan, about sixty-four miles to the northeast on the selected route to Missouri. He then ordered his entire command, which he had divided in order to facilitate collection of forage and to rid a wider area of bushwhackers, to rendezvous at Pocahontas, Arkansas.

On September 13 Price arrived in Pocahontas, having already traveled 356 miles from Camden, and there the entire army was concentrated. By September 18 the organization of the Army of Missouri had been completed and consisted of three divisions under Fagan, Marmaduke, and Shelby, totaling nearly 12,000 troops. Over 4,000 of these men were unarmed since Kirby Smith, intent upon transferring troops across the Mississippi, had been unable to furnish Price many men, thus compelling Price to fill his ranks with conscripts and deserters. Price had a nucleus of veterans in the three divisions and, because he hoped to obtain supplies and arms in Mis-

1. A day-by-day itinerary of the raid may be found in *O. R.*, XL, Pt. 1, 622–48.

souri as he advanced, decided to take the unarmed men along, perhaps expecting a repeat of Wilson's Creek. Four years of war had doomed this calculated risk to failure: then, his camp followers had been eager to accompany him in the hope of gaining weapons and getting into battle; now, most of his conscripts were forced to accompany him unwillingly and others joined only to plunder and gain revenge on the Federals for driving them from their homes. This last desperate effort was made up in great part of the dregs of a department that had been sapped of its strength throughout the war. The divisional commanders had reasonably good control of their regulars, but with many conscripts interspersed among them it became more and more difficult to maintain any kind of discipline. In addition there was friction among the commanders: Shelby quarreled with Marmaduke, and Fagan and Marmaduke distrusted Price.[2] Thus was Price's long-awaited Missouri raid inaugurated.

II

Once again, as a means of covering a wide sweep of territory to collect forage and provisions, Price decided to invade Missouri in three columns with Fredericktown, Missouri, as the rendezvous point. Fagan was to march along a central route, with Marmaduke on his right and Shelby on his left, each separated by a ten-to-twenty-mile interval. Price, accompanying Fagan, furnished each divisional commander with a map prepared by his engineer so that they would know his whereabouts at all times. When the army moved out it was followed by a curious entourage of carriages and wagons carrying many Missourians intent upon returning to their native state.[3]

On September 19 the army entered Missouri and on the twenty-fourth the central column arrived at Fredericktown. On their marches Shelby and Marmaduke encountered scattered resistance, fought several skirmishes, and Shelby managed to cut the southernmost telegraph line to northern Missouri at Patterson.[4] While in Fredericktown Price received word that Brigadier General Thomas Ewing was at Ironton with approximately 1,500 federal troops and that Union Major General A. J. Smith and his Sixteenth Corps, who had been diverted from Sherman in Georgia, were near St. Louis.[5] To prevent Smith from coming to the aid of Ewing, whom he meant to destroy, Price dispatched Shelby to wreck railroad bridges on the St. Louis and Iron Mountain Railroad between Ironton and St. Louis.

On the morning of September 26 Price pressed on with Marmaduke

2. Thomas C. Reynolds, "General Sterling Price and the Confederacy," 116.
3. *O. R.*, XLI, Pt. 1, 626–27.
4. *Ibid.*, 652.
5. *Ibid.*, 628.

and Fagan toward Ironton. Prior to his departure he sent a portion of Fagan's force ahead to capture a pass four miles from Ironton that could have been used by the enemy to slow his advance. On the evening of the twenty-sixth Fagan drove in the federal pickets at Arcadia and took a position facing the town. The next morning he pushed the enemy from Arcadia, through Ironton, and into Fort Davidson just west of Pilot Knob.[6]

When Price arrived at Pilot Knob he and his generals held a council to decide what should be done regarding Fort Davidson, a hexagonal earthen structure with heavy fixed batteries. The sandbagged rifle parapets of the fort stood nine feet above the surrounding plain, thus giving the troops inside a clear field of fire for almost 900 yards in every direction. All the cannons were mounted on open, wooden battery platforms on the parapet and the only shell-proof structure in the fort was a deep earth-covered powder magazine. Thus, the fort, while formidable against a frontal assault, was vulnerable to artillery fire from the crests of Pilot Knob Mountain and Shepard's Mountain, both within easy artillery range from the southeast and southwest.[7]

When Price held his council of war he was greatly disturbed by reports that Ewing had forced many Southern sympathizers into the fort, hoping to thwart any effort to shell his position.[8] Nevertheless, the Missourians were elated at the thought of having Ewing, the author of the hated Order Number Eleven that had cleared several Missouri counties of Southern sympathizers, trapped within the fort and they were eager to attack it. Price's engineer encouraged the idea by reporting that the fort was relatively weak and could easily be carried by a frontal assault.[9] Characteristically giving in to romantic impulse rather than military logic, Price ordered a frontal assault on the fort instead of shelling it into submission and possibly injuring fellow Southerners.

Price dismounted his troops and placed Marmaduke's division on the slopes of Shepard's Mountain and Fagan's on Pilot Knob. He then sent Colonel A. S. Dobbin and his mounted brigade to circle around north of the fort in order to block the road leading to Caledonia and Potosi. Price had earlier sent orders to Shelby to continue down the St. Louis and Iron Mountain Railroad and thus felt that this exit for Ewing was also blocked. He could not know that Shelby never received his communications.[10]

6. *Ibid.*, 628–29.
7. For an excellent description of the fort and the battle of Pilot Knob, see Richard S. Brownlee, "The Battle of Pilot Knob," *State of Missouri Official Manual for the Years 1861–1862.*
8. *O. R.,* XLI, Pt. 1, 714.
9. *Ibid.,* 707.
10. *Ibid.,* 629, 653.

At 2:00 P.M. on September 27, several puffs of smoke from Confederate cannon signalled the opening of the attack. With a high, screaming cheer, Price's men streamed on to the flat meadow surrounding the fort. As the federal guns opened up, the Confederates dashed forward discharging volley after volley. The vicious fire from the fort broke the Southern ranks several times but, urged on by their officers, they continued to advance. Fagan's division, composed mostly of conscripts, broke before nearing the fort and only Brigadier General William L. Cabell's brigade reached the moat surrounding the fort. Shattered, the Confederates fell back and Price, furious at the behavior of Fagan's men and grieved by the resulting decimation of his best troops, denied Marmaduke's plea for another frontal assault. Price realized that his troops lacked the spirit that had characterized his soldiers in earlier campaigns and so refused to continue the attack as originally planned. Twenty minutes of fighting had already resulted in a thousand casualties among his troops. The great bulk of these had been suffered by Price's crack brigades who had been cut to pieces in their gallant effort at the very edge of the fort.[11] That night Price changed his plan of attack and decided to entrench his artillery on Shepard's Mountain and use it to reduce the fort. However, he acted too late, since Ewing blew up his powder magazine during the night and escaped up the road that Price believed was blocked by Shelby.

The following day Price's men took possession of the fort, capturing sixteen pieces of artillery and a large amount of supplies, but it was a hollow accomplishment. With his best troops decimated and A. J. Smith's veteran corps of 8,000 men standing between him and St. Louis, Price had no alternative but to turn westward, hoping to add to his force and to gain supplies.[12] After a feint toward St. Louis and a futile chase of Ewing by Shelby and Marmaduke, Price turned his force westward toward Jefferson City. Believing that each day he remained in the state would result in additional recruits, he sought to avoid pitched battles and slowed his march. If his army could swell in size and he could gain needed supplies, his presence in the state might affect the outcome of the November presidential election. Thus, early in the campaign, the mixed motives involved in its very conception became glaringly apparent. A series of lightning-like cavalry strikes would accomplish the diversion desired by the Confederate command system and would very likely have resulted in a spectacularly successful, though short-lived, campaign, since the opposing Federals were so disorganized. This would not accomplish the personal and political desires of Price and he therefore eschewed a

11. *Ibid.*, 629, 679–80; Brownlee, "Pilot Knob."
12. *O. R.*, XLI, Pt. 1, 629–30.

strictly military procedure for a political one. The longer he could remain in the state, the greater the chance of affecting the November election and perhaps even liberating the state.[13]

On September 30, Price's force began its march toward the capital city. Along the way the rebels tore up miles of Pacific Railroad track and destroyed bridges. Many members of foraging parties began to loot and plunder promiscuously. When the troops first entered the state, they had been reasonably careful not to harm citizens of Southern sympathies and Price had commended several officers for shooting those who did.[14] However, by the time the army turned westward, many of Price's regulars had been killed or seriously wounded and their places had been taken by recruits or conscripts. These new additions, many of whom joined Price's army only to loot or to gain revenge on their Union tormentors, caused discipline to deteriorate.

Fewer men were joining his army than Price had anticipated. Four years of bitter partisan warfare in Missouri had caused much of the populace to become dispirited, many feeling that if they left their homes unprotected bushwhackers would destroy them and harm their families. Price temporarily gained some hope from a proclamation issued by the Supreme Commander of the Order of American Knights in Missouri on October 1 from his headquarters in St. Louis, naming Price military commander of the Knights and calling on all members to join his army.[15] Price, like many others, had considered the O.A.K. to be a powerful organization and must have expected a vast increase in his army. He was to be bitterly disappointed at the meager turnout.

Price's slow marches allowed the federal militia and regular troops time to fortify Jefferson City; thus he bypassed the city and headed for Boonville. This was a difficult decision to make, since capture of the state capital would have given prestige to his raid and might have had some effect on Northern opinion concerning the November election. Nonetheless, Price, still shaken by his experience at Pilot Knob, proceeded toward Boonville, reaching that town on October 10 and

13. Albert Castel claims that Price could have and should have marched from Pilot Knob to Jefferson City much faster in order to capture that city before it became heavily defended. He also feels that Price's failure to do this resulted in the failure of his political objective, which Castel saw as the installation of a Confederate government in the Missouri capital. Had this been Price's object, it seems likely he would have attacked the city. Since it was not his primary desire—his object being to remain in the state as long as possible in order to exert an influence on the November elections—the capture of the city, while prestigious, was not of essential importance. Castel, *General Sterling Price and the Civil War in the West*, 225.

14. *O. R.*, XLI, Pt. 1, 720–22.

15. John H. Taylor to the members of the Order of American Knights of the State of Missouri, October 1, 1864, *O. R.*, XLI, Pt. 3, 975–76.

receiving a warm welcome. In the center of an area sympathetic to the South, many men joined Price. He kept the Boonville ferry going night and day to bring in squads of recruits and a local citizen reported that Price's presence "acted like wildfire on the boys and men."[16] He gained some 2,000 recruits while at Boonville, although most came in unarmed and many intended to accompany the army only so long as it remained in Missouri. While in Boonville, Price dispatched "Bloody Bill" Anderson, one of the most vicious Southern guerilla leaders, to destroy railroads north of the Missouri River to prevent reinforcements from reaching his pursuers.[17]

By the time his army collected in Boonville, it had become little more than a mob. Officers and men had loaded themselves with their "rights" and now wanted to turn southward to save what they had.[18] Try as he and his officers might, Price could not gain control over more than the veteran core of his army, now consisting of less than 6,000 of the over 15,000 men attached in one manner or another to his command. Thomas C. Reynolds wrote Price in disgust that his army had ravaged the state to the point where Reynolds would find it very difficult to establish the rightful government in power. He continued that while he could not even find a horse or a blanket to purchase, camp followers were enriching themselves through their plunder of Southern families.[19]

Realizing the poor condition of his army, Price sent Brigadier General John B. Clark, Jr. across the Missouri River to attack Glasgow in the hope of capturing a large supply of guns known to be stored in the city hall. Price desperately needed these weapons to arm his recruits in order to give them an incentive to fight rather than loot. On October 14 Shelby took a brigade and a section of artillery across the river to reinforce Clark's effort, but before they could capture the town the federal commander destroyed the cache of weapons, and left the attackers nothing for their efforts except unwanted prisoners.[20]

Meanwhile Price had moved the remainder of his army on to Jonesborough, where he ordered Brigadier General M. Jeff Thompson to take a detachment to attack Sedalia. While en route Thompson discovered federal troop movements indicating that Union forces might be in front of Price's column and he sent word of this back to his commander.[21] By October 18 Price's entire force was again united and he

16. Mary G. C. Gordon to Jane Gentry Hudnall, October 25, 1864, Mary Gentry Clark Gordon Letter Diary.

17. *O. R.*, XLI, Pt. 1, 632.

18. M. Jeff Thompson, "Reminiscences," in M. Jeff Thompson Papers, 31.

19. Reynolds to S. Price, October 10, 1864, Thomas C. Reynolds Papers, Letter Book 4463.

20. *O. R.*, XLI, Pt. 1, 632, 656–57, 681–82.

21. Thompson to Price, October 15, 1864, *O. R.*, XLI, Pt. 3, 1013.

pushed on toward Lexington, but his time was beginning to run out.

By the time Price reached Boonville, General William Rosecrans, commander of the Department of Missouri, had formulated plans for his destruction. He sent General A. J. Smith's infantry in pursuit of Price and they were to be joined by Major General Joseph A. Mower with 4,500 veterans moving up from Arkansas. At the same time General Alfred Pleasonton, then in command of the Union forces in Jefferson City that numbered over 4,000 horse soldiers, was pursuing Price.[22] Pleasonton pushed Price closely all the way to Boonville, forced several skirmishes, and attempted to slow his advance in order to give other Union forces time to arrive.

While Price was marching across the state, Major General Samuel Curtis, Price's old opponent from Pea Ridge now commanding the Department of Kansas, gathered a large force for an advance into Missouri in hopes of trapping Price between Pleasonton, Smith, and himself. By October 15 Curtis had over 15,000 militiamen and regulars massed on the Kansas-Missouri border and ordered Major General James G. Blunt to move toward Lexington, Missouri, with three brigades. The Union strategy, however, ran into trouble when the bulk of Curtis' men would only go as far as the Big Blue River, six miles east of Kansas City.[23]

Price, aware that Smith was marching toward Sedalia from the south, that Blunt was in Lexington, Curtis farther west, and Pleasonton somewhere in his rear, had to determine some means of escape. He decided to move slightly southward so as to come between Smith and Blunt and prevent a juncture of their forces. He hoped to destroy Blunt and Smith in turn. With this accomplished he could move on Curtis, thus defeating each separate enemy force before they could effect a junction.

On October 19 Shelby's men pushed ahead toward Lexington, made contact with Blunt, and pushed him back. By the time that Price could move all his force forward darkness fell. Realizing that he was outnumbered, but determined to make a stand, Blunt fell back to the Little Blue River. However, Curtis instructed him to leave only 400 men and two howitzers on the Little Blue and to fall back with his main force to the Big Blue River, where Curtis was forced to remain by the stubbornness of his militia.[24]

On October 21 Price moved his force out toward the Little Blue and his forward elements had a sharp skirmish with Blunt's token force under Colonel Thomas Moonlight and his Eleventh Kansas cavalry. As Price's main force began to advance, the Federals were forced to retreat to the hills on the west bank of the river, but as the Confed-

22. *O. R.*, XLI, Pt. 1, 310–12.
23. *Ibid.*, 471, 474.
24. Curtis to Blunt, October 20, 1864, *O. R.*, XLI, Pt. 4, 145.

erates advanced in force, Blunt, who had earlier convinced Curtis to allow him to return to the Little Blue, arrived with his main force and engaged the Confederates with his entire command. The Union troops, with their breech-loading rifles and massed artillery, enjoyed superior firepower and thus managed to push the Rebels back nearly half a mile. However, the Confederate superiority in manpower began to tell as Price engulfed Blunt's flanks. Slowly Blunt gave way, retreating toward Independence, and by late afternoon he had removed his entire force from the field by withdrawing to the west.[25]

Blunt joined Curtis' force, which was entrenched in a north-south line from the mouth of the Big Blue River to Russell's Ford near Hickman Mills. There, on the west bank of the river, which was covered with brush and was much steeper than the east bank, the Federals enjoyed abundant protection. Curtis concentrated his forces at the main fords of the river, much to the discomfort of Blunt, who seriously doubted that Price would attack at the points of greatest concentration.[26]

In the meantime, Price saw his own problem as necessitating several moves. He must force a crossing of the Big Blue and defeat Curtis before Smith and Pleasonton could come to Curtis' aid, while at the same time holding off Pleasonton in his rear until he had defeated Curtis. All the while he must protect his supply train—by now a massive one of over 600 heavily-laden wagons. To do this he decided to send Shelby and part of Fagan's force to attack Curtis, while Fagan would bring up the wagon train with the other portion of his force and Marmaduke would keep Pleasonton at bay until Shelby finished with Curtis.

Price began the action on Saturday morning, October 22, by sending Colonel Sidney Jackman with his brigade of Shelby's division against Curtis at the main crossing of the Big Blue. At 9:00 A.M. Jackman, establishing contact, made a feint at the crossing. Curtis became suspicious of Jackman's half-hearted attempt at crossing and frantically sent word along his line to watch for a crossing upstream. While Jackman was attacking the main ford Shelby took Thompson's brigade and methodically probed Curtis' right for a weak spot. He was unsuccessful in that effort and by 11:00 A.M. felt he could delay no longer and would have to force a crossing. He decided to use Byram's Ford, where the Independence Road crossed the Big Blue, even though it would not be an easy task due to the narrowness of the road and the fact that the Union commanders had placed fallen timber in the river. Nevertheless, Shelby brought Jackman's brigade to the ford, dismounted it and, supported by Thompson's brigade, ordered an at-

25. *O. R.*, XLI, Pt. 1, 574–75, 657–58, 666.
26. James G. Blunt, "General Blunt's Account of his Civil War Experience," *Kansas Historical Quarterly*, I:3 (May, 1932), 257.

tempt to cross the river. They were sharply opposed by Colonel Charles Jennison with a full brigade of dismounted cavalry supporting a battery on a hill that rose above the ford. Again and again Jackman tried to force a crossing only to be thrown back. At 2:00 P.M. Shelby instructed Jackman to continue his efforts while he sent commands both up and downstream to attempt to find another crossing.[27]

Soon Lieutenant Colonel Alonzo Slayback found the little-used Hinckle Ford downstream, splashed his command across and thundered down on Jennison's exposed left flank. At that very moment Jackman was attempting a crossing and both forces struck at the same time, crushing the Union position. Jennison's men withdrew to the west and Curtis' line began to crumble as the Confederates massed for a drive northward. Shelby pushed his entire division across the river and struck out to the north, where he crushed militia that tried to resist him. Jennison's men never panicked and he consequently was able to keep Jackman and Slayback from completely routing his portion of the line. Night fell before the Confederates could complete their victory and they were forced to break off the engagement. This allowed Curtis time to reform his line around Westport. The Union position was now an east-west one just south of Brush Creek.

While Shelby was forcing a crossing of the Big Blue, Pleasonton attacked Marmaduke's position guarding Independence. He pushed Marmaduke back across the Big Blue to the ground at Byram's Ford where Jennison had stood earlier in the day. That same day Pleasonton asked Curtis to divert Smith's troops, who were south of Price, to Independence to support him. Curtis, complying with the request, had no way of knowing that this would cost him the complete destruction of Price's army. There were now no Union forces south of Price to cut off any possible retreat.

By the evening of October 22 Price found himself in a difficult position. Taking up headquarters in the Boston Adams house a mile and a half southwest of Byram's Ford, he thought out his situation. His troops under Shelby and Fagan, minus Cabell's brigade, were strung out facing the Union forces along the south bank of Brush Creek from the state line to the Big Blue. Marmaduke was concentrated against Pleasonton at Byram's Ford, and Cabell, with his brigade and a ragtag brigade of unarmed recruits, guarded Price's massive wagon train, still east of the Big Blue moving southward toward Little Santa Fe and the military road to Fort Scott, Kansas. Above all, Price wanted to avoid being crushed while at the same time attempting to protect his wagon train and herd of over 3,000 cattle. If he fell back on his wagons without delaying the Union forces his troops would be caught in a tangle and certainly would be destroyed. Therefore, Price

27. *O. R.*, XLI, Pt. 1, 478–84, 575–76, 584–86, 658–59, 667–68, 676.

decided to attempt to hold off Curtis and Pleasonton and take the chance that Smith would not attack his wagons. It was a stroke of good fortune for Price that Pleasonton had diverted Smith, since there would have been nothing between him and the meagerly-defended wagon train. Now only one brigade of Pleasonton's cavalry remained within striking distance of the wagons.

Saturday night, October 22, 1864, both armies remained tensed for the expected action. With the break of day the two lines moved toward one another in the gray light. As the lines came together Shelby and Fagan, attacking along Brush Creek, forced the Union line back from fence row to fence row until it had been pushed back to the north side of the creek. The tide of battle was running with the Confederates, but, due to Price's inattention to logistical matters, they were unable to press home their advantage. A shortage of ammunition at this critical moment compelled them to halt their attack. Within an hour ammunition had been obtained, but by that time the opportunity to press their advantage had passed as Curtis moved up reinforcements and more artillery. By 11:00 A.M. Curtis had great numbers of reinforcements stationed in the rear of the Union lines, waiting to charge the Southern positions. Fortunately for Curtis, a native of the region offered to guide his forces through a defile near the crest of the Confederate positions, thus enabling him to place artillery in a position to rake the Rebels.[28]

As the fighting along Brush Creek became intense the Confederate line, bending but not breaking, managed to push back repeated Union attacks. By noon, however, Price received word that Marmaduke was being pushed back by Pleasonton and also could see that Fagan was beginning to give way along Brush Creek. Word that his wagon train was being menaced necessitated removing Jackman's brigade from Shelby, thus leaving him to hold the line as best he could until Price could remove the wagons to safety. Price hurried toward the wagons, which were under attack from Brigadier General John McNeil's brigade of Union cavalry. Taking a desperate chance, Price rounded up several thousand unarmed men, formed them into a battle line, and advanced them toward the attacking Federals. The ruse was successful and McNeil, thinking himself to be outnumbered, retreated.[29]

In the meantime Shelby found himself in a precarious position. By 1:00 P.M. the Union line was beginning to engulf him from the front, right, and rear, where Marmaduke had given way. Fagan and Marmaduke retreated toward the wagon train while Shelby continued to fight for time. Although many of his men broke for the rear, his dogged withdrawal saved the Confederate army from complete destruc-

28. *Ibid.*, 484–91, 658–59, 667–68.
29. *Ibid.*, 372, 636.

tion. By the time Shelby left the field Price was moving with the wagon train southward toward the middle fork of the Grand River.[30]

Price had successfully evaded the pincers movement of Curtis, Smith, and Pleasonton, whose forces greatly outnumbered his own. While suffering a defeat at Westport, he kept his army intact and his wagon train secure, but his desire to protect the wagon train caused him to lose the opportunity to save his army and make good his escape. Instead of destroying the excess wagons and making forced marches, he chose to try to bring out his wagon train and thus slowed his march precipitously. Again, the romantic-egotistical desire to preserve this semblance of success clouded his military judgment.

Price's decision was to prove disastrous, even though Curtis did not order a pursuit until twelve hours after the Confederates had left the field at Westport. Price retreated across the state line into Kansas with his troops divided into parallel columns with his wagons and artillery between them. By this time his army was a tangle of cavalrymen, cattle, refugees, and wagons, interspersed with unarmed men, who now amounted to nearly his entire command. Many of his conscripts were deserting along the line of march. Encumbered in this manner Price's army made only twenty-four miles their first day, thus affording Curtis time to catch up.

On October 25 Pleasonton made contact with the fleeing Confederates on the banks of the Marais-des-Cygnes River. He immediately pressed the attack and caught Marmaduke and Fagan, protecting the rear of the train, off guard, routing them and pushing their troops back upon the wagons. Marmaduke and Cabell attempted to rally the fleeing troops with their veterans but were engulfed and captured, along with five pieces of artillery and over 500 of their men. The remnants of Fagan's and Marmaduke's troops fled toward the front of the column. Price, hearing the sounds of battle, mounted his horse and rode to the rear where he met the fleeing troops, but he could not rally them; they were deaf to his entreaties. Shelby, who was making a foray toward Fort Scott, received Price's frantic message to return and galloped with his men back to the scene of battle. His force crashed into the Union forces, stunned them, and gave Price time to regroup his men and continue his withdrawal. Continuing to fight a delaying action, Shelby gave Price time to move his troops and wagons out of danger, pushing them on until midnight. That night Price burned over a third of his wagons and made fifty-six miles the next day.[31]

Price's flight, with the Federals close on his heels, continued all day and most of the night of October 27–28. About 2:00 P.M. on the twenty-eighth Blunt, now heading the pursuit, caught up with the retreating Southerners just south of Newtonia, Missouri. Assuming

30. *Ibid.*, 636, 659.
31. *Ibid.*, 337–38, 491–95, 636–37, 659–60.

that the remainder of the Union troops would soon come to his assistance, Blunt pushed on too soon. Consequently, Shelby, commanding the rearguard, outnumbered Blunt and was able to defeat him soundly before Union assistance could arrive.[32]

On October 29 General Rosecrans provided Price and his harried troops with unexpected relief. He recalled all troops belonging to his Department of Missouri, leaving Curtis with only 3,500 men to continue the chase. Before this situation could be rectified by Curtis, Price was out of reach; he had crossed the Arkansas River on November 7 about thirty miles west of Fort Smith, Arkansas. Prior to this he sent three brigades of Fagan's division into northwest Arkansas to collect absentees and deserters and to return them within the lines during December. After crossing the river, Price furloughed Cabell's and Colonel W. F. Slemon's brigades and marched into Indian Territory as General Kirby Smith had ordered. However, instead of finding an abundance of supplies to be destroyed, Price and his men met only hunger, cold, and fatigue. The morale of his army suffered terribly and Price reported to Magruder from Boggy Depot in the Choctaw Nation that his troops were exhausted, with less than one-third of them armed and only one-half mounted.[33] They continued, nonetheless, and staggered into Bonham, Texas, on November 23, where they received supplies and the spirits of the men lifted.[34] From Bonham the Confederates turned eastward and arrived in Laynesport, Arkansas, on December 2, 1864. After an incredible march of 1,488 miles through enemy territory, Price's force limped back into Confederate territory.

III

With the raid completed it soon became apparent that the same dichotomy of thought regarding the objects of the mission colored the observations of those who analyzed it. Price, desirous of remaining in the state, gaining vast numbers of recruits, and being in a strong enough position to influence the presidential election, was bitterly disappointed. Missourians had not rallied to him as he had expected and those who did seemed to use his army only as an excuse to cover their lust for plunder. He was bitterly disillusioned with the results of his raid, especially the sacrifice of many of his best troops to bring out only unarmed recruits.[35]

32. *Ibid.*, 507–15, 661.
33. William G. Hazen to Alex R. Hazen, December 21, 1864, Miscellaneous Manuscripts; Dr. J. H. P. Baker Diary, 1864–1865, November 1, 1864; Sterling Price to Maj. Gen. J. B. Magruder, *O. R.*, XLI, Pt. 4, 1076–77.
34. Baker Diary, December 2, 1864.
35. Price to Kirby Smith, January 6, 1865, *O. R.*, XLVIII, Pt. 1, 1318; Kirby Smith to Davis, March 11, 1865, Kirby Smith Papers.

On the other hand, General Kirby Smith considered the raid a success. To Kirby Smith, the military man, the raid had fulfilled its intended purposes: A. J. Smith and Mower had been diverted from Sherman,[36] and Union troops in Arkansas had been neutralized, unable to send support east of the Mississippi River. The raid temporarily halted the siege of Mobile for lack of reinforcements, and freed General Nathan Bedford Forrest to operate against Sherman's communications. Kirby Smith informed President Davis that he had entertained no thought of Price remaining in Missouri and, since his raid had forced a concentration of from 40,000 to 50,000 Union troops and diverted reinforcements from Sherman, he "considered Gen'l. Price as having effected the objects for which he was ordered into Missouri and the expedition a success."[37] General John Magruder and others congratulated Price for his escape from the dangers encountered in Missouri.[38]

If the Confederate command was satisfied with the raid, Thomas C. Reynolds was not. He had been greatly shocked and disgusted by the pillaging and looting and feared that Missourians would now oppose the return of his exiled government. When he reached Boggy Depot, Reynolds wrote Kirby Smith that there might be an attempt to "whitewash the disgracefully managed expedition to Missouri," but when he returned he intended to handle the matter "*without gloves.*"[39] In an attempt to disassociate himself from the raid and disgrace Price, Reynolds published a lengthy public letter in the *Texas Republican* on December 23, 1864. This diatribe blamed Price for gross mismanagement and negligence at the expense of his men, and called for his removal from command. Reynolds, still feeling that Missouri might be retaken, wanted Price's power broken and his own reputation unsullied.[40]

Not willing to rest his case against Price on the public letter, Reynolds wrote to various Confederate officers and officials, attempting to stir up opposition to Price.[41] Still not content, Reynolds attempted to blackmail Price into resigning from the service by informing him that he was writing a memoir concerning what he considered to be trai-

36. Sherman to General A. J. Smith, September 12, 1864, *O. R.*, XXXIX, Pt. 2, 370.

37. Kirby Smith to Davis, November 21, 1864, Jefferson Davis Papers.

38. Magruder to Price, November 16, 1864; M. M. Parsons to Price, November 16, 1864, *O. R.*, XLI, Pt. 4, 1053–55.

39. Reynolds to Kirby Smith, November 19, 1864, Thomas C. Reynolds Papers, Letter Book 4464.

40. This letter may be found at the Conclusion of Reynolds' "Price and the Confederacy."

41. Reynolds to Captain Selden, January 7, 1865; Reynolds to Kirby Smith, January 7, 1865; Reynolds to Major General Ewing, January 16, 1865, Thomas C. Reynolds Papers, Letter Book 4464.

torous activity on the part of Price and his son Edwin in forming a Northwest confederacy. If Price did not resign Reynolds would make the memoir public and disgrace both father and son.[42]

At the time of Reynolds' attack, Price was on furlough in Washington, Texas. Already bitterly disappointed at the results of his campaign, Price was shocked and indignant at Reynolds' attempt to impugn both his military capabilities and his principles. Even in his disappointment Price could not permit such an attack to go unnoticed. He requested Kirby Smith to have Reynolds prefer charges against him and to convene a court-martial as soon as possible to air the charges and to decide if they were valid.[43] He meant to have his honor vindicated.

During this time Reynolds continued to seek support, none too successfully, in his vendetta against Price,[44] and simultaneously struck out against Confederate military authorities in the department. Writing to Governor Pendleton Murrah of Texas, he claimed it was "high time" that Confederate military authorities should learn that "they are the inferiors in rank to the executive of a sovereign state."[45]

By March 7, 1865, Price had reported back to active duty and assumed command of the Missouri division of infantry under Magruder. Finally, after constant insistence by Price, Kirby Smith ordered a court of inquiry to convene to discuss Reynolds' complaints against Price. A court-martial could not be held since Reynolds, as a civilian, could not bring charges against Price, and Kirby Smith himself saw no valid cause for such action.[46] Kirby Smith's refusal to call a court-martial should have been sufficient, but Price was bound to clear his name and so the court of inquiry was held. On March 12, 1865, Kirby Smith removed Price from active command, since he could not serve while attending the court of inquiry, which was to open its sessions on April 21, 1865, at Shreveport. The court's proceedings, however, were interrupted by the surrender of the department before the court could reach any conclusions.[47]

IV

Whether considered a success or a failure at the time, the raid did illuminate Price's strengths and weaknesses as a military commander.

42. Reynolds to Price, December 24, 1864, *O. R.*, XLI, Pt. 4, 1123.

43. Price to Kirby Smith, January 6, 1865, *O. R.*, XLVIII, Pt. 1, 1318.

44. See Thomas C. Reynolds Papers, Letter Book 4464, during the months of January and February, 1865.

45. Reynolds to Murrah, February 11, 1865, Thomas C. Reynolds Papers, Letter Book 4454.

46. Kirby Smith to R. W. Johnson, March 16, 1865; Kirby Smith to Samuel Cooper, March 16, 1865, *O. R.*, XLVIII, Pt. 1, 1427–29.

47. The minutes of the court of inquiry may be found in *O. R.*, XLI, Pt. 1, 701–29.

His most serious faults—his impulsiveness and lack of military subordination of his personal feelings—were glaringly apparent at Pilot Knob. Giving way to his passions rather than calculating the attack in strictly military terms, Price sent his men in an open assault against a heavily fortified position when it could have been shelled into submission, or even bypassed with no ill effects. As it was, he lost a considerable number of his best troops and jeopardized his expedition at the very outset.

While his impulsiveness had been a serious defect throughout much of his military career, it was at times a source of strength. This very impulsiveness had saved his army at Iuka and Westport. At Iuka he left his front facing Ord completely exposed, taking the chance that this would not draw an attack so that he could deal with Rosecrans. At Westport he left his wagon train exposed, risking an attack by Smith, in order to face Curtis and Pleasonton. In both instances his success was due in great part to chance, a northwest wind at Iuka, and an ill-advised order by Curtis at Westport. Nevertheless, a conservative commander might have reacted timidly in both cases and lost his entire army. In battle the difference between success and failure often rests on taking a bold risk when in difficulty.

Always holding an exalted view of his own military prowess, Price had, during the course of the war, demonstrated a reluctance to obey orders from his superiors. The Missouri raid represented an example of a coincidence of Price's own desires and the orders of Kirby Smith. His slow movement across the state, which allowed the Federals to mass against him, resulted from his desire to add recruits, assuming that the longer he was able to remain in one area the more men he could gain. This was also in consonance with Kirby Smith's orders to him to make the accession of recruits the main object of his mission. Further, his unwillingness to abandon his supply train stemmed from his own desire to emerge from the raid triumphant and Kirby Smith's orders to bring out all the supplies possible. Nonetheless, even here Price interpreted his orders rather loosely in order to serve his own ends.

His activity in Arkansas prior to the raid had, however, demonstrated his ability to occasionally overcome his impulsiveness. His evacuation of his tenuous position at Little Rock in the face of superior forces was judicious even while costing him prestige. Also, his actions in the Camden expedition, which entailed retreat without offering battle, demonstrated his ability as a tactical commander to obey his superior's orders. While with an independent command at Iuka, Price exercised tactical discretion in escaping Grant's trap rather than offering battle. Following Corinth, he advised the even more impulsive Van Dorn against a renewal of the battle.

Price's impulsiveness when uncurbed was both a strength and a weakness, as was his handling of volunteer troops. Price gained the affection and respect of his men by treating them kindly, with a minimum of discipline, and by his personal courage on the battlefield. While thus gaining the most from his men in battle, this led to serious problems when in bivouac or on the march. His men were notorious for their thieving and little was done about it. Their actions on the march into Missouri may have been beyond Price's or anyone's ability to curb; nonetheless, these were made easier by his manner of dealing with his troops.[48]

As a tactician Price demonstrated serious shortcomings, but his grasp of strategy was generally excellent.[49] He constantly insisted upon the value of putting troops into Missouri to take advantage of its flanking position and when he had entered the state, even with a meager force, he disrupted Union strategy. When the Confederate command finally ordered him into the state it was too late for anything except a diversion, but his raid did indicate what might have been achieved if attempted earlier with more troops. This pointed up Davis' and others' lack of understanding of the value of the Trans-Mississippi Department. Davis' policy of appointing someone from outside the area to command the department, while proper from the standpoint of keeping quarrels at a minimum, subordinated the department to the East. Kirby Smith, for example, was an excellent administrator and maintained good order within the department, but without a vital personal interest in the area he did not use its potential to the fullest. Instead, he subordinated it to the East, where he felt the most important results would come, not realizing he might ease military pressure on the East by vigorous action in his own department. Kirby Smith himself longed to be in service east of the Mississippi where he considered the laurels of combat were abundant.[50]

While serving under Bragg in Mississippi, Price had fully grasped the strategic importance of aiding Bragg rather than proceeding on a raid into Tennessee as Van Dorn suggested. While eager to enter Tennessee, Price realized that, without first taking Corinth, any raid into Tennessee would be jeopardized and would place Bragg in a

48. Shelby, whose official report is the most judicious of those submitted, commented to this effect even though he had no great respect for Price, *ibid.*, 662.

49. "Tactics" in this context means the maneuvering of troops in the presence of an enemy while "strategy" denotes the large-scale planning and directing of operations to secure the objects of war. Albert Castel presents a different evaluation of Price's capabilities as a general. Castel feels that Missouri was a lost cause and that Price should not have remained so dogmatically attached to it. This results in quite a different evaluation of Price's capabilities as a strategist. Castel, *General Sterling Price*, 283–85.

50. Joseph Howard Parks, *General Edmund Kirby Smith, C. S. A.*, 347–48.

perilous position. It was Price in this instance who wished to coordinate his movements with those of his superior rather than attempt a raid with Van Dorn.

As a military man Price represented an amalgam. While showing signs of growth as a commander during the war—especially throughout his retreat from Little Rock—just as often he displayed rash amateurism. Price simply did not mature consistently as a general during the course of the Civil War. He and his men fought well, in many instances heroically, but he could never gain respect in the Confederate command system. While this lack of respect was certainly due in part to the existing prejudice against his lack of military training, this could have been overcome. Price himself greatly injured his relationship with his superiors by his reluctance to subordinate his own ego and vanity, thus making it difficult to get along with him. Had he restrained his own ego, he might well have gained the respect necessary for his ideas regarding strategy to gain acceptance. In the final analysis, Price represented an excellent example of the natural ability with which the Confederacy abounded, only to be wasted. Caught up in the maze of individual egos, ambitions, and desires, which no one seemed either able or willing to overcome, Price epitomized the contentiousness that seriously damaged the Confederate military effort. Further, his loyalty to Missouri and his unwillingness to subordinate his state's interests for the whole, reflected a serious handicap under which the Confederacy labored. Its death was greatly hastened by the States rights disease and all its complications.

Price may best be described as a military romantic. His vision of a Southern aristocracy merged with his conception of military service. He had no practical military knowledge and was little concerned with logistics, as his failure to provide sufficient munitions at Westport made glaringly apparent, but instead glorified in the dashing charge. Price's image of the cavalier simply excluded the mundane.

V

At the time of Price's return from furlough, the Trans-Mississippi Department was in a weakened state, but the Confederate command still insisted that Kirby Smith transfer men east of the Mississippi River. The departmental commander himself favored this,[51] but Union control of the river made such action impractical and so military affairs in the department came to a virtual standstill. The financial, economic, and social demoralization that spread across the Confederacy entered the Trans-Mississippi Department also.

News of Lee's surrender on April 9, 1865, reached the Trans-

51. Kirby Smith's attitude regarding troop movements may best be seen in his letter to Davis of October 8, 1864, Jefferson Davis Papers.

Mississippi within ten days. The shock that spread over the department elicited varying responses. Many favored continued resistance while others wanted to surrender. Much discontent at the prospect of surrender developed among the Missouri troops and Kirby Smith was certain that Price was fomenting a plot to overthrow him, take command of the department, and continue to fight.[52] This, like previous power plots woven about Price, was simply loose talk.

As weeks passed, demoralization spread throughout the rapidly deteriorating department. Mutinous troops captured government stores and deserted to return to their homes. To end this situation Lieutenant General Simon B. Buckner, Price, and Brigadier General Joseph Brent proceeded to Baton Rouge on May 24 and then to New Orleans to meet with Major General E. R. S. Canby to discuss surrender terms. Meeting with Canby on May 25 the three generals signed surrender terms similar to those extended by Grant to Lee, with the condition that they would be subject to Kirby Smith's approval as commander of the department.[53] On June 2, Kirby Smith and Magruder signed the surrender terms on board a Union steamer off Galveston harbor. The war in the West came to an end.

52. Kirby Smith to Governor ——, "n.d.," Kirby Smith Papers.
53. *O. R.*, XLVIII, Pt. 2, 600–601.

· 18 ·

Flight to Mexico

At the time of the surrender, affairs in the Trans-Mississippi Department were deteriorating rapidly. Bands of unruly soldiers raided supply depots; many troops simply drifted away from their units and went home, and General Joseph Shelby was organizing much of his old brigade to accompany him to Mexico.

After the surrender Price also decided to go to Mexico. He was determined not to live in a society in which he felt he would be proscribed and in which he had lost all status.[1] He could have returned to Missouri where Edwin, who had purchased all his property at a sheriff's auction in 1863,[2] was running his business as profitably as possible under existing conditions. However, feeling that he could be part of a new aristocracy in Mexico, Price decided to turn his back on Missouri and his shattered society.

II

Because of unsettled conditions within the department, the uncertainties of a long trip through rough country, and unstable conditions in Mexico, Price decided to have his son Celsus take Martha, Stella,

1. For Price's thoughts on the prospect of living in Missouri after a Northern victory, see Price to Col. John H. Winston and John C. C. Thornton, January 3, 1864, *O. R.*, XXIV, Pt. 2, 817–18; Price to Dear Sir, December 16, 1865, published in *The* Liberty (Mo.) *Weekly Tribune*, January 25, 1866. While a great deal has been written on the Confederate movement to Mexico, little, if any, attention has been paid to the motivations of those who took part in this exodus. The standard interpretation maintains that these men feared reprisals if they remained in the United States. The most prominent works dealing with the Confederates in Mexico are: Andrew Rolle, *The Lost Cause: The Confederate Exodus to Mexico*; George D. Harmon, "Confederate Migrations to Mexico," *Hispanic American Historical Review*, XVII (November, 1937), 458–87; Lawrence Hill, "Confederate Exiles to Brazil," *Hispanic American Historical Review*, VII (May, 1927), 192–210; Lawrence Hill, "The Confederate Exodus to South America," *Southwestern Historical Quarterly*, XXXIX (October, 1935), 100–134 (January, 1936), 161–99 (April, 1936), 309–26; Carl Coke Rister, "Carlota: A Confederate Colony in Mexico," *Journal of Southern History*, XI (February, 1945), 33–50; J. Fred Rippy, "Mexican Projects of the Confederates," *Southwestern Historical Quarterly*, XXII (April, 1919), 291–317.
2. Chariton County (Mo.) Deed Book X, 104.

and Quintus home to Missouri to live with Edwin and his wife until he could send for them. While Celsus departed for Washington, Texas, where Martha had settled during the war, Price and several members of his staff, including his son Heber, began their journey toward Mexico. Driving a mule-drawn ambulance, Price left for San Antonio during the first week of June. On June 18 he left that city with a Mexican passport permitting him to enter and travel at will in Mexico.

Trusten Polk and Governor Isham Harris of Tennessee joined Price and his party at Salinas on July 9.³ Price had intended to proceed to Mexico City by way of Matamoras, but upon learning that the road was swarming with *Juaristas*, decided to go by way of San Luis Potosi. The small caravan, now consisting of two ambulances, Polk's carriage, and assorted mounted men, made between twenty and thirty miles a day and arrived in San Luis Potosi on July 24. Very favorably impressed with the city, the group stayed several days to rest their animals and make necessary repairs on their vehicles. They must have been cheered at the comfortable and inexpensive living conditions they discovered at San Luis Potosi and entertained great expectations for the success of their journey; while impressed with the countryside, they were still a bit uneasy about whether it was best for them to remain in Mexico. There was a feeling that the United States government would ask Mexico to return all Confederates who had fled there and that they would be given up. Moreover, although the French-controlled government was very courteous and polite to them, the exiles were not certain that the regime would last, and the *Juaristas* were unfriendly toward them.⁴

On July 27 the party left San Luis Potosi about noon and began its journey toward Mexico City. Shortly after their departure the travelers ran into heavy rains and Price, having sold his tent for needed supplies, slept in his ambulance with several others. The beautiful, lush countryside maintained their high spirits and Price and the others were much impressed by the imposing haciendas, many of which were owned by absentee landlords; several haciendas stretched out for miles and were worked by hordes of peons. Occasionally they would pass an especially impressive hacienda surrounded by beautiful gardens and orchards owned by an Englishman or a Frenchman. It seemed as if their search for a genteel society was to be rewarded and their lost status would be regained.

Continuing, occasionally making repairs or resting for a day or so, the Confederates approached mountainous regions during the first week of August. They spied an occasional group of bandits, but were

3. The account of Price's journey to Cordoba is drawn from the diary of Trusten Polk, Trusten Polk Papers.
4. M. M. Kimmel to his father, July 25, 1865, Glasgow Papers.

not bothered because they were sufficiently numerous and well-armed to discourage attacks. From time to time they took heart upon meeting ex-Confederate officers or officials along the way, some of whom had gained positions in the Mexican government.

On the afternoon of August 9 the party reached Mexico City and took lodgings at the San Carlos Hotel. They remained in the capital for more than six weeks and enjoyed a pleasant stay. Government officials treated them graciously and invited them to official functions and after-theatre gatherings.[5] Price and Harris received commissions from Maximilian to survey and plot lands for a settlement near Cordoba.

Early the morning of September 19, 1865, Price left Mexico City accompanied by Polk, Harris, Shelby—who had given up the thought of enlisting his entire brigade in Maximilian's service—and seven of Shelby's men. They reached Cordoba in the early evening of September 22. While they had been pleased with northern Mexico, they were not impressed with this city. Their accommodations were indifferent and the city was old, giving the impression it had seen its best days. Polk and Price were nonetheless hopeful that the Emperor's scheme of establishing settlements of immigrants would be successful in revitalizing the area. As soon as possible Price and Harris fitted themselves out with horses and began to execute their duties as land commissioners. They finally selected an area close to Cordoba and near the railroad running from Mexico City to Vera Cruz, some seventy miles to the east. The site was well-watered and some of the land was already under cultivation.

Within a few months the men finished surveying the land and the thirty ex-Confederates then at the colony gave Price the first choice of land. He selected a 640-acre section near a brook and a spring, and donated twenty-four acres of it for a townsite. The men laid this off into town lots and cleared away the brush to erect their homes. They named the town Carlota in honor of the Empress of Mexico.

By the second week in December Price felt settled enough to write his family and instruct them to join him as soon as they could raise the means. He also replied to a friend, who had evidently written a letter expressing concern about him and suggested his return to the United States to gain a pardon. Price declared that he could not think of returning and seeking a pardon since he was entirely satisfied with his part in the war and would act in the same way again under similar circumstances. Claiming that he had done all in his power to avert the war and had not favored secession, Price declared that once the war began he did not hesitate to take his stand with the South. Now he expressed great fear for the South's future. Price advised his friend

5. Several letters of invitation to these functions are in the Trusten Polk Papers.

that once the Negro was given his civil rights all Southerners would be better off in Mexico.

As to the situation in Mexico, Price declared that he had no doubt about the ability of the imperial government, since French troops were arriving weekly and the marauding bands that infested the country were fast being exterminated. Then, promoting his colony, Price expounded on the character of the land, stating that when its abundance became known many immigrants would join him and that land now selling cheaply would skyrocket. He mentioned a neighbor who had sold his last year's coffee crop for $16,000 and praised the lush vegetation in the surrounding area.[6]

Interest in the colony was not restricted to prospective immigrants. During the third week of December a correspondent of the New York *Herald* traveled to Cordoba to interview Price and to report on the colony's progress.[7] The reporter was impressed with the country along the way from Cordoba to Carlota, describing it as a "hothouse of huge dimension," abounding in orange groves, magnolias, lemon trees, and other lush vegetation. The ex-Confederate soldier who escorted him to Carlota assured him that the village would be as large as Richmond or New Orleans within a few years.

Upon entering the village the correspondent felt that only meager beginnings had been made, those consisting of a few scattered tents and a cluster of a dozen unfinished houses near a stream. As he approached Price's town lot he observed only a straw-roofed, low-built, massive cottage in half-finished condition. When Price saw him he assumed that he was from St. Louis and had come to join the colony. When he found out the visitor's purpose he made a gesture of impatience and seemed disappointed, but he did consent to an interview, and the two men sat down to a meal of game, fruits, and cream served by a Mexican servant. Price began by expounding on the wonders of the area, but soon began to talk of the war and, pointing to a large trunk containing all the papers relating to his campaigns, declared that he would like to find an historian to write them up as an "eternal monument" to the memory of his men.

Observing that Governor Harris' plantation as well as those of Shelby and Richard Ewell, an ex-lieutenant general under Lee, were close by, the correspondent inquired of Price if he and the others were not afraid that the *Juaristas* would upset their plans. Price passed off the *Juaristas* as insignificant and then began to expound on the nature of the Mexican people. He felt that the example of the French had revived sentiments of pride within the Mexicans and that they would

6. Price to ——, December 16, 1865, published in *The* Liberty *Weekly Tribune*, January 25, 1866.

7. Correspondent's report written from Cordoba on December 23, 1865, printed in *The* Jefferson City (Mo.) *Peoples' Tribune*, January 24, 1866.

soon become as invincible as the Spaniards of past eras. Obviously, Price's changed circumstances had drastically altered his opinion of the Mexican from that which he had held during the Mexican War.

When the correspondent inquired if Price felt that Mexico would resist an invasion from the United States, Price answered that it would not do so at the moment, and he felt that Mexico was shielded by the nation best suited to protect it. He thought that the French, being tied to Maximilian by treaty and by promise, intended to remain. He further believed that they would have the support of other European nations if the United States invaded Mexico.

Still on the subject of an invasion, Price declared emphatically that even if the United States did occupy the country the "landed aristocracy of Mexico would . . . ally itself with the landed aristocracy of the South" to thwart the permanent takeover of the country. He claimed that all landowners were in favor of an empire. Further, Price, becoming carried away by his bitterness toward the United States, claimed that Mexican Catholics would unite with American Catholics to create disturbances and unrest if the United States conquered Mexico.

At the conclusion of a five-hour interview, Price accompanied the correspondent on his return to Cordoba and showed him several fields he claimed to have developed. They were filled with coffee, tobacco, fruit, and beans, as well as cattle and horses. Since some of the land that Price purchased had already been under cultivation, he claimed to have exported a coffee crop worth $5,000 that year. In his eagerness to promote the colony Price evidently showed the reporter a field owned by a long-time resident, since his own fields were not as yet so productive.

It also became evident that the old feeling of *noblesse oblige* had not left Price. As he pointed out his Mexican field hands to the reporter he expressed a desire for the government to pass legislation enabling them to pass out of peonage and thus elevate themselves to an honorable position. A shift from Negro slavery to Mexican peonage would not call for any change in Price's attitude toward his workers, since he still adhered to the idea of Anglo-Saxon superiority. He announced that the Mexicans were faithful, lazy, required constant watching, and were childlike in the manner in which they responded well to kind treatment. He claimed to see an improvement in their work and general behavior each day.

Evidently this feeling of superiority and the idea that a new aristocracy was being formed were not unique to Price, since Thomas C. Reynolds, who had taken a position as an official on several of the railroads running out of Mexico City, felt that it was not the first time in history that civil strife in one country had sent "forth a swarm to regenerate or found another." In the past, Rome and Carthage had been founded by exiles, just as "Old Pap founded his Carlota." Respecting the United States and any return there, Reynolds felt that President Andrew Johnson represented the feelings and opinions of the "poor whites." This made Reynolds apprehensive, since he wished to return only as "one of the ruling class," and wanted the aristocratic South restored to equality and power within the Union.[8]

In April, 1866, Price's halcyon days ended and he endured severe anxiety. Celsus, with the intention of joining his father, had taken his mother, Stella, Quintus, and all their belongings to New York to board a boat for Havana and Vera Cruz. On April 10 they left on board the *Vera Cruz*, but, in a fog off the North Carolina coast, the ship ran aground, split in two, and sank with nearly all their possessions, including a fine piano belonging to Stella; this forced them to return to New York to take another boat. In the meantime Price, who had learned of the accident shortly after it happened, remained anxious regarding the welfare of his family.

Later in May, when the family finally arrived in Vera Cruz, Martha could barely recognize her husband because he had lost so much weight. He had been waiting in Vera Cruz for over three weeks for their arrival and during that time had suffered a severe recurrence of his stomach disorder.[9] After his family's arrival he recovered sufficiently to take them to Cordoba, where they took up residence until their home in Carlota could be completed.

Shortly after returning to Cordoba, Price, who had begun to recuperate, was requested by the colony to visit Mexico City to talk with the French authorities about outrages being committed on the colony by *Juaristas*. He spent nearly three weeks in Mexico City making arrangements for troops to be sent to the area to protect the settlers.

By the first week in July, Price and his family were evidently satisfied that the area was going to be safe and prosperous. Martha wrote a friend that the surrounding countryside was beautiful and that their unfinished home had a lovely grove of fruit trees surrounding it. She felt that their prospects for a "pleasant society" at Carlota were good and reported that there was an Episcopal service at Carlota every Sunday and Methodist preaching at Cordoba as well. She concluded that "if no unforseen accident occurs the Americans will do well, and most of them be comfortably settled in a few years."[10]

Sterling shared her hopes and told Edwin in a letter that every month that he lived in Mexico satisfied him still more, that it had a

8. Reynolds to Jubal A. Early, May 10, 1866, Thomas C. Reynolds Papers.

9. Martha Price to Mrs. B., July, 1866, published in *The* Liberty *Weekly Tribune*, August 31, 1866.

10. *Ibid.*

fine climate and wonderfully productive soil, and that with a stable government would be the most desirable country he had even seen. With regard to the stability of the country he felt that Edwin occupied as good a vantage point to determine this as he did. He did, however, state that when he visited the Emperor, Maximilian had become agitated when doubt was expressed that his government was fixed and permanently established. Feeling that Maximilian should know better than outsiders, Price expressed the opinion that another year would be necessary for the emperor to establish his authority fully. After stating that their losses were heavy in the shipwreck and could not be replaced in Mexico, he thanked Edwin for taking care of the family while they were in Missouri and transferred to him in fee simple all his claims to real estate in Missouri. Evidently he had forgiven Edwin for any shortcomings during the war, since he closed with an affectionate farewell.[11]

Within two months of such hopeful letters, Martha became concerned about her husband's health. She was heartsick at seeing him return from work completely fatigued from his efforts. Feeling that it would be several years before they could realize anything on their wild lands, Martha wrote a friend that since they were still living in Cordoba and found it very expensive, they had to economize at every point. The rent was high, provisions enormously costly and the little means left to her from the shipwreck had been greatly depleted. Sterling himself was completely out of funds. Martha was most distressed over "the general's" health and feared that it would be months before he was able to do anything at all. Price had labored industriously to complete his home before the rainy season but had not succeeded. His exertions in the rains weakened him to the point that he contacted typhoid fever, and his son Heber also fell severely ill with the disease.[12]

Conditions continued to worsen rather than improve. Price became steadily weaker and there was grave concern for his life if he remained in Cordoba. Moreover, the stability of the country no longer seemed assured. Most of the ex-Confederates were becoming disillusioned, concluding that they had been very foolish to undertake such a venture, and many were beginning to drift homeward.[13]

In December the Prices, though forced to leave Heber behind because of his poor condition, left for Missouri. Sterling was well enough to travel, and Martha feared for his life if he remained in Mexico any

11. Price to Edwin Price, July 2, 1866, letter in the Confederate Museum, Richmond, Virginia.
12. Martha Price to Mrs. Tyree, August 29, 1866, published in *The Peoples' Tribune*, October 3, 1866.
13. Jo. Shelby to Bob [R. J. Lawrence], February 2, 186[7], Civil War Papers, Missouri Historical Society.

longer. While en route from Cordoba, Sterling's friends back in Missouri began to consider what they could do for him. A committee was established to inquire if a pardon could be obtained for him and if he would accept and obey its provisions. In addition a "Price Fund" was started in hopes of raising $50,000 to buy the Prices a home in St. Louis and to get them re-established in Missouri. One Missouri newspaper commented that, since Virginia had provided for Lee, "Let Missouri not be behind in generosity to him who sacrificed his all in the same cause."[14]

Although his health was failing, Price had not lost his spirit or his bitterness toward the United States, and thus he refused to allow his friends to seek a pardon for him. Once again declaring that he had no apologies to offer for his past actions, Price announced that he would not accept a pardon even if his friends obtained one for him.[15] He was returning to Missouri alienated and determined to live within the society that had destroyed his way of life, but not to be a part of it.

III

On January 15, 1867, Price and his family boarded a steamboat bearing the ironic name *Olive Branch* at New Orleans to begin the last leg of their journey home. While in New Orleans Price had been honored and feted; several influential merchants gave him a large tract of land in Texas and other prominent commercial firms offered him agencies in Europe.[16] Intent upon returning home, he refused all such offers.

Upon their arrival in St. Louis on January 11, Price and his family took lodgings at the Southern Hotel while he attempted to regain his health. His old Boonslick friend William B. Napton barely recognized Price upon first seeing him, so emaciated was his condition.[17] A correspondent for a Cincinnati newspaper recognized the fifty-eight-year-old Price in the dining room of his hotel and described him as a poor old broken man, bald and lean, with his "shoulders bent under dwindled flesh, his feet were shrunken in their gaiters and rattled like a pair of spurs." He recalled that Price's voice was so low that the waiter had to bend down to hear his order.[18]

By March Price was making a remarkable recovery. During the second week of that month he and Celsus opened a commission busi-

14. *The Peoples' Tribune*, January 9, 1867.
15. Excerpt from a letter from Price to Thomas Snead published in *The Columbia Missourian*, May 31, 1924.
16. New Orleans *Times* and New Orleans *Daily Picayune*, January 5, 1867, reprinted in *The* Lexington (Mo.) *Weekly Caucasian*, January 16, 1867.
17. William B. Napton Diary, Missouri Historical Society, January 14, 1867.
18. *The Peoples' Tribune*, February 13, 1867.

ness, "Sterling Price & Co.," on the corner of Commercial and Chestnut streets. In no time they were doing a thriving business selling tobacco and purchasing plantation supplies for their customers. Price's name greatly enhanced the prospects of the firm and in June he was designated to award the prizes at Tobacco Premium Day in St. Louis.[19] By that time the Prices were comfortably settled in a home on Sixteenth Street. The house had been purchased by donations from hundreds of Missourians most of whom, in the hard times, had been able to make only small contributions.

Soon after this Price again began to complain of being unwell.[20] Although no definite symptoms of any disease were apparent, he became bent and feeble. In August he went to a spa at Baden Springs, Indiana, and seemed at first to recuperate, but he soon began to have severe attacks of diarrhea and returned to St. Louis. There he advised his family how to run the business so that, if he should die, "his name might shelter them from the poverty into which his allegiance to principles had thrown them." His health again improved and during the second week in September he visited the country home of General D. M. Frost near St. Ferdinand. On the way home he was in high spirits and commented that he had never felt better.

On Monday evening, September 23, cholera symptoms appeared, but to no alarming degree. By Tuesday morning his condition seemed favorable and the three attending doctors felt encouraged. He failed to rally, however, and by Wednesday night was having periodic lapses of short duration, during which he would call for "a prompt flank movement." The sound of a familiar voice would orient his wandering senses. Early on Thursday morning his mind was clear enough to recall that he had some hogsheads of tobacco to be sold, and he gave directions that Celsus should be awakened in time to see to that. He felt much better, although languid, and at times would rouse himself and even attempt to jest. Friday night his condition worsened again and by Saturday his doctors were convinced that there was no longer any hope for him, although they did not inform the family. That night Dr. J. C. Niedlet, who had served on Price's staff, remained by his couch, as did his favorite niece Lizzie and many of his old staff members. By midnight his entire family was in the room as he began to toss restlessly. Price's most intimate friends, knowing he had never been baptized, urged Martha to have that ceremony performed. She consented and an Episcopal priest was brought in to administer the ceremony. Price, able only to mumble in response to the priest, attempted to recite the Lord's Prayer, but had to desist from weakness. Everyone in the room knelt near the

19. St. Louis *Daily Missouri Republican,* June 14, 1867.
20. The following account of Price's last days is drawn from an anonymous eyewitness account in the Reynolds Papers.

couch and, when the final prayer was finished, only Price's hoarse breathing broke the silence. He attempted ineffectually to clear his throat several times and sank back on the couch. He lay still, but Dr. Niedlet found a weak pulse and continued to hold his wrist until 2:12 A.M. when he uttered in a low voice: "He is gone."

On October 3, 1867, Price's body rested in state in the First Methodist Episcopal Church on the corner of Eighth and Washington streets, where a constant throng of people passed to view the body. At 2:00 P.M. the funeral service began and shortly before 3:00 P.M. the Arnot brothers drove the hearse, drawn by matched blacks, and a carriage, drawn by grays, to the front of the church.

Epilogue

Old Pap

Although the Price family's arrival in St. Louis in 1867 occasioned no great reception, Price did receive a certain sympathy and became a figure with whom many Missourians could identify. Conditions and opinions had changed in Missouri in the year and a half since the end of the war. Immediately after the cessation of fighting, bitter feelings still existed between Unionist and ex-Confederate in Missouri. When Price's brother, Robert Pugh, returned to Brunswick in November, 1865, he was wounded by pro-Union men. Surviving five gunshot wounds, he fled with his family to Texas, where he had lived during the war. By the time that Sterling returned to the state, feelings had mellowed and many of his old enemies and pro-Union men had become disillusioned with Radical Reconstruction.[1] Price, broken in health, but defiant in attitude, symbolized the "lost cause" in Missouri, and after his death his stature as a symbol of the past grew even more pronounced.

When word of Price's death circulated throughout the state there was great mourning. Editors across Missouri eulogized him and many used his name to attack reconstruction policies.[2] In life Price had precipitated either violent hatred or unbending devotion; in death his named seemed to evoke only a nostalgia for a past that, either real or imagined, was somehow better. Caught up in the angry strife of the day, Missourians could only speak sympathetically of Price. In the future the mention of "Old Pap" would evoke only nostalgia; his weaknesses and human frailties would be forgotten.

1. This may best be seen by scanning the editorial policy of the St. Louis *Daily Missouri Republican*, from late 1865 through 1867.
2. Typical of these editorials was one appearing in *The* Jefferson City (Mo.) *Peoples' Tribune*, October 2, 1867: "But to have shed his best blood in Mexico does not prove a man's 'loyalty.' Nothing short of having assisted to violate the Constitution, destroy the equality of the States, free the negroes, and place them over and above the white race, now constitutes a *loyal man*. In this sense, Gen. Price never claimed to be loyal, and his true friends thank God that he never was."

Bibliography

Manuscripts

Lisbon Applegate Collection. Joint Collection of Western Historical Manuscripts and State Historical Society Manuscripts, University of Missouri, Columbia.

David Rice Atchison Papers. Joint Collection of Western Historical Manuscripts and State Historical Society Manuscripts, University of Missouri, Columbia.

J. H. P. Baker Diary. Joint Collection of Western Historical Manuscripts and State Historical Society Manuscripts, University of Missouri, Columbia.

Edward Bates Diary, 1848–1852. Missouri Historical Society, St. Louis.

P. G. T. Beauregard Papers. Duke University, Durham, North Carolina.

Thomas Hart Benton Papers. Missouri Historical Society, St. Louis.

Gist Blair Papers. Manuscript Division, Library of Congress, Washington, D.C.

James O. Broadhead Papers. Missouri Historical Society, St. Louis.

Civil War Papers. Missouri Historical Society, St. Louis.

Corbin Papers. Rutgers College Collection, Missouri Historical Society, St. Louis.

Jefferson Davis. Letter to Genl. Sterling Price, December 20, 1861. Confederate Museum, Richmond, Virginia.

Jefferson Davis Papers. Duke University, Durham, North Carolina.

Daniel Dunklin Collection. Joint Collection of Western Historical Manuscripts and State Historical Society Manuscripts, University of Missouri, Columbia.

Doctor Henry Dye, Journal. Josiah Trent Collection, Duke University Medical Center Library, Historical Collection, Durham, North Carolina.

Feazel and Lewis, Journal, 1843–1847. Microfilm in State Historical Society of Missouri, Columbia.

Hamilton R. Gamble Papers. Missouri Historical Society, St. Louis.

Glasgow Papers. Missouri Historical Society, St. Louis.

Mary Gentry Clark Gordon Letter Diary. Joint Collection of Western Historical Manuscripts and State Historical Society Manuscripts, University of Missouri, Columbia.

Memoirs of Major-General Henry Heth, C. S. A. Typescript in Heth-Selden Manuscripts, University of Virginia, Charlottesville.

Theophilus Holmes Papers. Duke University Library, Durham, North Carolina.

Hubard Family Papers. Southern Historical Collection, University of North Carolina, Chapel Hill.

Stephen Watts Kearny Papers. Missouri Historical Society, St. Louis.

James Keyte Papers. Joint Collection of Western Historical Manuscripts

and State Historical Society Manuscripts, University of Missouri, Columbia.
Abiel Leonard Collection. Joint Collection of Western Historical Manuscripts and State Historical Society Manuscripts, University of Missouri, Columbia.
Abraham Lincoln Papers. Missouri Historical Society, St. Louis.
Abraham Lincoln Papers. Robert Todd Lincoln Collection, Manuscript Division, Library of Congress, Washington, D.C.
Meredith M. Marmaduke Collection. Joint Collection of Western Historical Manuscripts and State Historical Society Manuscripts, University of Missouri, Columbia.
Mexican War Letters, Missouri Historical Society, St. Louis.
Miscellaneous Manuscripts, Joint Collection of Western Historical Manuscripts and State Historical Society Manuscripts, University of Missouri, Columbia.
Missouri History Papers, Missouri Historical Society, St. Louis.
William B. Napton Diary. Missouri Historical Society, St. Louis.
M. M. Parson Papers. Duke University, Durham, North Carolina.
Trusten Polk Papers. Southern Historical Collection, University of North Carolina, Chapel Hill.
Price Family Papers. Missouri Historical Society, St. Louis.
Sterling Price. Letter to Edwin Price, July 2, 1866. Confederate Museum, Richmond, Virginia.
Reynolds Papers. Missouri Historical Society, St. Louis.
Thomas C. Reynolds. Letters. Joint Collection of Western Historical Manuscripts and State Historical Society Manuscripts, University of Missouri, Columbia.
———. Papers. Manuscript Division, Library of Congress, Washington, D.C. (microfilm, University of Missouri).
———. "General Sterling Price and the Confederacy," Missouri Historical Society, St. Louis.
James S. Rollins Collection. Joint Collection of Western Historical Manuscripts and State Historical Society Manuscripts, University of Missouri, Columbia.
St. John's Parish Vestry Book 31. Archives Division, Virginia State Library, Richmond.
St. Patrick's Parish Vestry Book. Archives Division, Virginia State Library, Richmond.
Sappington Papers. Missouri Historical Society, St. Louis.
Shannon Family Papers. Joint Collection of Western Historical Manuscripts and State Historical Society Manuscripts, University of Missouri, Columbia.
Edmund Kirby Smith Papers. Southern Historical Collection, University of North Carolina, Chapel Hill.
George R. Smith Papers. Missouri Historical Society, St. Louis.
Dr. John F. Snyder Collection. Missouri Historical Society, St. Louis.
Sublette Papers. Missouri Historical Society, St. Louis.
Creed Taylor Papers. University of Virginia, Charlottesville.
M. Jeff Thompson Papers. Southern Historical Collection, University of North Carolina, Chapel Hill.
Judge Samuel Treat Papers. Missouri Historical Society, St. Louis.
Lewis T. Wigfall Papers. Manuscript Division, Library of Congress, Washington, D.C.

Published Collections

The Collected Works of Abraham Lincoln, Roy P. Basler, ed. New Brunswick, 1953, 8 vols.

Correspondence of John C. Calhoun, J. Franklin Jameson, ed. Annual Report of the American Historical Association for the Year 1899, Vol. II. Washington, D.C., 1900.

The Correspondence of Robert Toombs, Alexander Stephens, and Howell Cobb, U. B. Phillips, ed. Annual Report of the American Historical Association for the Year 1912, Vol. II. Washington, D.C., 1913.

Document Containing Correspondence, Orders, etc., in relation to the disturbance with the Mormons. . . . Fayette, Missouri, 1841.

The Messages and Proclamations of the Governors of the State of Missouri, Vol. II, Buel Leopard, and Floyd Shoemaker, eds. The State Historical Society of Missouri, Columbia, 1922.

Public Documents

United States Government

Senate Executive Documents, Thirtieth Congress, First Session. Washington, D.C., Wendell and Van Benthuysen, 1847–1848.

House Executive Documents, Twenty-Ninth Congress, Second Session. Washington, D.C., Ritchie and Heiss, 1846–1847.

House Executive Documents, Thirtieth Congress, First Session. Washington, D.C., Wendell and Van Benthuysen, 1847–1848.

The Adjutant General's Office. Letters Received, National Archives, Washington, D.C.

The Adjutant General's Office. Letters Sent, National Archives, Washington, D.C.

Congressional Directory for the First Session of the Twenty-Ninth Congress of the United States of America. Washington, D.C., T. and G. S. Gideon, 1846.

Congressional Globe, Twenty-Ninth Congress, First Session, Washington, D.C., Blair and Rives, 1846.

The War of the Rebellion: A Compilation of the Official Records of the Union and Confederate Armies. Washington, D.C., Government Printing Office, 1880–1900, 69 vols.

State Documents, Missouri

Journal of the Senate for various sessions from the Seventh to the Twenty-First, 1833–1861, inclusive, various places of publication.

Journal of the House of Representatives for various sessions from the Ninth to the Eighteenth, 1837–1855, inclusive, various places of publication.

Chariton County, Missouri, Deed Books C, D, and X.

Chariton County, Missouri, Tax Lists, 1833 and 1837. Missouri Historical Society, St. Louis.

Howard County, Missouri, Deed Book Q.

Journal and Proceedings of the Missouri State Convention Held at Jefferson City and St. Louis, March, 1861. St. Louis, George Knapp & Co., 1861.

Laws of the State of Missouri, Eleventh and Fifteenth General Assemblies, Jefferson City, 1841, 1849.

Missouri Censuses, 1830 and 1840.

State Documents, Virginia

Amelia County, Virginia, Deed Book 2. Archives Division, Virginia State Library, Richmond.
Muster Rolls of the Virginia Militia in the War of 1812, Archives Division, Virginia State Library, Richmond.
John Price, Will. Henrico County, Virginia, Records, Deeds and Wills, 1710–1714.
Pugh Price, Will. Prince Edward County, Virginia, Will Book 1.
Prince Edward County, Virginia, Deed Book 14.
Prince Edward County, Virginia, Legislative Petitions, Archives Division, Virginia State Library, Richmond.
Virginia Census, 1810.

Newspapers

American Farmer, Baltimore, Maryland
Arkansas State Gazette, Little Rock, Arkansas
Boon's Lick Democrat, Fayette, Missouri
Boon's Lick Times, Fayette, Missouri
The Columbia Missourian, Columbia, Missouri
Daily Missouri Democrat, St. Louis, Missouri
Daily Missouri Republican, St. Louis, Missouri
Daily Picayune, New Orleans, Louisiana
Daily Richmond Enquirer, Richmond, Virginia
Daily Richmond Whig, Richmond, Virginia
Fort Smith Weekly New Era, Fort Smith, Arkansas
Glasgow Weekly Times, Glasgow, Missouri
Illinois State Register, Springfield, Illinois
Jefferson Enquirer, Jefferson City, Missouri
Jefferson Examiner, Jefferson City, Missouri
Jeffersonian Republican, Jefferson City, Missouri
Lynchburg Daily Virginian, Lynchburg, Virginia
The Metropolitan, Jefferson City, Missouri
Missouri Argus, St. Louis, Missouri
Missouri Army Argus, single issue in Dr. James A. Gaines Papers, Miscellaneous Manuscripts, Joint Collection of Western Historical Manuscripts and State Historical Society Manuscripts, University of Missouri—Columbia.
Missouri Courier, Palmyra, Missouri
Missouri Register, Boonville, Missouri
Missouri Reporter, St. Louis, Missouri
Missouri Statesman, Columbia, Missouri
Natchez Daily Courier, Natchez, Mississippi
Niles Weekly Register, Baltimore, Maryland
Patriot, Columbia, Missouri
The Peoples' Tribune, Jefferson City, Missouri
The Randolph Citizen, Huntsville, Missouri
Richmond Daily Examiner, Richmond, Virginia
Saint Louis Daily Union, St. Louis, Missouri
Santa Fe Republican, Santa Fe, New Mexico. (Photostat at the Missouri Historical Society, St. Louis.)
Tri-Weekly Missouri Republican, St. Louis, Missouri

Washington Telegraph, Washington, Arkansas
The Weekly Brunswicker, Brunswick, Missouri
The Weekly Caucasian, Lexington, Missouri
Weekly Reveille, St. Louis, Missouri
Weekly Saint Louis Pilot, St. Louis, Missouri
The Weekly Tribune, Liberty, Missouri
The Western Monitor, Fayette, Missouri

Unpublished Studies

Kirkpatrick, Arthur Roy, "Missouri, the Twelfth Confederate State" (Ph.D. diss., University of Missouri, 1954).
Mering, John, "The Whig Party in Missouri" (Ph.D. diss., University of Missouri, 1960).
Morrow, Norman Potter, "Price's Missouri Expedition, 1864" (Master's diss., University of Texas, 1949).
Simmons, Lucy, "The Life of Sterling Price" (Master's diss., University of Chicago, 1922).
West, Alma, "The Earlier Political Career of Claiborne Fox Jackson, 1836–1851" (Master's diss., University of Missouri, 1941).

Books

Alexander, Thomas B., *Sectional Stress and Party Strength: A Study of the Roll-Call Voting Patterns in the United States House of Representatives, 1836–1869.* Nashville, 1967.
Allsop, Fred W., *Albert Pike, A Biography.* Little Rock, 1928.
Anderson, Ephraim M., *Memoirs: Historical and Personal, Including Campaigns of the First Missouri Confederate Brigade.* St. Louis, 1868.
Atherton, Lewis, *The Pioneer Merchant in Mid-America.* Columbia, Missouri, 1939.
Battles and Leaders of the Civil War, Robert U. Johnson, and C. C. Buel, eds. New York, 1884–1887, 4 vols.
Bearss, Edwin C., *Steele's Retreat from Camden and the Battle of Jenkins' Ferry.* Little Rock, 1967.
Bevier, R. S., *History of the First and Second Missouri Confederate Brigades, 1861–1865.* St. Louis, 1879.
Boggs, William R., *Military Reminiscences.* Durham, North Carolina, 1913.
Bradshaw, Herbert C., *History of Prince Edward County, Virginia.* Richmond, 1955.
Britton, Wiley, *The Civil War on the Border.* New York, 1899, 2 vols.
————, *The Union Brigade in the Civil War.* Kansas City, 1922.
Brownlee, Richard S., *Gray Ghosts of the Confederacy, Guerrilla Warfare in the West, 1861–1865.* Baton Rouge, 1958.
Cabell, William L., *Report of Gen. W. L. Cabell's Brigade in Price's Raid in Missouri and Kansas in 1864.* Dallas, 1900.
Cable, John, *The Bank of the State of Missouri.* New York, 1930.
Castel, Albert, *General Sterling Price and the Civil War in the West.* Baton Rouge, 1968.
Catton, Bruce, *Grant Moves South.* Boston, 1960.

Chambers, William N., *Old Bullion Benton, Senator from the New West*. Boston, 1956.
Confederate Military History, Clement A. Evans, ed. Atlanta, 1899, 12 vols.
Connelly, Thomas Lawrence, *Army of the Heartland: The Army of Tennessee, 1861–1862*. Baton Rouge, 1967.
Coulter, E. Merton, *The Confederate States of America*. Baton Rouge, 1950.
Davis, David B., *The Problem of Slavery in Western Culture*. Ithaca, 1966.
Davis, Jefferson, *The Rise and Fall of the Confederate Government*. New York, 1881, 2 vols.
Diary of James K. Polk, Milo M. Quaife, ed. Chicago, 1910, 4 vols.
Donald, David, *Lincoln Reconsidered: Essays in the Civil War Era*. New York, 1947.
Doniphan's Expedition and the Conquest of New Mexico and California, W. E. Connelley, ed. Topeka, 1907.
Down the Santa Fe Trail and into Mexico: The Diary of Susan Shelby Magoffin, 1846–1847, Stella M. Drumm, ed. New Haven, 1920.
Duke, Basil W., *Reminiscences of General Basil W. Duke*. Garden City, 1911.
Eaton, Clement, *A History of the Southern Confederacy*. New York, 1954.
Edwards, John N., *Noted Guerrillas, or the Warfare of the Border*. St. Louis, 1877.
————, *Shelby and his Men: or, The War in the West*. Cincinnati, 1867.
Edwards, Marcellus Ball, "Journal of Marcellus Ball Edwards," in Ralph Bieber, ed., *Southwest Historical Series*, IV. Glendale, California, 1935.
Eliot, Ellsworth, *West Point in the Confederacy*. New York, 1941.
Elliott, Richard Smith, *Notes Taken in Sixty Years*. St. Louis, 1883.
Ferguson, Philip Gooch, Diary, in Ralph Bieber, ed., *Southwest Historical Series*, IV. Glendale, California, 1935.
Freeman, Douglas Southall, *Lee's Lieutenants: A Study in Command*. New York, 1942–1945, 3 vols.
————, *R. E. Lee, A Biography*. New York, 1934–1935, 4 vols.
Garrard, Lewis, "Wah–To–Yah and the Taos Trail," in Ralph Bieber, ed., *Southwest Historical Series*, VI. Glendale, California, 1935.
General Catalogue of the Officers and Students of Hampden-Sidney College, Virginia, 1776–1906. Richmond, 1906.
Gibson, George R., "Journal of a Soldier under Kearny and Doniphan," in Ralph Bieber, ed., *Southwest Historical Series*, III. Glendale, California, 1935.
Grant, Ulysses Sidney, *Memoirs of U. S. Grant*. New York, 1885, 2 vols.
Green, Constance McLaughlin, *Washington: Village and Capital, 1800–1878*. Princeton, 1967.
Harding, Samuel B., *Life of George R. Smith*. Sedalia, Missouri, 1904.
Hartje, Robert G., *Van Dorn: The Life and Times of a Confederate General*. Nashville, 1967.
Hartz, Louis, *The Liberal Tradition in America*. New York, 1955.
Hinton, Richard Josiah, *Rebel Invasion of Missouri and Kansas and the Campaign of the Army of the Border Against General Sterling Price in October and November, 1864*. Chicago and Leavenworth, 1865.
History of Howard and Chariton Counties, Missouri. St. Louis, 1883.
Horn, Stanley F., *The Army of Tennessee*. Indianapolis and New York, 1941.

Hughes, John, *Doniphan's Expedition*. Cincinnati, 1848.

Inside the Confederate Government, Edward Younger, ed. New York, 1957.

Jefferson Davis, Constitutionalist: His Letters, Papers, and Speeches, Dunbar Rowland, ed. Jackson, Mississippi, 1923, 10 vols.

Jenkins, Paul B., *The Battle of Westport*. Kansas City, 1906.

Johnson, Ludwell H., *Red River Campaign: Politics and Cotton in the Civil War*. Baltimore, 1958.

Johnson's Universal Cyclopedia, Charles Kendall Adams, ed. in chief. New York, 1895.

Jones, Archer, *Confederate Strategy from Shiloh to Vicksburg*. Baton Rouge, 1961.

Jones, J. B., *A Rebel War Clerk's Diary at the Confederate States Capital*. Philadelphia, 1866, 2 vols.

Jordan, Winthrop D., *White Over Black: American Attitudes Toward the Negro, 1550–1812*. Chapel Hill, 1968.

Journals of Francis Parkman, Mason Wade, ed. London, 1946, 2 vols.

Kate: The Journal of a Confederate Nurse, Richard B. Harwell, ed. Baton Rouge, 1959.

Kirk, Russell, *Randolph of Roanoke*. Chicago, 1951.

Klement, Frank, *The Copperheads of the Middle West*. Chicago, 1960.

Lamers, William M., *The Edge of Glory: A Biography of General William S. Rosecrans*. New York, 1961.

"Laws of Hampden-Sidney College," printed pamphlet in Legislative Petitions, Prince Edward County, Virginia, 1800–1824. Archives Division, Virginia State Library, Richmond.

McClure, Clarence Henry, *Opposition in Missouri to Thomas Hart Benton*. Warrensburg, Missouri, 1926.

McCormick, Richard P., *The Second American Party System: Party Formation in the Jacksonian Era*. Chapel Hill, 1966.

McElroy, John S., *The Struggle for Missouri*. Washington, D.C., 1909.

McIlwain, Richard, *Memories of Three Score Years and Ten*. New York, 1908.

McWhiney, Grady, *Braxton Bragg and Confederate Defeat: Field Command*. New York, 1969.

Mering, John Volmer, *The Whig Party in Missouri*. Columbia, Missouri, 1967.

Merk, Frederick, *Manifest Destiny and Mission in American History: A Reinterpretation*. New York, 1966.

Meyers, Marvin, *The Jacksonian Persuasion*. Palo Alto, 1957.

Monaghan, Jay, *Civil War on the Western Border, 1854–1865*. Boston, 1955.

Monnett, Howard N., *Action Before Westport, 1864*. Kansas City, 1964.

Nevins, Allan, *Frémont: The West's Greatest Adventurer*. New York, 1928.

———, *The Emergence of Lincoln*. New York, 1950, 2 vols.

———, *The War for the Union*. New York, 1959.

———, *The Statesmanship of the Civil War*. New York, 1950.

O'Flaherty, Daniel, *General Jo Shelby: Undefeated Rebel*. Chapel Hill, 1954.

Parks, Joseph Howard, *General Edmund Kirby Smith, C. S. A.* Baton Rouge, 1954.

Parrish, William Earl, *David Rice Atchison of Missouri, Border Politician*. Columbia, Missouri, 1961.

———, *Missouri Under Radical Rule, 1865–1870*. Columbia, Missouri, 1965.

———, *Turbulent Partnership: Missouri and the Union, 1861–1865*. Columbia, Missouri, 1964.

Patrick, Rembert, *Jefferson Davis and His Cabinet*. Baton Rouge, 1944.

Peterson, Cyrus A., and Joseph M. Hanson, *Pilot Knob, The Thermopylae of the West*. New York, 1814.

Peterson, Norma L., *Freedom and Franchise: The Political Career of B. Gratz Brown*. Columbia, Missouri, 1965.

Picturesque Fayette and Its People, Verne Dyson, ed. Fayette, Missouri, 1905.

Pollard, Edward R., *The First Year of the War*. Richmond, 1862.

Pratt, Parley Parker, *Autobiography*. Salt Lake City, 1964.

Price, Benjamin Luther, *John Price the Immigrant*. Alexandria, Louisiana, n.d.

Quincy, Edmund, *Life of Josiah Quincy*. Boston, 1867.

Rawley, James, *Turning Points of the Civil War*. Lincoln, 1966.

Rea, Ralph R., *Sterling Price, The Lee of the West*. Little Rock, 1959.

Robert, Joseph Clark, *The Story of Tobacco in America*. New York, 1949.

———, *The Tobacco Kingdom*. Durham, North Carolina, 1938.

Roberts, B. H., *History of the Church of Jesus Christ of Latter Day Saints*, III. Salt Lake City, 1948.

Rolle, Andrew F., *The Lost Cause: The Confederate Exodus to Mexico*. Norman, Oklahoma, 1965.

Rose, Victor M., *The Life and Services of Gen. Ben McCulloch*. Philadelphia, 1888.

Ruxton, George, *Adventures in Mexico and the Rocky Mountains*. New York, 1948.

Scharf, John T., *History of St. Louis City and County from the Earliest Period to the Present Day*. Philadelphia, 1883, 2 vols.

Seward, Frederick, *Seward at Washington*. New York, 1891.

Shannon, James, *An Address delivered before the Pro-Slavery Convention of the State of Missouri, July 13, 1855 on Domestic Slavery*. St. Louis, 1855.

———, *The Philosophy of Slavery as Identified with the Philosophy of Human Happiness*. Frankfort, Kentucky, 1849.

Silbey, Joel H., *The Shrine of Party: Congressional Voting Behavior, 1841–1852*. Pittsburgh, 1967.

Smith, Elbert, *Magnificent Missourian: The Life of Thomas Hart Benton*. New York, 1958.

Smith, Justin H., *The War With Mexico*. New York, 1919, 2 vols.

Smith, William E., *The Francis Preston Blair Family in Politics*, New York, 1933, 2 vols.

Snead, Thomas L., *The Fight for Missouri*. New York, 1886.

A Soldier's Honor: With Reminiscences of Major General Earl Van Dorn, E. Van Dorn Miller, ed. New York, 1902.

Stickles, Arndt M., *Simon Bolivar Buckner, Borderland Knight*. Chapel Hill, 1940.

Strode, Hudson, *Jefferson Davis, Confederate President*. New York, 1959.

Sydnor, Charles, *The Development of Southern Sectionalism*. Baton Rouge, 1948.

———, *Gentlemen Freeholders*. Chapel Hill, 1952.

Taylor, Creed, *Journal of the Law School and the Moot Court Attached at Needham, Virginia*. Richmond, 1822.

Taylor, William R., *Cavalier and Yankee.* New York, 1961.
Twitchell, Ralph Emerson, *Leading Facts of New Mexican History,* Cedar Rapids, Iowa, 1963, 2 vols.
Vandiver, Frank, *Rebel Brass: The Confederate Command System.* Baton Rouge, 1958.
Von Abele, Rudolph, *Alexander H. Stephens.* New York, 1946.
Ward, John, *Andrew Jackson: Symbol for an Age.* New York, 1962.
Warner, Ezra, *Generals in Blue.* Baton Rouge, 1964.
————, *Generals in Gray.* Baton Rouge, 1951.
Washington During War Time, Marcus Benjamin, ed. Washington, D.C., n.d.
The West Point Atlas of American Wars, I, Colonel Vincent J. Esposito, ed. New York, 1959.
Wetmore, Alphonso, *Gazetteer of the State of Missouri.* St. Louis, 1837.
Why the North Won the Civil War, David Donald, ed. Baton Rouge, 1960.
Wiley, Bell I., *The Road to Appomattox.* Memphis, 1956.
Williams, T. Harry, *Americans at War: The Development of the American Military System.* Baton Rouge, 1960.
————, *P. G. T. Beauregard: Napoleon in Gray.* Baton Rouge, 1955.
Woolman, John, *The Journal of John Woolman; Plea for the Poor,* with Introduction by Frederick Tolles. Corinth paperback edition. New York, 1961.
Yearns, Wilfred Buck, *The Confederate Congress.* Athens, Georgia, 1960.

Articles

Barry, Louise, "Kansas Before 1854: A Revised Annals." *Kansas Historical Quarterly,* 30 (Autumn, 1964), 62–91.
Bearss, Edwin C., "The Battle of Helena." *Arkansas Historical Quarterly,* 20 (Autumn, 1961), 258–93.
————, "The First Day at Pea Ridge, March 7, 1862." *Arkansas Historical Quarterly,* 17 (Summer, 1958), 132–54.
————, "From Rolla to Fayetteville With General Curtis." *Arkansas Historical Quarterly,* 19 (Autumn, 1960), 225–59.
"Letters of George Caleb Bingham to James S. Rollins," C. B. Rollins, ed. *Missouri Historical Review,* 32:1 to 33:4 (October, 1937–July, 1939).
Blunt, James G., "General Blunt's Account of His Civil War Experience." *Kansas Historical Quarterly,* 1:3 (May, 1932), 211–65.
Britton, Wiley, "Resume of Military Operations in Missouri and Arkansas, 1864–65." *Battles and Leaders of the Civil War,* 4:364–77.
Brown, A. F., "Van Dorn's Operations in Northern Mississippi-Recollections of a Cavalryman." *Southern Historical Society Papers,* 6 (Richmond, 1878), 151–61.
Brown, Walter L., "Pea Ridge: Gettysburg of the West." *Arkansas Historical Quarterly,* 15 (Spring, 1956), 3–16.
Brownlee, Richard S., "The Battle of Pilot Knob." *State of Missouri Official Manual for the Years 1961–1962* (Jefferson City, Missouri, 1962).
"Campaign in Southern Arkansas: A Memoir by C. T. Anderson," Roman J. Zorn, ed. *Arkansas Historical Quarterly,* 8 (Autumn, 1949), 240–44.
Castel, Albert, "A New View of the Battle of Pea Ridge." *Missouri Historical Review,* 62:2 (January, 1968), 136–51.
Cheetham, Francis, "The First Term of the American Court in Taos, New Mexico." *New Mexico Historical Review,* 1 (January, 1926), 23–41.

Cotterill, R. S., "The National Railroad Convention in St. Louis, 1849." *Missouri Historical Review*, 12:4 (July, 1915), 203–15.

Covington, James W., "The Camp Jackson Affair: 1861." *Missouri Historical Review*, 55 (April, 1961), 197–212.

Cowen, Ruth Caroline, "Reorganization of Federal Arkansas, 1862–1865." *Arkansas Historical Quarterly*, 18 (Summer, 1959), 32–57.

Darr, John C., "Price's Raid into Missouri." *Confederate Veteran*, 11 (August, 1903), 359–62.

Davis, David B., "Some Themes of Counter-Subversion: An Analysis of Anti-Masonic, Anti-Catholic, and Anti-Mormon Literature." *Mississippi Valley Historical Review*, 47:2 (September, 1960), 205–24.

Donald, David, "The Confederate as a Fighting Man." *Journal of Southern History*, 25 (May, 1959), 178–93.

"Elkhorn to Vicksburg: James H. Fauntelroy's Diary for the Year 1862," Homer L. Calkins, ed. *Civil War History*, 2 (January, 1956), 7–43.

Frémont, John C., "In Command in Missouri." *Battles and Leaders of the Civil War*, 1:278–88.

Geise, William R., "Missouri's Confederate Capital in Marshall, Texas." *Missouri Historical Review*, 58 (October, 1963), 37–54.

Grover, George S., "Civil War in Missouri." *Missouri Historical Review*, 8 (October, 1913), 1–28.

———, "The Price Campaign of 1864." *Missouri Historical Review*, 6 (July, 1912), 167–81.

———, "The Shelby Raid, 1863." *Missouri Historical Review*, 6 (April, 1912), 107–26.

Hamilton, C. S., "The Battle of Iuka." *Battles and Leaders of the Civil War*, 2:734–36.

Harmon, George D., "Confederate Migration to Mexico." *Hispanic American Historical Review*, 17 (November, 1937), 458–87.

Hartje, Robert G., "A Confederate Dilemma Across the Mississippi." *Arkansas Historical Quarterly*, 17 (Summer, 1958), 119–31.

Hill, Lawrence, "Confederate Exiles to Brazil." *Hispanic American Historical Review*, 7 (May, 1927), 192–210.

———, "The Confederate Exodus to South America." *Southwestern Historical Quarterly*, 39 (October, 1935), 100–134; (January, 1936), 161–99; (April, 1936), 309–26.

Huff, Leo E., "The Last Duel in Arkansas: The Marmaduke-Walker Duel." *Arkansas Historical Quarterly*, 22 (Spring, 1964), 36–49.

———, "The Union Expedition Against Little Rock, August–September, 1863." *Arkansas Historical Quarterly*, 22 (Fall, 1963), 223–37.

Kirkpatrick, Arthur Roy, "The Admission of Missouri to the Confederacy." *Missouri Historical Review*, 55 (July, 1961), 366–86.

———, "Missouri in the Early Months of the Civil War." *Missouri Historical Review*, 55 (April, 1961), 235–66.

———, "Missouri on the Eve of the Civil War." *Missouri Historical Review*, 55 (January, 1961), 99–108.

———, "Missouri's Delegation in the Confederate Congress." *Civil War History*, 5 (March, 1959), 188–98.

Langsdorf, Edgar, "Price's Raid and the Battle of Mine Creek." *Kansas Historical Quarterly*, 30 (Autumn, 1964), 281–306.

Lyon, William H., "Claiborne Fox Jackson and the Secession Crisis in Missouri." *Missouri Historical Review*, 58 (July, 1964), 422–41.

McCausland, Susan A. Arnold, "The Battle of Lexington as Seen by a Woman." *Missouri Historical Review*, 6 (April, 1912), 127–35.

Maury, Dabney H., "Recollections of a Campaign Against Grant in North Mississippi, 1862–1863." *Southern Historical Society Papers*, 13:285–311. Richmond, Virginia, 1885.

————, "Recollections of General Earl Van Dorn." *Southern Historical Society Papers*, 19:191–201. Richmond, Virginia, 1891.

————, "Recollections of the Elkhorn Campaign." *Southern Historical Society Papers*, 2:180–92. Richmond, Virginia, 1876.

Mudd, James A., "What I Saw at Wilson's Creek." *Missouri Historical Review*, 7 (January, 1913), 87–113.

Mulligan, James A., "The Siege of Lexington, Missouri." *Battles and Leaders of the Civil War*, 1:307–13.

Pearce, N. Bartlett, "Arkansas Troops in the Battle of Wilson's Creek." *Battles and Leaders of the Civil War*, 1:298–303.

Perkins, J. R., "Jefferson Davis and Gen. Sterling Price." *Confederate Veteran*, 19 (October, 1911), 473–77.

Richards, Ira Don, "The Battle of Poison Spring." *Arkansas Historical Quarterly*, 18 (Winter, 1959), 1–12.

Rippy, J. Fred, "Mexican Projects of the Confederates." *Southwestern Historical Quarterly*, 22 (April, 1919), 291–317.

Rister, Carl C., "Carlota, a Confederate Colony in Mexico." *Journal of Southern History*, 11 (February, 1945), 33–50.

Rosecrans, William S., "The Battle of Corinth." *Battles and Leaders of the Civil War*, 2:743–56.

Scroggs, Jack B., and Donald E. Reynolds, "Arkansas and the Vicksburg Campaign." *Civil War History*, 4 (December, 1959), 390–401.

Shalhope, Robert E., "Jacksonian Politics in Missouri: A Comment on the McCormick Thesis." *Civil War History*, 15:3 (September, 1969), 210–25.

————, "Thomas Hart Benton and Missouri State Politics: A Re-examination." *Missouri Historical Society Bulletin*, 25:3 (April, 1969), 171–91.

Sigel, Franz, "The Flanking Column at Wilson's Creek." *Battles and Leaders of the Civil War*, 1:304–6.

————, "The Pea Ridge Campaign." *Battles and Leaders of the Civil War*, 1:314–34.

Smith, W. Wayne, "An Experiment in Counterinsurgency: The Assessment of Confederate Sympathizers in Missouri." *The Journal of Southern History*, 25:3 (August, 1969), 361–80.

Snead, Thomas L., "The Conquest of Arkansas." *Battles and Leaders of the Civil War*, 3:441–61.

————, "The First Year of the War in Missouri." *Battles and Leaders of the Civil War*, 1:262–77.

————, "With Price East of the Mississippi." *Battles and Leaders of the Civil War*, 2:717–34.

Snyder, J. F., "The Capture of Lexington." *Missouri Historical Review*, 7 (October, 1912), 1–9.

————, "Missouri Democratic Convention of 1860," *St. Louis Globe-Democrat*, February 13, 1898, 37.

Wherry, William M., "Wilson's Creek and the Death of Lyon." *Battles and Leaders of the Civil War*, 1:289–99.

Index